THE LOGIC OF THE
HISTORY OF IDEAS

Human cultures generate meanings, and the history of ideas, broadly conceived, is the study of these meanings. An adequate theory of culture must therefore rest on a suitable philosophical enquiry into the nature of the history of ideas. Mark Bevir's book explores the forms of reasoning appropriate to the history of ideas, enhancing our understanding by grappling with central questions such as: what is a meaning? What constitutes objective knowledge of the past? What are beliefs and traditions? How can we explain why people held the beliefs they did? The book ranges widely over issues and theorists associated with post-analytic philosophy, post-modernism, hermeneutics, literary theory, political thought, and social theory.

MARK BEVIR is Reader in Political Theory at the University of Newcastle upon Tyne.

T0381627

THE LOGIC OF THE
HISTORY OF IDEAS

MARK BEVIR

CAMBRIDGE
UNIVERSITY PRESS

PUBLISHED BY THE PRESS SYNDICATE OF THE UNIVERSITY OF CAMBRIDGE
The Pitt Building, Trumpington Street, Cambridge, United Kingdom

CAMBRIDGE UNIVERSITY PRESS
The Edinburgh Building, Cambridge CB2 2RU, UK
40 West 20th Street, New York NY 10011–4211, USA
477 Williamstown Road, Port Melbourne, VIC 3207, Australia
Ruiz de Alarcón 13, 28014 Madrid, Spain
Dock House, The Waterfront, Cape Town 8001, South Africa

http://www.cambridge.org

First published 1999
Reprinted 2000
First paperback edition 2002

Typeface Baskerville 11/12½ pt.

A catalogue record for this book is available from the British Library

Library of Congress Cataloguing in Publication data
Bevir, Mark.
The logic of the history of ideas / Mark Bevir.
p.   cm.
Includes bibliographical references and index.
ISBN 0 521 64034 2 (hb)
1. Idea (Philosophy) – History.   I. Title.
B822.B48   1999
190–dc21   98-38079   CIP

ISBN 0 521 64034 2 hardback
ISBN 0 521 01684 3 paperback

TO LAURA

Contents

Preface

Many of us find it hard to disentangle our interest in certain questions from our commitment to a particular approach. Certainly I do not know whether my decision to focus on the forms of justification and explanation appropriate to the history of ideas came before or after my decision to do so in a manner indebted to analytic philosophy. Perhaps the two cannot be separated. What I do know is that the work of Quentin Skinner, itself clearly influenced by analytic philosophy, first stirred my curiosity about issues germane to the logic of the history of ideas. My decision to draw on analytic philosophy to undertake a normative study of the forms of reasoning appropriate to the history of ideas has taken me away from the dominant concerns of the hermeneutic tradition, and, in particular, the ontological hermeneutics developed by Hans-Georg Gadamer. Whereas hermeneutic theorists typically concentrate on phenomenological and descriptive issues about the process of understanding, I have tried to provide a logical and normative analysis of the ways in which we should justify and explain the understandings we reach. Whereas they concentrate on the nature of understanding as an intellectual activity, I have grappled with the logical forms appropriate to arguments within the history of ideas. To have concerns other than those that dominate the hermeneutic tradition is not, however, to deny the validity of that tradition. Whatever quarrels I may have with the specific arguments of hermeneutic theorists, and those quarrels will become clear, I hope my logic of the history of ideas remains compatible with a hermeneutic study of the process of understanding. Surely analytic and other forms of philosophy need not always compete with one another?[1] Surely they can complement one another as different approaches suited to explorations of different issues?

[1] Elsewhere I have suggested that the post-modern rejection of given truths could inspire a type of phenomenology closely resembling the post-analytic philosphy I defend. See M. Bevir, 'Meaning, truth and phenomenology', *Teorema* 16 (1997), 61–76.

Although the debates surrounding the work of Skinner, and also J. G. A. Pocock, first stirred my curiosity about the logic of the history of ideas, I soon found myself leaving their ambit. Skinner and Pocock aim primarily to define a method for the history of ideas. They seek to describe the appropriate manner in which to recover the meaning of a text. It is their particular methods that then enable them to dismiss other ways of doing things, notably those which deny the autonomy of the history of ideas, focus on the coherence of texts, or consider the contemporary relevance of texts. In contrast, I decided that no method can constitute a form of justification. A method can perform a useful heuristic role, but it cannot give us a logical guarantee of the objectivity of an understanding of a work. Once again I do not want to deny the interest of the issues raised by Skinner and Pocock.[2] However, because my concern is with the logic of the history of ideas, not its heuristics, I have come to rely at many points less on the secondary literature that surrounds their work than on analytic philosophers who have written on epistemology and the philosophy of mind, notably Ludwig Wittgenstein and Donald Davidson.

So, my work has a strange relationship to much of the existing literature on the nature of the history of ideas. The existing literature, whether studying the process of human understanding or defending a particular method, focuses on ways in which we can come to grasp the meaning of a text. I engage with this literature when I consider the nature of the meanings we try to grasp, arguing that such meanings are equivalent to individual viewpoints understood as expressed beliefs. After this, however, I leave its concerns behind by arguing against the possibility of a logic of discovery. I suggest that no answer to the question of how we can grasp the meaning of a text can have a place in a logic of the history of ideas. My interest shifts, therefore, to the question of how we can explain the beliefs we postulate as the meanings of past works. Here I break with the established agenda in a way which gives my ensuing arguments at best a tangential relationship to the work of scholars such as Gadamer and Skinner. Thus, for instance, when I explore the nature of a tradition, I do so to give content to a concept of tradition that helps us to explain beliefs, not one that helps us to analyse the process of understanding, or one that specifies a pre-condition of all

---

[2] I have considered many of these issues elsewhere. See M. Bevir, 'The errors of linguistic contextualism', *History and Theory* 31 (1992), 276–98; 'Are there perennial problems in political theory?', *Political Studies* 42 (1994), 662–75; and 'Mind and method in the history of ideas', *History and Theory* 36 (1997), 167–89.

historical knowledge. The tangential relationship of my work to the existing literature means that although I contrast my concepts as they address my concerns with those of other authors, I often do so without thereby denying the validity of their concepts as tools for addressing their rather different concerns. After all, to say that a particular concept of tradition does not help us to explain beliefs need not be to say that it tells us nothing about the process of human understanding or the pre-conditions of historical knowledge.

Acknowledgements

I am grateful to all those whose professional and emotional support made my work easier and more enjoyable than it otherwise would have been. Newcastle University awarded me a research fellowship during the tenure of which I wrote much of the manuscript. The editors of *History and Theory*, *Journal of Political Ideologies*, and *Political Studies* kindly allowed me to use material that first appeared therein. John Haslam helped to steer the manuscript through the editorial process.

CHAPTER I

On analytic philosophy

INTRODUCTION

Patterns of family life, debates in politics, religious observances, techno-
logical inventions, scientific beliefs, literature, and the arts – all of these
things are aspects of human culture. Typically we define a broad
concept of human culture in contrast to physical and biological processes. One key feature differentiates the cultural, even if the precise
boundaries between it, the physical, and the biological sometimes remain blurred. Cultural phenomena convey meanings, and they do so
because cultures are composed at least in part of beliefs. Some components of a culture, such as political tracts and literary works, usually
stand as self-conscious attempts to convey meanings through language.
Other components of a culture, such as sculpture and painting, usually
stand as self-conscious attempts to convey meanings through non-
linguistic forms. Yet other components of a culture, such as habits of
association and sporting activities, do not usually represent any sort of
self-conscious attempt to convey meanings. In each of these cases,
however, the objects and activities in question constitute cultural phenomena precisely because they do convey meanings. Students of culture
concentrate on the meanings conveyed by patterns of behaviour, forms
of social organisation, economic systems, technical inventions, and the
like, not on these things in themselves.

To study the history of ideas is to study meaning, and so culture, from
a historical perspective. But then the study of culture must always be
parasitic on history. Although scholars can evaluate cultural phenomena epistemically, morally, or aesthetically, they cannot evaluate what
they do not know, and the only way they can acquire knowledge of
cultural phenomena is through historical studies. Thus, a recognition of
the meaningfulness of human life combines with a historical consciousness to place questions of interpretation at the centre of the human

sciences. Because human life is meaningful, students of the human sciences have to undertake the interpretation of cultural phenomena. Because cultural phenomena exist and are handed down in time, students of the human sciences have to interpret cultural phenomena in terms of historical processes. Given that we can define the history of ideas as the study of meaning, an adequate theory of culture requires a suitable grasp of the nature of the history of ideas. Equally we can say that a philosophical inquiry into the logic of the history of ideas can provide us with the beginnings of a theory of culture.

How should we conduct a philosophical inquiry into the logic of the history of ideas? This is a metaphilosophical question. Just as we uncover the logic of any particular discipline by engaging in a philosophical analysis of that discipline, so to uncover the logic of philosophy we have to engage in a philosophical analysis of philosophy itself. Before we can turn our attention to the particular logic of the history of ideas, therefore, we have to examine, first, the nature of philosophy, and, second, the types of arguments proper to philosophy. I will argue that to identify the logic of any discipline one has to uncover the forms of reasoning appropriate to it by means of a study of the grammar of the concepts operating in it. In addition, I will argue that we can draw out the grammar of a set of concepts by means of both deductive and inductive arguments.

THE NATURE OF A LOGIC

Different philosophers conceive of their discipline in different ways. To lay down the law as to what philosophy is would be beyond the scope of this study. None the less, I can identify and defend a particular approach to the task of analysing the logic of the history of ideas, where this approach stands as one of many legitimate approaches to philosophy within a pluralist account of the discipline of philosophy. Indeed, I already have gone some way towards doing just this by taking as my subject matter the logic of the history of ideas. The logic of a discipline consists of the forms of reasoning appropriate to it. Thus, my subject matter commits me to a view of philosophy as in part a second-order discipline concerned with the forms of reasoning appropriate to first-order disciplines. Most analytic philosophers are familiar and happy with the view of their discipline as in part a second-order one. Other philosophers, however, generally conceive of philosophy in rather different ways. Phenomenologists typically define philosophy in terms of the inspection of one's own consciousness, especially one's own intellectual processes.[1] Their work concentrates on what they regard as the essences of the objects and capacities available to all minds. Similarly, and in part because of a debt to phenomenology, hermeneutic theorists often conceive of philosophy primarily in terms of a study of the activity of understanding.[2] Their work concentrates on the nature of our being and how it circumscribes the ways we can reach an understanding of our world.

As a general rule, one can treat analytic philosophy, phenomenology, and hermeneutics as compatible activities.[3] They do not give conflicting answers to a shared set of questions in a way that would place them in opposition to one another. On the contrary, they represent different approaches to philosophy, where each approach is designed to deal with a distinct set of questions. Even if one cannot always reconcile the answers particular exponents of these different approaches give to their respective questions, one still need not define the approaches themselves as intrinsically hostile to one another. Consider, for example, scholars influenced by hermeneutics who argue that we must reject intentionalist accounts of hermeneutic meaning because the nature of our understanding implies that we cannot grasp past intentions as they were.[4] Later I will reject their conclusion on the grounds that we cannot grasp anything as it is, so that in this respect past intentions are no different from any of the other objects of which we have knowledge. But to reject their conclusion as based on an untenable ideal of pure perception is not to reject hermeneutics as an approach to questions about the activity of understanding. When we take the logic of the history of ideas as our subject matter, we do not thereby deny the validity of non-analytic approaches to philosophy, we just commit ourselves to issues that have arisen most prominently in the context of the analytic tradition. The point of my metaphilosophical explorations, therefore, is not to deny that philosophy has a role to play other than as a second-order discipline. It is rather to

---

[1] E. Husserl, *Ideas: General Introduction to Pure Phenomenology*, trans. W. Gibson (London: George Allen & Unwin, 1931).

[2] H.-G. Gadamer, *Truth and Method*, trans. W. Glen-Doepel (London: Sheed & Ward, 1979).

[3] I believe anti-foundationalism encourages us to reformulate phenomenology in a way that brings it closer to post-analytic philosophy. See M. Bevir, 'Meaning, truth and phenomenology', *Teorema* 16 (1997), 61–76.

[4] J. Gunnell, *Political Theory: Tradition and Interpretation* (Cambridge, Mass.: Winthrop Publishers, 1979); D. LaCapra, 'Rethinking intellectual history and reading texts', in *Rethinking Intellectual History: Texts, Contexts, Language* (Ithaca, N.Y.: Cornell University Press, 1983), pp. 23–71; and P. Ricœur, *Interpretation Theory: Discourse and the Surplus of Meaning* (Fort Worth, Tex.: Texas Christian University Press, 1976).

identify and to defend the particular procedures scholars should use to pursue a second-order study of the history of ideas.

A concern with the logic of the history of ideas places us within the analytic tradition. However, even within the analytic tradition, philosophers do not agree about the nature of their discipline. Before we can devise a logic, we need to specify more clearly what we are after and how best we might obtain it. We need to identify the particular conception of analytic philosophy that should guide a study of the logic of the history of ideas. Many scholars still associate analytic philosophy far too closely with the particular commitments of the logical positivists. The logical positivists argued that the truth-value, or semantic meaning, of any proposition consists in the method of its verification, so that if no facts could show a given proposition to be true or false, then that proposition must be meaningless or tautological.[5] This verifiability principle led the logical positivists to distinguish sharply between the synthetic and the analytic conceived as contrasting types of knowledge with different forms of justification. A synthetic proposition is true or false according to whether or not it is verified: synthetic truths, those of science, rest on empirical facts. An analytic proposition is true or false according to whether it can be proved or disproved from definitions using only the laws of formal logic: analytic truths, those of mathematics and logic, are tautologies. If a proposition is neither synthetic nor analytic, it has no truth-value, so it is meaningless. The logical positivists insisted, therefore, that the whole of philosophy has to be a second-order discipline. Traditional arguments in metaphysics, ethics, and aesthetics are either meaningless or expressions of things such as emotional attitudes. Real philosophy draws out logical truths; it elucidates the meanings found in first-order disciplines; it is analytic in that the knowledge it gives us consists of tautologies.

Much contemporary analytic philosophy renounces the commitments of the logical positivists. Early critics of logical positivism asked about the status of the verifiability principle. They pointed out that this principle is neither a synthetic proposition to be verified by empirical investigation nor an analytic proposition to be grasped as a tautology. By now logical positivism has given way to approaches to analytic philosophy inspired by work as diverse as that of Thomas Kuhn on the

---

[5] A. Ayer, *Language, Truth and Logic* (London: Victor Gollancz, 1936); and R. Carnap, 'The old and the new logic', in A. Ayer (ed.), *Logical Positivism* (Glencoe, Ill.: Free Press, 1959), pp. 133–46. Also see L. Wittgenstein, *Tractatus Logico-Philosophicus*, trans. D. Pears and B. McGuiness (London: Routledge & Kegan Paul, 1960).

sociology and philosophy of science, W. V. O. Quine working within the empiricist tradition of the logical positivists, and the linguistic approach found in the later writings of Ludwig Wittgenstein.[6] Despite their many differences, Kuhn, Quine, and Wittgenstein all agree that semantic meanings depend on their contexts in a way that undermines logical positivism. What we would count as a verification of a given proposition depends at a minimum on some of the other beliefs we accept as true. Most contemporary analytic philosophy denies, therefore, that semantic meanings have the stability necessary to sustain reductionist programmes such as logical positivism. The arguments of Kuhn, Quine, and Wittgenstein challenge the account of philosophy given by the logical positivists in two crucial ways. For a start, a rejection of the verifiability principle makes it difficult to reject as meaningless disputes in areas such as metaphysics and ethics. Philosophy is not just a second-order discipline. In addition, the dependence of semantic meanings on particular contexts undermines any significant distinction between the synthetic and the analytic conceived as contrasting types of knowledge.[7] (Indeed, one might describe analytic philosophy done in the wake of Kuhn, Quine, and Wittgenstein as post-analytic precisely because it undermines the logical positivists' concept of the analytic.) A synthetic proposition cannot be true or false simply by virtue of being verified by the facts since what we accept as a verification must depend on the way our other beliefs stabilise our definitions of the terms of that proposition. An analytic proposition cannot be true simply by virtue of definitions and the laws of formal logic since how we define something must depend on our other beliefs, where these other beliefs might alter as a result of further empirical investigations. All of our knowledge arises, therefore, in the context of our particular web of beliefs.[8]

The argument that all of our knowledge arises in the context of our particular web of beliefs suggests there are no given truths.[9] If all of our

[6] T. Kuhn, *The Structure of Scientific Revolutions* (Chicago: University of Chicago Press, 1970); W. Quine, *Word and Object* (Cambridge, Mass.: MIT Press, 1960); and L. Wittgenstein, *Philosophical Investigations*, trans. G. Anscombe (Oxford: Basil Blackwell, 1972).

[7] Compare W. Quine, 'Two dogmas of empiricism', in *From a Logical Point of View* (Cambridge, Mass.: Harvard University Press, 1961), pp. 20–46.

[8] The image of our beliefs as forming an interconnected web derives primarily from W. Quine and J. Ullian, *The Web of Belief* (New York: Random House, 1970).

[9] That all roads – Dewey and pragmatism, Heidegger and continental philosophy, and Wittgenstein and analytic philosophy – lead not just away from logical positivism, and more generally Cartesian and Kantian philosophy, but towards anti-foundationalism is suggested by R. Rorty, *Philosophy and the Mirror of Nature* (Princeton: Princeton University Press, 1979), particularly pp. 5–13.

knowledge depends on a particular context, surely no empirical fact and
no principle of reason can possibly be given to us as an unquestionable,
self-evident, and basic truth. By and large, I will go along with the
anti-foundational (or post-analytic) conclusion that there are no given
truths. However, I will reject the irrationalist anti-foundationalism
found in post-structuralists and post-modernists such as Jacques Derrida, Michel Foucault, and Jean-François Lyotard.[10] A rejection of pure
observations, and so given empirical truths, will play a key role in many
of my later arguments. Moreover, because I have repudiated a sharp
distinction between the synthetic and the analytic conceived as contrasting types of knowledge, a rejection of given empirical truths must make
me suspicious of the idea that there are given truths of reason. I will
eschew, therefore, any commitment to a simple presence, an ultimately
privileged representation. There is no self-evident truth or set of truths
capable of providing our knowledge with absolutely secure foundations.[11] All of our beliefs are in principle open to revision. Such anti-
foundationalist sympathies clearly require one to adopt a much less
restrictive view of philosophy than did the logical positivists. For a start,
once one accepts that philosophers legitimately can ask questions other
than second-order ones, one no longer should be hostile to non-analytic
approaches to the discipline. My interest lies in questions about the
forms of reasoning appropriate to a first-order discipline, and such
questions are prominent in analytic philosophy, but this does not mean I
have to dismiss as illegitimate questions more commonly explored by
phenomenologists, hermeneutic theorists, and the like. In addition, once
one rejects a sharp distinction between the analytic and the synthetic as
contrasting types of knowledge, one thereby raises questions about the
nature of (post-)analytic philosophy – questions about the type of knowledge it provides and the means of its doing so. To answer these
questions, I will adopt a (post-)analytic view of philosophy drawing on
the later work of Wittgenstein while avoiding the more outlandish forms
of the ordinary language approach with which it sometimes is associated.

[10] A degree of tentativeness is appropriate here precisely because some scholars contrast an
irrationalist post-modernism with a post-analytic approach, and in this context post-analytic
philosophy can seem to reintroduce a notion of the given. See M. Lilla, 'On Goodman, Putnam,
and Rorty: the return to the given', *Partisan Review* 51 (1984), 220–35.
[11] Compare J. Derrida, *Speech and Phenomena, and Other Essays on Husserl's Theory of Signs*, trans. D.
Allison (Evanston, Ill.: Northwestern University Press, 1973); and Rorty, *Philosophy and the Mirror
of Nature*. However, to reject foundationalism is not necessarily to reject the very idea of our
having justified knowledge. Compare L. Wittgenstein, *On Certainty*, trans. D. Paul and G.
Anscombe (Oxford: Basil Blackwell, 1974).

The logic of an academic discipline consists of an analysis of the forms of reasoning appropriate to it. Philosophers try to arrive at such analyses by reasoning about reasoning in a way that makes part of philosophy a second-order discipline concerned to investigate the nature of first-order reasoning. We can accept this much without thereby subscribing to the logical positivists' view of the whole of philosophy as a second-order investigation. It is just that the topic I have chosen happens to be a second-order study. My concern happens to be with the logic of the history of ideas, where the subject matter of any logic is the reasoning appropriate to the data studied by a first-order discipline, not the data itself. Logics analyse the forms of reasoning associated with acceptable conclusions in first-order disciplines. They do not examine the acceptability of particular conclusions in first-order disciplines. For example, a literary critic might ask whether Hamlet is reasonably or unreasonably irresolute, a literary historian might ask whether Shakespeare intended to portray Hamlet as reasonably or unreasonably irresolute, and a philosopher might ask whether or not these two questions are the same. The philosopher can debate the third question as a conceptual puzzle without first answering either of the questions of literary and historical fact. The third question centres on the abstract relationship between our concept of the meaning of a work and our concept of the intentions of its author.

Philosophers determine what forms of reasoning are appropriate to a discipline by studying the concepts operating within it. To say this is not to commit oneself to the sharp distinction drawn by logical positivists between analytic and synthetic knowledge. Even if the terms analytic and synthetic cannot refer to two different types of knowledge, however, they can refer to two different ways of coming to know things. After all, any web of beliefs we accept provides us with a context that goes a long way towards fixing the semantic meaning of its individual components. Against the background of any particular web of beliefs, moreover, we can come to know things either by further empirical investigations of the world or by exploring the logical implications of the beliefs we already hold. The latter approach differs from both science and formal logic, the synthetic and the analytic, as they are defined by logical positivists. Clearly it does not require any further empirical studies of the world, but equally clearly it does not consist in the elucidation of tautologies impervious to such empirical studies. Rather, it draws out the logical implications of beliefs that we currently hold true but might change at a later date.

Wittgenstein's account of philosophy as the study of the grammar of our concepts closely resembles this latter approach to knowledge.[12] Unfortunately, however, Wittgenstein's image of a grammar can wrongly suggest that his interests are linguistic, not conceptual. Really we should see Wittgenstein's philosophy as a means of unpacking categories or theories and intuitions or facts that are embedded in our concepts. Philosophy, so understood, gives us knowledge which is true for us purely by virtue of semantic meaning, that is, purely by virtue of being implied by the concepts we use to make sense of the world.[13] The knowledge philosophy gives us is not self-evident in the sense anti-foundationalists reject, since someone who did not share our concepts would not accept it as true. Equally, however, we cannot question the knowledge philosophy gives us since our acceptance of our concepts makes it true for us by virtue of semantic meaning alone. Even if Wittgenstein's discussions of what he means by the grammar of our concepts can seem a bit too metaphorical, the bold outline of his position is clear. And even if this bold outline can seem to leave unanswered questions about the precise status of philosophical knowledge, it will suffice for us; after all, fully to explore the nature of the knowledge philosophy gives us would take one far from a study of the logic of the history of ideas. My approach to philosophy is (post-)analytic in that the knowledge it gives us derives from the grammar of our concepts.

Philosophers construct the logic of a discipline by exploring the grammar of the concepts operating within it. They do not have to study the actual subject matter of the disciplines they investigate. Thus, when we investigate the logic of the history of ideas, our concern must be with the way historians of ideas reason about historical data, not with historical data itself. Moreover, because the logic of a discipline consists of the forms of reasoning appropriate to it, and because the practitioners of a discipline might not reason in the appropriate manner, philosophers must concentrate on what the practitioners ought to do, not what they actually do. A logic provides us with a normative account of reasoning, not a historical, sociological, or psychological one.[14] For

---

[12] One of the first works to explore this account of philosophy is L. Wittgenstein, *Philosophical Grammar*, ed. R. Rhees, trans. A. Kenny (Oxford: Basil Blackwell, 1974).

[13] On Wittgenstein's position in relation to Quine's critique of analyticity, see C. Wright, *Wittgenstein on the Foundations of Mathematics* (London: Duckworth, 1980), particularly pp. 358–63. Also see H. Putnam, 'Analyticity and apriority: beyond Wittgenstein and Quine', in *Philosophical Papers*, 3 vols. (Cambridge: Cambridge University Press, 1975–83), vol. III, *Realism and Reason*, pp. 115–38.

[14] Something close to a view of philosophy as the empirical study of human reasoning inspired D. Hume, *A Treatise of Human Nature*, ed. L. Selby-Bigge, rev. P. Nidditch (Oxford: Clarendon Press, 1978). Hume described his work in its subtitle as 'an attempt to introduce the experimental method of reasoning into moral subjects'.

example, philosophers cannot determine whether or not the meaning of a literary work corresponds to the intentions of its author simply by seeing whether literary critics and literary historians have or have not equated the question of whether Hamlet is reasonably or unreasonably irresolute with that of whether Shakespeare intended to portray Hamlet as reasonably or unreasonably irresolute. No doubt exemplary instances of what the practitioners of a discipline actually do often provide philosophers with examples they can refer to when justifying their logics. Indeed, such instances can act as examples philosophers must account for if their logics are to be convincing. Philosophers must take account of exemplary instances of reasoning because to show that their logics outline the forms of reasoning that make for acceptable conclusions within a discipline, they must relate the forms of reasoning they advocate to the main characteristics of good practice in the relevant discipline. None the less, even a description of exemplary instance followed by exemplary instance will degenerate into a mere list unless it is accompanied by a normative, philosophical elucidation of the features that make these instances, and not others, exemplary. When philosophers analyse the logic of any discipline, they outline the conceptual form and content of an ideal type of reasoning. They do not describe the historical, social, or psychological processes involved in an actual type of reasoning. Thus, neither phenomenological nor metahistorical accounts of actual, historical reasoning can sustain a logic.[15] The most they can do is to suggest limits to the possible, where, because 'ought' implies 'can', these limits would operate on a logic. When we investigate the logic of the history of ideas, our concern must be with what historians of ideas ought to do, not what they do do.

The logic of a discipline consists of a normative account of the reasoning appropriate to it. Disciplines generally have forms of justificatory and explanatory reasoning as the two constitutive parts of their logics. A form of justification consists of an analysis of the characteristics that make a certain body of facts and theories objective, or authoritative, within a discipline. It specifies the way in which scholars can justify their claims to knowledge. Thus, a form of justification might consist of a method by which scholars can arrive at suitable facts and theories, or a test for evaluating the facts and theories scholars put forward, or criteria for comparing rival bodies of facts and theories. A method, in a strong

---

[15] Works that muddle phenomenological and metahistorical issues with logical ones include respectively R. Collingwood, *The Idea of History*, ed. T. Knox (Oxford: Clarendon Press, 1946); and H. White, *Metahistory: The Historical Imagination in Nineteenth-Century Europe* (Baltimore: Johns Hopkins University Press, 1973).

sense, is a special procedure that enables scholars to reach a correct conclusion about something. Spectrometry, for example, is a method that enables scientists to measure the absorption of energy by gases, liquids, and solids. A method, in a weak sense, is a special procedure without which scholars can not reach a correct conclusion about something. Some Marxists, for example, argue that class analysis provides a method without which historians cannot understand political conflicts in capitalist societies. All methods differ from heuristic techniques in that they are either sufficient or necessary to ensure a correct conclusion about something, whereas heuristic techniques merely provide a potentially fruitful way of reaching a correct conclusion about something. Usually philosophers can leave questions concerning heuristic techniques to methodologists precisely because heuristic techniques do not have the same logical, and so normative, force as do methods.

Philosophers study the forms of reasoning appropriate to first-order disciplines. They do not study the mnemonics or cues scholars use to make their tasks easier. The exclusion of heuristics from philosophy restricts the expectations we should have of a logic of the history of ideas. Properly understood, many of the debates scholars engage in about the nature of the history of ideas will not concern us since they are matters of heuristics, not logic. Consider, for instance, debates about the procedures historians ought to adopt to understand an unfamiliar work. Such procedures enter into logic only if they constitute a form of justification, that is, only if we can justify or reject a view of a work simply by saying it was or was not reached using the relevant procedure. Theories of how we should come to understand a work move from heuristics to logic only if they constitute a sufficient or necessary condition of an objective understanding of a work. If they provide us only with sensible advice, they remain matters for heuristics alone. Consider also debates about how far historians should go to make a work, or group of works, seem sincere, coherent, or rational. Such questions become matters of logic only if their resolution depends on the grammar of our concepts. In so far as the extent to which we ought to treat beliefs as sincere, coherent, and rational remains a matter for interpretative judgement, it too must remain a matter of heuristics alone. Heuristic concerns are legitimate and interesting, but they have no place in the logic of the history of ideas.

Let us turn now from forms of justification to the other main component of a logic. A form of explanation consists of an analysis of the thing (or things) that explains the objects of concern to us, together with an analysis of the relationship of this thing (or these things) to these objects. It specifies the way in which scholars can explain the data they uncover. Some Marxists, for example, analyse the form of explanation appropriate to political conflicts in capitalist societies in terms of social class together with a theory of historical materialism which defines the relationship of class-structure to political conflict in capitalist society. More generally, philosophers interested in the explanation of human action often debate whether actions should be explained causally or conditionally. Causal explanation is the form appropriate to the natural sciences. It appears in cases where the occurrence of one thing makes the occurrence of another necessary because of the operation of physical laws. Conditional explanation is defined in contrast to causal explanation as the form appropriate to rational action. It appears in cases where one thing does not necessitate another but merely gives someone a reason to act in a way that brings about the other. Philosophers sometimes prescribe for a discipline forms of justification and explanation that closely resemble each other. Some Marxists, for example, ground both their methodological and explanatory reasoning on the concept of class. When this happens, the close resemblance between the two usually arises because they both reflect the nature of the object being investigated. Certainly Marxists adopt forms of justification and explanation based on the concept of class because they believe that capitalist societies are constituted by a given class-structure. None the less, we have no general reason to assume that the forms of justification and explanation appropriate to a discipline will resemble one another. Indeed, they can differ dramatically. Although spectrometry provides scientists with a method for measuring the absorption of energy by gases, liquids, and solids, scientists explain the absorption of energy by reference to theories about the structure of gases, liquids, and solids, not by reference to spectrometry.

A concern with forms of justification and explanation sometimes appears to involve the study of language rather than reality; or, to be exact, because language is a part of reality, it sometimes appears to involve the study of language to the exclusion of other parts of reality. For example, a philosopher who studies the relationship of the meaning of a literary work to the intentions of its author can appear to be studying the role of words such as 'meaning' and 'intention' within our ordinary language. Some exponents of analytic philosophy make great play of the close relationship between philosophy and language. Once one understands why philosophy often appears to take a linguistic form, however, one will find that doing philosophy is not the same thing as studying language. Why does philosophy often take a linguistic form? Earlier I argued that philosophers study the grammar of our concepts, not the actual phenomena so conceptualised, or an actual process of thinking. The only way philosophers can discuss the grammar of our concepts, however, is by using the words we use to convey concepts. Philosophers cannot rely on mystical or introspective revelations of inexpressible truths about the nature of things. Even if they thought they had grasped a truth as a result of such a revelation, they could not examine its validity except by considering it as a statement couched in a language embodying concepts. In a sense, therefore, philosophers cannot help but take an interest in language. Every time they consider a conceptual issue, they confront language as the medium in which we deal with concepts. More controversially, because many of the concepts of concern to philosophers have established linguistic expressions, some philosophers find they benefit from approaching concepts through a study of the operation of their linguistic expressions. For example, a philosopher concerned with the nature of meaning and its relationship to authorial intention might benefit from considering how we use the word 'meaning' and how our use of it relates to our use of the word 'intention'.

There are, therefore, good reasons why philosophy often takes a linguistic form. Yet these reasons do not enable us to reduce philosophy to a study of language. When the legendary critics denounce philosophy as a mere matter of words, or how one chooses to define things, they invariably miss their target. On the one hand, if words are taken to be combinations of sounds arbitrarily associated with particular concepts, it simply is not true that philosophy is a mere matter of words or of how one chooses to define things. When philosophers discuss a word such as 'truth', their interest lies in the concept of truth, not the sounds we conventionally use to convey it. Philosophers rarely mistake bogus questions about words defined exclusively in terms of sounds for genuine questions about words defined to include the concepts conventionally linked to sounds. On the other hand, if words are defined to include ideas and concepts, then it is no fault in philosophers that words provide the subject matter of the majority of their studies and debates. On the contrary, every intellectual debate concerns ideas and concepts, so in this respect philosophers do not differ from anyone else. The legendary critics complain: philosophy concerns conventional definitions, so when philosophers say the nature of truth is such and such, their conclusion merely implies that we use 'such and such' to denote our concept of truth, so if we decided to use 'XYZ' to denote our concept of truth, philosophers would say the nature of truth was XYZ. But this criticism establishes only that we could express our concepts using different patterns of sounds from those we do use. It does not establish that no genuine philosophical issues arise about our concepts whatever patterns of sounds we use to express them. After all, even if we decided to use 'XYZ' to denote our concept of truth, philosophers still would want to know whether XYZ consisted in correspondence with reality, a perfectly coherent set of propositions, or something else again.

Philosophers who investigate the way we use words do so principally in order to obtain insights into the grammar of our concepts, not insights into words and their place in ordinary language. Unfortunately, however, a few extreme linguistic philosophers appear to make stronger claims than this. These stronger claims are at the very least misleading, and more often than not wrong. Moreover, although the philosophers who make these stronger claims typically associate them, with some reason, with the views of Wittgenstein, one can at least as reasonably draw on Wittgenstein to reach an account of philosophy close to that I am defending.[16] Extreme linguistic philosophers sometimes suggest that philosophy deals with the place of words in ordinary language, not the nature of the world as we conceive it.[17] Actually, however, the fact that we usefully can approach some philosophical issues through an examination of ordinary language does not imply that philosophical issues are issues about ordinary language. On the contrary, I have suggested that most philosophers discuss questions of linguistic usage only in order to discover things about the best understanding of reality currently available to us. They turn to language as a way of investigating the grammar of our concepts and thereby exploring further our understanding of the world. Their real concern is with the presuppositions and implications of the concepts that we use to make sense of the world. Thus, while philosophers construct the logic of a discipline on the basis of the concepts deployed within it, not the data uncovered by it, they do so to examine what these concepts imply about the nature of the world, not to record how we use the words that embody these concepts.

Because our concepts apply to reality, we can extend our understanding of reality by exploring the implications of the concepts we believe

---

[16] Compare R. Newell, *The Concept of Philosophy* (London: Methuen, 1967).
[17] Wittgenstein, *Philosophical Investigations*, # 43. On his actual method see Newell, *Concept of Philosophy*, pp. 145–52.

best capture reality. Surely this is what philosophers typically do. Certainly Wittgenstein's philosophical practice often fits this analysis in a way that suggests that his description of his philosophy as a study of ordinary language is partially misleading. On the one hand, his description of philosophy as a study of ordinary language helps to distance his position from logical positivism.[18] It underlines his view that philosophy uncovers truths given to us by our existing concepts, rather than by further empirical studies or pure reason. On the other hand, however, a study of Wittgenstein's philosophical practice shows his concern typically to have been with concepts, theories, and habits of thinking, not words and their uses. Whereas he rarely appeals to our standard forms of speech to clarify actual norms of usage, he often appeals to unusual situations to clarify our grasp of the limiting cases to which we would apply various concepts. Perhaps philosophers now need less to distance themselves from logical positivism than to emphasise that their discipline concerns concepts and the relationships between them. We need to dispel the unfortunate impression that philosophy is an imprecisely defined study of language.

Extreme linguistic philosophers also sometimes say the point of philosophy is to unravel the intellectual confusions created by the bewitching effects of language.[19] They argue that philosophical problems arise only when philosophers place words in contexts other than those they can occupy in ordinary language. Because the words do not belong in these contexts, they have no true meaning therein, and this absence of true meaning generates apparent paradoxes. Thus, they continue, we can dissolve philosophical problems simply by revealing them to be pseudo-problems which arise only when we fail fully to grasp the workings of ordinary language. Philosophers should not develop theories: they should remind us of how our language works so as to stop us worrying about meaningless paradoxes. In contrast, I have suggested that philosophers who clarify the meaning of words, whether or not they start with ordinary usage, do so principally in order to unpack the grammar of our concepts. Moreover, when they do so, the implications they thereby derive from our concepts constitute theories about reality, not reminders of how we normally use words. No doubt it is possible for

---

[18] On the contrast between Wittgenstein's view of philosophy as a study of grammar and his earlier concern with logical syntax, see P. Hacker, *Insight and Illusion: Themes in the Philosophy of Wittgenstein* (Oxford: Clarendon Press, 1986), pp. 179–206.

[19] Wittgenstein, *Philosophical Investigations*, # 126. Again on his actual method, see Newell, *Concept of Philosophy*, pp. 145–52.

a description of the way we use certain words to draw our attention to a particular theory without further ado, and this theory might suggest an obvious answer to a philosophical problem. None the less, we have no reason to assume such a procedure will enable us to resolve all, or even most, of our philosophical problems. Here Wittgenstein's description of his philosophy as concerned to undo the bewitching effects of language is again partially misleading. Although it distances his work from logical positivism, it does so at the expense of giving far too many hostages to an extreme linguistic philosophy.[20] The philosophical problems Wittgenstein considers rarely resemble cases in which we use one word when we should have used another. They are more like cases in which we know what words to use but are confused about the concepts we thereby apply. Typically he aims not to clarify the way our language works, but to highlight the limitations of some of the theoretical models of the world that are suggested to us by our language. At most we should say that Wittgenstein shows how ordinary language prompts us to adopt theories which philosophical reflection reveals to be mistaken.

Facts about our ordinary use of language by themselves cannot answer philosophical questions for the simple reason that these questions concern the grammar of our concepts not our use of words. Philosophers try to enhance our knowledge of reality by exploring the nature and implications of the way in which we conceptualise it. They focus on the grammar of the concepts that express what they believe to be the best understanding of the world available to us. What is more, there is no reason why the best set of concepts available to us should be the ones embodied in ordinary language. Sometimes the practitioners of a discipline may have refined certain concepts in order to ensure greater precision than ordinary usage allows. In these cases, what I will call the descriptions of ordinary language have been superseded by what I will call the accounts of scholars. Sometimes philosophers, too, may have refined certain concepts because they were frustrated by a lack of rigour in our ordinary or scholarly usage. In these cases, descriptions and accounts alike have been superseded by what I will call the analyses of philosophers. Of course, critics can challenge the refinements a philosopher makes to any given concept, but such challenges will be convincing only if they are suitably rigorous. To achieve the necessary rigour, moreover, critics usually have to introduce refinements of their own instead of relying exclusively on ordinary language. When philosophers

---

[20] On the contrast between Wittgenstein's view of philosophy as a study of grammar and a view of philosophy as aiming at systematic theories, see Hacker, *Insight and Illusion*, pp. 175–8.

study the nature and implications of a particular understanding of reality, they usually benefit from identifying it as precisely as possible. Thus, if our everyday descriptions and scientific accounts fail to provide them with a clear understanding of the concepts involved, they have to analyse these concepts for themselves. We must allow, therefore, that philosophers can work quite legitimately with concepts other than those embodied in ordinary language.

What set of concepts should we use to construct the logic of the history of ideas? Well, whereas the natural sciences rely heavily on specialised languages which contain concepts more precisely defined than those of ordinary language, the history of ideas relies on the concepts of ordinary language to describe beliefs, actions, and the like. When we investigate the logic of the history of ideas, therefore, we should do so principally by drawing out the implications of ordinary language. We should do so not because philosophers must always do so, but rather because ordinary language embodies the concepts that provide the best available understanding of the material studied by historians of ideas. Thus, in so far as the relevant parts of ordinary language lack precision, we can legitimately clarify them further before deriving logical conclusions from them.

A logic is a normative account of the forms of justificatory and explanatory reasoning appropriate to a given discipline. The characterisation of a logic generally relies on analysis to clarify the concepts of our everyday descriptions and scholarly accounts of the data uncovered by the relevant discipline. When we develop a logic for the history of ideas, we aim to enhance our understanding of reality by exploring the grammar of a refined set of the concepts operating in that discipline. The logical implications we draw out from these concepts constitute theories about the world – for example, that human beings are agents who typically have reasons for holding the beliefs they do. It is these theories about the world that provide us with grounds for identifying certain forms of reasoning as appropriate to the history of ideas.

PHILOSOPHICAL ARGUMENT

Now that I have analysed the abstract nature of logics, I will consider what sorts of reasoning are appropriate for constructing them. Because logics identify valid forms of reasoning without explaining phenomena, a logic of logics should consist of a form of justification but not a form of explanation. What justifies a claim to philosophical knowledge? Philosophical arguments cannot rest on formal logic if only because the logics of disciplines do not consist solely of logical deductions from the principles of formal logic. In addition, an anti-foundational suspicion of all self-evident truths suggests that even the truths of formal logic are not simply given to us, so they too need justifying. Philosophers cannot base logics on formal logic itself. They cannot identify the forms of reasoning appropriate to a discipline by reference to logical principles alone.[21] Rather, they must construct a logic by drawing out the implications of a given set of concepts. They must rely on an acceptance of the particular concepts that operate in a discipline as a basis for identifying the forms of reasoning appropriate to it. Likewise, philosophical arguments cannot rest on our experiences of the world if only because the logics of disciplines do not consist solely of statements of empirical fact. In addition, of course, an anti-foundational suspicion of all self-evident truths suggests that our experiences are not simply given to us, so they too need justifying.

I already have rejected the possibility of philosophers proceeding by describing facts about the data studied by a discipline, or historical, sociological, or psychological facts about processes of reasoning, or even facts about ordinary language. Instead, philosophers must proceed by drawing out the nature and implications of the concepts operating in a discipline, and this suggests that these concepts provide the foundation of the logic they construct. The foundation of philosophical knowledge is a prior acceptance of the understanding of the world expressed by the concepts that philosophers take as their subject matter. When philosophers successfully show that the grammar of a set of concepts entails such and such, people must accept such and such if they accept the understanding of the world expressed by the relevant set of concepts. If our view of the world is valid, the implications of the concepts making up this view of the world must also be valid.

---

[21] Contrast B. Russell, 'The philosophy of logical analysis', in *History of Western Philosophy* (London: George Allen & Unwin, 1971), pp. 783–9. For an indication of the way the early thought of Wittgenstein reinforced this view, see B. Russell, 'The philosophy of logical atomism', in *Logic and Knowledge*, ed. R. Marsh (London: George Allen & Unwin, 1956), pp. 175–281. Russell emphasised that he arrived at his view of philosophy through his work on the philosophy of mathematics. In the view I am defending, a logic of mathematics would consist of drawing out the grammar of the concepts operating in mathematics. Because these concepts closely resemble those of formal logic, one can see why someone might approach the philosophy of mathematics through an analysis of the logical implications of formal logic. In fact, however, the view I am defending would divorce even the philosophy of mathematics from logical analysis. Compare Wittgenstein, *Philosophical Grammar*; L. Wittgenstein, *Remarks on the Foundations of Mathematics*, ed. G. Anscombe, R. Rhees, and G. von Wright (Oxford: Basil Blackwell, 1978); and, for detailed discussion, Wright, *Wittgenstein*.

It is because philosophical knowledge rests on a prior acceptance of a given understanding of the world that so many philosophers find the challenge of the sceptic peculiarly pertinent. Because philosophical argument rests on a prior acceptance of an understanding of the world, the sceptic who denies that we have valid grounds for accepting any understanding of the world thereby undermines the very basis of philosophical argument. How can we meet the challenge of the sceptic? A move away from logical positivism makes the question of how we can justify philosophical knowledge a part of the more general question of how we can justify knowledge as a whole. We cannot distinguish between two types of knowledge in need of different forms of justification; the synthetic or scientific to be defended by reference to our experiences, and the analytic or philosophic to be defended by reference to the principles of reason itself. Instead we must see our knowledge as a single whole in need of a single form of justification. In addition, a shift away from logical positivism precludes the adoption of a foundationalist form of justification. We cannot justify philosophical arguments by reference to given, self-evident truths, either empirical facts or principles of pure reason. Later I will consider in some detail how we should justify our knowledge. For now, however, I will observe only that my response to scepticism will draw on the nature of our being in the world. People could not survive if they did not act in the world, and to act in the world they must have some sort of view of the world. Thus, the nature of our being in the world requires us to commit ourselves, no matter how provisionally, to an understanding of the world, and this commitment provides a basis for philosophical argument. Once people commit themselves, no matter how tentatively, to a set of concepts, they must also commit themselves to the implications of that set of concepts. Consider, for example, how one might rebut the sceptical position developed by Hayden White.[22] White implies that we have no rational grounds for preferring one philosophy of history to another. He argues that our decisions about the forms of reasoning a historian should adopt rest on aesthetic judgements about the rival merits of various linguistic tropes. The failings of his scepticism, however, appear in his neglect of semantics. In a work that discusses competing philosophies of history in terms of their linguistic properties, he does not once consider the way we use language to represent the world. White has thus to neglect semantics because if he acknowledged that we use language to represent the world, he would recognise that to commit oneself to a philosophy of history as a

---

[22] White, *Metahistory*.

language is necessarily to commit oneself to a view of the world. He would see that the nature of our being in the world compels us to accept a set of concepts as true. He would undermine his own scepticism.

No doubt relativists will object that to have to adopt a view of the world is not to have a reason to take as true any particular view of the world. I will consider the problem posed by relativism in greater detail later. For now, I want to point out only that relativism, unlike scepticism, does not undermine the very basis of philosophical argument. Relativism queries the strength and nature of our attachment to our view of the world, and thereby the strength and nature of our attachment to the philosophical implications of our view of the world. But it does not undermine the basic point that we must accept a view of the world, and once we do so, we also must accept the implications of this view of the world. Relativism queries the strength of the basis of philosophical argument, but it does not cast doubt on its very existence. We can justify our philosophical conclusions by reference to our prior acceptance of the set of concepts on which they are based, where our life commits us to at least a tentative acceptance of some set of concepts.

Now that we have identified the foundations of philosophical argument, we can proceed to examine how such argument works. Philosophers can tease out the grammar of a set of concepts using both deductive and inductive procedures. A rejection of the logical positivists' sharp distinction between analytic and synthetic propositions influences the way in which we conceive of deduction and induction. We cannot define deduction and induction as ways of arriving at contrasting types of belief, respectively the analytic and the synthetic. Instead, we must define deduction and induction as different procedures deployed in a single web of beliefs.[23] Deduction typically draws out the implications of our most entrenched beliefs – the categories that govern whole clusters of concepts. In contrast, induction typically highlights the implications of our beliefs about the differences that can appear within clusters of concepts. The procedures of deduction and induction operate on, and generate, beliefs that might differ in degree, but certainly do not differ in kind.

Deductive arguments demonstrate the implications of general propositions.[24] They are of most use when philosophers want to discuss a set

---

[23] Thus, the traditional problem of induction, that is, of how to justify the knowledge it generates, disappears to become part of the larger problem of how to justify our web of beliefs as a whole.

[24] Because our understanding of concepts rests on our ability to apply them to particular cases, deductive arguments, like inductive ones, ultimately rest on particular cases. On the importance of particular cases, see J. Wisdom, 'A feature of Wittgenstein's technique', in K. Fann (ed.), *Wittgenstein: The Man and His Philosophy* (New York: Dell, 1967), pp. 353–65.

of concepts as a single, coherent whole. On these occasions, philosophers can often deduce consequences from the categories that govern the relevant cluster of concepts. Whenever a group of concepts form a coherent whole, they entail categories which define clear limits to what one can say using them. Categories demarcate the boundaries of the intelligible.[25] For example, we cannot make sense of the statement 'the red table is unhappy' simply because our categorical understanding of inanimate objects, such as tables, precludes our attributing to them emotions, such as unhappiness. Philosophers can use deductive arguments to explicate the implications that categories have for a whole discipline. A critic might suggest that we successfully transgress categorical limits to the intelligible whenever we use language metaphorically.[26] But this would be to miss the point. Categorical limits restrict our grasp of conceptual possibilities rather than our use of words. Thus, although we undoubtedly can use words in metaphorical ways to express concepts other than those they normally express, this does not provide any evidence of the latter concepts successfully transgressing categorical limits to the intelligible. Metaphors play about with our use of words, not our understanding of concepts. Another critic might suggest that because we use words in diverse ways, we cannot make any general assertions about the ways we can and cannot use them. But this would be to make much the same mistake as the first critic. Categorical limits apply to our use of concepts, not words, and typically each of the different ways we use a given word evokes a different concept. Thus, although our words undoubtedly have a plurality of meanings, this does not imply that our concepts have a plurality of meanings. Yet another critic might suggest that our concepts are too imprecise to enable us to identify categorical limits to the intelligible. Certainly the majority of our concepts do not have precise, necessary, and sufficient conditions of application. They consist of vague, imprecise collections of family resemblances, as Wittgenstein showed with respect to the concept of a game.[27] None the less, the imprecise nature of many of our concepts does not preclude their fixing limits to what we can find intelligible. For a start, some of our concepts, including 'mother' and 'bachelor', surely do have necessary and sufficient conditions of

---

[25] Compare G. Ryle, 'Categories' and 'Philosophical argument', in *Collected Papers*, vol. II, *Collected Essays 1929–1968* (London: Hutchinson & Co., 1971), pp. 170–84 and 194–211.

[26] Some philosophers argue that all language is metaphorical since meanings do not have sharp boundaries. See J. Derrida, 'Differance', in *Margins of Philosophy*, trans. A. Bass (Brighton, Sussex: Harvester Press, 1982), pp. 1–27.

[27] Wittgenstein, *Philosophical Investigations*, ## 66–9.

application.[28] More importantly, even when we cannot specify precise conditions of application for our concepts, we can specify limiting conditions, and this alone is sufficient to create a space for deductive, categorical argument. For instance, although we cannot say precisely what counts as a game, we can say that a game must be played by living beings, which implies that we cannot make sense of the idea of a table playing a game with a chair. Our concepts entail categories which define limits to what we can conceive as possible. Consequently, philosophers can sometimes deduce the necessity or impossibility of something simply from the limits our categories impose on the intelligible.

On one view, a deductive argument ends in an acceptable conclusion if, and only if, the premises of the argument entail the conclusion and the premises are true. In contrast, I will take a more conventionalist view of deduction, according to which a deductive argument ends in an acceptable conclusion if, and only if, the premises entail the conclusion and we take the premises to be true. I must adopt this conventionalist view because I am suspicious of the idea of given truths. If there are no given truths, we cannot be certain of the truth of the everyday and scientific theories informing our understanding of the world, so we cannot be certain of the truth of the categories embedded in our understanding of the world. However, a conventionalism grounded on the absence of given truths is not a problem for philosophers. Philosophers can premise their deductive arguments on the conceptual structure the practitioners of a discipline take to be true without themselves worrying about its truth. When they do so, their arguments will presuppose the truth of the conceptual structure, which might not be true – but then none of our knowledge of the world is absolutely certain. When philosophers premise their arguments on the conceptual structure that governs a discipline, their conclusions will follow from the categories that underpin the very possibility of scholars engaging in the discipline; after all, without categorical limits to the intelligible, there would be no limit to what could explain what, and so no identifiable discipline. Thus, if we denied the conclusion of a valid deductive argument, we would overturn the whole of the discipline that operates using the relevant set of concepts. Successful deductive arguments prove their conclusions as effectively as is possible.

[28] Surely Wittgenstein can not have meant his argument about family resemblances to apply to all concepts if only because he saw mathematics as a form of deductive or categorical argument conducted within a language of stipulated definitions? See Wittgenstein, *Philosophical Grammar* and *Foundations of Mathematics*.

Philosophical arguments can work inductively as well as deductively. Indeed, Wittgenstein's recognition that concepts such as 'game' are held together by family resemblances actually serves not to question the role within philosophy of deduction, but rather to highlight the role therein of induction. To analyse many of our concepts, we have to explore the range of circumstances they can cover. We have to do so precisely because we cannot specify these circumstances in terms of necessary and sufficient conditions.[29] Inductive arguments move from particular cases to general propositions. Thus, they are of most use when philosophers want to discuss either the diverse types of circumstances we can describe using a given set of concepts or the diverse sets of concepts we can use to describe a particular type of circumstance. On these occasions, particular cases can provide philosophers with pertinent reminders of the complexity of the conceptual structures with which we make sense of the world. Sometimes we accept particular cases as valid on the basis of our intuitions, that is, our pre-philosophical or untutored reasoning. When we do so, these cases can act as tests for our philosophical theories. Intuitions thus provide philosophers with data. For example, Wittgenstein asks us to imagine that someone doodles but that nobody regards the doodle as meaningful until a psychoanalyst talks to the doodler, comes up with an interpretation of the doodle, and, together with the doodler, finds correlations between elements of the doodle and elements of the interpretation.[30] Wittgenstein suggests that because we would intuitively describe the psychoanalyst's account of the doodle as an interpretation, we should therefore conceive of psychoanalysis as a process concerned with the speculative interpretation of meanings, not the scientific diagnosis of causes. He uses our intuitions about a particular case to tell us something about the form of explanation found in psychoanalysis.

A critic might argue that our intuitions are purely subjective so philosophers have no reason to trust them. But this would be to misunderstand the epistemic status of our intuitions. Intuitions here refer to the concepts with which we understand the world as they are before we explore them philosophically. For example, we will describe the psychoanalyst's account of the doodle as an interpretation if we think our concept of an interpretation fits the case better than our concepts of a diagnosis or a hypothesis. Our intuitions derive from our pre-philo-

---

[29] L. Wittgenstein, *The Blue and Brown Books* (Oxford: Basil Blackwell, 1969), pp. 19–20.
[30] L. Wittgenstein, 'Conversations on Freud', in R. Wollheim and J. Hopkins (eds.), *Philosophical Essays on Freud* (Cambridge: Cambridge University Press, 1982), pp. 1–11.

sophical grasp of shared concepts, not from personal choice or subjective fancy. Another critic might argue that philosophers have no reason to assume that our intuitive grasp of shared concepts provides us with a suitable source of knowledge. But this would be to make much the same mistake as the first critic. Intuitionism here describes a way of testing philosophical theories against the knowledge contained in the concepts with which we understand the world. It does not claim to provide us with a phenomenological account of the nature of knowledge as such. Of course, our pre-philosophical grasp of a shared concept might be inadequate if only because our understanding of the world might be inadequate. Equally, however, scientific data might be inadequate if only because it depends on theories about the world which might be inadequate. The possibility of our being wrong about something we believe to be true should not prevent us proceeding as though what we believe to be true is true. Thus, although our intuitions might be false, this does not imply that they are of no relevance to philosophical theorising. Philosophers must modify their theories to take account of our intuitions in much the same way as scientists must modify their theories to take account of the results of experiments.

On one view, an inductive argument leads to an acceptable conclusion if, and only if, the premises support the conclusion and the premises are true. In contrast, I again will take a more conventionalist view, according to which an inductive argument leads to an acceptable conclusion if, and only if, the premises support the conclusion and we take the premises to be true. Philosophers can ground inductive arguments on our intuitions about particular cases without worrying about the epistemic adequacy of these intuitions. When they do so, their conclusions will rest on the implications of particular cases whose significance other philosophers might question, but then all of our knowledge of the world is open to question. None the less, philosophers can sidestep a valid inductive argument based on our intuitions in two special ways that they cannot use to counter a valid deductive argument. The first is that they can challenge aspects of the everyday or scientific understanding of the world underlying the relevant intuitions. The second is that they can adopt a speculative hypothesis to reconcile their favoured perspective with the relevant intuitions. These two procedures enable philosophers to repudiate the conclusion of a valid inductive argument without thereby overturning a whole discipline. Thus, successful inductive arguments do not have the force of deductive ones.

The role of examples differs in deductive and inductive arguments. Deductive arguments start out from general propositions which cannot be individual examples precisely because of their generality. None the less, we can illustrate the way a deductive argument draws out the implications of general propositions by showing how it works when we put an individual example in the place of the relevant general propositions. Examples illustrate deductive arguments. Consequently, the best examples for deductive arguments are usually both simple and realistic. A simple example illustrates clearly how a deductive argument works, which is the role of examples in deductive arguments. A realistic example highlights the general applicability of a deductive argument throughout the discipline being considered, where the strength of deductive arguments lies in just such general applicability. Inductive arguments, in contrast, start out from our intuitions, and although these intuitions can be responses to either general or specific propositions, our intuitions about general propositions always depend for their validity on our having similar intuitions about a number of specific propositions, so that ultimately all inductive arguments rest on intuitions about particular cases. Examples constitute the substance of inductive arguments. Consequently, the best examples for inductive arguments can be complex and far-fetched. Inductive arguments work by testing philosophical theories in much the same way as experiments test scientific theories, so philosophers should design examples in the light of their inductive arguments in much the same way as scientists design experiments in the light of their hypotheses. When philosophers make an inductive argument, they rarely can rely on the simple and realistic examples that arise in the ordinary run of things because these examples rarely provide the best tests of the relevant theories. Usually philosophers have to manipulate examples in order to isolate as far as possible the particular theories they want to test. Indeed, there are times when only a complex and far-fetched example, or set of examples, will eliminate all the other features one might consider relevant. Thought experiments epitomise such complex, far-fetched examples.[31] They postulate an extraordinary set of circumstances, and ask us to use our intuitions to discover how we would talk about these circumstances. They aim to advance our philo-

---

[31] For two exemplary thought experiments, see the use of 'Gavagi' in Quine, *Word and Object*, and 'Twin-Earth' in H. Putnam, 'The meaning of meaning', in *Philosophical Papers*, vol. II, *Mind, Language and Reality*, pp. 215–71. On the role of thought experiments in science, see T. Kuhn, 'A function for thought experiments', in I. Hacking (ed.), *Scientific Revolutions* (Oxford: Oxford University Press, 1981), pp. 6–27.

sophical theorising by clarifying the detailed content of our concepts through the exploration of our intuitions about an extreme case or set of cases. The role of examples in inductive arguments indicates once again the relationship of philosophy to the study of ordinary language. Inductive philosophical arguments deploy complex, far-fetched examples precisely because philosophical theories concern the grammar of our concepts, not the way we use words. When philosophers invoke our intuitions about various situations, their aim should be not to describe how we use words, but to clarify our conceptualisation of reality. Thus, they need not record every feature of our ordinary use of language. They can concentrate instead on situations, whether real or imaginary, that provide suitable tests for our philosophical theories.

Clearly deductive and inductive arguments best fulfil slightly different roles. Although philosophers use both types of argument for the same ultimate purpose, namely, to elucidate the content and implications of our concepts, the two types of argument best serve this purpose in different ways. We cannot define precise limits to the proper place of either type of argument, but we can identify the broad outline of their ideal roles. The generality of deductive arguments fits them for the construction of sweeping theories covering the whole of a discipline. Again, their generality makes them an ideal tool for criticising philosophical theories whose confusions result in logics completely inapplicable to the relevant discipline. For example, the argument that our categorical understanding of inanimate objects precludes our attributing emotions to them implies that physicists cannot use forms of explanation referring to emotional states. Philosophers are most likely to generalise when they draw out the implications of a set of concepts, arguing that such and such applies to the whole of a discipline by virtue of the categories informing the discipline. Thus, deductive arguments are particularly suited to theorising about forms of explanation in the light of a refined set of concepts. In contrast, the particularity of inductive arguments fits them for the analysis of the various possibilities or approaches that have a place in a discipline. Again, their particularity makes them ideal for criticising philosophers who generalise too quickly and so extend to the whole of a discipline what really is a feature only of a special part of it. For example, if we conclude, with Wittgenstein, that the psychoanalyst interprets the doodle, then we will query any attempt to describe all of psychotherapy in terms of the cure of mental illnesses using diagnostic techniques. Philosophers are most likely to discuss the varied nature of the material considered in a discipline when they refine the concepts operating in it, arguing that a given concept can refer to this sort of thing, that sort of thing, or whatever. Thus, inductive arguments are particularly suited to analysing concepts as they appear in our everyday descriptions or scholarly accounts of the world.

Philosophical arguments rest on a prior acceptance of the sets of concepts that philosophers take as their subject matter. We accept these concepts in so far as they appear in either our everyday descriptions or our scholarly accounts of the world. Philosophers can draw out the content and implications of a set of concepts using both deductive and inductive arguments. Deductive arguments draw out the implications of the general propositions or categories embodied in particular sets of concepts, and they usually do so using simple, clear examples. Typically they sustain sweeping theories about the nature of a discipline as a whole. Inductive arguments draw out the implications of the particular propositions or intuitions associated with particular sets of concepts, and they often have to do so using complex, far-fetched examples. Typically they sustain taxonomic analyses of the various different approaches that have a place in a discipline. I will explore the logic of the history of ideas, therefore, using both deductive and inductive arguments with the different types of examples they require. Sometimes I will use simple, realistic examples, but at other times I will have to introduce complex, far-fetched ones designed to isolate a particular feature of our concepts.

THE LOGIC OF THE HISTORY OF IDEAS

When we study the logic of the history of ideas, we undertake a second-order study of the reasoning appropriate to a first-order discipline. My analysis of the nature of a logic has drawn on a moderate (post-)analytic philosophy. It avoids not only the excesses of the logical positivists, but also those of the more ardent of the linguistic philosophers who have succeeded them. I have argued that philosophers construct logics on the basis of an acceptance of the understanding of the world expressed by a given set of concepts. They do so by using deductive and inductive arguments, first, to analyse the concepts that operate in a discipline, and, second, to show how these concepts sustain theories that assign certain forms of justificatory and explanatory reasoning to the discipline. When I explore the logic of the history of ideas, I will follow this procedure. Perhaps, however, some critics might object to the very idea of a distinctive logic for the history of ideas on the grounds that a single logic applies to all human reasoning. They might argue that the logic of the history of ideas cannot consist of anything more than an analysis of the forms of reasoning appropriate to all disciplines. Actually, however, this criticism would presuppose at the beginning of our inquiry what could be established only at its conclusion. Perhaps the forms of reasoning appropriate to the history of ideas are indeed forms of reasoning applicable to all disciplines. But we cannot assume this without any argument. Our critics must establish that the forms of reasoning appropriate to the history of ideas apply to all other disciplines. To do this, moreover, they must examine the forms of reasoning appropriate to the history of ideas. Our critics cannot show that the history of ideas has no distinctive logic apart from by investigating the nature of its logic. Thus, the possibility of its not having a distinctive logic cannot possibly count as a reason not to investigate its logic.

Historians of ideas study relics from the past in the hope of recovering their meaning. In the next chapter, I will analyse the concept of meaning, for meanings constitute the subject matter of the history of ideas. The hermeneutic meanings of concern to historians need to be distinguished from both semantic meanings, understood in terms of truth conditions, and also linguistic meanings, understood in terms of conventional usage. In addition, the occasion of an utterance needs to be seen as entering into its hermeneutic meaning only indirectly by way of the understanding of the speaker, not directly as a result of how things actually are. An analysis of hermeneutic meaning in these terms leads to intentionalism. The hermeneutic meaning of an utterance derives from the intentions of the author in making it. However, we should distinguish here between an acceptable, weak intentionalism and stronger versions of the theory. Whereas strong intentionalists regard intentions as conscious and prior to utterances, a weak intentionalism allows for the unconscious and for changes of intent during the act of making an utterance. Weak intentionalism consists of little more than a principle of procedural individualism according to which hermeneutic meanings exist only for specific individuals. Weak intentions are individual viewpoints.

In chapter 3, I will move on to the problem of objectivity in the history of ideas. My aim will be to outline a form of justification appropriate to the history of ideas understood as the study of hermeneutic meanings. How can historians defend the claim that a work has a given meaning? I will begin by arguing that objectivity cannot rest on a particular method, or on a logic of vindication or refutation. We cannot justify historical knowledge by reference to the procedures we use to reach it, or by tests against pure facts designed to identify true theories or to exclude false ones. Instead, we should develop a general concept of objectivity based on appeals to shared perceptions of certain facts, a critical attitude, and the possibility of comparing rival webs of theories. Once we do so, we can relate our concept of objectivity to truth by means of an anthropological turn that appeals to the nature of our being in the world. Finally, I will defend the application of this general concept of objectivity to the history of ideas, thereby countering both the post-modern sceptics, who argue that we cannot have objective knowledge of any meaningful work, and the phenomenological sceptics, who argue that we cannot have objective knowledge of the past.

What is the nature of a weak intention defined in the context of a principle of procedural individualism? In chapter 4, I will reduce individual viewpoints to expressed beliefs, thereby eliminating from them both pro-attitudes and illocutionary forces. A pro-attitude is a preference for a state of affairs.[32] Whereas David Hume saw the constituents of actions as beliefs and desires, I will refer to the constituents of actions as beliefs and pro-attitudes. The term pro-attitude highlights the fact that desires are just one of several possible bases for preferences and motives. Thus, historians of ideas study works in order to recover hermeneutic meanings understood as expressions of beliefs. They do not study works to recover actions understood as expressions of pro-attitudes as well as beliefs. Once we thus reduce weak intentions to beliefs, we can proceed to establish the conceptual priority of sincerity over deception, of conscious beliefs over unconscious ones, and of rational beliefs over irrational ones. In doing so, we will define conscious beliefs to include pre-conscious ones, and we will define rational beliefs in terms of consistency, not in terms of objectivity or an appropriate means to any subjective end. The crucial point here is that the conceptual priority of sincere, conscious, and rational beliefs implies that historians initially should presume the beliefs expressed in works are sincere, conscious, and rational.

In chapter 5, therefore, I will turn to an analysis of the form of explanation appropriate to sincere, conscious, and rational beliefs. How can historians account for the meanings they reconstruct from the relics available to them? I will reject all forms of scientism, including physical-

---

[32] I have taken concept of a pro-attitude from D. Davidson, 'Actions, reasons, and causes', in *Essays on Actions and Events* (Oxford: Clarendon Press, 1980), pp. 3–19.

ism, understood as the claim that we can reduce matters of belief to physiology, and also including social positivism, understood as the claim that we can discuss matters of belief using the scientific concept of causation. Instead, I will identify a synchronic form of explanation that makes sense of individual beliefs by relating them to wider webs of belief, and that makes sense of these wider webs of belief by relating them to intellectual traditions. Because beliefs relate to one another in webs, we can present a belief as rational by describing the web to which it belongs. Similarly, because people reach the webs of belief they do against the background of inherited traditions, we can present a web of beliefs as rational by relating it to the tradition from which it arose.

Synchronic explanations cannot account for changes of belief or developments in traditions. In chapter 6 I will proceed to identify a diachronic form of explanation that makes sense of these things by reference to the impact of specifiable dilemmas on webs of belief. Dilemmas arise for individuals when they accept as authoritative a new understanding that, merely by virtue of being new, poses a question for their existing web of beliefs. Dilemmas explain changes of belief simply because people who accept something as true have to extend or modify their existing beliefs to accommodate the newcomer. We cannot reduce the concept of a dilemma any further since we cannot identify an area of experience that possesses a privileged status as an influence on our beliefs. On the contrary, dilemmas can arise from, and so affect, all areas of human life, including politics, work, and faith. Finally I will explore the nature of the link between antecedent and consequent in explanations of belief. Because our synchronic and diachronic forms of explanation presume rationality, they work by uncovering the conditional links between various beliefs. Conditional links are neither necessary, as are those defined in terms of the scientific concept of causation, nor arbitrary, as are those defined in terms of pure chance. Rather, they are those we postulate when we explain human beliefs as rational phenomena.

In chapter 7 I will consider the forms of explanation appropriate to cases in which the presumption of sincere, conscious, and rational belief fails. Deception, self-deception, and irrationality all should be analysed in terms of rogue pro-attitudes, that is, pro-attitudes which exercise an illegitimate influence on the beliefs people express. Deception occurs whenever a rogue pro-attitude leads someone to express beliefs other than their actual ones. Self-deception occurs whenever a rogue pro-attitude acts as a censor, screening out actual, unconscious beliefs that contradict the expressed, actual ones. Irrationality occurs whenever a rogue pro-attitude prompts rogue beliefs that contradict the main web of beliefs. Pro-attitudes, whether rogue ones or not, can arise from any one of need, desire, or reason. Finally I will argue that all pro-attitudes are tied to the actions they inspire by volitional connections. Volitional connections are neither necessary nor arbitrary. Equally they are not conditional since they lead to a change in one's stance towards a given propositional content, not a change in propositional content. Volitional connections are what a will creates whenever it makes a decision and then issues a corresponding command.

The result of all these arguments will be a complete logic for the history of ideas. Historians should adopt, first, the form of justificatory reasoning detailed in the discussion of objectivity; second, the form of explanatory reasoning for sincere, conscious, rational beliefs detailed in the discussion of webs of belief, traditions, and dilemmas; and, third, the form of explanatory reasoning for deception, self-deception, and ir-rationality detailed in the discussion of the operation of rogue pro-attitudes.

CHAPTER 2

On meaning

INTRODUCTION

Historians have before them various relics left over from the past. There are government documents, newspapers, the natural landscape, paintings, tools and utensils, books, items of clothing, films, and the like. All these relics were made into what they are by processes which began in the past even if they have not yet ended. Historians study these relics in order to obtain an understanding of the past from which they derive. Historians cannot have direct access to the past, in the way we can to the present, simply because it has gone. Instead they must begin by recreating, or perhaps creating, the past from relics available to them in the present. A newspaper article exists as a relic from the past, and historians use it to identify as a historical object an action that was performed or an event that did occur in the past. A ruin exists as a relic from the past, and historians use it to identify as a historical object a building as it was in the past. A ship's logbook exists as a relic from the past, and historians use it to identify as a historical object a voyage made in the past. A tumulus exists as a relic from the past, and historians use it to identify as a historical object a human encampment that existed in the past. Historians study relics from the past. They use them to reconstruct historical objects, or, perhaps we should say, to construct historical objects.

Historians of ideas study relics from the past in order to recover historical meanings. They seek to reconstruct ideas or meanings from the past. This account of the history of ideas would meet with widespread acceptance provided we defined the concept of a relic broadly so as to include things like paintings and utensils as well as books, and provided we did give substantial content to the concept of a historical meaning. We can adopt a suitably wide definition of a relic from the past without much difficulty. Historians are free to study whatever

artefacts they want. Although other historians may question the importance of a chosen artefact, they are unlikely to object as a matter of
principle to its being studied. Everyone will agree that innumerable
types of artefacts can act as evidence from which to postulate a meaning
as a historical object. To devise a suitably broad concept of historical
meaning is a much more problematic task. Not only do historians
disagree about the importance of different sorts of meaning, they also
have incompatible views about what constitutes a historical meaning.
There is no consensus as to the nature of the meanings we identify as
historical objects through our studies of relics from the past. Indeed, one
historian might argue that the objects other historians take as their
subject matter are not only unimportant but also non-existent. Disputes
about the nature of historical meaning often represent disagreements
about the very nature of the history of ideas. Before we can consider
what forms of justification and explanation are appropriate to the
history of ideas, therefore, we must be clear about the nature of the
discipline. We must define the nature of the objects it postulates. We
must analyse the concept of historical meaning as it appears in our
everyday descriptions and scholarly accounts. What, we must ask, is the
nature of a historical meaning?

HERMENEUTIC MEANING

When we say something, we normally assume we are communicating
our thoughts. If people paraphrased what we said in a way which did
not tally with our thoughts, we normally would complain that they had
misunderstood us. Moreover, because we generalise from our own case,
we typically assume that other people also use language to express their
thoughts. When we wonder what people meant by what they told us, we
normally want to know what ideas they hoped to convey to us by saying
what they did. It is, therefore, a common-sense view that the meaning of
a given utterance derives from the intentions of its author, although the
exact nature of an intention remains to be determined. Intentionalism,
however, has been challenged from a variety of perspectives. For a start,
there are contextualists who see meanings as the product of the relevant
linguistic contexts, and there are conventionalists who see meanings as
the product of the relevant set of social conventions. In addition, there
are occasionalists who think intentionalism fails properly to take account of the way the occasion of an utterance influences its meaning.
Finally, there are scholars who deride intentionalism for ignoring the

possibility of actual meanings differing from intended meanings, a possibility best exemplified by cases in which authors are unaware of the influence of their unconscious designs on the utterances they make. These criticisms of intentionalism have become so widely accepted that intentionalists have been reduced to a besieged minority.

Much of the current distrust of intentionalism draws, with varying degrees of self-awareness, on a hostility to the idea of given empirical truths secured by pure perceptions. A profound appreciation of the fact of cultural diversity, a recognition of differences in our own society, the dethronement of Newtonian physics, and various other things, have combined to leave many scholars sceptical of any claim that we can perceive things as they are. Instead scholars have become more and more conscious of the extent to which one's social context influences the way one sees the world. Intentionalism appears to many scholars to embody a discredited faith in the self-sufficient autonomy of the isolated individual. It evokes images of atomistic individuals who fix the meaning of their utterances beyond the reach of all social influences. Critics of intentionalism typically emphasise, therefore, both that speech requires language conceived as a social inheritance, and that utterances constitute actions in a public realm over which speakers have little control. Society gives individuals the language in which they make their utterances and in terms of which their utterances acquire public significance.

Earlier I accepted there are no self-evident empirical truths, so now I must reject the atomistic individualism many scholars associate with intentionalism. Indeed, when I come to outline the form of explanation appropriate to the history of ideas, I will emphasise that individuals necessarily reach the beliefs they do against the background of a social tradition. At the moment, however, the important question to ask is whether intentionalism fails along with atomistic individualism. I do not think it does. We do not have to give up intentionalism to accept that individuals can neither reach the understandings they do nor make the utterances they do in isolation from society. Intentionalism is compatible with a belief that the social context necessarily influences what people see, believe, and say. Crucially, we can repudiate atomistic individualism without thereby denying the ability of human beings to act creatively in any given social context. Just because one's social context influences one's beliefs does not mean that it determines them. Just because society gives people a language with which to express their beliefs does not mean that it determines how they use language on any particular occasion. Thus, we can stick with an intentionalist analysis of historical meaning provided we do not argue that society determines either our beliefs or how we use language on any particular occasion. To retain an intentionalist analysis of meaning while repudiating atomistic individualism, we have only to say that meanings derive from intentions which are influenced by social contexts, though they cannot be reduced to them. Intentionalism fails only if we conclude that society determines our beliefs or the way we use language on a particular occasion, and to reject atomistic individualism is not to embrace this conclusion. Indeed, if we can use language creatively, the meaning of what we say surely must derive from our intentional use of language, even if the social context influences the way we use language. The virtues and vices of intentionalism must be decided independently of those of atomistic individualism. The starting point for a defence of intentionalism is, therefore, a recognition of the fact that, no matter how much society influences what individuals say, we still cannot reduce what individuals say to facts about their social locations. It is from this starting point that I will defend intentionalism against contextualists, conventionalists, and occasionalists, before modifying it to allow for possibilities raised by its other critics.

Contextualists denounce intentionalist accounts of historical meaning on the grounds that the meaning of an utterance derives from things they describe variously as 'epistemes', 'forms of discourse', or 'paradigms'. They believe that the meanings available to authors depend on the ways of thinking, writing, or speaking that exist in the community. Authors cannot break out of socially given structures, so what they can say hinges on the theoretical structures to which their community gives them access. What they can say depends on the concepts with which they work, and these concepts do not neutrally reflect an external reality, but rather embody socially transmitted assumptions about the world. Some contextualists declare the concept of the author to be redundant on the grounds that authors merely follow discursive practices. The quasi-structuralism of Foucault's early work, for example, led him to argue that a theoretical and linguistic structure 'governs the appearance of statements as unique events' in a way that makes language, not the author, 'the first law of what can be said'.[1] Other contextualists, notably J. G. A. Pocock, allow authors to creep back on to the historical stage, only to restrict them to bit parts as the

---

[1] M. Foucault, *The Archaeology of Knowledge*, trans. A. Sheridan-Smith (London: Tavistock, 1972), p. 129. Also see M. Foucault, 'What is an author?', in *Language, Counter-Memory, Practice*, trans. D. Bouchard and S. Simon (Oxford: Basil Blackwell, 1977), pp. 113–38.

mouthpieces of the script-writing paradigms which constitute their conceptual frameworks.[2] They argue that even if authors remain the actors of history, the units of history must be theoretical and linguistic structures because these structures determine what authors may say. Pocock, for example, talks of the way languages function 'paradigmatically to prescribe what he [the author] might say and how he might say it': languages 'give him [the author] the intentions he can have, by giving him the means he can have of performing them'.[3] The clear implication of such talk is that languages decide not only form but also content. They fix not only the words we use but also the ideas or meanings we express using words. It is true that Pocock sometimes seems to adopt a different position by insisting that texts have multiple meanings and thereby suggesting that no language can fix an author's intentions. Actually, however, he ascribes the open, multiple nature of the meaning of a text not to the ability of authors to use language creatively to convey their particular ideas, but rather to the fact that any linguistic context typically includes several languages each of which gives the text a different meaning. As Pocock explains, 'the more complex, even the more contradictory, the language context in which he [the author] is situated, the richer and more ambivalent become the speech acts he is capable of performing'.[4] All contextualists, therefore, despite the important differences between them, argue that historical meanings derive from the linguistic structures present in society. Historical meanings do not derive from the mental activity of individuals.

All the various justifications for a contextualist theory of historical meaning refer to arguments in semantics. The semantic meaning of a proposition comes from the truth conditions by which we assign it a truth-value. In order to give a semantic interpretation of a natural language, for instance, we might assign objects to names and specify satisfaction conditions to indicate when we can predicate particular properties of any given object. An example will make things clearer.

---

[2] J. Pocock, 'The history of political thought: a methodological enquiry', in P. Laslett and W. Runciman (eds.), *Philosophy, Politics and Society*, second series (Oxford: Basil Blackwell, 1962), pp. 183–202; 'Languages and their implications: the transformation of the study of political thought', in *Politics, Language and Time* (London: Methuen, 1972), pp. 3–41; and 'State of the art', in *Virtue, Commerce and History* (Cambridge: Cambridge University Press, 1985), pp. 1–34. Pocock himself, unlike many commentators on his work, distances his contextualism from Skinner's conventionalism. See, for example, Pocock, 'State of the art', pp. 4–5.
[3] Pocock, 'Languages and their implications', in *Politics, Language and Time*, p. 25; 'State of the art', in *Virtue, Commerce and History*, p. 5.
[4] Pocock, 'State of the art', in *Virtue, Commerce and History*, p. 5.

The semantic meaning of the proposition 'Jane is a hallelujah lass' derives from both the object named by the word 'Jane' and the satisfaction conditions that specify when we correctly may describe someone as a 'hallelujah lass'. If we define our satisfaction conditions in terms of criteria for the application of the predicate, we will say the basic condition for applying the predicate 'hallelujah lass' is that the named object should be a female member of the Salvation Army. If we define our satisfaction conditions in terms of the consequences of the application of the predicate, we will say the basic condition for applying the predicate 'hallelujah lass' is that the named object should be a zealous female Protestant committed to social work among the poor. The semantic meaning of a proposition depends on what would have to be the case in reality for it to be true of reality.

Because semantics concerns the relationship of propositions to reality, some philosophers, including many of the logical positivists, analyse semantic meanings as a nomenclature.[5] They argue for something akin to a one to one correspondence between our concepts and the features of reality they denote. The meaning of a concept is a corresponding thing, quality, relation, or whatever, such that the presence of this thing in reality makes it correct to predicate the concept of reality. In contrast, semantic holists such as Ferdinand de Saussure look on concepts as changeable and flexible entities that do not have a one to one correspondence with features of reality.[6] They see a concept as an abstract category that on its own cannot tell us what we should include and what we should exclude as an example of it. In this view, concepts are relational entities defined principally by their difference from each other. The semantic meaning of a concept comes from its structural relationships with other concepts. Similarly, because semantics concerns the relationship of propositions to reality, some philosophers, again including many of the logical positivists, analyse semantic meanings in terms of a theory of confirmation. They argue that any given proposition is confirmed by a particular set of experiences so that the semantic meaning of a proposition is given by the relevant experiences precisely because they are what would have to be the case for it to be true.[7] In contrast, semantic holists such as Thomas Kuhn and W. V. O.

---

[5] Some proponents of a nomenclature theory of semantic meaning regard our concepts as composites of atomic units that then have the requisite one to one correspondence with reality. See, in particular, Wittgenstein, *Tractatus Logico-Philosophicus*.

[6] F. de Saussure, *Course in General Linguistics*, ed. C. Bally and A. Sechehaye, trans. W. Baskin (New York: McGraw-Hill, 1966).   [7] See, for example, Ayer, *Language, Truth and Logic*, pp. 19–20.

Quine argue that no experience can ever force us to reject a proposition because we can always devise an auxiliary hypothesis to reconcile any troublesome experience with any initial proposition.[8] We cannot specify truth conditions for single sentences because what experiences we would accept as showing a given sentence to be true always will depend on our broader, theoretical outlook. Single sentences have no fixed meaning. Their semantic meaning depends on the theoretical context in which we locate them.

The contextualists typically defend their view of hermeneutic meaning by appealing to the arguments of semantic holists. Foucault owes a debt to Saussure, and also to Gaston Bachelard and Georges Canguilhem, two French philosophers whose views closely resemble those of Kuhn.[9] Pocock originally grounded his methodology on the philosophy of science of Kuhn before later shifting to a position based on the linguistic theory of Saussure.[10] Anyway, we do not need to get bogged down in questions of who influenced whom to recognise that the contextualists try to take us from a view of semantic meanings as dependent on linguistic context to a view of hermeneutic meanings as also dependent on linguistic context. Arguments taken from semantics provide the justification for contextualist theories of hermeneutic meaning. Followers of Saussure argue that concepts have no core meaning but rather acquire meaning by virtue of being distinguished from other concepts: meanings come from linguistic contexts. Followers of Kuhn argue that sentences have no core meaning but rather acquire meaning from broader theories: meanings again come from linguistic contexts.

Actually, however, questions of hermeneutics are different from questions of semantics, so neither the Saussurian nor the Kuhnian variety of semantic holism can support a contextualist analysis of hermeneutic meaning. Questions in hermeneutics concern the meanings of particular utterances, not the truth conditions of a proposition abstracted from its particular instances. In semantics, we examine the truth conditions of abstract propositions: we ask 'What state of affairs has to be the case for such and such to be true?' In hermeneutics, we examine the ideas conveyed by a particular utterance: we ask 'What did an author mean

[8] Kuhn, *Structure of Scientific Revolutions*, and Quine, 'Two dogmas of empiricism'.
[9] G. Gutting, *Michel Foucault's Archaeology of Scientific Reason* (Cambridge: Cambridge University Press, 1989).
[10] Pocock, 'Languages and their implication', in *Politics, Language and Time*, pp. 3–41; and Pocock, 'State of the art', in *Virtue, Commerce and History*, pp. 1–34. Kuhn himself later adopted a more nuanced view of paradigms. See T. Kuhn, 'Second thoughts on paradigms', in F. Suppe (ed.), *The Structure of Scientific Theories* (Urbana, Ill.: University of Illinois Press, 1974), pp. 459–82.

when he said such and such?' There are two vital differences between hermeneutic and semantic meanings. The first is that hermeneutic meanings are concrete and specific whereas semantic meanings are abstract and general. Imagine that Paul and Susan are walking through the East End of London puzzling over a problem. As they turn a corner, Susan suggests a solution to the problem, and, at exactly the same moment, sees a religious hostel for the homeless staffed by women whose uniform closely resembles that of the Salvation Army. Paul says 'hallelujah lass'. If Susan ponders the hermeneutic question of what he meant, she is unlikely to wonder about the truth conditions for the predicate 'hallelujah lass'. She is unlikely to wonder whether we should define a 'hallelujah lass' as a member of the Salvation Army or a zealous Protestant committed to social work among the poor. She might wonder, however, whether Paul was enthusiastically endorsing her suggested solution to the problem or drawing her attention to the hostel. Moreover, if she decided he was drawing her attention to the hostel, she might wonder whether he thought the women staffing the hostel belonged to the Salvation Army or to another group of zealous Protestants committed to social work. Susan would not want to know about the truth conditions for the predicate 'hallelujah lass' abstracted from all particular instances. She would want to know what Paul meant by saying 'hallelujah lass' at a particular time in a particular place. She would ponder the hermeneutic meaning of his specific utterance, not the semantic meaning of an abstract proposition. Clearly, therefore, questions of hermeneutics differ from questions of semantics.

The second vital difference between hermeneutic and semantic meanings is that hermeneutic meanings do not have to be as precise as semantic ones. This is because hermeneutic meanings describe what someone meant by a given utterance, not what would have to be the case in reality for a proposition to be true. Consider the proposition 'two is the number of dogs I have'. This proposition deploys 'two' as an object of which we can predicate properties such as 'being equal to the number of dogs I have'. Thus, as Gottlob Frege suggested, its semantic interpretation should refer to numbers as objects. It entails an ontological commitment to numbers as objects with a real existence.[11] Now consider the proposition 'I have two dogs'. This proposition refers to 'two' only as a property predicated of the object 'my dogs'. Thus, as

---

[11] G. Frege, *The Foundations of Arithmetic: A Logico-Mathematical Enquiry into the Concept of Number*, trans. J. Austin (Oxford: Basil Blackwell, 1950), particularly pp. 67–70.

Frege again suggested, its semantic interpretation need not refer to numbers as objects. It does not entail an ontological commitment to numbers, but rather allows for numbers existing solely as properties of objects. From a semantic perspective, therefore, 'two is the number of dogs I have' and 'I have two dogs' possess significantly different meanings.[12] From a hermeneutic perspective, however, we do not recognise such precise differences between utterances. If someone said 'two is the number of dogs I have' and someone else said 'I have two dogs', we would usually assume they both meant the same thing. Quite reasonably, we would take both utterances to mean 'I have two dogs', although we might regard the first as an unnecessarily long-winded way of expressing this idea. After all, neither someone who says 'two is the number of dogs I have', nor someone who says 'I have two dogs', is likely to be expressing a belief about the ontological status of numbers. When we consider the semantic meanings of the two propositions, we have to concern ourselves with their truth-value and so perhaps their ontological import, but when we consider the hermeneutic meanings of the two utterances, we normally will dismiss their different ontological implications as irrelevant. Clearly, therefore, questions of hermeneutics differ from questions of semantics.

Contextualists might argue that although hermeneutic meanings differ from semantic meanings, the relationship between the two is such that if semantic meanings derive from linguistic contexts, hermeneutic meanings must also do so. They might say that if 'dog' did not refer to something in reality, we could not make a meaningful utterance using the word 'dog'. Actually, however, hermeneutic and semantic meanings differ in such a way that the semantic meaning of a proposition is neither sufficient nor necessary to fix the hermeneutic meaning of a particular utterance of it. Semantic meanings are not sufficient to fix hermeneutic meanings because they are general and abstract whereas hermeneutic ones are particular and concrete. Because semantic meanings are general and abstract, we can specify them using precisely stated alternatives. For example, if Susan asked us what is the semantic meaning of 'hallelujah lass', what has to be the case for the exclamation 'hallelujah lass' to be true, we could say it is the presence of a female who is either a

---

[12] Of course, one can accept that the two propositions have different semantic meanings without thereby committing oneself to Frege's logical analysis of natural numbers, for which see Frege, *The Foundations of Arithmetic*, particularly pp. 73–95. Indeed, we must do so if we are to maintain our doubts about the existence of given truths.

member of the Salvation Army or a zealous Protestant committed to social work. In contrast, because hermeneutic meanings are particular and concrete, when we specify them we must decide between these sorts of precisely stated alternatives. For example, even if Susan knows the semantic meaning of 'hallelujah lass', she still might not know whether Peter means 'what a superb solution to the dilemma', or 'there is a female member of the Salvation Army', or 'there is a zealous Protestant committed to social work'. In such cases, listeners do not understand the hermeneutic meaning of a statement for which they can give a semantic interpretation. Thus, semantic meanings cannot be sufficient to fix hermeneutic meanings. Likewise, semantic meanings are not necessary to fix hermeneutic meanings because hermeneutic meanings are less precise than semantic ones. When we are concerned with hermeneutic meanings, we can slide over ambiguities and other imprecisions people concerned with semantic meanings must resolve. For instance, we can imagine someone saying 'the number of dogs I have is exactly the same as the number of cats I have', and other people understanding the hermeneutic meaning of the utterance, without the author or the audience ever having thought about the ontological status of numbers. People often can grasp the hermeneutic meaning of an utterance even if they remain ignorant of the semantic meaning of the corresponding proposition. In such cases, listeners understand the hermeneutic meaning of a statement for which they cannot give a semantic interpretation. Thus, semantic meanings cannot be necessary to fix hermeneutic meanings.

Once we grasp the nature of the relationship between semantics and hermeneutics, we can identify the fallacy in contextualism. Because hermeneutic meanings differ from semantic ones, and because semantic meanings are neither sufficient nor necessary to fix hermeneutic ones, we can therefore rule out the possibility of the relationship between the two being such that if semantic meanings derive from linguistic contexts, hermeneutic ones also must do so. Thus, we can accept, with Saussure and Kuhn, that the semantic meaning of a proposition depends on its linguistic or theoretical context, and still deny, against the contextualists, that hermeneutic meanings also do so. The relative autonomy of hermeneutics implies that no argument from semantics by itself can sustain an account of the nature of hermeneutic meaning. Contextualists have no justification for their theory of historical meaning. They do not give us any reason to reject intentionalism.

Conventionalists such as Quentin Skinner propose a slightly different alternative to intentionalism from that of contextualists.[13] They argue that the hermeneutic meaning of a given utterance comes from its conventional meaning. To be precise, Skinner argues that to understand an utterance we have to grasp both its meaning and its illocutionary force, where its meaning comes from its sense and reference, and its illocutionary force derives from the conventions that determine what the author was doing in making it. Skinner here equates intended illocutionary force with actual illocutionary force. He identifies what an author intended in making an utterance with what he did do in making it by virtue of the ruling set of conventions. Sometimes Skinner does not seem to have any reason for doing this. In the best-known statement of his position, for example, he just says: because 'the essential aim, in any attempt to understand the utterances themselves, must be to recover this complex intention on the part of the author', therefore 'the appropriate methodology for the history of ideas must be concerned, first of all, to delineate the whole range of communications which could have been conventionally performed on the given occasion by the utterance of the given utterance, and, next, to trace the relations between the given utterance and this wider linguistic context as a means of decoding the actual intentions of the given writer'.[14] At other times, however, Skinner justifies equating intended illocutionary force with actual illocutionary force on the grounds that authors must follow the ruling conventions since they want to be understood. He says: because 'any writer must standardly be engaged in an intended act of communication', therefore 'whatever intentions a given writer may have, they must be conventional intentions in the strong sense that they must be recognizable *as* intentions to uphold some particular position in argument, to contribute in a particular way to the treatment of some particular theme, and so on'.[15] Surely, however, people might fail to follow the ruling conventions either by design or inadvertently. It seems to be these possibilities that lead Peter Strawson, to whom Skinner refers for support, to say only

---

[13] Most of Skinner's philosophical articles are collected in J. Tully (ed.), *Meaning and Context: Quentin Skinner and His Critics* (Cambridge: Polity Press, 1988). Also see Q. Skinner, 'Conventions and the understanding of speech-acts', *Philosophical Quarterly* 20 (1970), 118–38; and 'On performing and explaining linguistic actions', *Philosophical Quarterly* 21 (1971), 1–21. Skinner himself, unlike many commentators on his work, distinguishes his conventionalism from Pocock's contextualism. See, for example, 'Some problems in the analysis of political thought and action', in Tully, *Meaning and Context*, p. 106.

[14] Q. Skinner, 'Meaning and understanding in the history of ideas', in Tully, *Meaning and Context*, pp. 63–4.

[15] Q. Skinner, 'Motives, intentions, and the interpretation of Texts', in Tully, *Meaning and Context*, p. 77.

that 'the aim, if not the achievement, of securing uptake is essentially a *standard, if not invariable*, element in the performance of the illocutionary act'.[16] If the aim of securing uptake is not invariable, authors need not always even try to follow the ruling conventions, let alone succeed in doing so. No doubt Skinner is right to suggest authors standardly perform intended acts of communication, but this does not allow him to conclude that intentions always must be conventional; or at least it allows him to do so only if he conflates standardly with invariably, in which case his premise is false.

In any case, the important point is that conventionalists accept that we use particular utterances to express our intentions only then to argue that the way we express our intentions depends on conventional meanings. Although we select words in accord with our intentions, the meanings of the words we select comes from established conventions, not our intentions. If, for example, we want to communicate something like 'the woman over there is a member of the Salvation Army', we might choose to say 'hallelujah lass', but the meaning of 'hallelujah lass' derives from social conventions, not our intentions. All the various justifications for a conventionalist theory of hermeneutic meaning refer to arguments in linguistics. If we look up a word in a dictionary, we find a definition of it. We discover, for instance, that 'hallelujah' means something such as 'praise to God'. The definitions given by dictionaries are the linguistic meanings of the words concerned. Linguistic meanings differ from semantic meanings in that they do not have to be so precise. Thus, for example, people can know the linguistic meaning of the words 'the number of dogs I have is exactly the same as the number of cats I have' without knowing that in semantic terms these words imply an ontological commitment to numbers. Linguistic meanings also differ from semantic meanings because semantics concerns the truth conditions of a proposition about reality, whereas language might fulfil a multiplicity of roles of which conveying propositions about reality might be only one. If this is so, some words and phrases might have a linguistic meaning but not a semantic interpretation. For example, some philosophers argue that when people cry 'help' or priests say 'praise be to God' their utterances have linguistic meanings even though the corresponding propositions do not have semantic meanings. We know what their utterances mean even though we cannot say what would have to be the case for them to be true.

[16] P. Strawson, 'Intention and convention in speech-acts', *Philosophical Review* 73 (1964), 439–60.

Philosophers who defend a particularly sceptical form of empiricism generally look upon linguistic meanings as a nomenclature. According to sceptical empiricists, we have no reason to assume that our impressions are a true guide to external reality.[17] We have knowledge only of our own experiences, not a reality which produces them. We have knowledge only of the impressions we have of external things, not the things in themselves. Sceptical empiricism implies that we must be able to have a purely private language because we can express our knowledge in language and our knowledge rests on purely private experiences. Indeed, a private language in which we record our private sensations must be the model of our actual languages. All users of an actual language must come to know the meaning of the words in it through the private process of correlating a particular word with a particular, private sensation. They must do so because they have knowledge only of their private experiences, so that they cannot connect meanings with anything else. According to sceptical empiricists, therefore, the linguistic meaning of a word depends on a naming process in which it is correlated with a private experience. Wittgenstein attacked this sort of sceptical empiricism on the grounds that language, and so linguistic meanings, depends on social conventions. He argued that there could not be a purely private language. People could not refer successfully to their private sensations using terms whose meanings could be known only to them.[18] Suppose, Wittgenstein wrote, I decide to write 'S' in my diary every time I have a particular sensation. In these circumstances, I will have no proper criteria by which to decide whether or not I use 'S' correctly. For instance, I will be unable to distinguish between the case in which I write 'S' in my diary every time I have the requisite sensation, and the case in which I write 'S' in my diary if I have either the requisite sensation on a weekday or a different sensation on a Saturday or Sunday. What is more, Wittgenstein continued, if I cannot distinguish between a case in which I stick to the rules and a case in which I merely seem to stick to the rules, then there are no genuine rules, and if there are no genuine rules to limit the reference of my terms, the use of my terms is arbitrary so I do not have a genuine language. Without social conventions there cannot be a language.

---

[17] B. Russell, 'Knowledge by acquaintance and knowledge by description', *Proceedings of the Aristotelian Society* 11 (1911), 108–28.

[18] Wittgenstein, *Philosophical Investigations*, ## 243–363. On how Wittgenstein's argument against a private language undermines the solipsism implicit in sceptical empiricism, see Hacker, *Insight and Illusion*, pp. 264–72.

Conventionalists typically defend their view of hermeneutic meaning by appealing to the arguments of Wittgenstein against the possibility of a purely private language. James Tully, a disciple of Skinner, has explained, for instance, that 'the horizon and general orientation' of conventionalism rests on Wittgenstein's philosophy of language.[19] In any case, we do not need to get bogged down in questions of who influenced whom to recognise that conventionalists try to take us from a view of linguistic meaning as dependent on a prior set of social conventions to a view of hermeneutic meanings as equally dependent on social conventions. Arguments from linguistics provide the justification for conventionalist theories of hermeneutic meaning. Actually, however, questions of hermeneutics are different from questions of linguistics, so Wittgenstein's argument against a purely private language does not undermine intentionalism. Questions in hermeneutics concern the meanings of particular utterances, not the conventional meanings of words, phrases, and propositions abstracted from particular instances. We have already covered much of the ground that establishes the two are not the same. Linguistic meanings may not be as precise as semantic meanings, but they are just as abstract, and so just as capable of being specified in terms of a number of alternatives. For example, the linguistic or conventional meaning of 'hallelujah lass' includes all of 'good one, girl', 'a female member of the Salvation Army', and 'a zealous female Protestant given to social reform'. In our example, however, the hermeneutic meaning of 'hallelujah lass' will be whichever one of these alternatives Peter intends to convey. Clearly, therefore, questions of hermeneutics differ from questions of linguistics.

Conventionalists might argue that although linguistic meanings differ from hermeneutic meanings, they still fix boundaries to hermeneutic meanings. They might say that if linguistic meanings derive from conventions, hermeneutic meanings also must do so. Perhaps if 'a female member of the Salvation Army' was not part of the linguistic meaning of 'hallelujah lass', we would be unable to convey the idea 'there is a female member of the Salvation Army' by saying 'hallelujah lass'. Actually, however, hermeneutic and linguistic meanings differ in a way that implies that linguistic meanings are neither sufficient nor necessary to fix hermeneutic meanings. Consider the case of Mrs Malaprop, a character who constantly muddles her words in a play by

[19] J. Tully, 'The pen is a mighty sword: Quentin Skinner's analysis of politics', in Tully *Meaning and Context*, p. 8.

Richard Sheridan.[20] In one scene, Captain Absolute reads out a letter complaining about Mrs Malaprop's dull chat full of words she does not understand. Mrs Malaprop responds by proclaiming her pride in her use of language, and, more particularly, her ability to present 'a nice derangement of epitaphs'. The hope is that the audience will laugh at this additional instance of Mrs Malaprop tripping over her tongue. They will recognise that she meant to say 'a nice arrangement of epithets'. Sheridan's joke relies on the audience distinguishing between a linguistic and a hermeneutic meaning. The linguistic meaning of Mrs Malaprop's utterance is 'a nice derangement of epitaphs': when people say 'a nice derangement of epitaphs', they conventionally mean 'a nice derangement of epitaphs'. But the hermeneutic meaning of her utterance is 'a nice arrangement of epithets': although she said 'a nice derangement of epitaphs', she obviously meant 'a nice arrangement of epithets'. To grasp the joke, members of the audience must recognise that the hermeneutic meaning of her utterance differs from its linguistic one. They must recognise that the hermeneutic meaning of an utterance can vary from the linguistic meaning of the corresponding proposition. Linguistic meanings cannot be sufficient to fix hermeneutic meanings because we might fail to understand a particular instance of a proposition of which we know the linguistic meaning. For instance, people watching Sheridan's play might fail to grasp that Mrs Malaprop meant 'a nice arrangement of epithets' even if they knew the conventional meaning of 'a nice derangement of epitaphs'. Furthermore, linguistic meanings cannot be necessary to fix hermeneutic meanings because we can understand a particular instance of a proposition of which we do not know the linguistic meaning. For instance, people watching Sheridan's play might grasp that Mrs Malaprop meant 'a nice arrangement of epithets' even if they did not know 'epitaph' conventionally means 'words inscribed on a tomb'.

We can illustrate the gap between linguistic and hermeneutic meanings in another way. Linguistic meanings cannot fix hermeneutic meanings because if they could, we could have a convention to signal sincerity, which we cannot. Imagine that Mr Sarcasm shouts 'hallelujah lass' when he hears Kate describe her plan for increasing company profits. Kate wonders: is he being sincere or not? She asks herself: does

---

[20] R. Sheridan, *The Rivals*, ed. E. Duthie (London: E. Benn, 1979), p. 64. The example, and aspects of the argument, are taken from D. Davidson, 'A nice derangement of epitaphs', in E. LePore (ed.), *Truth and Interpretation: Perspectives on the Philosophy of Donald Davidson* (Oxford: Basil Blackwell, 1987), pp. 433–46.

he mean 'hallelujah lass (sincere)' or 'hallelujah lass (sarcasm)'? She decides that to avoid confusion they should introduce a convention whereby he will say 'really' when he is being sincere but not when he is being sarcastic. A week later Mr Sarcasm shouts 'hallelujah lass, really'. But his meaning is no clearer. Kate still wonders: is he being sincere or not? She asks herself: does he mean 'hallelujah lass, really (sincere)' or 'hallelujah lass, really (sarcasm)'? And so they might go on indefinitely. No convention can signal sincerity because whenever someone makes a particular utterance any agreed signal of sincerity necessarily becomes available for subversion as well as for use. Thus, no system of conventions, no set of linguistic meanings, can ever fix the hermeneutic meaning of a particular utterance.

Now that we have considered the relationship between linguistics and hermeneutics, we can identify the fallacy in conventionalism. Conventionalism rests on a failure to distinguish the prerequisites which must be met for language to be possible at all from the prerequisites which must be met for communication to occur on a particular occasion. Conventionalists argue from Wittgenstein's belief that language presupposes social conventions to the conclusion that an author must follow existing social conventions. But to establish that shared conventions are necessary for a language to exist is not to establish that authors cannot successfully express their intentions unless they respect the ruling conventions. If Wittgenstein is right, the fact that we have a language implies that there are social conventions governing its use: thus, the phrase 'a nice derangement of epitaphs' has a conventional meaning. Furthermore, the existence of these social conventions suggests authors usually have prior theories about the meanings of the words they use: thus, if we had asked Mrs Malaprop, prior to her speaking, what 'a nice derangement of epitaphs meant', she might well have said 'a set of words taken from a tomb and put out of order in an agreeable fashion'. None of this establishes, however, that authors must use words in accord with their prior theories, let alone the dominant prior theories in their community: thus, Mrs Malaprop still used 'a nice derangement of epitaphs' to mean 'a nice arrangement of epithets'.

We cannot assimilate Wittgenstein to the conventionalist position. Indeed, his discussion of what is involved in following a rule shows him to have been hostile to the idea of conventions fixing performances.[21]

---

[21] Wittgenstein, *Philosophical Investigations*, ## 143–242. A controversial discussion of the argument in relation to that against private languages is S. Kripke, *Wittgenstein on Rules and Private Language* (Oxford: Basil Blackwell, 1982).

His analysis of rule-following implies that no convention could have the determinate nature presupposed by conventionalism. All the correct past uses of a word can never determine how we should use it in the future because one can always devise a rule under which they would be consistent with our using it to refer to any object. Conventions are too vague to fix performances. In any case, whatever the merits of Wittgenstein's analysis of rule-following, his argument against the very possibility of a private language certainly does not sustain a conventionalist account of meaning. The necessity of there being social conventions governing language does not establish that authors or audiences must follow these conventions when they respectively make or understand particular utterances. Moreover, we can make exactly the same point in the terms of the speech-act theory deployed by Skinner. Just as the ruling set of conventions cannot fix hermeneutic meanings even though the latter presuppose a language the existence of which requires there to be conventions, so illocutionary forces cannot be reduced to conventions even though they require a background of conventions. Philosophers such as Strawson argue that illocutionary force requires a background of conventions. Conventionalists such as Skinner misuse their argument in the same way that they misuse the private language argument.[22] They move illegitimately from the necessity of a conventional background to the necessity of authors following, and readers having, correct prior knowledge of the relevant conventions.

An intentionalist analysis of hermeneutic meaning is, therefore, perfectly compatible with the belief that the existence of a language presupposes a background of shared conventions governing its use. After all, if linguistic meanings are merely conventional, they are not fixed, and if they are not fixed, they can be subverted or broken in particular utterances, so they cannot determine the hermeneutic meaning of particular utterances. Thus, even if we agree that linguistic meanings derive from conventions, so that conventions are necessary for a language to exist, we can still insist that hermeneutic meanings derive from intentions, not conventions. No doubt because people usually want to be understood, they often express themselves in what they believe to be the conventional manner. No doubt, moreover, because people typically have a fairly accurate grasp of the conventions governing the languages they use, this means that we should expect hermeneutic meanings often to overlap with linguistic ones. None the less, because people sometimes

---

[22] Strawson, 'Intention and convention'.

misunderstand the conventional way of using certain words, or even use words in ways they know to be unconventional, we cannot assume that hermeneutic meanings will always overlap with linguistic ones. The relative autonomy of hermeneutics implies that no argument from linguistics by itself can sustain an account of the nature of hermeneutic meaning. Conventionalists have no justification for their theory of historical meaning. They do not give us any reason to reject intentionalism.

So far, I have distinguished hermeneutic meanings from semantic and linguistic ones. Next I want to point to a general failing of any theory that attempts to fix hermeneutic meanings by reference to another sort of meaning. Any theory that reduces hermeneutic meanings to a type of meaning beyond particular utterances confronts insurmountable difficulties in accounting for linguistic and conceptual change. A meaning lying outside of a particular utterance must be a hypostatisation merely by virtue of its abstract nature. A meaning must be an ideal type unless it is the meaning of a particular utterance. Thus, if hermeneutic meanings derived from another type of meaning, the meaning of particular utterances would have to correspond to ideal types. But if the meaning of particular utterances corresponded to ideal types, then because ideal types must be static, the variety of utterances available to us would remain forever the same. If the meanings of particular utterances derived from those of abstract propositions, we could never use words innovatively to convey novel concepts. Nobody could use a word innovatively if its meaning was already fixed by an ideal type. Any theory reducing hermeneutic meaning to some other type of meaning cannot account for change. Thus, the fact of change proves that hermeneutic meanings are irreducible. Perhaps a critic might argue that if we conceived of ideal types as abstract norms, we would open up the possibility of explaining linguistic change as a product of numerous incremental changes. He might argue that as more and more people use a word in a novel fashion, so this novel usage becomes part of the norm, until the norm itself changes. But this still will not do, since the small changes would have to be particular utterances departing from existing norms, and if particular utterances could depart from norms, hermeneutic meanings could not derive from norms. Because change occurs, we cannot accept a theory of meaning that cannot account for change, and we cannot account for change unless we recognise the irreducibility of hermeneutic meaning. Thus, we have to abandon all attempts to fix hermeneutic meanings by reference to any type of social meaning. Change occurs because people deliberately or inadvertently make innovations, so we cannot explain change unless we allow for innovations, and we cannot allow for innovations if we try to fix the meanings of utterances by reference to abstract social meanings. Hermeneutic meanings must be irreducible.

Of course, contextualists such as Pocock and conventionalists such as Skinner have written histories that trace conceptual and linguistic change.[23] My point is not that they cannot write such histories. It is that when they do so, their accounts of change cannot be based on the theories of meaning they avow. Properly to account for linguistic and conceptual change they must depart from their stated methods. Skinner, however, denies that his method precludes our accounting for innovation and change. He does so by distinguishing his 'unexceptionable' claim that an 'agent who is engaged in an intended act of communication must be limited by the prevailing conventions of discourse' from the stronger one that the agent 'must be limited only to *following* these conventions'.[24] Surely, however, this distinction lacks any significant force; after all, if, as seems reasonable, we analyse what is involved in one's following a convention in terms of one's remaining within the limits set by it, an agent who is limited by the prevailing conventions of discourse must be limited to following these conventions.

Problems arise here from a confusion between two types of convention which an utterance might break. This confusion manifests itself in Skinner's sudden shift from talk of 'conventions' to talk of 'conventions and attitudes' when he goes on to insist 'it is open to any writer to indicate that his aim is to extend, to subvert, or in some other way to alter a prevailing set of accepted conventions and attitudes'.[25] On the one hand, authors can challenge conventional beliefs or attitudes. They can use words to convey concepts in a conventional manner but do so to question established beliefs. As Skinner has pointed out, for example, Machiavelli's utterance 'Princes must learn when not to be virtuous' broke a convention governing the advice to princes literature. It challenged the established belief that princes should be advised always to act virtuously. Machiavelli used words conventionally 'to challenge

---

[23] J. Pocock, *The Machiavellian Moment: Florentine Political Thought and the Atlantic Republican Tradition* (Princeton: Princeton University Press, 1975); and Q. Skinner, *The Foundations of Modern Political Thought*, 2 vols. (Cambridge: Cambridge University Press, 1978). Other contextualists and conventionalists disavow any interest in the process of change. See, for example, M. Foucault, *The Order of Things: An Archaeology of the Human Sciences* (London: Tavistock, 1970).
[24] Skinner, 'Analysis of political thought and action', p. 105.   [25] *Ibid.*

and repudiate an accepted moral commonplace'.[26] On the other hand, authors can use words unconventionally. They can divorce words from the concepts they normally convey, and they can do so without challenging an established belief. For example, Mrs Malaprop used the phrase 'a nice derangement of epitaphs' unconventionally to convey the idea of 'a nice arrangement of epithets'. In the first type of case, illustrated by Machiavelli, authors express unorthodox opinions, but they do not use language innovatively. Rather, they follow linguistic conventions to indicate their rejection of a prevailing set of attitudes. Because they neither introduce a new concept nor use a word to convey a concept other than the one it conventionally conveys, they do not initiate a process of linguistic or conceptual change. We should accept, with Skinner, that contextualist and conventionalist historians can account for these cases. They can say the meaning of the utterance was fixed by the meaning of its words in the relevant language, and then show how this meaning expressed a challenge to established beliefs. What contextualist and conventionalist historians cannot account for is the second type of case, illustrated by Mrs Malaprop, in which authors use words unconventionally. After all, if we accepted Skinner's contention that illocutionary intentions 'must be conventional intentions in the strong sense of being recognisable *as* intentions to uphold some particular position in argument', we would have to conclude authors could indicate an intention to challenge prevailing attitudes only by following the conventions governing linguistic meanings.[27] Clearly if the words in an utterance are used unconventionally, that is, to convey meanings other than those they have in the relevant language, then historians cannot say that the meaning of the utterance is limited by the meaning of its words in the language. Historians must depart from the principles of contextualism and conventionalism if they are to explain unconventional uses of language. We have to accept the irreducibility of hermeneutic meaning if we are to allow for linguistic and conceptual change.

Perhaps it is conceivable that hermeneutic meanings could be irreducible but not intentional. None the less, our distinction between hermeneutic and other forms of meaning effectively justifies intentionalism. Whereas semantic and linguistic meanings are abstract and social, hermeneutic meanings are defined by what an author meant by a particular utterance on a particular occasion. When we ask about a

---

[26] Q. Skinner, '"Social meaning" and the explanation of social action', in Tully, *Meaning and Context*, p. 86.   [27] Skinner, 'Motives, intentions, and the interpretation of texts', p. 77.

hermeneutic meaning, we do not want to know about truth conditions or linguistic conventions. Rather, we want to know what Peter meant by 'hallelujah lass', what our interlocutor meant by 'two is the number of dogs I have', and what Mrs Malaprop meant by 'a nice derangement of epitaphs'. Furthermore, when we ask what someone meant by a particular utterance on a particular occasion, we ask about their intentions in making it. When we ask about hermeneutic meanings, we want to know what ideas Peter, our interlocutor, and Mrs Malaprop intended to convey by saying what they did when they did. Thus, hermeneutic meanings differ from semantic and linguistic meanings precisely because the former are individual and intentional whereas the latter are social and abstract. The hermeneutic meaning of an utterance comes from the ideas the author intended to express in making it. When Peter says 'hallelujah lass', the meaning of his utterance depends on whether he intends to convey either pleasure at Susan's suggestion or information about a women running a hostel for the homeless. When our interlocutor says 'two is the number of dogs I have', the meaning of his utterance depends on whether he intends to express an ontological commitment to numbers or tell us about his pets. And when Mrs Malaprop says 'a nice derangement of epitaphs', the meaning of her utterance is 'a nice arrangement of epithets' precisely because that is what she intends to convey. Hermeneutic meanings are intentional.

Our arguments for the irreducibility and intentionality of hermeneutic meanings point to a general theory of language. Because hermeneutic meanings are particular or unique, whereas linguistic meanings are abstract or multiplex, we always have to use language to make an utterance – we can never merely apply language in making an utterance. Words, propositions, and the like do not possess precise functions, so we cannot merely pick out the ones whose functions happen to coincide with our purposes. Language does not resemble a set of nuts and bolts, with the size and shape of each unit being fixed so that all we need to do is to pick out the requisite units for the task before us. Instead, words and sentences can play numerous different roles in language, so we necessarily attach a particular content to them when we use them to fulfil a particular purpose. Individuals constantly mould and redefine the parts of a language as they use them to meet new needs in new contexts. Moreover, because hermeneutic meanings can be attached to new words and new sentences used in new ways, therefore our use of language cannot be contained within boundaries set by social conventions. Because the roles that words, sentences, and the like can play do not have prescribed limits, individuals are not restricted in the content they can attach to them when they use them to fulfil particular purposes. Language does not consist of a set of clearly defined units we combine to build the sentential structures we choose. Instead, words and sentences are indeterminate in that we can redesign them or even invent them to meet our needs. We can use the parts of a language to convey content that they have not conveyed before. Individuals constantly extend and develop the parts of a language by using them to express ever new hermeneutic meanings in ever new circumstances.

What all of this implies is that we know language as a faculty, not just an object. Although we can have knowledge of particular languages, we can do so only because we have capacity-knowledge of language as such. We have a linguistic faculty, where a faculty is an ability that transcends any given content or situation, an ability to do something in general, not just an ability to do something in particular instances, no matter how broadly defined. A faculty entails creative agency in that we can exercise it on novel content in novel circumstances. The faculty of language, for example, enables us to use words to convey and to understand hermeneutic meanings in general, and this means that we cannot identify a limit to the ideas we may convey and understand using language. As language users, we do not have recourse only to a list of words and propositions already possessing given meanings, either a list we already possess, or one we can construct using a fixed set of rules. Rather, we possess an ability to devise and to understand new words and new sentences so as to convey and grasp new meanings which lie beyond all established rules. Although we have only a finite number of words, each with a finite set of linguistic meanings, the creative nature of our linguistic faculty enables us to use this finite set to express an infinite range of ideas. Any particular language constitutes a resource on which we draw in attempts to express the ideas we choose. Any particular language is like an instrument that our linguistic faculty enables us to play in search of the tune we want. Our intentions give content to the words we utter, understood as form. After all, there would be no point asking someone 'what do you mean?' if authors did not have some kind of ability to fix hermeneutic meanings in accord with their intentions.

PROCEDURAL INDIVIDUALISM

Hermeneutic meanings derive from intentions. As yet, however, I have not shown that historians need concern themselves solely with hermeneutic meanings. A critic might say that historians need focus at most in part, and perhaps not at all, on hermeneutic meanings. If the critic were correct, to have identified hermeneutic meanings with intentions would not be to have rescued an intentionalist analysis of historical meaning. Next, however, I will argue that only hermeneutic meanings concern historians. Hermeneutic meanings exist for specifiable people, so they have a historical existence. Semantic and linguistic meanings are abstractions derived from hermeneutic meanings. Indeed, any attempt to ascribe to any form of meaning an existence independent of hermeneutic meanings seems to fail, and, at the very least, requires one to deny that the relevant form of meaning has a historical existence.

I want to approach the question of what sorts of meaning concern historians tangentially by way of a study of the nature of the meaning an utterance has for a reader. The meaning of an utterance to a reader cannot be its semantic meaning because readers sometimes find meanings in statements whose semantic properties elude them. Similarly, the meaning of an utterance to a reader cannot be its linguistic meaning because readers sometimes find meanings in statements whose linguistic properties elude them. More generally, when someone understands an utterance to have a particular meaning, that meaning is not necessarily the same as the truth conditions for, or the conventional meaning of, the utterance abstracted from the particular instance being considered. Imagine, for instance, that Susan does not know that 'hallelujah lass' is a name for a female member of the Salvation Army, so she takes Peter to mean 'well done, what a brilliant idea'. Her understanding of his utterance does not enable us to declare the semantic or linguistic meaning of 'hallelujah lass' to be 'well done'. 'hallelujah lass' means 'well done' to her on a particular occasion, but this tells us little about the semantic or linguistic properties of 'hallelujah lass'. It would appear, therefore, that the meaning of an utterance to a reader is a particular meaning, not an abstract one. It would appear that the meaning of an utterance to a reader is a hermeneutic meaning, not a semantic or linguistic one. Certainly, the meaning of an utterance to a reader has many similarities with the meaning of an utterance to its author. Both are meanings individuals place or find in particular utterances, where the abstract propositions embodied in the utterances already have certain semantic and linguistic properties. The only difference is that authors appear to play a more active role than readers. Moreover, one might want to capture the comparative passivity of the reader by saying that whereas speakers intend to convey meaning, listeners merely happen to grasp meaning. Because this is the only difference, however, we can classify the meaning of an utterance to a reader as a form of hermeneutic meaning provided we adopt a weak form of intentionalism. We have to expand our concept of an intention from the idea of wanting to convey meaning to embrace also the idea of happening to grasp meaning.

Because the concept of an intention usually suggests a prior design to do something, intentionalism often appears to equate hermeneutic meanings exclusively with what authors want their utterances to mean. In contrast, I will adopt a weak intentionalism that equates hermeneutic meanings with the meanings utterances have for particular individuals, whether they be authors or readers. Weak intentionalism implies only that hermeneutic meanings have no existence apart from individuals. Utterances have hermeneutic meanings only because individuals take them so to do. The important point here is that weak intentionalism makes any meaning an utterance has for any individual an intentional, hermeneutic one. The meaning of an utterance to any reader, as well as to its author, is a hermeneutic meaning, not a semantic or linguistic one. Once we accept this, we can redefine what is at stake in the question of whether historians should concern themselves exclusively with hermeneutic meanings. To argue that they should do so is to defend a principle of procedural individualism in the history of ideas. Weak intentionalism implies that historians need study only the meanings utterances have for specific individuals whether authors or readers. This procedural individualism follows solely from the doctrine that historical meanings are always meanings for specific individuals. It does not presuppose any of the other doctrines that have gone by the name of individualism. It commits us, for instance, neither to an atomist individualism according to which individuals could exist, grasp meanings, or perform actions apart from society, nor to a methodological individualism according to which we should study society without referring to social wholes.[28]

To defend an intentionalist analysis of historical meaning, and so a principle of procedural individualism in the history of ideas, one has to show that historians need concern themselves only with hermeneutic meanings. I will do this in two ways. In the first place, I will defend an analysis of linguistic and semantic meanings that reduces them to hermeneutic ones. Historians who study linguistic or semantic meanings

[28] On varieties of individualism, see S. Lukes, *Individualism* (Oxford: Basil Blackwell, 1973).

explore abstractions derived from hermeneutic ones. However, because my argument about the nature of various types of meaning will be an inductive one focusing on semantic and linguistic meanings, someone might argue that there is another type of meaning we cannot reduce to the hermeneutic. Thus, I will support my initial argument with a second one to show that any meaning we could not reduce to hermeneutic ones would be ahistorical. If a meaning was neither hermeneutic nor an abstraction based on hermeneutic meanings, it would be atemporal and so of no concern to historians.

If we can reduce semantic and linguistic meanings to hermeneutic ones, we can say that historians who study them concern themselves with weak intentions defined as the meanings utterances have for individuals. Consider first the case of semantic meanings. The semantic meaning of an utterance comes from what would have to be the case for it to be true. Because there are no self-evident empirical truths, what would have to be the case for an utterance to be true must be relative to some conceptual framework. Thus, because what would have to be the case for an utterance to be true can be decided only relative to a conceptual framework, semantic meanings cannot exist apart from for individuals. Utterances can acquire semantic meanings only within a set of concepts held by one or more individual. Semantic meanings are abstractions based on hermeneutic ones. When we say the semantic meaning of an utterance is such and such, we imply that a group of individuals, usually including ourselves, share a conceptual framework within which they would accept the utterance as true if such and such was the case. This analysis of semantic meanings explains why they have the properties we have already ascribed to them. Semantic meanings are attached to abstract propositions, not particular utterances, because they are abstractions we can reduce to hermeneutic meanings. Semantic meanings are more precise than hermeneutic meanings because to ask people what would make such and such true is to ask them to elucidate their concept of such and such. It is, for example, to ask our interlocutor who says 'two is the number of dogs I have' whether his concept of two is of an independent existent. Finally, semantic meanings are holistic because people would elucidate their concept of such and such by reference to their other beliefs. Our interlocutor, for example, would answer us by describing his beliefs about the ontological status of numbers. The holistic nature of semantic meanings derives from the holistic nature of the beliefs of any individual. It does not show that the meanings of particular utterances derive from a social language.

Consider now the case of linguistic meanings. The linguistic meaning of a word comes from the concept to which it conventionally refers: thus, the linguistic meaning of 'bachelor' is an unmarried man. The bond between a word and the concept that constitutes its linguistic meaning is a purely conventional one without any natural foundation: thus, social convention could decree that the word 'bac' rather than 'bachelor' refer to an unmarried man. Although some words might seem to be a peculiarly apt expression for a given concept, as in cases of onomatopoeia, even here there could clearly be a convention binding a different word to the relevant concept. Crucially, because linguistic meanings are purely conventional, they are given simply by what individuals do and do not accept as a convention. Their existence is a function solely of the fact that a number of individuals take certain words to refer to certain concepts. Linguistic meanings are abstractions based on hermeneutic ones. When we say that the linguistic meaning of an utterance is such and such, we imply that a group of individuals accept certain conventions under which they understand it to refer to such and such. This analysis of linguistic meanings explains why they have the properties we already have ascribed to them. Linguistic meanings are attached to abstract propositions, not particular utterances, because they are abstractions we can reduce to hermeneutic meanings. Linguistic meanings are not as precise as semantic ones, and perhaps not attached only to statements about reality, because they derive solely from the general ways individuals use and understand words, not from the specific truth conditions individuals believe apply to words. Finally, the existence of linguistic meanings depends on social conventions because they themselves are conventional. They are based on the agreement of a number of individuals about how we use various words, phrases, sentences, and the like. The conventional nature of linguistic meanings follows from their being abstractions based on hermeneutic meanings. It does not show that the meanings of particular utterances derive from social conventions.

Ironically the theorists on whom contextualists and conventionalists draw, namely, Saussure and Wittgenstein, argue for something very like the reduction of semantic and linguistic meanings to hermeneutic ones. Saussure does so in his account of the arbitrary nature of the sign.[29] He argues that the bond between signifiers and signifieds, words and concepts, is an arbitrary one. The bond is set up by social conventions,

---

[29] Saussure, *Course in General Linguistics*, pp. 67–9.

where the sole constraint on these conventions is that our signifiers must differ from each other. Thus, he suggests the linguistic meaning of a word derives from a purely arbitrary convention upon which individuals happen to agree. Saussure also argues that our signifieds gain their semantic content not from a natural bond between them and a feature of the world, but rather from their place in a system of signifieds. Thus, he suggests that the semantic meaning of an utterance derives from the set of concepts within which individuals happen to locate it. Wittgenstein's analysis of meaning as use provides us with the basis of a similar argument to the effect that we can reduce all forms of meaning, including the semantic and linguistic, to hermeneutic ones.[30] He argues that the linguistic meaning of an utterance derives from the way people use it on particular occasions within an existing, public game. Words refer to particular concepts only by virtue of the fact that people use them to do so. Wittgenstein also argues that the semantic meaning of an utterance derives from circumstances in which people will assent to its use. Utterances acquire a truth-value only in relation to the conceptual system in which people locate them. Indeed, Wittgenstein's flirtation with behaviourism takes him close to the conclusion Quine adopts as a result of combining his semantic holism with behaviourism, that is, that meanings cannot be Platonic or mental entities existing apart from the assent and dissent people give to particular utterances.[31]

We can conclude, therefore, that semantic and linguistic meanings are reducible to hermeneutic ones. Historians who study them concern themselves with weak intentions defined as the meanings utterances have for individuals. Critics might suggest, however, that there is another form of meaning we cannot reduce to the hermeneutic. To counter such a criticism, I will argue that any form of meaning we could not reduce to the hermeneutic would have to be atemporal and so of no concern to historians. From now on I will simplify my argument by adopting a single contrast between a hermeneutic meaning, defined as the meaning an utterance has for a particular individual, and a structural meaning, defined as any other form of meaning an utterance might bear. Scholars can approach utterances in one of two contrasting ways depending on which sort of meaning interests them. If they want to know about the hermeneutic meaning of an utterance, they will consider it as a work, that is, a set of words written, or spoken, or understood

[30] On meaning as use, and for a consequent attack on structural meanings that are not abstractions based on hermeneutic ones, see respectively Wittgenstein, *Philosophical Investigations*, ## 43 and 79–88.   [31] Quine, *Word and Object*, particularly pp. 26–79.

in a particular way on a particular occasion. If they want to know about
the structural meaning of an utterance, they will consider it as a text,
that is, a set of phonemes, words, and sentences possessing, say, certain
linguistic and semantic properties. Of course, if scholars wish to do so,
they can choose to define a text in a different way from me. They might
define a text, for example, as the site of a variety of works – the site of the
work of its author and the total works of all those who ever read it. If
they define a text in this way, however, they must recognise that
intentionalists and historians inspired by reception theory undertake
compatible tasks designed to unpack different aspects of the text.[32] More
importantly, because we cannot establish any limits to the works a text
so defined might inspire, their definition of a text makes it an indeterminate entity which always possesses a 'surplus meaning'.[33] The indeterminate nature of a text so defined makes it irrelevant to historians. A
historian cannot recover a text so defined if only because its nature
remains to be decided by the meanings future readers attach to it. A
historian can recover only the particular, determinate works the author
and earlier readers have already placed at the site that is the text.
Moreover, because the part of the text so defined of concern to historians consists solely of past works, such a definition of a text does not
suggest that historians need concern themselves with anything other
than hermeneutic meanings.

Let me return now, therefore, to my contrast between a work possessing a hermeneutic meaning and a text possessing a structural meaning. To vindicate an intentionalist analysis of historical meaning, we
have to show that historians need concern themselves only with hermeneutic meanings not structural ones, with works not texts. It is not
necessarily that there is anything wrong with the study of structural
meanings. It is just that such studies are not historical, and the business
of historians is, of course, to study history. Imagine that someone in the
eighteenth century wrote an essay, containing a section entitled 'Hallelujah Lass'. If we study the essay as a text, we must abstract the words
and phrases in it from the occasion of its appearance. We must investigate the linguistic and semantic properties of the essay considered as a
series of abstract propositions. Moreover, when we identify the abstract, structural meaning of the essay, we must allow for the fact that
the phrase 'hallelujah lass' can refer to a female member of the

---

[32] Compare M. Thompson, 'Reception theory and the interpretation of historical meaning',
History and Theory 32 (1993), 248–72.
[33] A variety of forms of surplus meaning are analysed in Ricœur, *Interpretation Theory*.

Salvation Army. The structural meaning of the text of the essay must
include a reference to the idea of a female member of the Salvation
Army. There might not be anything untoward about this provided we
did not put the structural meaning of the text back into history. But if
we try to ascribe a historical existence to the structural meaning of the
text, we will find that an essay written in the eighteenth century refers
to an organisation that was not established until the late nineteenth
century. We will be stuck with an unacceptable anachronism. In order
to locate a text in time, we have to appeal to something outside of it,
but as soon as we do this, we necessarily switch our attention from the
text and its structural meaning to a work and its hermeneutic meaning.
Imagine that we have two essays, one written in the eighteenth century
and one written in the twentieth century, containing exactly the same
words and punctuation in exactly the same order. Any fact enabling us
to distinguish between the two essays would have to refer to the particular occasion of the appearance of one or other of them; it would
have to be a fact about the essays as works, not texts. Moreover,
because the two essays have identical texts, they must share the same
structural meaning. Thus, if the twentieth-century essay contains a
section headed 'hallelujah lass' so that 'a female member of the Salvation Army' is part of the structural meaning of its text, the structural
meaning of the text of the eighteenth-century essay also must include
mention of the Salvation Army. Once again, therefore, we cannot
ascribe historical existence to texts without falling into unacceptable
anachronisms. We cannot do so because texts do not have a historical
existence. As soon as we consider an utterance as a historical object, we
necessarily focus our attention on its hermeneutic meaning as a work.
The obvious way to fix an utterance in history is to consider the
meaning it had for certain people. We might say, for example, that our
two identical essays have different historical meanings because the
words they contain meant different things to people in the eighteenth
and twentieth centuries. To ask about the meaning an utterance had
for a particular group of people, however, is to ask about the hermeneutic meaning of various works. To ask what the essay meant to
people in the eighteenth century is to ask how they understood the
essay, which is to ask about their weak intentions. We can conclude,
therefore, that only hermeneutic meanings and works have a historical
existence.

   The ahistorical nature of structural meanings and texts should
not surprise us. It was this that prevented any attempt to reduce

hermeneutic meanings to any other type of meaning from providing an adequate account of linguistic change. Just as any attempt to reduce hermeneutic meanings to another sort of meaning necessarily involved postulating ideal types to which hermeneutic meanings had to conform, so we can identify a simple dichotomy between hermeneutic and structural meanings. And just as postulating ideal types to which hermeneutic meanings had to conform precluded an adequate account of change, so structural meanings are ahistorical. We cannot identify structural meanings with any specific instance of an utterance, so they must exist outside of time, and being outside of time, they cannot be said to alter with time. Thus, if we focus on structural meanings, we leave ourselves with no way of explaining linguistic change. Structural meanings and texts are of no concern to historians.

Once one adopts a weak intentionalism according to which the meaning of an utterance to any given individual becomes a species of intentional meaning, there is only one way to avoid an intentionalist analysis of historical meaning. One must identify a magical language-x with an equally magical meaning-x existing in history, as do hermeneutic meanings, but existing independently of particular individuals, as do structural meanings. Although there are brave souls who seek to defend something akin to language-x, their endeavours seem doomed to fail.[34] Consider what is involved in abandoning the idea that historical meanings exist only for individuals. When we talk of a social language, we typically have in mind a set of inter-subjective meanings shared by various people. For example, when two people talk of a female friend who is a member of the Salvation Army by saying 'Jane is a hallelujah lass', they share a set of meanings which constitute the language they use to communicate. Thus, although we might describe their shared language as a social structure, we do not thereby commit ourselves to the claim that it exists independently of particular individuals. On the contrary, it exists only because they, as individuals, share certain meanings. Because language-x does not embody this sort of inter-subjectivity, its ontological status remains extremely vague. It cannot be a concrete entity; nor can it be an emergent entity, since if it were it would have to emerge from facts about individuals. Indeed, language-x must exist independently of human thought, since our thoughts are facts about us, so if language-x depended for its existence on our thoughts, it would not

[34] For something very like a language-x, see Foucault's account of epistemes as 'historical aprioris' that exist in time in a world free of subjectivity. Foucault, *Order of Things*, particularly pp. xx–xxii.

exist independently of us as individuals. Language-x must be a Platonic form; it must be an abstract entity with a real and independent existence. Although Platonic forms have had an honoured place in the history of philosophy, a suspicious stance towards the very possibility of self-evident truths undermines any belief in them. (Certainly Wittgenstein's dislike of the idea of self-evident truths informs his analysis of all forms of meaning as reducible to the way in which we use language.[35]) Moreover, the opponents of intentionalism face special difficulties since a belief in a language-x existing in time requires them to ascribe a historical existence to a Platonic form. They must explain how a Platonic form can exist for some time and then wither. How can a Platonic form be subject to natural processes such as those of growth and decay? Surely any theory of meaning that finds itself having to answer this question has gone wildly astray.

All historical meanings are either meanings for individuals or abstractions derived from meanings for individuals. A principle of procedural individualism operates in the history of ideas such that historians need concern themselves only with the meanings utterances have for individuals. Thus, because we have adopted a weak form of intentionalism, we can conclude all historical meanings are intentional. Our weak intentionalism thus provides us with the beginnings of an analysis of historical meaning. It implies that individuals associate historical meanings with statements, books, films, and events: statements, books, films, and events do not of themselves embody historical meanings. Objects come to mean something only because someone understands them so to do. Perhaps the idea of historical meanings being human constructs might seem uncontroversial, but even if it does, this uncontroversial idea has controversial corollaries. For a start, it implies that we cannot ascribe historical meanings to texts. Because historical meanings are always meanings for individuals, we cannot ascribe a historical meaning to a text in itself. We can ask only about the historical meaning a text had for so-and-so, that is, the meaning of a work. Moreover, the idea that hermeneutic meanings are human constructs implies that we must reject the possibility of a collective consciousness being greater than its individual constituents. It makes sense to talk of a classical mentality, a proletarian ideology, or a national outlook, only if we aim thereby to highlight the fact of various individuals sharing certain beliefs. As a

---

[35] See Wright, *Wittgenstein*, particularly pp. 19–20.

matter of principle, we must be able to translate any statement about a collective consciousness into a series of statements about specific individuals. Meanings can be inter-subjective, but an inter-subjective meaning is just a result of specific individuals attaching the same meaning to a given object. Although our weak intentionalism provides us with this partial analysis of hermeneutic meaning, it leaves a number of questions unanswered. In particular, it has no implications for the question in philosophical psychology of how exactly individuals attach hermeneutic meanings to utterances. They may do so by having images in their head, by using a language of thought, by deploying a public language, or by some other means.

THE OCCASIONALITY OF INTENTIONS

Historians study the hermeneutic meanings of works, and these meanings derive from the intentions of individuals. This leaves an important question still to be answered. Are intentions fixed exclusively by reference to the individual concerned? Can we identify and individuate an intention solely in terms of facts about the person whose intention it is? Perhaps I was too quick to adopt a principle of procedural individualism for the history of ideas. I have established only that historians can focus exclusively on hermeneutic meanings defined in terms of weak intentions, and this does not necessarily allow me to conclude that we can fix a weak intention solely by reference to the individual whose intention it is. If we cannot individuate intentions solely by reference to the individuals whose intentions they are, historians will be unable to define a hermeneutic meaning without going beyond the relevant individual. It is this line of argument that leads hermeneutic occasionalists to reject intentionalism.

Utterances are situated historically. They are made in, and refer to, specific occasions which exist irrespective of the intentions of their authors. For example, when Peter says 'hallelujah lass', he does so in the context of, and with reference to, an occasion composed of specific objects and events, including both Susan's suggestion and the hostel for the homeless. Occasionalists argue that the situated nature of utterances implies that their meaning necessarily reflects aspects of the occasions of their being made. Most occasionalists argue this with respect to semantic meanings. Hilary Putnam, for instance, invites us to imagine a twin-earth where a substance called 'water' plays exactly the same role as water does on earth even though it is chemically different from water on earth.[36] Twin-earth water looks, tastes, sounds, and behaves just like water, but it has the chemical composition XYZ, not H_2O. Thus, if both my *doppelgänger* on twin-earth and I talk about water in terms of the role it plays, it seems that we express the same belief but refer to different things. We both believe that 'water plays such and such a role', but whereas he refers to XYZ, I refer to H_2O. Putnam concludes that because identical beliefs can refer to different things, mental content cannot fix reference. Clearly Putnam's occasionalism applies only to semantic meanings, not hermeneutic ones. Both my *doppelgänger* and I intend to express the idea that water plays such and such a role, and anyone on our respective earths who so understands us will have grasped correctly the hermeneutic meaning of our utterances. It is just that the truth conditions of our utterances treated abstractly as propositions will differ. Whereas the abstract proposition embodied in my utterance on earth will be true if H_2O plays such and such a role, the abstract proposition embodied in his utterance on twin-earth will be true if XYZ plays such and such a role. Putnam certainly does not suggest that the occasion of an utterance enters into its hermeneutic meaning. On the contrary, he concludes that mental content does not fix reference precisely because he thinks the occasion of an utterance enters into its semantic meaning or reference but not its hermeneutic meaning or mental content. Clearly, therefore, semantic occasionalism does not undermine an intentionalist analysis of hermeneutic meaning.

Unfortunately, however, we cannot leave the matter there since some philosophers defend a hermeneutic version of occasionalism. They argue that languages group objects together in ways which permeate mental content so as to preclude our individuating beliefs individualistically. They do not deny that hermeneutic meanings derive from intentions. They deny that we can individuate intentions solely by reference to facts about the individuals whose intentions they are. Tyler Burge, for instance, invites us to imagine Ms Patient who uses the word 'arthritis' to describe rheumatoid diseases of the bones as well as of the joints although she belongs to our linguistic community in which 'arthritis' conventionally refers only to rheumatoid disease of the joints.[37] Ms Patient says to us 'I have arthritis in my thigh', we explain to her that she is wrong because arthritis occurs only in the joints, and she accepts she

---

[36] Putnam, 'Meaning of meaning'.
[37] T. Burge, 'Individualism and the mental', in P. French, T. Uehling, Jr, and H. Wettstein (eds.), *Studies in Metaphysics*, Midwest Studies in Philosophy 4 (Minneapolis: University of Minnesota Press, 1979), pp. 73–121.

was mistaken. In this case, we would say Ms Patient believed she had arthritis in her thigh. Next Burge invites us to imagine Ms Patient* who is physically and mentally identical to Ms Patient although she belongs to a linguistic community the members of which use the word 'arthritis' to describe rheumatoid diseases of the bones as well as of the joints. Ms Patient* says to us 'I have arthritis in my thigh', but because her utterance makes sense in the language of her linguistic community, we do not tell her that arthritis occurs only in the joints so she is wrong. In this case, we would say Ms Patient* believed she had a rheumatoid disease in her thigh, not Ms Patient* believed she had arthritis in her thigh. Burge concludes, therefore, that we ascribe different beliefs to Ms Patient and Ms Patient* despite their being physically and mentally identical. More generally, hermeneutic occasionalists present us with two individuals who differ solely in their linguistic communities, and who make identical utterances only for us to identify these utterances as expressions of different beliefs. They conclude, therefore, that we cannot individuate an intention solely by reference to the individual concerned. To fix the hermeneutic meaning of a given utterance, we have to refer to the author's linguistic community understood as a part of the occasion of its being made.

Hermeneutic occasionalists misconstrue the import of their thought experiment. They do so because they fail to distinguish properly between the roles of hermeneutic and linguistic meanings in human discourse. Consider again the case of Ms Patient. She says 'I have arthritis in my thigh' because she believes that she has a rheumatoid disease in her thigh and that the word 'arthritis' refers to rheumatoid diseases of the bones. Because these are her beliefs, when she says 'I have arthritis in my thigh', she intends to express the idea 'I have a rheumatoid disease in my thigh', and anyone who so understands her will have correctly understood the hermeneutic meaning of her utterance. Hermeneutic occasionalists, in contrast, suggest that we would treat her utterance as an expression of the mistaken belief 'I have arthritis in my thigh', and, more surprisingly, that she would accept our doing so. None the less, the fact that we would treat her utterance as such and such does not establish it is such and such. When we treat her utterance as an expression of a mistaken belief, we treat it in terms of its linguistic, not hermeneutic, meaning; after all, the conventional meaning of 'I have arthritis in my thigh' is 'I have arthritis in my thigh', not 'I have a rheumatoid disease in my thigh'. Similarly, when she accepts our treatment of her utterance, she treats it in terms of its linguistic meaning, not its hermeneutic meaning. Hermeneutic occasionalists establish only that we sometimes treat utterances as though their hermeneutic meaning was given by their linguistic meaning. They do not establish that hermeneutic meanings actually depend on linguistic meanings.

Why do people sometimes treat an utterance whether made by themselves or someone else in terms of its linguistic, not its hermeneutic, meaning? People treat utterances in this way because they recognise that conventional usage has a certain authority. The authority of linguistic meanings, and the distinction between them and hermeneutic ones, appears whenever we talk of someone having said one thing and meant something else. Whenever we do this, we distinguish what someone said, defined in terms of the authority of the conventional or linguistic meaning of the utterance, from what he meant, defined in terms of the intentional or hermeneutic meaning of the utterance. This distinction implies another between two forms of discourse. On the one hand, we have dialogue, defined as the form of discourse in which we try to recover hermeneutic meanings without paying homage to the authority of linguistic meanings. On the other hand, we have argument, defined as the form of discourse in which we accept the authority of linguistic meanings. When we engage in dialogue, we want to understand other people, so we typically treat their utterances charitably. We try to grasp the hermeneutic meaning of their utterances even if doing so involves our attaching an unconventional meaning to their words.[38] When we engage in argument, we want to show other people to be mistaken, so we treat their utterances uncharitably. We try to hold them to the linguistic meanings of their utterances even if doing so involves our ignoring the beliefs they intended to express.

Now we can identify the error made by hermeneutic occasionalists. Whereas their thought experiments rely on our treating utterances as we would in argument, their conclusion purportedly applies to how we would treat utterances in dialogue. Whereas their thought experiments rely on our equating the meaning of an utterance with its linguistic meaning, their conclusion purportedly applies to hermeneutic meanings. Their argument exhibits a confusion between different types of meaning. If we treat Ms Patient's utterance as a contribution to an argument, we will hold her to the belief that she has arthritis in her thigh,

---

[38] To say this is not to subscribe to any particular account of how we should treat utterances charitably. In particular, it is not to accept Davidson's principle of charity, for which see D. Davidson, 'Radical interpretation', 'Belief and the basis of meaning', and 'Thought and talk', all in *Inquiries into Truth and Interpretation* (Oxford: Clarendon Press, 1984), pp. 125–39, 141–54, and 155–70.

but we will do so because we will identify the meaning of her utterance with its linguistic meaning, not her intentions. In this case, therefore, the occasionalists have no grounds for applying their conclusion to hermeneutic meaning. Likewise, if we treat Ms Patient's utterance as a contribution to a dialogue, we will concern ourselves with hermeneutic meanings, but we will take the meaning of her utterance to be that she has a rheumatoid disease in her thigh. In this case, therefore, there is no difference between the beliefs and meanings we ascribe to Ms Patient and those we ascribe to Ms Patient*. The hermeneutic occasionalists fail, therefore, to establish that we cannot individuate intentions solely by reference to the individuals whose intentions they are. Historians can fix hermeneutic meanings understood as intentions without referring to the occasions of their being made.

Although utterances are made on particular occasions, objective facts about the occasions do not directly influence their hermeneutic meanings. They do not do so because hermeneutic meanings refer to occasions as they are perceived by individuals, not occasions as they really are or as we believe them to be. A hermeneutic meaning is what an individual intends by an utterance, and when an individual responds to an occasion, he necessarily does so in terms of his perception of it, which might not be accurate. Imagine, for example, that Peter says 'hallelujah lass' in order to indicate the presence of a female member of the Salvation Army, although the woman to whom he refers is not in fact a member of the Salvation Army. Susan will grasp his intention if she recognises that he is describing the woman in question as a female member of the Salvation Army. She will understand his utterance providing she grasps what he believes about the occasion. Indeed, even if she does not recognise the true nature of the occasion, even if she too believes the woman is a member of the Salvation Army, she still will grasp the hermeneutic meaning of his utterance provided she rightly understands his intention as it expresses his view of the occasion. The occasionality that counts for hermeneutic meanings is itself, therefore, a part of the intention of the author.

Of course, the reality of an occasion, as we see it, will often be a good guide to the way authors perceive it and so the occasionality of their intentions. Authors often view occasions more or less accurately, or at least more or less as we do, and when they do so, we will be able to make sense of the occasionality of their intentions by reference to the actual nature of the occasion, or at least the nature of the occasion as we see it. Thus, occasions are often reliable guides to hermeneutic meanings even though they never influence them directly. It is important to recognise here the diverse nature of the things that can enter into the occasion of an utterance. Other utterances, personal reflections, social experiences, and numerous other things can provide the occasion for an utterance. Moreover, there are no logical reasons why we should privilege one aspect of an occasion over all others. Neither the socio-economic aspect beloved of Marxists, nor the linguistic aspect beloved of conventionalists, nor any other favoured aspect of an occasion has a legitimate claim to a privileged status based on the grammar of our concepts. All aspects of an occasion can influence the way authors understand the things they discuss. None the less, no aspect of an occasion can ever be of more than indirect relevance to the hermeneutic meaning of an utterance. When we describe an occasion, we fill out the meaning of an utterance only in so far as the author perceived the occasion as we describe it. We can conclude, therefore, that historical meanings are either intentions or abstractions derived from intentions. When other things, such as the linguistic or economic context of an utterance, enter into a historical meaning, they do so only indirectly by virtue of their relationship to such intentions. In order to justify this intentionalism, however, we have to adopt a weak concept of an intention. We have to conceive of an intention not as the prior purpose of the author, but rather as the meaning an utterance has for a particular individual whether he be its author or reader. The crux of intentionalism is, therefore, a principle of procedural individualism for the history of ideas.

WEAK INTENTIONALISM

According to weak intentionalism, historians should concern themselves only with hermeneutic meanings defined as meanings that consist of the understanding of a specific individual and are identifiable exclusively by reference to that individual. I can fill out this weak version of intentionalism by showing how it avoids the errors widely associated with a stronger one. As I do so, I will also reject several other purported reasons for denying that the meaning of an utterance derives from the intentions of its author. Strong intentionalists typically argue that a text has a meaning only by virtue of the determining will of its author, so that to understand what a text says, we must recover what its author meant.[39] The main difficulties with this argument arise because it assumes texts

---

[39] E. Hirsch, *Validity in Interpretation* (New Haven, Conn.: Yale University Press, 1967); and P. Juhl, *Interpretation* (Princeton: Princeton University Press, 1980).

have hermeneutic meanings. The strong intentionalists are right to insist that hermeneutic meanings require the action of the will or mind of a specific individual. Yet because they look for the meaning of a text, they mistakenly focus exclusively on the mind of the author, thereby neglecting the fact that the mind of a reader also can act to determine a hermeneutic meaning. In most other respects, strong intentionalism looks rather like a straw man constructed by critics who should be aiming their fire at weak intentionalism but have failed to locate their target. In distinguishing between two varieties of intentionalism, therefore, I am concerned less to distance myself from other intentionalists than to disarm critics who have misunderstood intentionalism.

Strong and weak intentionalists take different views of authorial intentions. Strong intentionalists typically identify authorial intentions with prior purposes.[40] For example, when authors set out to write a poem expressing sadness, their prior purpose is to write a sad poem; thus, according to strong intentionalists, the hermeneutic meaning of their poems must incorporate a notion of sadness. In this way, strong intentionalists identify the meaning of an utterance with an authorial purpose antecedent to it – first the poets want to write a sad poem, then they do so. Really, however, because authorial purposes are antecedent to utterances, they must be related only contingently to the meanings utterances have for their authors. Poets might set out to write a sad poem only later to come to look on what they are writing as joyous, and if this happens, their poems will come to have a meaning for them different from their prior purpose. Thus, the New Critics are quite right to condemn strong intentionalism.[41] Strong intentions are related only contingently to the meanings of utterances to their authors, and this implies that they cannot be constitutive of hermeneutic meaning. Consider the example of a poet who sets out to write a sad poem, but while writing comes to think of it as joyous. It would be a foolish historian who insisted we understand the hermeneutic meaning of the poem to include a feeling of sadness simply because the original purpose of the author had been to write a sad poem. More generally, strong intentions cannot determine the meaning of an utterance for its author because authors often change their minds about what they are doing while they are

---

[40] One source of an equation of authorial intentions with prior purposes seems to be the interest of literary critics in the emotional effects authors hope their works will have. See I. Richards, *Practical Criticism* (London: Routledge & Kegan Paul, 1929), particularly pp. 180–3.

[41] W. Wimsatt and M. Beardsley, 'The intentional fallacy', in W. Wimsatt (ed.), *The Verbal Icon: Studies in the Meaning of Poetry* (Lexington, Ky.: University of Kentucky Press, 1954), pp. 3–18.

engaged in the act of writing. Prior purposes cannot fix hermeneutic meanings because the final intentions of authors need bear no relation whatsoever to their original intentions. Strong intentions, therefore, have no necessary bearing on the meanings utterances have for their authors, let alone anyone else. They are merely biographical facts about authors.

Weak intentionalism avoids the errors in strong intentionalism identified by the New Critics. It does so by equating authorial intentions with the meaning an utterance has for its author rather than the prior purpose of its author.[42] This distinction has two important components. The first is that weak intentionalism focuses on the final intentions of authors as they make an utterance. It does not consider the original intentions of authors when they first contemplate making an utterance. For example, if a poet set out to write a sad poem but during the course of writing came to look on what he was writing as a joyous poem, then a description of the meaning of the poem to its author must refer to the final conception of a joyous poem but it need not refer to the original conception of a sad poem. Of course, it is possible for authors to alter their view of the meaning of their utterances long after they have made them – few people never change their minds. But when this happens, the revised meaning of the utterance to its author will be a meaning to its author as reader, not as author; and, although the recovery of the meaning of an utterance to a reader is a legitimate historical task, for the moment I will restrict myself to the meaning an utterance has for its author. The second important component of the distinction between the meaning of an utterance to its author and the prior purposes of its author is that the former goes beyond a purposive view of authorial intentions to embrace the substantive beliefs of the author. Weak intentions are not reducible to a concern to have a certain effect or bring about a state of affairs. They incorporate the ideas that animate the actual content of the utterance. For example, if a poet writes a poem describing the sadness felt at the death of a friend, the meaning of the poem to its author might include not only a final intention to express the

---

[42] Skinner has made a closely related distinction between an intention in doing something and an intention to do something, where the former, but not the latter, enters into the meaning of an utterance. See, in particular, Skinner, 'Motives, intentions, and the interpretation of texts', pp. 68–78. The difference between my distinction and his is that my weak intentions consist exclusively of beliefs, whereas his intentions in doing something also include the illocutionary force of an utterance. The basis of this difference is not that I want to exclude all desires from the intentional aspect of an action, but rather that I do not think such desires enter into the meaning of a work.

idea of sadness but also beliefs about the nature of sadness. Weak intentionalism implies that hermeneutic meanings derive from the ideas authors hope to communicate through their utterances. We can say, therefore, that weak intentions are the final intentions authors have as they make their utterances. Weak intentions are the result of the process by which authors develop their ideas during the act of speaking, writing, painting, or whatever. They are not antecedent to utterances: rather, they emerge along with utterances. Moreover, because a weak intention comes into being along with an utterance, it is constitutive of the meaning of the utterance to its author. Weak intentions are what utterances mean to their authors at the time they are made. It is because weak intentions are thus constitutive of the meaning of utterances to their authors that the arguments of the New Critics have no bearing on weak intentionalism. If we want to grasp the meaning of an utterance to its author, we must grasp the final intention of the author in making it.

Strong and weak intentionalism also differ in their account of the conscious nature of authorial intentions. Strong intentionalists identify all authorial intentions exclusively with conscious ones.[43] They imply that authors have infallible knowledge of their own intentions, not just privileged access to them. Authors must be right about what their utterances mean to them. What is at issue here is not whether or not historians should accept every pronouncement authors make about their intentions. Authors may lie deliberately, and even the most virulent intentionalist would not want historians to perpetuate a lie. What is at issue is, rather, whether or not to know what authors think they intend is to know what they do intend. Strong intentionalists argue that it is. They reduce intentions to conscious intentions. Psychoanalytical theorists, in contrast, argue, quite rightly, that authors may not consciously grasp the meanings their utterances have even for them. An author's pre-conscious and unconscious mind can influence what he writes without his being aware of this happening.[44] For a start, authors can be

---

[43] Actually intentionalists often emphasise the importance of the preconscious and unconscious. See, for example, Hirsch, *Validity in Interpretation*, pp. 51–7. Likewise, although Skinner initially argued that historians could not overturn any statement authors made about their intentions – Skinner, 'Meaning and understanding', p. 40 – he soon rejected this view and began to allow for the possibility not only of preconscious intentions but also unconscious ones – Skinner, 'Motives, intentions, and the interpretation of texts', pp. 76–7.

[44] An influential, psychoanalytic approach to hermeneutics derives from J. Lacan, 'The function and field of speech and language in psychoanalysis' and 'The agency of the letter in the unconscious or reason since Freud', in *Ecrits: A Selection*, trans. A. Sheridan (London: Tavistock, 1977), pp. 30–113 and 146–78.

ignorant of certain beliefs expressed by their utterances, and when this is so, a historian will have to modify the self-understanding of the authors in order to grasp their actual intentions. For example, a literary histor- ian who found frequent allusions to divorce in a poem about the sadness felt on the death of a friend might conclude an essential part of the meaning of the poem to its author to consist of certain pre-conscious beliefs about divorce. More dramatically still, authors can be wrong about the beliefs that inspired their work, and when this happens, a historian will have to overturn the self-understanding of the authors in order to grasp their actual intentions. For example, a literary historian who found that a poem about the sadness felt on the death of a friend was actually a joyous poem might conclude the poet actually welcomed the death of his friend. Psychoanalytic theorists are quite right, there- fore, to condemn strong intentionalism on the grounds that the con- scious intentions of authors do not necessarily constitute the meaning of their utterances for themselves, let alone anyone else.

Weak intentionalism avoids the errors in strong intentionalism identi- fied by the psychoanalytic theorists. It does so by equating authorial intentions with the meanings utterances have for their authors, and leaving open the question of whether these meanings are conscious, pre-conscious, or unconscious. Weak intentionalism does not commit itself to any particular view of the awareness authors have of their intentions. Later I will argue that we should hesitate before ascribing hidden intentions to authors, but this later argument has nothing to do with a defence of intentionalism. A concern with intentions remains central irrespective of whether or not authors are always conscious of their intentions, and irrespective also of the status of any other intentions they might have. To say that an utterance meant such and such to its author either pre-consciously or unconsciously is still to say it meant such and such to its author. Imagine a literary historian finds constant allusions to divorce in a poem ostensibly about the sadness caused by the death of a friend, and after some consideration, decides that these allusions reflect certain unconscious beliefs of the poet. Clearly the historian is still describing the ideas, and so weak intentions, of the author. The arguments of the psychoanalytic theorists do not impinge on weak intentionalism because pre-conscious and unconscious inten- tions are still intentions.

Strong and weak intentionalists disagree not only about the nature of authorial intentions, but also about the relationship of such intentions to hermeneutic meanings. Strong intentionalists argue that the meaning of

an utterance to its author exhausts its historical meaning.[45] They say
that authorial intentions, and authorial intentions alone, constitute
hermeneutic meanings. Weak intentionalists, in contrast, adopt a procedural individualism according to which hermeneutic meanings must
be meanings for specific individuals but not necessarily for the authors of
the relevant utterances. According to weak intentionalists, utterances
can have non-authorial meanings. Moreover, because utterances can
have non-authorial meanings, they can come to possess public meanings of greater historical import than the meanings they have for their
authors. Imagine that an author intends an utterance to mean one thing
but a reader understands it to mean another. When this happens, weak
intentionalists will say that as a matter of historical fact the utterance
meant what the reader understood it to mean, although, of course, it did
so for the reader, not the author. The qualification is important. Non-
authorial historical meanings still have to be meanings for specific
individuals. Historians can attribute a non-authorial meaning to an
utterance only if they can show someone really did understand it in the
relevant way. Moreover, the evidence they give to show someone really
did understand it in the relevant way surely must be the writings, or just
possibly the actions, of the person concerned. Generally, therefore,
historians must base any claim that an utterance had a non-authorial
meaning on an argument about the authorial meaning of one or more
works by the person who understood it in the way they describe. The
attribution of a non-authorial meaning to an utterance typically depends on an analysis of the authorial meaning of at least one other
utterance.

Because authorial meanings do not exhaust historical meanings, we
can talk if we like of the meaning of a text going beyond the intentions of
its author. We can talk of the author having very little control over the
meaning of a text. Similarly, because every time someone reads a text,
he takes it to have a particular meaning, we can talk if we like of each
reading being a creative act. We can talk of the gradual unfolding of a
text's significance, the constant proliferation of its meanings, and the
impossibility of pinning down every meaning it might bear. Such talk is

---

[45] Theological concerns led many early hermeneutic theorists to tie the correct interpretation of a
text to its original meaning, understood in terms of either its author alone or its author and his
particular linguistic community. See especially F. Schleiermacher, *Hermeneutics: The Hand Written
Manuscripts*, ed. H. Kimmerle, trans. J. Duke and J. Forstman (Missoula, Mont.: Scholars Press,
1977), particularly p. 68. Later intentionalists have been more circumspect about such matters.
See, for example, E. Hirsch, 'Three dimensions in hermeneutics', *New Literary History* 3 (1971–72),
247.

extremely popular at the moment, especially with scholars influenced by reception theory.[46] None the less, while such talk is not wrong, it is lopsided in a way that obscures the true nature of the history of ideas. Consider first the fashionable suggestion that historians cannot study authorial intentions. Reception theorists sometimes draw on phenomenological scepticism to suggest that historians can understand the past only by engaging in dialogue with it. They argue that historians of ideas must renounce a concern with authorial intentions in favour of one with the text conceived as a product of multiple readings.[47] According to phenomenological sceptics, the way in which a reader understands a text always reflects his presuppositions.[48] Reception theorists imply that this phenomenological scepticism shows we can never recover the authorial intention behind a text. We should concentrate instead on the meaning of the text as it has been produced by a continuous stream of creative readings. Later I will consider phenomenological scepticism in detail. For the moment, I want to point out only that phenomenological scepticism cannot do the work reception theorists here ask it to. If we cannot have access to past meanings, we cannot recover not only authorial intentions, but also the ways readers responded to texts. There are only two possible responses to phenomenological scepticism. The first is: if we believe the limitations of human understanding make history impossible, we will focus solely on what texts mean to us, knowing full well we cannot recover either the intentions of the authors of these texts or the meanings these texts have had for past readers.[49] The second is: if we think the limitations of human understanding make history difficult but not impossible, we will try to recover the meaning of texts to authors and readers alike. Unless we reject the very possibility of studying historical meanings, we must allow that historians can study the meaning of a text to its author.

Reception theory seems to be on firmer ground when it relies solely on the suggestion that the history of ideas cannot just be a study of authorial intentions. Certainly texts can be read in ways their authors did not intend. Even here, however, reception theory is lopsided. Clearly reception theory so understood is of most relevance to historians who want to write a study of the way people have understood a given text

---

[46] See LaCapra, 'Rethinking intellectual history', in *Rethinking Intellectual History* pp. 23–71. and Ricœur, *Interpretation Theory*.

[47] Critiques of intentionalism based on this argument, include LaCapra, 'Rethinking intellectual history', in *Rethinking Intellectual History* pp. 23–71, and J. Keane, 'More theses on the philosophy of history', in Tully, *Meaning and Context*, pp. 204–17.   [48] Gadamer, *Truth and Method*.

[49] See S. Fish, *Is There a Text in This Class?* (Cambridge, Mass.: Harvard University Press, 1980).

through the ages. Surely if anyone has to go beyond authorial intentions to describe the way other people have read a text, it is these historians. But reception theory does not adequately describe the task of these historians. When historians want to know what someone took a text to mean, they will study the writings, or possibly the actions, of that person. They will be interested in the meaning of the utterances of this person, not the meaning of the original text. Thus, when historians study the way people have understood a given text through the ages, they still concern themselves with authorial intentions. It is just that the relevant authorial intentions now lie in the texts in which the readers of the primary text expressed their understanding of the primary text. In this way, whenever we shift our focus away from the author, we turn our attention to another work, and presumably another text, so we can also talk if we like of the meaning of a work being bound by the intentions of its author. Similarly, because every time someone reads a text, he creates new meanings, we can also talk if we like about every reading of a text producing a new work with a meaning composed of the weak intention of the reader.

The prevalent confusion over how we should describe the historical task of delineating the way people have understood a particular text through the ages arises largely because of the bad habit of referring to the hermeneutic meaning of a text.[50] It is because scholars wrongly talk as though a text had a hermeneutic meaning that they are tempted to refer to the meaning of a text as something going beyond the intentions of its author. It is because scholars wrongly ascribe hermeneutic meanings to texts that they are tempted to refer to the meaning of a text as something which develops and alters as time passes. Really hermeneutic meanings are always meanings for individuals, so texts do not have hermeneutic meanings. Whenever we are tempted to talk about the hermeneutic meaning of a text, we should talk instead of the meaning of the text for someone, that is, the meaning of a work. Once we start to do this, we will dispel the confusion over how to describe the way people have understood a text through the ages. Authorial intentions are not the only historical meanings because utterances can mean things to

---

[50] This bad habit is remarkably common. Earlier we saw how it led strong intentionalists astray, as in Hirsch, *Validity in Interpretation*. Now we have seen how it leads reception theorists astray, as in LaCapra, 'Rethinking intellectual history', in *Rethinking Intellectual History*, pp. 23–71. In addition, it informs the mistaken call by the New Critics for a focus on the poem or text itself on the grounds that it at least is 'indubitably there'. See F. Leavis, 'The responsible critic: or the function of criticism at any time', in *A Selection from Scrutiny*, 2 vols. (Cambridge: Cambridge University Press, 1968), vol. II, p. 292.

people other than their authors. But to talk of a text having various hermeneutic meanings over which the author has no control is mislead-ing because texts do not have hermeneutic meanings.

Although weak intentionalism does not restrict the role of the histor-ian to the recovery of authorial intentions, it does allow us to declare some ways of approaching relics from the past to be ahistorical. A principle of procedural individualism requires a historian who wants to ascribe a meaning to an utterance to specify for whom it had that meaning. Because hermeneutic meanings are meanings for individuals, any claim that a hermeneutic meaning existed must entail a claim that it existed for one or more individuals who, at least in principle, could be specified. Thus, the ascription of a meaning to an utterance is ahistorical if the individuals for whom it had that meaning are not historical figures. There is nothing wrong with people saying that an utterance means something to them or their contemporaries: it is just that these meanings are contemporary, not historical. Likewise, there is nothing wrong with people finding interesting ideas in an utterance and writing about these ideas: it is just that unless they give evidence to suggest that a historical figure understood the utterance to convey the ideas, these meanings too will be contemporary, not historical. More generally, there is no reason why people should not treat utterances as something other than histori-cal objects: it is just if they do so, they are not doing history. As historians, we must study meanings that actually existed in the past. A principle of procedural individualism implies that as historians we must study meanings that existed for specific individuals in the past.

I have analysed our everyday description of meaning in order to develop a more rigorous understanding of the objects historians of ideas recon-struct from the relics of the past available to them in the present. Much of this analysis consisted of a series of distinctions between semantic, linguistic, and hermeneutic meaning, and between strong and weak intentionalism. To establish these distinctions I relied mainly on induc-tive arguments which deployed examples to illustrate the relevant con-trasts. In addition, my analysis divided the different types of meaning and intention according to whether or not they concern historians. To make this division I relied mainly on deductive arguments to demon-strate that structural meanings have a temporal existence only when they are reducible to hermeneutic ones. The result of my analysis is the core of a theory of historical meaning. Any historical meaning must be based on what a given individual took an utterance to mean. It must derive from the weak intentions of a specific individual. All historical meanings are either hermeneutic meanings or else abstractions based on hermeneutic meanings, where hermeneutic meanings are the meanings particular utterances have for particular individuals. Once we stretch our account of an intention to include the way a reader understands an utterance, we can adopt a straightforward dichotomy between hermeneutic meanings which exist in time and structural meanings which do not. We can do so because meanings can exist in time only if they are reducible to the way in which a specific group of readers understand an utterance. Thus, all historical meanings must derive from hermeneutic meanings since hermeneutic meanings alone have a temporal existence. Historical meanings are always meanings for certain individuals, and we cannot reduce the meaning an individual attaches to an utterance to either the truth conditions or the conventional meaning of the utterance.

The hermeneutic meaning of a work derives from the intentions of the person for whom the text has that meaning. We can defend this conclusion, however, only because we have defined the way readers understand an utterance as a species of intentional meaning. We have moved from a strong concept of intention defined as the conscious, prior purposes of authors to a weak concept of intention defined as the meaning, conscious or otherwise, an utterance has for someone, whether its author or a reader. However, because we typically think of intentions as prior purposes, to call a weak intention an intention is somewhat misleading. From now on, therefore, I will talk instead of the meaning of a work deriving from an individual viewpoint. By expanding intentionalism to equate historical meanings with individual viewpoints, we avoid many of the criticisms raised against intentionalism by New Critics, psychoanalytic critics, and reception theorists. We do so because an individual view of a text need not be prior to the utterance, conscious, or the view of the author.

Some criticisms of intentionalism arise from a phenomenological scepticism I am yet to consider. Ontological hermeneutic theorists such as Gadamer, and critical hermeneutic theorists such as Paul Ricœur, argue that the very nature of human understanding precludes our having knowledge of the intentions of past writers.[51] Our concrete

[51] Gadamer, *Truth and Method*, particularly pp. 245–74; Ricœur, *Interpretation Theory*, particularly pp. 43–4 and 89–95.

situation in the present or an inherent gap between hermeneutic and semantic meanings implies that we are at a distance from past works so that we can come to understand them only by appropriating them in a productive act. Many opponents of intentionalism draw on a phenomenological scepticism they associate with Gadamer and Ricœur. Phenomenological scepticism appears to challenge my analysis of historical meaning by denying that one can have knowledge of historical meanings as I have defined them. Because this challenge rests on an epistemological argument, however, I will not deal with it until I have considered what constitutes objective knowledge of the past. Before I continue with my analysis of the meanings studied by historians, therefore, I must ask what sort of knowledge historians can have of past works. Before I look more closely at the nature of an individual viewpoint, I need to provide a logic of justification appropriate to the history of ideas. For the moment, however, I can provide at least a provisional answer to my initial question about meaning. What is a historical meaning? A historical meaning is a hermeneutic meaning or an abstraction based on a number of hermeneutic meanings, where a hermeneutic meaning is an individual viewpoint.

CHAPTER 3

On objectivity

INTRODUCTION

The first task of historians of ideas is to use relics from the past to reconstruct as historical objects the weak intentions that constitute the hermeneutic meanings of utterances made in the past. Only afterwards do they turn to the task of relating these historical objects to one another in narratives or theories, although, of course, the theories they already hold will influence the way they reconstruct historical objects, and no doubt as they devise further theories so they will modify their understanding of the relevant historical objects. No account of the tasks of a practice, however, can tell us everything we want to know about it. In particular, I have said nothing to answer the question of how historians should set about, first, reconstructing historical meanings from the relics available to them, and second, justifying the narratives or theories they develop around the hermeneutic meanings they thus reconstruct. Consider a group of students who want to know what a particular utterance means. Suppose they consult the works of several eminent historians only to find that the historians disagree among themselves. What the students need is a way of deciding which historian best describes the meaning of the utterance.

At one extreme, some scholars suggest that historians can justify or condemn an individual theory as conclusively true or false, with every reasonable person then being bound to accept that theory. Some of these objectivists pin their faith on a particular method. They argue that the use of a particular method will always reveal the meaning of an utterance, or, more usually, that it is a prerequisite of reconstructing the meaning of an utterance. Thus, they conclude that historians can justify a theory by showing it was reached using a special method which necessarily produces a true understanding of utterances, or, more usually, that historians can begin to justify a theory by showing that the alternatives were reached by methods which cannot generate a true understanding of utterances. Other objectivists pin their faith on pure perceptions of the relevant facts. They argue that once we have a theory in front of us, we can see whether or not it accords with the facts. Historical theories rest on historical objects that are founded on facts given to us by our pure perceptions of relics from the past. Thus, they conclude that historians can justify a theory by showing that the facts prove it to be true, or at least that the facts do not prove it to be false. At the other extreme, some scholars deny that historians have any way of justifying their theories; they imply that we cannot make any sort of informed decision between rival historical theories. All of these sceptics argue that if we define the history of ideas as the study of the intentions of historical figures, we make the history of ideas an impossible practice. Some of them reject the very possibility of our having knowledge of other people's minds: they argue that historians cannot recover hermeneutic meanings because hermeneutic meanings are intentional. Others reject the very possibility of our having knowledge of the past: they argue that historians cannot recover hermeneutic meanings because hermeneutic meanings are historical.

I will oppose the extremes of objectivism and scepticism. Much recent scholarship has emphasised the problems inherent in all representation, the subjective and constructed nature of all experience, and the historical and social specificity of all reasoning. The debates generated by this scholarship often focus on post-modernism. Post-modernists reject all foundationalist epistemologies: they deny that we ever can justify our knowledge by reference to given empirical facts or self-evident logical truths. I adopted something akin to this post-modern view by arguing that all semantic meaning, and so knowledge, depends on a particular context. After all, if all knowledge depends on a particular context, neither an empirical fact nor a principle of reason can be given to us as an unquestionable and basic truth. Unfortunately, however, post-modernism has produced a widespread, unhealthy dichotomy in the way we think about the problem of objectivity. On the one hand, far too many post-modernists promote a playful nihilism. They condemn the traditional ideal of objectivity not only as intellectually untenable, but also as inimical to freedom, and in its place they champion an 'anything goes' attitude to truth.[1] They would have us abandon the very idea of

---

[1] In addition to the works mentioned elsewhere by Derrida, Foucault, and arguably Rorty, see J. Baudrillard, *Simulations*, trans. P. Foss, P. Patton, and P. Beitchman (New York: Semiotext[e], 1983).

objectivity. On the other hand, far too many opponents of post-modernism insist on a traditional ideal of objectivity as the only bulwark against an invidious culture of relativism and irrationalism, perhaps even social chaos.[2] They would have us ignore the manifest problems in the traditional concept of objectivity. Actually, however, we can accept the absence of any given truths capable of providing foundations for our knowledge without thereby adopting an irrationalist relativism. We can do so simply by shifting the focus of our epistemology from a search for given truths to a defence of a human practice. In analysing the form of justification appropriate to the history of ideas, therefore, I will oppose both foundationalist objectivism and irrationalist relativism.[3] In accord with my anti-foundationalism, I will deny that there is either a particular method or a decision procedure that we can use as a criterion of good history. But I also will argue that there is no reason why we should assume that we cannot have accurate knowledge of past intentions. Objectivity in the history of ideas rests on a combination of agreement on certain facts, an extensive use of criticism, and a comparison of rival views in relation to clearly defined criteria. Historians cannot pronounce their particular theories to be decisively true or false, but they can make rational decisions between rival webs of theories, and thereby pronounce their theories to be the best currently available to us.

THE PLACE OF METHOD

We want to know how historians should set about reconstructing historical objects from the relics available to them in the present. Numerous scholars have tried to promote a logic of discovery for the history of ideas. They argue either that their favoured method is a foolproof way of reconstructing historical objects, or, more usually, that their favoured method is a prerequisite of reconstructing historical objects. They conclude that historians can go at least some way towards justifying their theories by reference to their adherence to the favoured method. Consider, for example, the New Critics. They insisted that works were

---

[2] A much discussed example is A. Bloom, *The Closing of the American Mind* (New York: Simon & Schuster, 1987). In many ways, however, the same might be said of J. Habermas, *The Philosophical Discourse of Modernity*, trans. F. Lawrence (Cambridge: Polity Press, 1987).

[3] For an attempt to avoid these two extremes by drawing on the hermeneutic tradition, see R. Bernstein, *Beyond Objectivism and Relativism: Science, Hermeneutics, and Praxis* (Philadelphia: University of Pennsylvania Press, 1983). For an earlier version of my position, see M. Bevir, 'Objectivity in history', *History and Theory* 33 (1994), 328–44.

verbal icons, defined as self-sufficient entities, so that literary historians should concentrate exclusively on a close reading of the work before them.[4] They dismissed all appeals to extrinsic materials as irrelevant to a proper understanding of a work. No doubt the New Critics typically insisted on a close reading of the work itself mainly to preclude references to biographical and social facts. No doubt their point was less that close reading guaranteed understanding than that other approaches were irrelevant, or even damaging, to understanding. None the less, they still ended up defining a particular method as a prerequisite of understanding. They still argued that we should reach an understanding of a work solely by studying the work itself.

Consider also the more recent example of the conventionalists. They believe that we cannot discover what a work means unless we locate it in the linguistic conventions governing the treatment of the issues it considers. Indeed, the widely recognised overlap between conventionalists and contextualists consists in the fact that both regard the study of the linguistic context of a work as a prerequisite of understanding it. Skinner, a conventionalist, says, 'to understand what any given writer may have been doing in using some particular concept or argument, we need first of all to grasp the nature and range of things that could recognizably have been done by using that particular concept, in the treatment of that particular theme, at that particular time'.[5] Similarly, Pocock, a contextualist, says, 'it seems a prior necessity [of historical understanding] to establish the language or languages in which some passage of political discourse was being conducted'.[6] Sometimes conventionalists even suggest that their preferred method might be sufficient to ensure historical understanding, as when Skinner says, 'if we succeed in identifying this [linguistic] context with sufficient accuracy, we can eventually hope to read off what the speaker or writer in whom we are interested was doing in saying what he or she said'.[7]

Despite Skinner's numerous statements to the effect that he provides us with a method we must adopt if we are to understand a work, some scholars still insist that his work deals with epistemological rather than

---

[4] Leavis, 'Responsible critic'; and Wimsatt and Beardsley, 'Intentional fallacy'. The New Critics sometimes gave history a strictly limited role in relation to their project of evaluating supposed verbal icons by reference to supposed universal standards. See, in particular, W. Wimsatt, 'History and criticism: a problematic relationship', in Wimsatt, *The Verbal Icon*, pp. 253–65.

[5] Skinner, 'Motives, intentions, and the interpretation of texts', p. 77.

[6] Pocock, 'State of the art', in *Virtue, Commerce and History*, p. 7.

[7] Q. Skinner, 'A reply to my critics', in Tully, *Meaning and Context*, p. 275.

methodological issues.[8] What these scholars fail to recognise is that because Skinner offers us his method as a logic of discovery, he necessarily fuses epistemology with methodology. His method constitutes a form of justification. Conventionalists such as Skinner argue that the meaning of an utterance derives not only from the meanings of the words used in it – meanings they equate with linguistic meanings – but also from its intended illocutionary force – a force they equate with the author's intention in making it. According to Skinner, for instance, the meaning of the words in Defoe's tract on *The Shortest Way with the Dissenters* is clear. Defoe argued that we should regard religious dissent as a capital offence, and this means that we should regard religious dissent as a capital offence. None the less, Skinner continues, to understand a work, we have to grasp not only the meaning of the words in it, but also its intended illocutionary force. To understand *The Shortest Way with the Dissenters*, we have to recognise that it has the force of a parody. Defoe was being ironic: he was mocking religious bigots by making fun of the arguments they used; he was ridiculing contemporary arguments against religious toleration, not recommending the hanging of dissenters. Crucially, conventionalists argue that the expression and reception of intended illocutionary force requires a background of shared conventions. Thus, they conclude that if historians are to understand a given utterance, they must focus on the prevailing conventions governing discussion of the issues it addresses. As Skinner explains, the recovery of the intended illocutionary force of an utterance requires 'a separate form of study, which it will in fact be essential to undertake if the critic's aim is to understand "the meaning" of the writer's corresponding works'.[9]

The New Critics, the conventionalists, and all others who put their faith in a favoured method, are wrong to do so. Here I will begin by developing a general argument to establish that there cannot be a logic of discovery for the history of ideas – no method can be a prerequisite of good history. Then I will go on to apply this general argument to the specific case of conventionalism – knowledge of the relevant linguistic context is not a prerequisite of good history. Any putative logic of

---

[8] See, for example, Gunnell, *Political Theory*, particularly pp. 98–103; and J. Gunnell, 'Interpretation and the history of political theory: apology and epistemology', *American Political Science Review* 76 (1982), 317–27. Skinner, reacting critically to Gunnell's characterisation of his work, has reaffirmed yet again that he offers us a method as a logic of discovery. He writes, 'I have sought to argue that, if our aim is to acquire this kind of understanding [of the historical meaning of a text], we have no option but to adopt an historical and intertextual approach'. Skinner, 'Reply to my critics', p. 232.   [9] Skinner, 'Motives, intentions and the interpretation of texts', p. 75.

discovery for the history of ideas must rest either explicitly or implicitly on the assumption that to understand an utterance a reader must have a correct prior theory. One can insist on a specific method only if one assumes that historians will be unable to reconstruct meanings as historical objects if they approach relics from the past without suitable knowledge or preparation. Proponents of logics of discovery must argue that to grasp the meaning of an utterance we have to approach it already knowing certain things. Depending on their particular predilections, they might insist on our having knowledge of things such as linguistic conventions, the psychological make up of the speaker, or the relevant socio-economic background. Against all logics of discovery, I will argue that a correct prior theory is neither necessary nor sufficient to ensure a correct understanding of an utterance, so that historians may manage to recover the meaning of an utterance no matter what prior knowledge they possess, no matter what method they adopt.

To start we should distinguish the prior theories with which people approach an utterance from the passing theories in terms of which they understand it. Consider the case of Mrs Malaprop. Most members of an audience to Sheridan's play probably have a prior theory that 'a nice derangement of epitaphs' means 'a nice derangement of epitaphs', but no doubt some of them develop a passing theory that Mrs Malaprop means 'a nice arrangement of epithets'. Prior theories differ from passing theories because in reaching conclusions we characteristically go beyond the evidence before us; indeed, if we did not do so, the conclusion would be a mere restatement of the evidence, and not a conclusion at all. For example, neither Mrs Malaprop's words, nor the context of her words, provide conclusive evidence that she means 'a nice arrangement of epithets'. Members of the audience necessarily go beyond the evidence when they decide this is what she means. Indeed, it is because the evidence does not prove conclusively she means 'a nice arrangement of epithets' that we can imagine other members of the audience thinking she means 'a nice derangement of epitaphs', or, perhaps more plausibly, simply being confused as to her meaning. Whenever we come to understand an utterance, we necessarily go beyond the evidence in a manner that points to a distinction between prior and passing theories. Critics might suggest that the distinction between prior and passing theories comes down to nothing more than the impact of a particular context. Perhaps, for example, members of the audience reach the passing theory that Mrs Malaprop means 'a nice arrangement of epithets' simply because they have a prior theory that this is what people mean when they say 'a nice derangement of epitaphs' in the context in which she does so. Actually, however, this criticism will not do. Consider a group of people who hold a prior theory that someone in Mrs Malaprop's situation who says 'a nice derangement of epitaphs' means 'a nice arrangement of epithets'. We must grant that one of them might go to see Sheridan's play and then understand Mrs Malaprop to mean 'a nice derangement of epitaphs'. If we did not grant this, we would have to postulate a necessary connection between one's prior expectations and one's actual understanding, where, because we do not know what causes actual understandings, any such postulate would be an inappropriate matter of faith. Different people react differently to the same utterance, and we cannot explain why. Moreover, because we do not know why people understand an utterance in the way they do, we cannot guarantee that a particular prior theory will lead to a particular understanding. Thus, we must be able to distinguish prior theories from passing theories no matter how tightly we specify the situations to which prior theories refer. We will not be able to reduce passing theories to prior theories until we know what leads people to understand utterances in the way they do, and it seems unlikely that we will ever have such knowledge.

The distinction between prior and passing theories of itself shows that correct prior knowledge is neither necessary nor sufficient to ensure a correct passing theory. A correct prior theory is not necessary for understanding because we might always set out with a faulty prior theory and yet arrive at an adequate passing theory. For example, some members of the audience might reach the passing theory that Mrs Malaprop means 'a nice arrangement of epithets' even if their prior theory suggested she meant 'a nice derangement of epitaphs'. Likewise, a correct prior theory is not sufficient for understanding because we always might set out with an adequate prior theory and yet arrive at a faulty passing theory. For example, some members of the audience might reach the passing theory that Mrs Malaprop means 'a nice derangement of epithets' even if their prior theory suggested she meant 'a nice arrangement of epitaphs'. Finally, because a correct passing theory is neither necessary nor sufficient to ensure understanding, therefore, no method can be either a guarantee or a prerequisite of good history. No method can guarantee good history because someone who sets out with a correct prior theory might reach a faulty passing theory. And no method can be a prerequisite of good history because someone who sets out with an erroneous prior theory might reach an adequate passing theory. There cannot be a logic of discovery for the history of ideas.

The foregoing argument against a logic of discovery for the history of ideas can be fleshed out in relation to the specific method proposed by the conventionalists. The conventionalists argue that historians cannot recover the intended illocutionary force of an utterance unless they have prior knowledge of its linguistic context. Clearly we should accept that shared conventions are necessary for communication if only because authors and readers who had no shared conventions would speak different languages. However, the necessity for shared conventions if communication is to occur cannot sustain by itself a logic of discovery: after all, even if it is necessary for author and reader to share some conventions, there may still be no method that is necessary or sufficient to ensure they come to share these conventions. Conventionalists must establish that historians can come to share the relevant conventions with an author only if they study the relevant linguistic context. Conventionalism presupposes that historians must set about reconstructing the meaning of an utterance already knowing the conventions the author used to convey his illocutionary intention in making it.

In contrast, we have found correct prior knowledge to be neither necessary nor sufficient to ensure an accurate passing theory. A correct prior theory is not necessary for understanding because a historian might set out with a faulty prior theory and still arrive at an adequate passing theory. Thus, a historian who knew nothing about the linguistic context of a particular utterance still might grasp the illocutionary intention of the author in making it. Consider, for example, a group of historians who know that Annie Besant was a prominent figure in the National Secular Society who condemned religion in general and Christianity in particular. Imagine they discover that Besant wrote a book on Christianity, Islam, Hinduism, and Buddhism, in which she said she wanted 'to help members of each of the four religions to recognise the value and beauty of the three faiths which are not their own, and to demonstrate their underlying unity'.[10] Was Besant being sincere? Some of the historians might conclude she was. They would be right. Besant left the National Secular Society for the Theosophical Society, and her utterance expresses the theosophists' faith in the fundamental unity and value of all religions. The historians who are right not only know nothing about the conventions governing theosophical works, their

[10] A. Besant, *Four Great Religions* (London: Theosophical Publishing, n.d.), p. 1.

prior theory actually inclines them to locate the work in the wrong context. But despite having a woefully inadequate prior theory, they arrive at a correct passing theory. Clearly, therefore, knowledge of the linguistic context is not necessary to ensure recovery of the intended illocutionary force of an utterance.

A correct prior theory is not sufficient for understanding because a historian might set out with an adequate prior theory and yet arrive at a faulty passing theory. Moreover, conventionalists imply that the meanings historians attach to works by placing them in their linguistic contexts are necessarily the meanings intended by their authors; but this need not be so because contexts do not fix intentions. A historian who knew all about the linguistic context of an utterance still might fail to grasp its intended illocutionary force. Consider, for instance, a group of historians who know that E. M. Forster signed off a novel with the words 'Weybridge, 1924'. Imagine they study the linguistic conventions of the time and thereby discover that his fellow writers often signed off with a romantic flourish, typified by James Joyce's 'Trieste–Zurich–Paris, 1914–21'. Was Forster parodying his fellow novelists? Some of the historians might conclude, with Skinner, that Forster did indeed intend to deflate a pretentious habit of his fellow novelists.[11] Surely, however, the evidence is not strong enough to warrant this conclusion. Maybe he did write the novel in Weybridge in 1924, and maybe he intended simply to record this fact. We have alternative views, and to decide between them, we must consider things other than the linguistic context of the novel. The historians need to investigate Forster's life. If they discover that he wrote the novel in Cambridge and India from 1922 to 1924 without ever visiting Weybridge, the case for understanding the utterance as a parody would seem more or less conclusive. But if they discover that he wrote the novel in Weybridge in 1924, the idea that his utterance was a parody would begin to look rather more doubtful. Clearly, therefore, knowledge of the linguistic context is not sufficient to ensure recovery of the intended illocutionary force of an utterance.

Crucially, because prior knowledge of the linguistic context is neither necessary nor sufficient to ensure recovery of the intended illocutionary force of an utterance, the conventionalists have no valid reason for insisting on their favoured method. Their favoured method is not a prerequisite of good history because someone who set out without knowledge of the linguistic context might still reach an adequate passing theory. Their favoured method is not a guarantee of good history

[11] Skinner, 'Reply to my critics', p. 285.

because someone who set out with knowledge of the linguistic context might still reach a faulty passing theory. Finally, because their favoured method is neither a prerequisite nor a guarantee of good history, a historian might do as well using some other method.

There cannot be a logic of discovery for the history of ideas. Because there is no mechanical procedure appropriate to the retrieval of past meanings, historians cannot justify their theories by reference to the method they use. This should not surprise us. Earlier we found that people possess a linguistic faculty enabling them to generate novel sentences conveying novel meanings in a way we cannot reduce to fixed procedures. Now we have found that this linguistic faculty also enables them to understand novel sentences conveying novel meanings in a way we cannot reduce to fixed procedures. Because our linguistic faculty is a skill we exercise, not a set of rules we apply, therefore, when we move from prior theories to passing theories, we necessarily do so creatively. The creative nature of our understanding implies that we might end up with correct passing theories even if we begin with faulty prior theories, and that we might end up with incorrect passing theories even if we begin with adequate prior theories. No method can fix the way our linguistic faculty operates. Thus, historians always come to understand a work by a creative process in which success can be a result of insight, intuition, or good luck. Fortunately, however, the limits of historical method need not worry us; after all, scientists do not claim that the objectivity of their knowledge rests on a logic of discovery, and historians need not aim at more secure knowledge than do scientists. The particular process by which a historian comes to believe in the historical existence of certain objects has no philosophical significance. Historians can try to systematise past experience in methodological hints, or they can try something new; they can rely on instinct and guesswork, or they can wait for inspiration. What matters is the result of their endeavours. Just as we judge mathematical proofs and scientific theories without asking how their exponents hit upon them, so we should evaluate accounts of historical objects without considering the methods used by historians. We should concentrate on the reasonableness of the histories people write, not the reasons why they write what they do.

The proper contribution of method is neither to legislate to historians, nor to decide between good and bad history. It is rather to draw the attention of historians to sources of evidence and fruitful ways of thinking about the past.[12] Methodologists should develop the craft of

---

[12] To reject the possibility of a logic of discovery is not to repudiate any role for theory. Contrast S. Knapp and W. Michaels, 'Against theory (literary criticism)', *Critical Inquiry* 8 (1982), 723–42.

their discipline instead of addressing philosophical issues about its logic.[13] Just as carpenters can make chairs however they wish provided the results are acceptable, so historians can arrive at theories however they wish provided the results are acceptable. But just as carpenters practise a craft with a lore that often provides useful guidance when they come to work on a piece of wood, so historians practise a craft with a lore composed of heuristic techniques, knowledge of which facilitates the study of the past. Historians learn their craft as they pick up hints on how to locate sources, on how to deal with different types of source, and even on what types of sources are most likely to provide evidence pertinent to certain types of question. They master their craft as they become more and more attuned to the history, controversies, norms, and institutions of their discipline. None the less, because skilled crafts-manship always requires supplementation with imagination and luck, mastery of a craft can never be a guarantee or prerequisite of success. We should not mistake the craft-lore of a discipline for a part of its logic. Methodologists propose heuristic techniques rather than prescriptive rules. Once we thus recognise the proper contribution of method, we will see how a rejection of conventionalism leaves open the possibility of the linguistic context providing historians with useful evidence about the meaning of an utterance. Although historians might grasp the intention of an author without paying any heed to the linguistic context, they also might not do so. The linguistic context might provide the crucial piece of evidence that leads a particular historian to grasp the meaning of an utterance. Certainly historians might illuminate Besant's work by telling us about the state of comparative religion at the time she wrote. It is just that they might succeed in recovering her illocutionary intention even if they knew nothing about the linguistic context. Moreover, because the linguistic context might provide a crucial piece of evidence, prudent historians will always examine it. None the less, there is nothing special about linguistic contexts in this respect.[14] Prudent historians will im-

---

[13] The distinction between logic and heuristics lends support to methodological pluralism since it suggests that a variety of methods could lead one to an objective understanding of a work. A stronger defence of methodological pluralism, drawing on Quine, but sensibly avoiding his physicalism, is P. Roth, *Meaning and Method in the Social Sciences* (Ithaca, N.Y.: Cornell University Press, 1987).

[14] I can extend to linguistic contexts an argument conventionalists make about social contexts. Cf. 'despite the possibility, therefore, that a study of social context may *help* in the understanding of a text, which I have conceded, the fundamental assumption of the contextual methodology, that the ideas of a given text should be understood *in terms of* its social context, can be shown to be mistaken, and to serve in consequence not as the guide to understanding, but as the source of further very prevalent confusions in the history of ideas'. Skinner, 'Meaning and understanding', p. 59.

merse themselves in the ideas, habits, and social and economic structures of the periods they study so as to stimulate and check their
intuitions. We should not dismiss the search for evidence. We should
reject only the idea that the search for evidence must take a particular
form. Method can sustain helpful hints. It cannot sustain a logic of
discovery.

AGAINST VINDICATION AND REFUTATION

Logical empiricists argue that historians can justify their theories using a
logic of either vindication or refutation. Whereas logical positivism
refers to the doctrines associated with the Vienna circle of the 1920s and
1930s, logical empiricism refers to the doctrine that we can determine
conclusively the truth or falsity of propositions by reference to facts that
are given to us by pure experiences. Because the logical positivists were
influenced by the empirical tradition, there is a strong overlap between
the two. However, while almost all the logical positivists were also
logical empiricists, several logical empiricists, such as Karl Popper, are
not logical positivists. The most important doctrinal difference between
the two is that the logical positivists were committed strongly to the
verification principle in a way logical empiricists need not be. Logical
empiricists argue only that historians can justify their theories using a
logic of either vindication or refutation. Whereas a logic of discovery
tells us how to find the truth, a logic of vindication tells us how to
determine whether a given theory is or is not true, and a logic of
refutation tells us how to determine whether a given theory is or is not
false. Logics of vindication and refutation ignore the question of how a
historian constructed a given object or theory. They concentrate instead
on whether or not a given object or theory corresponds to pure facts.
Verificationists defend an ideal of vindication. They believe that we can
decode all meaningful theories into a series of observation statements.
Thus, a theory is true if it consists of observation statements that are
true; or, as probabilists would say, a theory is more or less probably true
depending on the number and nature of the observation statements with
which it is in accord.[15] Falsificationists agree about the importance of
breaking down theories into observation statements, but they insist that
no number of positive observations can prove a theory to be true.[16]
Thus, they defend an ideal of refutation. They believe that the objective

[15] A probabilist example of verificationism is R. Carnap, *The Logical Syntax of Language* (London: Routledge & Kegan Paul, 1937).
[16] K. Popper, *The Logic of Scientific Discovery* (New York: Basic Books, 1959).

status of theories derives from our ability to make observations showing other theories to be false.

We need not worry ourselves too much with the differences between verificationists and falsificationists, differences which derive from their respective stances towards the Humean problem of induction. What matters to us is something they have in common. Verificationists and falsificationists alike ground objective knowledge on confrontations with given facts. All logics of vindication and refutation rely on our confronting a theory with facts in a test that proves it to be true or false, or not-false or false. Verificationists argue that if we consider any individual theory, we can decide whether it is true or not true. Falsificationists argue that if we consider any individual theory, we can decide whether it is false or not-false. Thus, the proponents of logics of vindication and refutation must defend the idea of basic facts against which we can determine conclusively the truth or the falsity of individual theories. Logical empiricists guarantee our knowledge of basic facts by arguing that we have pure experiences of an external world. Our perceptions are of the world as it is. The process of experience does not affect the way we perceive the world. Logical empiricists disagree about whether the pure experiences that decide issues of truth or falsity are either particular experiences of individuals or inter-subjective experiences within a community; but whichever view they take, they invariably appeal to pure experience as the foundation of objective knowledge. Indeed, philosophers must defend the idea of pure experiential data if they are to argue that we can determine either truth or falsity conclusively.

There cannot be a logic of either vindication or refutation for the very general reason that we do not have pure experiences.[17] This argument applies to all areas of knowledge, not just the history of ideas. The nature of a perception depends on the perceiver. A sensation can become the object of a perception only when our intelligence identifies it as a particular sensation both distinct from and in relation to other sensations. We can become aware of a sensation only when we attend to it, and when we attend to it, we necessarily use abstract categories to identify it as a particular sort of sensation. Thus, our perceptions always incorporate elements of our theoretical understanding of the world. Certainly our everyday accounts of our experiences embody numerous

---

[17] A related problem with logical empiricism is that experience does not take the form of propositions so it cannot justify beliefs since they do take such a form. Compare D. Davidson, 'A coherence theory of truth and knowledge', in LePore, *Truth and Interpretation*, p. 310; and Rorty, *Philosophy and the Mirror of Nature*, p. 178.

realist assumptions, including: objects exist independently of our per-
ceiving them; objects persist through time; other people can perceive the
objects we perceive; objects sometimes act causally upon one another.
All of these theoretical assumptions are embodied in our everyday
experiences. This does not mean that our categories determine what
experiences we have: objects really do force various sensations upon us.
But it does mean that our categories influence the way we experience
the sensations we have: we make sense of the sensations objects force
upon us by using our categories. The important point here is that
because experiences embody theoretical assumptions, they cannot be
pure, so they cannot provide criteria for determining conclusively either
the truth or the falsity of theories. When we look at the facts to see if a
theory is true, what we find there will depend in part on us.

Logical empiricists might respond to such criticism by giving a phenomenological account of pure experience.[18] They might define their
ideal of pure experience solely in terms of the content of our sensations
without evoking any realist assumptions about the relationship of our
sensations to an external world. This response will not do for two
reasons. First, a phenomenological account of an experience cannot
capture its actuality. When we see an object falling, we see an object
falling. We cannot give a simpler description of the experience, and we
cannot have a more fundamental experience. If we could deprive people
of the theoretical assumptions entwined within their experience, we
would be left with people so disorientated they would not be able to make
coherent sense of the world in the way they have to if they are to describe
their sensations. Second, the very idea of a phenomenological account of
experience presupposes an acquaintance with realist theories. We cannot make sense of the idea of people who have sensations that do not
embody realist assumptions except in contrast to the idea of people who
have experiences that do embody realist assumptions. We cannot
bracket off something unless we already know what it is we are to bracket
off. To identify experiences with pure sensations bereft of intelligent
resolution is to identify experiences with things we cannot conceive of
precisely because they cannot be objects of experience. All attempts to
abstract the notion of sensation from the experiences of individuals end
in the dismissal of the idea of sensation. They do so because sensation
always occurs in the context of the experiences of individuals. The idea
of experiences without prior theories is, therefore, incomprehensible.

[18] Husserl, *Ideas*.

Logical empiricism also presupposes a semantic theory based on a particular analysis of confirmation according to which we can assign truth-values to individual propositions. After all, a proposition must refer to a definite state of affairs if we are to decide conclusively its truth or falsity by comparing it with our experiences. If the precise nature of the state of affairs to which it refers depends on other propositions, our experiences cannot determine conclusively its truth or falsity. They can determine its truth or falsity only relative to these other propositions. The possibility of a logic of vindication or refutation relies on our matching propositions with experiences individually. Thus, semantic holism, properly understood, challenges not an intentionalist analysis of historical meaning, but rather the analysis of confirmation required by logical empiricism.[19] Semantic holists such as Kuhn argue that the truth-value of a proposition depends on its context. Our theories can confront our experiences in tests of verification or falsification only as interconnected webs.[20] Likewise, one feature of Wittgenstein's argument against a private language is a holistic critique of the possibility of pure meaning and so pure experience.[21] One key feature of his discussion of pain, moreover, is to establish that we do not have pure experiences even of our own mental states.[22] The important point here, however, is not how we should understand Wittgenstein's arguments, but that the semantic holists are right. There cannot be a logic of either vindication or refutation because our theories can confront our experiences only holistically, never individually. Because we cannot have pure experiences, observation and theory necessarily go along together. Thus, propositions can confront the world only in clusters. Whenever we use observations to test a hypothesis, the way we interpret the observations and their relation to the hypothesis presupposes the truth of various theories. To test a hypothesis against observations, we must accept the truth of the bundle of theories that acts as background knowledge in the test. Any test must apply, therefore, not to a single hypothesis, but to an interconnected web of hypotheses, composed of the theories being assumed as background knowledge as well as the

---

[19] If, like Frege, one takes semantic holism to imply that words have meaning only in sentences, one can reconcile semantic holism with logical empiricism by assimilating sentences to names. But if, as I am, one takes semantic holism to imply that the truth conditions of words, and sentences, depend on the other theories one holds true, semantic holism necessarily undermines the idea of confirmation found in logical empiricism. See P. Hacker, 'Semantic holism: Frege and Wittgenstein', in C. Luckhardt (ed.), *Wittgenstein: Sources and Perspectives* (Hassocks, Sussex: Harvester Press, 1979), pp. 213–42.

[20] Kuhn, *Structure of Scientific Revolutions*. Also see Quine, 'Two dogmas of empiricism'.

[21] Wittgenstein, *Philosophical Investigations*, ## 243–363.   [22] *Ibid.*, ## 403–9.

theory being tested. Of course, during the test we can distinguish the theory we are testing from the background theories we assume to be true. But this distinction has no logical significance. It does not allow us to determine conclusively whether a hypothesis is true or false by a test against observations. To see this, we need to recognise only that when a test shows a hypothesis to be true or false in a manner we did not expect, we still have a choice about how to accommodate the result of the test within our web of beliefs. Either we can accept the result of the test with respect to the hypothesis, or we can reconsider the theories on which the test depended, or we can introduce a speculative theory to explain the discrepancy between the hypothesis and the result of the test. Because observation entails theory, we cannot decide conclusively whether a theory is true or false, or even not-false or false.

Some logical empiricists defend the possibility of our testing individual theories by suggesting that we make any relevant background theories immutable by convention.[23] They think that we can fix our empirical base by taking certain theories to be true. Actually, however, this defence of logical empiricism will not do. It will not do even if we accept the rather implausible idea that a proof of the conventional immutability of our background theories would introduce logical significance into the distinction between the hypothesis being tested and the theories being assumed for the sake of the test. The problem is that our background theories do not possess the required immutability. Indeed, our background theories appear to be so highly flexible that there are an indefinite number of ways in which we might tinker with our belief system in order to accommodate any unexpected observation. Not one single theory appears to be appropriately immune from revision. All theories seem to be available for re-evaluation. Consider, for instance, the theory that fire heats things up. Surely we believe this theory with as much certainty as we do any evidence we could offer to support it. Indeed, it is so important to our understanding of reality that we cannot conceive of any one observation that would overturn it. It is, therefore, a perfect candidate for the role of a background theory we could make immutable by convention. None the less, the theory that fire heats things up remains a proposition we could come to reject as false, as the logical empiricists recognise in saying it is immutable only by convention. Imagine we did come to reject it. Clearly we would have to be able to explain the process by which we had done so. Provided we rejected

---

[23] Popper appeals to conventionalism to defend the idea of a background of hardened theories in the *Logic of Scientific Discovery*.

the very idea of immutable theories, we could explain this process in the same way we would our coming to reject any other theory. In contrast, if we believed in theories made immutable by convention, we would have to identify a moment when the theory that fire heats things up had ceased to count as immutable and so become a candidate for rejection. But, of course, we would not be able to identify such a moment. Moreover, because we have no way of deciding whether or not a theory is immutable by convention, we must conclude that none of our theories is immutable by convention. A logic of vindication or refutation that depends on a hardened background established by convention is, therefore, a mere methodological fiction of no relevance to our actual practice. All our theories might prove false. None of them is immutable.

How dramatic is the claim that we cannot take any theory to be immutable? Does it apply to formal logic? A holistic critique of logical empiricism relies only on a denial that empirical propositions can be immutable. But because philosophers such as Quine use semantic holism to challenge the traditional distinction between empirical or synthetic propositions and logical or analytic ones, their denial of immutability applies to the latter as well as the former.[24] The strength of Quine's position lies in the damage semantic holism does to the traditional distinction between the analytic and the synthetic conceived as contrasting types of knowledge.[25] Because we can continue to believe in a proposition despite evidence to the contrary simply by adjusting our background theories, we seem to be able to treat any given proposition as if it were either analytic or synthetic provided only that we are prepared to make suitably drastic changes to our other theories. There seem to be no logical criteria for deciding whether a proposition is synthetic or analytic. There are only the behavioural criteria of how we actually treat it. This failure of the traditional distinction between the analytic and synthetic explains why we have to unpack the idea of philosophical knowledge in terms of a grammar of concepts rather than logical tautology. The weakness of Quine's position, however, lies in his relative neglect of the role played in all webs of belief by a concept of

[24] Quine, 'Two dogmas of empiricism'. Also see W. Quine, *Philosophy of Logic* (Englewood Cliffs, N.J.: Prentice-Hall, 1970), particularly pp. 85–6 and 100. Quine discusses deviant logics in the latter work. Some of his followers suggest that quantum mechanics might be the sort of intractable phenomenon that forces us to revise our logic. See H. Putnam, 'The logic of quantum mechanics', in *Philosophical Papers*, vol. I: *Mathematics, Matter, and Method*, pp. 174–97.
[25] On even a moderate reading, Quine's argument implies there are no truths that it never would be rational to give up. Compare H. Putnam, 'It ain't necessarily so', in *Philosophical Papers*, vol. I: *Mathematics, Matter and Method*, pp. 237–49.

best belief. Our ability to argue, to explain, and to predict, all rely on our allowing one or more of our beliefs to act as a reason for accepting another belief. Even Quine acknowledges that we necessarily concern ourselves with the consistency of our beliefs, and some of his followers acknowledge that something like a concept of best belief must play a crucial role in any web of beliefs if only because we have an interest in justifying our beliefs.[26] The very idea of an interconnected web of beliefs presupposes that some beliefs can justify other beliefs. To have a web of beliefs at all simply is, therefore, to have a concept of best belief that guides the way we treat other beliefs. Although the concept of best belief is not analytic in the sense of being a formal logical truth immune from revision, any web of beliefs must include norms that define an ideal web of beliefs, and one of these norms always must be some sort of concern with consistency. Although we should reject the traditional concept of the analytic that went with attempts to ground objectivity on conclusive tests of individual theories, we should retain a lax concept of the analytic that draws on our concern to hold justified, consistent webs of belief. This concern with consistency explains why we can conceive of philosophy as drawing out the implications of the concepts we already hold true in a way that makes philosophical knowledge true for us by virtue of meaning alone.

The arguments of the semantic holists undermine the attempts of logical empiricists to construct logics of vindication or refutation. They do so, moreover, irrespective of the precise analysis we give of the epistemological status of formal logic and philosophical knowledge. Semantic holism starts by rejecting pure experience and ends by insisting that beliefs confront reality only as interconnected webs. Observation entails theory, so if an observation disproved a favourite theory, we could rescue the theory by insisting that the observation rested on a false theory; or if an observation proved a detested theory, we could jettison the theory by insisting that the observation rested on a false theory. Our ability thus to isolate theories from observations should not surprise us. We believe in some theories as certainly, if not more certainly, than we could any evidence we might offer in support of them. Some of our theoretical beliefs are so central to our view of the world that we cannot think of a single observation that would refute them, although, of course, we can imagine their being gradually eroded by a series of observations until they were not so central to our view of the world, at

---

[26] See respectively Quine, *Word and Object*, p. 59; and H. Putnam, *Reason, Truth, and History* (Cambridge: Cambridge University Press, 1981), particularly pp. 155–68.

which point we might jettison them. If one stone did not fall when dropped, we would not conclude that things do not fall when dropped. If one pan of water did not boil when put over a gas flame, we would not conclude that fire does not heat things up. Yet once we accept that observations cannot determine conclusively the truth or falsity of a proposition, we must give up all hope of devising a logic of vindication or refutation. The real message of semantic holism is, therefore: because the semantic interpretation of an individual theory depends on other theories, we cannot determine the truth-value of individual theories. We cannot determine conclusively whether an individual proposition is true or false. We cannot do so because any such judgement always depends on theoretical assumptions embodied in our observations.

There cannot be a logic of vindication or refutation either for the history of ideas or for any other discipline. Neither historians nor anyone else can justify their theories by reference to pure facts. We cannot have a mechanical procedure by which to determine whether our historical theories are true or false. Fortunately, however, the limits of tests against facts need not worry us; after all, the arguments of semantic holists are entirely general, so they apply to science as much as history, and historians certainly need not aim at more secure knowledge than do scientists. Few scientists would say they can give us conclusive answers to scientific questions. Most of them recognise that even their most cherished theories remain open to change, open to improvement, revision, and rejection. Most scientists would say that their theories were the best currently available. In doing so, they would imply that objectivity rests not on a particular method or conclusive tests against allegedly pure facts, but rather a process of comparison between rival theories.

OBJECTIVITY THROUGH COMPARISON

Clearly we need a logic of justification that does not rely on either a method or allegedly given facts.[27] Because semantic holism shows that our theories always might be mistaken, we must define an objective theory as one we accept as correct on the basis of defensible criteria. An objective theory cannot be one we are certain is true. Our logic of

---

[27] Despite the significant differences in their views, the following have inspired my analysis of objectivity: Kuhn, *Structure of Scientific Revolutions*; I. Lakatos, 'Falsification and the methodology of scientific research programmes', in *Philosophical Writings*, vol. I: *The Methodology of Scientific-Research Programmes* (Cambridge: Cambridge University Press, 1978), pp. 8–101; Quine, *Word and Object*; and, especially, Wittgenstein, *On Certainty*.

justification must describe a practice of comparison. For a start, an objective theory must be one that compares well with its rivals. No doubt there will be times when we have no way of deciding between two or more theories, but this will not always be the case, and even when it is, we will still be able to decide between these two or more theories and innumerable other, inferior ones. Moreover, a logic of comparison must refer to a practice or activity. Logical empiricists defend a foundationalism that grounds human knowledge on pure experience. They argue that experience provides us with certainties, perhaps certainties about what is so, perhaps certainties about what is not so, but definitely certainties. Really, however, the inevitable infusion of theory in experience means that certainty or knowledge always requires something more than experience. Once we reject the possibility of pure experience, we must allow for an irreducible subjectivity in the concept of certainty. We must allow that because our observations do not record reality neutrally but rather make sense of reality through a theoretical understanding, therefore, our knowledge must depend at least in part on us. Because experience contains human elements, knowledge must contain human elements, and because we cannot eradicate these human elements, objectivity must be a product of our behaviour, not just our experiences. We must portray objectivity as a product of a human practice. Besides, because the nature of experience is such that future experiences can overturn alleged certainties based on prior experiences, we cannot define justified knowledge in terms of an ever-increasing number of certainties. We must recognise rather that objectivity represents a particular orientation towards experience. Objectivity depends on our making reasonable comparisons between rival theories, where comparison is a human activity. An account of justified knowledge cannot end with a growing history of information, or theories, or putative certainties. It must end with a description of a particular attitude or stance towards information, or theories, or putative certainties. Epistemology must be anthropocentric.[28]

The apparent danger is that if we define objectivity in terms of a human practice, we leave ourselves no rational control over the beliefs the practice generates as objective. Once we allow subjective elements into our epistemology, we seem to threaten the very idea of rational, objective belief; we raise the spectre of an out and out relativism in

---

[28] An anthropological turn with respect to 'conceptual structures' lay at the heart of Wittgenstein's development as he moved from his early to his later philosophy. See Hacker, *Insight and Illusion*, pp. 146–78.

which anything goes. What we need is an anthropocentric epistemology that provides us with rational criteria for accepting or rejecting beliefs. It is important to recognise, however, that all epistemologies ultimately confront the same threat of an out and out relativism. They do so because they all ultimately rest on claims about human practices. Even the logical empiricist account of objectivity describes a human practice consisting of human judgements: after all, even if we had pure experiences, and even if there were clear, inductive rules for developing general laws out of these experiences, we would still have to decide to accept these experiences and these inductive rules as the criteria of objective knowledge. The foundations of human knowledge must be human judgements, so all epistemologies must be anthropocentric; so my difficulty with an out and out relativism is everybody's difficulty. Thus, my analysis of objective knowledge will begin by identifying a human practice that gives us rational criteria for accepting or rejecting beliefs. Only afterwards will I go on to confront the question of what grounds we can give the out and out relativist for accepting the results of this practice.

Objective knowledge arises from a human practice in which we criticise and compare rival webs of theories in terms of agreed facts. An agreed fact is a piece of evidence nearly everyone in a given community, especially any of them present as witnesses, would accept as true. This definition of a fact follows from a recognition of the role of theory in observation. Because theory enters into observation, we cannot describe a fact as a statement of how things really are. Observation and description entail categorisation: for example, when we see or describe a stone falling, we categorise the falling object as a stone. In addition, categorisation entails decisions about what things resemble that being categorised: for example, when we categorise a falling object as a stone, we decide it resembles other stones, or at least our idea of other stones, not slates. Even if we had described nothing more than an object falling, we would still have used the categories 'object' and 'falling', and they would still have embodied theoretical assumptions about the nature of objects and what happens when things fall. Facts always entail categorisation. Thus, because our categorisations can be wrong, facts can differ from how things are. None the less, the role of theories in observation does not mean, as some idealists suggest, that facts depend solely on theories. We cannot describe a fact as a theoretical deduction because observations enter into our theories about the world. Even a theoretical argument must rest on premises, the content of which will come from observations in so far as the argument employs terms that refer to states of affairs and events. Facts entail observations, and observations stick to the world, so facts too must attach themselves to the world. Thus, we can fend off idealism simply by insisting on the presence of an independent reality, correspondence with which constitutes truth. Whether or not we can equate facts directly with the truth is another matter. Moreover, because I have argued that we cannot do so, I will need to find another way of relating facts to the truth if I am to avoid out and out relativism.

A fact is something the members of a community accept as a fundamental proposition. Typically, facts are observations that embody categories based on the recognition of similarities and differences between particular cases. However, not all observations that embody categories constitute facts. If, for instance, two backpackers catch a glimpse of an animal they believe to be a wolf, they might say they saw a wolf, but when pressed further not go so far as to say it is a fact they saw a wolf. Their uncertainty about their classification might hold them back. Observations that embody categories constitute facts only when they are exemplary, that is, when the circumstances in which they are made are trustworthy. If, for instance, two naturalists watch a wolf through binoculars for an hour or so, they will say it is a fact they saw a wolf even though they thereby make theoretical assumptions about the optical reliability of binoculars. A fact is an exemplary case of a classification. When we say such and such is a fact, we are not simply asserting such and such, we are also saying that such and such is either an exemplary case or a case tested against exemplary cases. Theories explain facts by postulating significant relationships – parallels, overlaps, and distinctions – between them. A fact acquires its particular character from its relationship to the other facts that fix its content. Theories reveal the particular character of a fact by uncovering its relationship to these other facts. They describe a fact in its relationship to the other facts that locate it in time and space and thereby define the preconditions of its unfolding. Of course, just as theories reveal the particular character of facts, so they often help to define the way we regard a fact. Theories do not reveal pre-given facts; rather, they create the character of facts and even guide our decisions as to what should count as a fact. Because there are no pure observations, facts do not hold out their character to us; rather, we construct their character in part through the theories we incorporate in our observations. Thus, we cannot say simply that such and such a theory does or does not fit the facts. All we can do is to compare bundles of theories in terms of their relative ability to relate innumerable facts to one another by highlighting pertinent similarities and differences, and continuities and disjunctions.

Objectivity arises from our criticising and comparing rival webs of theories in terms of generally accepted facts. The possibility of such comparison exists because people agree on a wide number of facts which collectively provide sufficient overlap for them to debate the merits of their rival views. For instance, even if Peter's view entails theoretical assumptions with which Paul disagrees, and even if Paul's view entails theoretical assumptions with which Peter disagrees, they still might agree on enough facts to make debate worthwhile, and perhaps even to enable them to reach a decision as to the respective merits of their rival views. Because they agree on numerous facts, these facts constitute an authority to which they can refer in their attempts to justify their views. The facts provide the basis of a comparison of their alternative theories. Someone might complain that if facts embody theories, theories end up determining the nature of the facts they explain, which means that we cannot judge theories by reference to their success in explaining the facts. The whole process looks perilously circular. Really, however, the nature of criticism enables us to escape from this circle. The practice of criticism means that no theory can determine the facts it encounters. Critics can point to facts the proponents of a theory have not considered. They can demand that the theory explain uncomfortable facts. Critics can highlight what they take to be counter-instances to a theory, and the theory must meet the challenges they thereby set. Criticism gives facts a relative autonomy from any set of theories. It ensures that the process of comparing theories in terms of facts is not circular. None the less, we still have to deal with the problem that appeals to the facts are never decisive. For instance, if Peter refers to a fact that supports his view and contradicts Paul's, Paul need not admit Peter is right. Paul might either question the fact or introduce a speculative theory to reconcile the fact with his theory. It is at this point that epistemology must take an anthropological turn. We must define objectivity as a human practice based on intellectual virtues. When people debate the merits of rival theories, they engage in a human practice governed by rules of thumb which define a standard of intellectual honesty. Although people obviously do not always live up to this standard, their failure to do so does not imply that it is naive or irrelevant. It would be naive only if our anthropological epistemology was an empirical account of a human practice. Yet we have seen that a logic is a normative account of reasoning. Our anthropological epistemology constitutes an account of a practice that would generate objective knowledge if it were followed. The rules of thumb that govern our practice of debate are neither decisive nor independent of us: they neither compel us to give up our theories in specific situations, nor force us to comply with their vaguer strictures. On the contrary, they represent a normative standard that exercises a control on our behaviour only because we often recognise its reasonableness. Whenever we contrast objective belief with biased belief, we implicitly recognise that objectivity constitutes a normative standard operating within a human practice.

Let us define more precisely the rules of thumb that constitute our normative standard of intellectual honesty. The first rule is that objective behaviour requires a willingness to take criticism seriously. If Paul does not take Peter's criticism of his theory seriously, we will say he is biased. None the less, as we have seen, Paul could respond to a fact or argument against his theory either by denying the validity of the fact or argument or by deploying a speculative theory so as to reconcile the fact or argument with his favoured theory. Thus, the second rule is that objective behaviour implies a preference for established standards of evidence and reason, backed up by a preference for challenges to these standards which themselves rest on impersonal, consistent criteria of evidence and reason. This rule limits the occasions when we can deny the validity of a fact or argument that contradicts our views. In particular, it sets up a presumption against exceptions: it implies that we should try to avoid responding to uncomfortable facts or arguments by declaring them to be exceptions which prove our theories; it implies that we should try instead to modify our theories so as to accommodate troublesome cases. Likewise, the third rule is that objective behaviour implies a preference for positive speculative theories which suggest exciting new predictions rather than negative ones which merely block criticisms of existing theories. This rule limits the occasions when we can deploy speculative theories to reconcile our views with evidence that contradicts them. In particular, it sets up a presumption against purely face-saving responses to criticism: it implies we should try to avoid meeting criticism by personalising the issue, fancy word play, vacuous waffle, special pleading, or makeshift apologetic; it implies we should try instead to modify our webs of theories in ways that extend the range and vigour of our core ideas.

The rules of thumb that define intellectual honesty describe preferred behaviour, not required behaviour. Semantic holism shows that the truth criteria of any given statement depend on its theoretical context. Because our theories map on to reality only as interconnected webs, we cannot evaluate a single theory except as part of a larger web. Thus, if people either reject a fact or introduce a speculative theory in a way outlawed by our rules of thumb, the arguments they use to do so might still be part of a web of theories that our rules of thumb pass as sound. We should show a general respect for our rules of thumb as we develop our whole web of theories, but we need not follow them slavishly on each and every occasion when we encounter an obstacle. Rules of thumb are rules of thumb, not unbreakable laws.

Our analysis of intellectual honesty sustains clear criteria for the comparison of rival webs of theories. These criteria fall into two groups. The first group deals with the synchronic features of webs of theories. Because we should respect established standards of evidence and reason, we should prefer webs of theories that are accurate, comprehensive, and consistent. Our standards of evidence require us to try to support our theories by reference to as many facts as we can. An accurate web of theories has a close fit to the facts that support it. A comprehensive web of theories covers a wide range of facts, with few outstanding exceptions; more particularly, it may bring together facts from different areas or areas we previously had not related to one another. Our standards of reasoning require us to try to make our theories intelligible and coherent. A consistent web of theories holds together without contravening the accepted principles of logic. Critics might worry that when we thus define objectivity in terms of consistency, we suggest that any inconsistency in any part of a web of beliefs would undermine the whole web.[29] Actually, however, we would do so only if we equated objectivity with absolute consistency by, say, adopting a coherence theory of truth and equating objective knowledge with truth so defined. In contrast, we have made consistency only one of several criteria in terms of which we should compare rival webs of belief to decide which is objectively valid. From our perspective, therefore, inconsistencies in a web of beliefs can be acceptable because they are fewer than those in rival webs or because they are counter-balanced by the success of the web in terms of our other criteria. The second group of criteria for comparing rival webs of theories deals with their diachronic features. Because we should favour positive speculative theories over those that merely block criticism, we should prefer networks of theories that are progressive, fruitful, and

[29] A. Goldman, *Epistemology and Cognition* (Cambridge, Mass.: Harvard University Press, 1986), p. 197.

open. Speculative theories are positive in so far as they inspire new avenues of research and suggest new predictions. A progressive web of theories is one characterised by positive speculative theories that suggest new predictions not previously associated with it. A fruitful web of theories is one in which the new predictions suggested by the relevant speculative theories typically receive support from the facts. Because fruitful progress comes from speculative responses to criticism, the more a web of theories cuts itself off from all possible criticism, the more it becomes a dead end unable to sustain further progress. An open web of theories stands by clearly defined propositions in a way that facilitates criticism.

Although we can evaluate rival views using our criteria of comparison, we cannot do so either definitively or instantly. For a start, because objectivity rests on criteria of comparison, the web of theories we select will be the one that best meets our criteria, not the one that constitutes the truth. We make sense of the world as best we can. We do not discover certainties. Thus, no matter how badly a web of theories does by our criteria, we will not reject it unless there is a better alternative on offer. This is why effective criticism must usually be positive: there is little point in people attacking a web of theories unless they also champion a suitable alternative.[30] When critics challenge our theory of such and such, we are right to ask them how they would account for such and such. What is more, because objectivity rests on criteria of comparison, our selection of theories will be gradual. How well a web of theories does in comparison with others is something that typically changes over time as its protagonists and critics alike turn up new facts and propose new speculative theories. A single criticism can rarely demolish a reigning web of beliefs if only because we must give the adherents of the reigning web time to develop a speculative theory to counter criticism in a fruitful way. Thus, dogmatism has a positive role in our quest for knowledge. People can stand by a web of theories while they develop suitable responses to the challenges confronting it. A web of theories triumphs over time by winning an increasing number of adherents, but as it triumphs new alternatives emerge and old alternatives return with new modifications, and it has to fight off these new rivals. We make better and better sense of the world through a continuous process of dialectical competition between rival webs of theories which themselves are being constantly modified and extended.

[30] We should allow some role to purely negative critiques if only because to show how a web of theories fails is a way of encouraging people to develop a better alternative.

Our logic of comparison contains a form of justification appropriate to the history of ideas. Historians can justify their theories by showing them to be objective, where objectivity arises not out of a method, nor a test against pure facts, but rather a comparison with rival theories. Historians can justify their theories by relating them, in a comparison with their rivals, to criteria of accuracy, comprehensiveness, consistency, progressiveness, fruitfulness, and openness. We can fill out this analysis of the form of justification appropriate to the history of ideas by briefly showing how historians deployed something akin to it in a well-known debate about John Locke's views on property. Historians generally agree on various facts about Locke and his work. Historians agree that Locke used the idea of a state of nature to present his political views, that he argued that men have rights including those to life and property, and that he defended the moral legitimacy of revolution in some, albeit exceptional, circumstances. Historians agree on these facts and others like them irrespective of matters such as their political affinities, their theories of meaning, and their professional standing. Moreover, because any number of historians accept these facts, they can use them as a starting point for a comparison of their rival theories. Most theories in the history of ideas concern either the meaning of particular works or the general nature and place of ideas in human life. C. B. Macpherson, for example, marshalled various facts in order to portray Locke as a philosopher who defended the rationality of unlimited desire, and so capital accumulation, in a way that provided a moral basis for capitalism. Moreover, he located this portrait of Locke in a Marxist historiography according to which all political theorists in Britain during the seventeenth and eighteenth centuries adopted ideas which reflected the emergence of a capitalist economy.[31]

Historians can criticise and compare theories in terms of generally accepted facts using our criteria of accuracy, comprehensiveness, consistency, progressiveness, fruitfulness, and openness. Alan Ryan, for example, criticised Macpherson for inaccuracy.[32] He argued that Macpherson was wrong to say Locke thought rationality was restricted to the one class of people who go in for the acquisition of capital goods. Locke explicitly said that all adults apart from lunatics are rational enough to understand what the law of nature requires of them. Ryan also criticised Macpherson, at least implicitly, for not being comprehensive: he used

[31] C. Macpherson, *The Political Theory of Possessive Individualism* (Oxford: Oxford University Press, 1962).
[32] A. Ryan, 'Locke and the dictatorship of the bourgeoisie', *Political Studies* 13 (1965), 219–30.

various passages in Locke's text to show that Locke said things quite contrary to those found in Macpherson's account. More generally, Ryan argued that Macpherson's errors stemmed from an unfruitful method. Macpherson's approach led to an emphasis on things other than Locke's text as a basis for a reading of the text; but when Ryan evaluated this reading against the text, he found passages that showed it to be wrong. Macpherson's approach was unfruitful because it inspired predictions that received no support from the facts. Ryan himself recommended a method based on reading the text alone to uncover what Locke said, if not what Locke intended to say. John Dunn, too, criticised Macpherson for not being comprehensive, arguing that he ignored the religious faith which provided the unifying theme of Locke's thought.[33] According to Dunn, Locke could not have intended to demonstrate the overriding rationality of capital accumulation because his view of rationality derived from his religious faith. For Locke, the rationality of any action in this world depended on its effect on the hereafter. Tully later developed Dunn's critique of Macpherson by presenting Locke's political thought in the context of his religious faith as an attempt to defend a self-governing community composed of small proprietors who enjoy the security to harvest the fruits of their labour.[34] Tully argued that Locke's ideal was radically different from capitalism.

Because people can respond to criticism in ways that strengthen their theories, the comparison of rival theories must be diachronic as well as synchronic. Our criteria of comparison certainly prompt us to scrutinise the way in which historians deal with criticism to see whether or not their theories are progressive, fruitful, and open. If Macpherson had responded to Ryan, Dunn, and Tully, we would want to know whether his revisions represented a progressive development of his theory or a defensive move to block their criticisms. Although Macpherson has not replied to his critics, Neal Wood has defended an interpretation of Locke that we might take as a revised version of Macpherson's original view in so far as it occurs within a similar, Marxist historiography.[35] Wood criticises Tully's interpretation of Locke for being incomplete, and possibly inconsistent. He argues that we cannot reconcile Tully's interpretation with many established facts about Locke and his beliefs, such as that Locke charged interest on loans to his friends, served the

---

[33] J. Dunn, *The Political Thought of John Locke* (Cambridge: Cambridge University Press, 1969).

[34] J. Tully, *A Discourse on Property: John Locke and His Adversaries* (Cambridge: Cambridge University Press, 1980).

[35] N. Wood, *John Locke and Agrarian Capitalism* (Berkeley: University of California Press, 1984).

Whig aristocracy faithfully, supported slavery, and did not condemn wide income differentials. Because Wood's criticisms of Tully do not suggest new insights, but merely counter a rival to the Marxist view, by themselves they would represent a purely defensive attempt to block criticism. Actually, however, Wood also extends the Marxist outlook by offering us a revised theory, which, he claims, explains the failings of Macpherson's earlier account of Locke. Wood portrays Locke as a theorist of agrarian capitalism, not an apologist for the mercantile and manufacturing bourgeoisie. How progressive Wood's view of Locke really is, and whether or not Marxist historiography as a whole is characterised by progressive responses, are issues we need not consider. What matters to us is the way the debate on Locke's views on property illustrates how historians might deploy our criteria of comparison to justify their theories. Historians of ideas should justify their work by comparing it with its rivals, using the criteria of accuracy, comprehensiveness, consistency, progressiveness, fruitfulness, and openness.

TRUTH AND COMMENSURABILITY

Numerous debates could have illustrated how historians might deploy our criteria of comparison to justify their theories. Any example I chose, however, would probably meet similar objections. Critics will complain that a form of justification based solely on generally accepted facts and criteria of comparison is not acceptable because we have no reason to assume that the theories we thus select give us knowledge of the world as it is. Critics will complain that I have divorced objectivity from truth defined in terms of correspondence with reality or how things really are. I have enabled historians to justify their theories as objective, but perhaps I have done so by denying them the possibility of defending them as true, and surely truth is what historians want. Any explicitly subjective analysis of objectivity such as mine invariably arouses the two dreaded phantoms of relativism – irrationality and incommensurability. Critics complain, first, that even if we generally agree on the facts, and even if we have definite criteria for comparing webs of theories, we still cannot make rational decisions on the basis of these facts and these criteria. After all, a general acceptance of certain facts does not make them true. On the contrary, if facts depend on human practices, facts can differ from the truth, so our webs of theories are conventional, and our knowledge is thus irrational. Foucault certainly embraced a form of irrationalism on the grounds that all knowledge, or truth, becomes such only within a discursive formation produced not by a reliable cognitive method, but by a struggle for power, a 'hazardous play of dominations'.[36] Critics complain, secondly, that even if we generally agree on the facts, and even if we have clear criteria for comparing webs of theories, other people might still reject these facts and these criteria. After all, if our webs of theories rest on conventional facts, our theories will be acceptable only to people who accept our conventions, so our knowledge is incommensurable with the knowledge of people from other cultures or other times. Kuhn certainly embraced a thesis of incommensurability on the grounds that 'the proponents of competing paradigms practice their trades in different worlds', so 'before they can hope to communicate fully, one group must experience conversion' to the paradigm of the other.[37] I will consider these two complaints in turn.

Let me begin with the problem of irrationality. Any attempt to defend objectivity by invoking generally accepted facts must steer a course between the Scylla of arbitrariness and the Charybdis of circularity. If we do not attempt to justify our facts as true, if we rely solely on people generally accepting them, they will appear arbitrary and so incapable of justifying our theories. But if we justify our facts as true by reference to our theories, we will have a circular argument whereby we justify the facts in terms of the theories and the theories in terms of the facts. I should point out, however, that this predicament is not mine alone. Every epistemology runs up against an equivalent problem of final justification. We can give evidence and reasons for holding our theories, and often we can give evidence and reasons for accepting our initial evidence and reasons, but there always comes a time when the regress ends, a time when we no longer can give any fresh evidence and reasons for accepting our earlier evidence and reasons. For example, logical empiricists defend knowledge by reference to perceptions; but critics could ask why we should accept the evidence of our perceptions, and so on, until finally the logical empiricists would run out of evidence and reasons. Any epistemology must defend the rationality of the human practice in terms of which it defines objective knowledge.

[36] M. Foucault, 'Nietzsche, genealogy, history', in *Language, Counter-Memory, Practice*, p. 151.
[37] Kuhn, *Structure of Scientific Revolutions*. I would not quarrel with a weak thesis of incommensurability according to which we have no algorithm by which to compare all rival paradigms; after all, this leaves open the possibility of our making a rational comparison of any two rival paradigms. For this weak thesis, developed in relation to Kuhn's work, see Rorty, *Philosophy and the Mirror of Nature*, pp. 315–33. Kuhn's own repudiation of the stronger thesis appears in T. Kuhn, 'Postscript – 1969', in *Structure of Scientific Revolutions*; and T. Kuhn, 'Reflections on my critics', in I. Lakatos and A. Musgrave (eds.), *Criticism and the Growth of Knowledge* (Cambridge: Cambridge University Press, 1970), pp. 231–78.

We can secure generally accepted facts so as to avoid the charge of irrationalism by pointing out that our perceptions must be fairly reliable. Doing so also enables us to avoid a charge rightly levelled against an analysis of justified knowledge in terms of pure coherence, namely, that it cannot account for the special status of our perceptual beliefs.[38] Crucially, our perceptions must be fairly reliable because we act moderately successfully in pre-given natural and social environments. Our perceptions must be reasonably accurate because they inform our understanding of the world, which guides our actions in the world, which generally work out more or less as we expect them to. If our perceptions were completely unreliable, they would lead us to a radically false understanding of the world, and a radically false understanding of the world would prove unsustainable because it would lead us to act in ways we could not do for long. Again, our natural environment limits the actions we can perform successfully and so the ways in which we can make sense of the world. Because we must act in the world, the actions we can perform successfully are limited by the nature of the world. Thus, because our knowledge and perceptions inform our actions, they too are constrained by the nature of the world. Imagine John operates a dog-sleigh in the Arctic Circle, but he does not perceive any difference between dogs and wolves. Before long, John would run into serious trouble. Imagine now that all humans have perceptions as unreliable as John's. Humanity as a whole would have run into serious trouble long ago. Thus, our very existence suggests that our perceptions must be fairly reliable. Furthermore, because we can rely on the broad content of our perceptions, we have good reason to assume that the facts we agree upon will generally be true; after all, facts are exemplary perceptions. Finally, because we can assume that the facts we agree upon generally will be true, knowledge based on a comparison of theories in terms of these facts is secure. We can ground objective knowledge on facts, facts on perceptions, and perceptions on our ability to interact successfully with our environment.

It is important to recognise that our interaction with our environment secures only the broad content of our perceptions, not particular instances of perception. This is why we can adopt criteria for comparing rival webs of theories, but not a logic of vindication or refutation. Our ability to interact with our environment implies that our perceptions must fall

---

[38] P. Moser, *Knowledge and Evidence* (Cambridge: Cambridge University Press, 1989), particularly pp. 172–83. To accept that our perceptual beliefs have a special status is not, however, to accept Moser's defence of a given element in experience.

within the limits that demarcate the point beyond which such interaction would not be possible. Thus, most of the facts we agree upon must be more or less true. However, although the broad content of our perceptions must fall within these limits, no particular perception need be foolproof. Thus, the facts we agree upon are not secure enough to enable us conclusively to determine the truth or falsity of any individual theory. We can make the same point in a different way. Our knowledge has a perceptual basis, but this perceptual base embodies both the theories we use to categorise things according to their similarities and differences and also the theories we use to ascribe certain qualities to the things we thus categorise. The perceptual base of our knowledge secures the general accuracy of the facts upon which we agree, and thereby makes sense of our efforts to compare rival webs of theories. But the theoretical component of the perceptual base prevents us being certain about any particular fact, and so about the truth or falsity of any individual theory. We can secure the broad sweep of human knowledge, but not any single part thereof.

We can relate objective knowledge to truth because our ability to find our way around the world vouches for the broad content of our perceptions. Although the anthropological epistemology I have defended might appear to resemble naturalistic and pragmatic ones, there are in fact important differences between them. Naturalised epistemologies equate the philosophy of knowledge with psychological or sociological studies of the way people, especially scientists, actually do reach what we take to be justified knowledge.[39] Pragmatic epistemologies equate justified knowledge with a pragmatic concept of truth, understood as a psychological or sociological account of the beliefs that actually do work best for people.[40] In contrast, an anthropological epistemology provides a normative analysis of justified knowledge. It says that people should justify their claims to knowledge in terms of our criteria of comparison because our theories suggest that these criteria provide a means of approaching the truth. It does not say either that people actually do justify their beliefs in this way, or that knowledge is true by virtue of

---

[39] W. Quine, 'Epistemology naturalized', in *Ontological Relativity and Other Essays* (New York: Columbia University Press, 1969), pp. 69–90; and, more recently, W. Quine, *The Pursuit of Truth* (Cambridge, Mass.: Harvard University Press, 1990). On the way naturalised epistemology excludes normative considerations, see Goldman, *Epistemology and Cognition*, particularly pp. 2–3.

[40] Although the founder of pragmatism, Charles Peirce, took his doctrine to be an analysis of meaning, later theorists developed it as a theory of truth. 'The true', they said, 'is only the expedient in the way of our thinking, just as 'the right is only the expedient in the way of our behaving'. W. James, *Pragmatism: A New Name for Some Old Ways of Thinking* (New York: Longman, Green, 1907), p. 222.

meeting our criteria. All I have argued is that after people justify their claims to knowledge using our criteria of comparison, they can fend off the charge of irrationalism by referring to the nature of our being in the world.

An anthropological epistemology also differs from an evolutionary one: it applies only to knowledge in general, so, unlike an evolutionary epistemology, it can relate objectivity back to truth. Evolutionary epistemologists argue that we should take individual theories to be validated by their fitness to survive as guides to action in the world. They regard a theory as one of an infinite number of possible, more or less random, responses to a problem. Our actions test our theories, perhaps deliberately or perhaps not. When a theory fails a test, it is falsified. Our remaining theories are valid because they have survived all the tests they have faced. Thus, as Popper concludes, 'our knowledge consists, at every moment, of those hypotheses which have shown their (comparative) fitness by surviving so far on their struggle for existence'.[41] Two problems confront evolutionary epistemology. The first is that it assumes that theories can face tests individually whereas semantic holism implies they cannot. An individual theory might survive tests because we rearranged our other theories to account for its failures, not because of its intrinsic fitness. Thus, no evolutionary mechanism can work on individual theories. The second problem with evolutionary epistemology is that it portrays truth as a regulative ideal for human knowledge but fails adequately to relate objective knowledge to truth. Because there are an infinite number of possible theories, the failure of any number of theories still cannot give us a reason to assume our remaining theories are true. Our remaining theories appear as random responses to problems, not products of rational intelligence going to work on broadly accurate perceptions. Thus, evolutionary epistemologies can portray our theories as guesses that serve us well, but they cannot portray them as guesses that are more or less true. We cannot adequately relate objective knowledge to truth unless we defend the accuracy of our perceptions.

Critics might bemoan the weakness of our response to the charge of irrationalism. They might argue that although our criteria of comparison give us a method for approximating truth, methods can go wrong, so we cannot rely on them to lead us to truth. They might argue that

[41] K. Popper, *Objective Knowledge: An Evolutionary Approach* (Oxford: Clarendon Press, 1972), p. 261. A similar approach informs S. Toulmin, *Human Understanding: The Collective Use and Evolution of Concepts* (Princeton: Princeton University Press, 1972).

because any particular perception could be mistaken, any particular theory could be wrong, so we cannot treat any of our theories as true. We must accept the conclusions of these critics. It is just that we cannot guarantee the truth of any one of our theories in the way they imply we should do. Semantic holism implies that none of our theories is immutable, so any one of them might be wrong, so we cannot tie objectivity to truth in the way the critics want us to. The critics set us an unattainable goal. We cannot relate our knowledge to truth in a substantive fashion. But this does not mean that we have to give up the very idea of truth conceived as knowledge that corresponds to the world as it is. Some philosophers, notably Richard Rorty, argue that a rejection of given facts should lead us to renounce as an empiricist dogma the idea of a neutral, mind-independent world to which our knowledge might correspond.[42] But Rorty's conclusion is far too dramatic. The best understanding of the world available to us is surely one that postulates a world existing independently of us. A process of inference to the best explanation allows us, therefore, to retain our idea of a neutral, mind-independent world.[43] Truth can still play a role as a regulative ideal for human knowledge. The success of our actions in the world guarantees the broad accuracy of our perceptions, so we have good reason to assume that our criteria of comparison will lead us to objective knowledge that approximates to truth.

Let me turn now to the problem of incommensurability. Some scholars suggest that semantic holism entails the incommensurability of different conceptual schemes.[44] They argue that because both the meaning of a proposition and the content of a belief depend on the contexts in which we locate them, no belief can retain its content if we move it from one conceptual scheme to another, so we cannot possibly compare beliefs from rival conceptual schemes. Really, however, semantic holism need not commit us to a thesis of incommensurability.[45] For a start, the fact that those we seek to understand have beliefs whose content depends on the other beliefs they hold does not preclude their beliefs

[42] R. Rorty, 'The world well lost', *Journal of Philosophy* 69 (1972), 649–65.

[43] On this form of reasoning see P. Lipton, *Inference to the Best Explanation* (London: Routledge, 1991).

[44] For the suggestion that a thesis of incommensurability follows from Quine's holism, see C. Condren, *The Status and Appraisal of Classic Texts* (Princeton: Princeton University Press, 1985), pp. 49–50; and R. Kirk, *Translation Determined* (Oxford: Oxford University Press, 1986), pp. 206–9.

[45] It seems that if we really had to define conceptual schemes as incommensurable with each other, we would have to reject the very idea of conceptual schemes. See D. Davidson, 'On the very idea of a conceptual scheme', in *Inquiries into Truth*, pp. 183–98. To evoke Davidson here is not, however, to imply that his argument works against all notions of a conceptual scheme. See M. Lynch, 'Three models of conceptual schemes', *Inquiry* 40 (1997), 407–26.

overlapping with ours in a way that makes translation possible. In addition, the creative nature of our linguistic faculty implies that even if our beliefs do not overlap with theirs, we could still set out from ours and end up being able to make sense of theirs. So far, therefore, we have not committed ourselves to a position for or against a thesis of incommensurability.[46] We have found, however, that objective knowledge arises from our exercising the virtue of intellectual honesty within a practice of comparing rival webs of theories. If we disagree about the relative merits of different views, we should draw back from the point of disagreement until we can agree upon a platform from which to compare them, where the platform at which we arrive will consist of agreed facts, standards of evidence, and ways of reasoning.

As anti-foundationalists, we cannot specify in advance the substantive content of this platform. We cannot insist, for instance, that everyone accept the validity of our criteria of comparison as if they at least were self-evident truths given to us by the very nature of belief, language, or speech.[47] Yet the absence of a universal platform does not entail the possibility of cases in which there is no such platform. Proponents of incommensurability argue that it is possible we might not agree on any platform with people from other cultures – we might not be able to compare our theories with theirs. For the sake of argument, therefore, imagine that a group of anthropologists discover a lost tribe the members of which oppose all our standards of evidence and all our ways of reasoning. Perhaps the anthropologists have no beliefs at all in common with the members of the tribe. None the less, even complete disagreement does not preclude the possibility of meaningful comparison, so the mere existence of the tribe would not establish a thesis of incommensurability. The relativist still has to show that the anthropologists and members of the tribe could not compare their worldviews.

The grounds for a refutation of relativism lie, once again, in the way our beliefs guide our actions in pre-given environments. Crucially, because the beliefs a group hold inform their practices, members of all cultures must recognise similarities and differences in the things they encounter. All groups have practices composed of repeatable patterns of behaviour, and such practices can exist only if the practitioners recog-

---

[46] For a fuller analysis of semantic holism's compatibility with meaning determinacy, see E. Lormand, 'How to be a meaning holist', *Journal of Philosophy* 93 (1996), 51–73.
[47] Contrast J. Habermas, *The Theory of Communicative Action*, 2 vols., trans. T. McCarthy (Boston: Beacon Press, 1984–87). On how one can reject Habermas's universalism without falling into relativism, see M. Hesse, 'Habermas and the force of dialectical argument', *History of European Ideas* 21 (1995), 367–78.

nise at least some situations as similar to, and others as different from, at least some previous situations. Furthermore, because the perception of similarities and differences must ultimately rest on exemplary perceptions, people from all cultures must take their own exemplary perceptions to be facts. Everybody must be as certain about the things they take to be exemplary perceptions as they are about anything. All worldviews must rest on facts, where facts are the exemplary perceptions that inform the way one categorises things by their similarities and differences. Thus, even if the anthropologists and the tribe disagree with each and every fact the other group believes in, the structures of their worldviews must be broadly similar. No matter what the content of their respective sets of belief, both must embody exemplary perceptions of similarities and differences. Thus, the anthropologists and the tribe can come to understand each other's beliefs provided only that they can perceive the similarities and differences informing each other's categories. Here the ability of the tribe and the anthropologists to interact with their respective environments guarantees the broad content of their perceptions. Moreover, this suggests that they can come to perceive the similarities and differences informing each other's categories. A broad guarantee of the perceptions of the tribe implies that many of the similarities and differences contained in their worldview must be true of reality, while a broad guarantee of the perceptions of the anthropologists implies that they can recognise similarities and differences found in reality, including the true ones contained in the worldview of the tribe. Thus, the anthropologists can come to understand the beliefs of the tribe, and, of course, by parallel reasoning, the tribe can come to understand the beliefs of the anthropologists. The ability of the anthropologists and the tribe thus to come to understand one another should not surprise us. Just as our linguistic faculty enables us to generate and understand novel utterances made in novel circumstances, so the linguistic faculty of the anthropologists and the tribe enables them to come to understand one another. The fact that they have radically different beliefs does not preclude their being able to express each other's beliefs in terms of their own concepts.[48] On the contrary, because both of their languages are able to express novel content, each language can convey

---

[48] Even philosophers who defend a weak version of 'untranslatability' typically do so only by eliding the distinction between what has to happen for us to 'understand' the beliefs of others with what has to happen for us to accept their beliefs, that is, not to regard their beliefs as 'in some ways defective'. See A. MacIntyre, *Whose Justice? Which Rationality?* (London: Duckworth, 1988), p. 380.

the beliefs of the other group. Our linguistic faculty enables us to extend, modify, and use our language to convey any other worldview. All groups can come to understand the worldview of all other groups.

After the anthropologists and the tribe have understood each other's worldview, they can compare the respective merits of their worldviews by trying to account for the practices inspired by each in terms of the other. As the anthropologists come to grasp the similarities and differences informing the worldview of the tribe, so they will devise explanations of the beliefs held by the tribe. Either they will incorporate a belief of the tribe into their own worldview, or they will dismiss it as illusion, in which case they will try to explain its persistence in the worldview of the tribe. Similarly, as the members of the tribe come to understand the beliefs of the anthropologists, so they will either incorporate new beliefs into their worldview, or dismiss them as illusions, in which case they will try to explain their place in the worldview of the anthropologists. Thus, the anthropologists and the tribe will acquire a stock of shared facts, or, at the very least, they will develop explanations of each other's worldviews. They will acquire an agreed platform from which they can compare their worldviews in terms of their respective ability to account for shared facts or for one another. Imagine the comparison of their worldviews using our criteria shows the beliefs of one to be preferable to those of the other. Might not the losers refuse to accept the comparison? Yes, they might, but we have seen that there is a place for such dogmatism. The selection of a web of theories by our criteria can be neither instant nor conclusive. The adherents of a defeated web must be allowed time to devise a suitable, fruitful response to the criticisms put forward by the adherents of the victorious one. What matters, therefore, is the broad movement of knowledge over time. Here we find most plausible a scenario in which the initial dogmatism of the losers wears down so that they gradually move towards the worldview of the winners. Moreover, we would expect the losers to move towards the worldview of the winners irrespective of whether or not their own worldview was suffering from an 'epistemological crisis'.[49] We would expect them to do so just because they are capable of recognising as valuable the practical achievements tied to the worldview of the winners.

Because humans share a common physiology, they must interact with nature to broadly similar effect. Because all humans must secure food and drink, and no doubt try to avoid and cure disease, some of the

---

[49] Contrast *ibid.*, pp. 361–6.

practices of the winners must have broadly similar results to some of the practices of the losers. Thus, the losers will presumably recognise that some of the practices of the winners have results which they too value. Members of the losing group will see the comparative ease with which the others acquire food and cure disease. Thus, over time we would expect some of the losers to adopt some of the practices of the winners, and we would expect the achievements of these pioneers to inspire others from among the losers to do likewise. Finally, as the losers thus adopted the practices of the winners, so they would have to adopt some of the beliefs informing these practices simply in order to perform them adequately. The fact is, therefore, that our need to interact with our environment influences our reactions to the beliefs of other cultures in a way that sustains a weak concept of commensurability. The need to interact with our environment pulls different worldviews towards one another so as to make them comparable. We can always compare rival views, even if in extreme cases we first have to go through a learning process in which we come to perceive things as members of another culture do. We should note, however, that even in such extreme cases we need not accept the beliefs of the others, but only learn to perceive things as they do: the anthropologists and the tribe do not have to accept each other's beliefs. We should note also that we do not have to use any particular method to learn their way of seeing things: the anthropologists and the tribe might grasp a similarity or distinction drawn by the other as a result of innumerable things, including intuition, guesswork, or luck.

Once again critics might bemoan the weakness of our response to the thesis of incommensurability. They might argue that because some beliefs make little or no difference to how people behave, the need to act in a given environment is unlikely to level all disagreements, so some incommensurability remains probable. Because people can act in more or less the same way even though they have different beliefs, people from one culture can adopt the practices of another culture without adopting the precise beliefs associated with that other culture. Once again we must accept the conclusions of these critics. It is just that we cannot remove all traces of relativism from our epistemology in the way they imply we should. According to semantic holism, no theory is immutable; thus, we cannot insist that people adopt any individual theory, so there always remains some latitude of interpretation within which different cultures can introduce their own special emphases. Once again our critics set us an unattainable goal. We cannot point to truths that people from all cultures must acknowledge. But this does not mean we have to give up the quest for truth altogether. On the contrary, truth can still play the role of a regulative ideal around which all cultures coalesce. An encounter with alien cultural practices we admire compels us to reach a compromise with the beliefs informing these practices. We do not have to adopt carbon copies of the beliefs, but we do have to adapt our beliefs so as to enable us to adopt the practices. Our culture need not become identical to the other culture, but equally our culture cannot remain as it was. What happens is that our culture adjusts to take account of the other culture in a way that takes us closer to truth understood as a regulative ideal.

DEALING WITH SCEPTICISM

I have argued that historians should justify their claims to objective knowledge by comparing rival webs of theories in terms of the specific criteria identified. Some sceptics deny that such comparison is possible in the history of ideas. Much of the inspiration for my account of objectivity comes from the practice of science. The sceptics argue that we cannot approach the history of ideas through the model of science because the history of ideas concerns past intentions whereas science does not. Contextualist sceptics, such as Foucault, combine an argument about intentions being unknowable with their argument that meanings derive from linguistic contexts, which if it were true would suggest that we need not worry about intentions being unknowable.[50] Other sceptics do not necessarily want to reject an intentionalist theory of meaning. They argue baldly that we can never recover historical meanings. All we can study is the meaning a text has for us. Here, because there is no logical connection between scepticism and contextualism, and because we already have dealt with contextualism, we will take scepticism to be the bald claim that we cannot recover the viewpoints of historical figures.

Post-modern and phenomenological sceptics conclude that we cannot have objective knowledge of historical meanings for quite different reasons. Post-modern sceptics proudly pronounce the history of ideas to be a chimera. They say that there are no fixed meanings. Texts are open ended and we can do what we like with past works. Typically they defend their scepticism by arguing that we cannot have knowledge of

---

[50] Foucault, *Archaeology of Knowledge*.

individual viewpoints, or other minds more generally, because all meanings are unstable. In contrast, phenomenological sceptics regard any
reading of a historical work as a product of a fusion of horizons. They
say that historians necessarily approach the past from the perspective of
the present. Our preconceptions invariably influence what we find in
the past. Typically they defend their scepticism by arguing that we
necessarily distort the past by bringing to it contemporary prejudices.
When we consider these two forms of scepticism, we will find, first, that
there is no reason to assume that we cannot know other minds, and,
second, that although historians approach their material with current
prejudices, this does not preclude objective knowledge of the past.
Before turning to scepticism, however, I should make clear my concern
to avoid metaphysical issues in philosophical psychology. Although I
equated hermeneutic meanings with individual viewpoints, I said nothing about the nature of an individual viewpoint. I want as far as
possible to avoid taking a stance on the metaphysical nature of psychological states such as individual viewpoints. Scholars can define them
more or less as they choose: they can follow the mentalists and define
them in terms of mental states, or they can follow the behaviourists and
define them in terms of actual or possible behaviour, or they can adopt
some other position again. Scepticism fails irrespective of considerations
in philosophical psychology.

Post-modern sceptics, such as Derrida, argue that there can be no
correct understanding of a work. They do so on the grounds that all
meanings are unstable so that we do not have an authorised source by
which to judge a claim to correctness. All meanings are unstable, they
say, because signification presupposes that 'each so-called "present"
element . . . is related to something other than itself, thereby keeping
within itself the mark of the past element, and already letting itself be
vitiated by the mark of its relation to the future element'.[51] The rhetoric
of the post-modern sceptics tends to slide unnoticed, however, between
a weak claim which is true and a strong claim which is false. The weak
claim is that texts do not have fixed meanings so we can understand
them in different ways. Few people would disagree. We are at liberty to
understand a text as we wish rather than as the author intended. It is
just, as we have seen, that we will not be doing history unless we identify
the way we understand a text with the view a past figure took of it. The

[51] Derrida, 'Differance', p. 13. Examples of reception theory inspired in part by post-modern
scepticism, include Fish, *Is There a Text in This Class?*, and LaCapra, 'Rethinking intellectual
history', in *Rethinking Intellectual History*, pp. 23–71.

weak claim of the post-modernists establishes only that we can approach texts in ahistorical ways. It does not establish that we cannot approach them in historical ways. Thus, because few historians want to insist that everyone who reads a text must do so with a historical eye, few historians need feel threatened by this weak claim. None the less, much of the drama of post-modern scepticism arises from an equivocation whereby a strong position is asserted but only this weak position is defended. The strong claim is that the history of ideas is impossible because we cannot hope to identify the view a past figure took of a text. Clearly this strong claim does not follow from the fact that texts do not have fixed meanings. There is no obvious reason why historians should not be able to understand how a particular individual viewed a text just because it has had a variety of meanings over time. In order to sustain their strong claim, post-modern sceptics must show that historians cannot recover the viewpoints of people from the past. Generally they try to do this by defending at least one of the following three positions: individual viewpoints are not stable entities, we cannot climb out of language, and we cannot have knowledge of other minds. I will consider these three positions in turn.

Post-modern sceptics sometimes argue that we cannot have knowledge of intentions because intentions are unstable. 'Suppose', they say, 'I ask what an author's intention means, and then what the meaning of the author's intention means, and so on.'[52] They argue that individual viewpoints cannot be constitutive of meanings because individual viewpoints themselves have meanings. Any attempt to equate meanings with individual viewpoints allegedly runs into an infinite regress. We can undermine this argument simply by asking what exactly the sceptics refer to when they talk about the meaning of an individual viewpoint. Individual viewpoints are behavioural or mental states which do not have meanings in the sense that utterances have meanings. Thus, although we can ask someone what a particular description of an individual viewpoint means, we cannot ask what an individual viewpoint itself means. If we adopt the behaviourist view of psychological states, then to ask about the meaning of an agent's viewpoint will be to ask about the meaning of an agent's action; but behaviourists deny that we can ask about the meaning of an action as though there were

---

[52] T. Eagleton, *Literary Theory: An Introduction* (Oxford: Basil Blackwell, 1983), p. 69. On the instability of intentions also see J. Derrida, 'Signature, event, context', in *Limited Inc.*, ed. G. Graff, trans. S. Weber and J. Mehlman (Evanston, Ill.: Northwestern University Press, 1988), pp. 1–23.

something behind it when there is not.[53] Thus, behaviourism implies that individual viewpoints do not have meanings. If we adopt the mentalist view of psychological states, then when people describe a mental state, they make an utterance and we can ask what they mean by this utterance; but asking about the meaning of an utterance describing a mental state is not the same thing as asking about the meaning of the mental state itself. Imagine that a passer-by who overhears Peter saying 'hallelujah lass' asks him what he means. Peter explains that he intended to praise Susan's suggestion – he makes a statement about his viewpoint. Although the passer-by can ask Peter what he means by this statement about his viewpoint, he cannot ask him what he means by his viewpoint. Thus, mentalism too implies that individual viewpoints do not have meanings. Whether we identify individual viewpoints with behavioural or mental states, we look on them as things that exist in a world outside of human discourse and so do not have hermeneutic meanings. Individual viewpoints seem to be unstable only because we must use language to describe them and we can always ask about the meaning of the words we so use. Because we can use various combinations of words to describe individual viewpoints, our descriptions of them are unstable; but because individual viewpoints exist outside of language, they themselves are fixed. Although we can use various combinations of words to describe an individual viewpoint, it remains the same whatever words we use to describe it. Individual viewpoints are part of the reality to which our language refers. They are not part of our language.

Post-modern sceptics sometimes argue that we cannot have knowledge of individual viewpoints precisely because they exist outside of language, whereas we always remain within language. As Derrida puts it, there is only writing, 'there is no "outside" to the text'.[54] Here too, however, the rhetoric of post-modern scepticism has an unfortunate tendency to slide from arguments for a weak claim which is true to a defence of a strong claim which is false. Few people would deny the weak claim that we must use language, conceived as a set of signs, if we are to refer to anything at all. But this weak claim does not establish the strong claim that we cannot penetrate the linguistic fog to acquire knowledge of the things to which our signs refer. On the contrary, if our signs refer to reality, presumably we can have knowledge of reality. The real issue, therefore, is whether our signs refer to reality. The post-

[53] Compare Quine, *Word and Object*, particularly pp. 26–79.
[54] J. Derrida, *Of Grammatology*, trans. G. Spivak (Baltimore: Johns Hopkins University Press, 1976), p. 158.

modern sceptics who argue that we cannot have knowledge of anything outside of language must do so on the grounds that our language does not refer to reality. But this seems highly implausible. Certainly, although we have championed semantic holism against the picture theory of language, and although semantic holism shows that concepts do not have a one to one correspondence with reality, none of this suggests that our concepts do not refer to reality at all. Rather, it suggests that our concepts refer to reality within a theoretical context.

As a last resort, post-modern sceptics sometimes accept that we can penetrate the linguistic fog engulfing reality only to deny that we can thereby acquire knowledge of individual viewpoints. Derrida, for example, occasionally suggests that individual viewpoints are 'in principle inaccessible' because we cannot know anything about other people's minds.[55] Behaviourists can easily rebut this argument for post-modern scepticism. Given that we define psychological concepts by reference to actual or possible behaviour, we can have knowledge of individual viewpoints simply because we can observe behaviour. The fact that we cannot know other minds is irrelevant because individual viewpoints are not mental states. Mentalists, too, can rebut this argument for scepticism provided only that they reject logical empiricism. The sceptics' position derives from the twin assertions that we can know things only if we perceive them directly, and that we cannot perceive other minds directly. Yet the logical empiricism contained in these assertions does scant justice to our everyday notion of experience. When we say we have experienced something, we imply that it exists and that we have had sensations we could not have had if it did not exist, but we do not necessarily imply that we have perceived it in itself. For instance, if we say we have experienced radio waves, we imply that they exist and that we have listened to the radio, but we do not imply that we have perceived radio waves directly. We imply that we have heard the sounds the radio waves produce in our ear, not the radio waves themselves. Thus, provided mentalists accept our everyday, realist understanding of experience, they too can argue that we can have knowledge of other people's minds. They can say that we have knowledge of other people's minds because we encounter their minds indirectly in their behaviour. Mentalists can defend the possibility of indirect knowledge of other minds simply by rejecting the logical empiricists' insistence on direct experience as the basis of objective knowledge in favour of a more

---

[55] See, for example, J. Derrida, *Spurs: Nietzsche's Styles*, trans. B. Harlow (Chicago: University of Chicago Press, 1979), p. 125.

relaxed, realist epistemology. Thus, the last resort of the post-modern sceptic falls along with logical empiricism.

We can turn now to the phenomenological sceptics who argue that we cannot recover the viewpoints of people from the past because the historicity of our being prevents us escaping from our own historical horizon. Many phenomenological sceptics set out from an argument about the peculiar nature of historical events conceived as things that constantly unfold through time. They refer us to Gadamer's analysis of historical knowledge as dependent on 'the inner historicity that belongs to experience itself', an analysis that itself points back to Wilhelm Dilthey's belief that a historical event 'gains meaning from its relationship with the whole, from the connection between past and future'.[56] Actually, however, whereas Gadamer's followers often take him to have proven the irrelevance and futility of any attempt to recover an authorial intention, he himself focused on the implications of human ontology for human understanding as such. His concern lay less with the specific methodological problems we face in acquiring knowledge of the past than in very general issues about the nature of all our understanding. Indeed, he sometimes appears explicitly to deny that his work can sustain methodological conclusions of the sort his followers derive from it.[57] We should distinguish, therefore, between the ontological or philosophical hermeneutics we earlier accepted as legitimate and the methodological hermeneutics we are now rejecting as an unreasonable scepticism.[58] Whereas the former explores the nature of human understanding and thus the sort of knowledge we can have, the latter draws conclusions about the nature of the history of ideas from the assumption that the former shows that past intentions are things we are peculiarly unable to know. Phenomenological sceptics are committed to the former, methodological variety of hermeneutics. They argue that later historical events alter the meaning of earlier historical events so that we always understand history from a wider perspective than our ancestors but a narrower one than our heirs. When Petrarch climbed Mount

---

[56] Gadamer, *Truth and Method*, p. 195; W. Dilthey, *Selected Writings*, ed. and trans. H. Rickman (Cambridge: Cambridge University Press, 1976), pp. 235–36. Examples of reception theory inspired in part by phenomenological scepticism include Gunnell, *Political Theory*, particularly pp. 110–26; and Ricœur, *Interpretation Theory*, particularly pp. 89–95.

[57] See Gadamer, *Truth and Method*, pp. 267–8.

[58] A similar distinction is suggested by R. Palmer, *Hermeneutics: Interpretation Theory in Schleiermacher, Dilthey, Heidegger, and Gadamer* (Evanston, Ill.: Northwestern University Press, 1969), particularly p. 46. Moreover, Gadamer himself explicitly drew on Heidegger in order to shift the hermeneutic tradition from an epistemological orientation to an ontological one. See Gadamer, *Truth and Method*, particularly pp. 214–34.

Ventoux, for example, he and his contemporaries did not have a concept of the Renaissance in terms of which to understand his action; but today we recognise that his climb inaugurated the Renaissance precisely because later events have transformed its meaning. Phenomenological sceptics argue that the current meaning of a historical event depends on a grasp of history as a unity culminating in the present. Thus, because the nature of the present constantly changes, to grasp the full meaning of a historical event, we would have to see history as a whole, which we cannot do. Phenomenological sceptics argue that because the meaning of past events depends on the future course of history, historical events do not have fixed meanings, so our historical knowledge remains trapped within the limits of our particular historical horizon. Our historical situation restricts our historical knowledge.

Phenomenological scepticism relies on our conceiving the meaning of historical events in terms of their later significance. But we will do this only if we continue to confuse texts with works. Because texts are timeless, because they might acquire a different meaning every time they are read, it is tempting to see their nature or meaning as something that constantly unfolds through time, and so to conclude that we cannot know them fully since part of their nature always remains to be decided by the future. Actually, however, because texts are timeless, because they can acquire a historical meaning only when a particular individual reads them as works, therefore, they are of no interest to the historian. Historians need concern themselves only with works, and the meaning of a work does not depend on its later significance, so historians can have objective knowledge of the meanings that concern them. Historians study the hermeneutic meanings of works – the meanings texts had for specific individuals in the past – and these meanings do not alter with later events. It is true that because authorial intentions do not exhaust historical meanings, we can talk of the historical meanings of texts going beyond the intentions of their authors. Still, this does not affect my argument. When people understand a text in a particular way, their understanding of it becomes a work the meaning of which does not depend on later events; thus, future historians can study that work without bothering about the later significance of the text. Historians can know, for example, why Petrarch climbed Ventoux, what his climb meant to him, and what his climb has meant to other people in the past, without knowing anything about the future consequences, let alone the final significance, of his climb. We cannot predict the future, so we cannot know how our heirs will react to texts. We can discover, however, what an author meant by a text, what another person has taken a text to mean, and what particular consequences a reading of a text has had. The inability of historians to know the future does not prevent their knowing the past. The fact is that once we distinguish the future significance of an event or work from both its nature and its previous consequences, we no longer have any reason to draw a qualitative distinction between objectivity in history and objectivity in the natural sciences. There is a fixed historical reality: an author did mean such and such by his work. Future events might lead historians to revise their view of this fixed historical reality: either new evidence or a new climate of opinion might prompt historians to adopt a new understanding of a work. But then scientific wisdom can change as a consequence of new evidence or a new climate of opinion. In all areas of knowledge, the future will cast new light on things, thereby encouraging further reflection, which will often lead people to revise their beliefs. In no area of human knowledge, however, does the likelihood of our revising our beliefs prevent us comparing rival sets of beliefs to decide which is the best currently available.

Phenomenological sceptics sometimes give a simpler argument against the possibility of objective historical knowledge. They argue that our contemporary presuppositions enter into our understanding in a way that prevents us having real knowledge of the past. They refer us to Gadamer's insistence that 'there is no understanding or interpretation in which the totality of this existential structure [the historicity of being] does not function, even if the intention of the knower is simply to read "what is there" and to discover from his sources "how it was"'.[59] Once again, however, we should note that whereas Gadamer's followers often take him to have proven the futility of recovering authorial intentions, he actually seems to have been concerned to highlight the positive role played by prejudice in all forms of human understanding. He does indeed suggest that we cannot have unmediated access to the past, but that is something I granted when I rejected the very idea of given facts. Whether or not we regard the absence of pure historical facts as a problem depends on whether or not we contrast history with some other area of human understanding in which people do have access to such facts. I argued that we cannot do so, and it is not clear that Gadamer would disagree with me, even though his followers often seem to do so. Whereas Gadamer appears to think that prejudice plays a positive role

[59] Gadamer, *Truth and Method*, p. 232.

in all knowledge, his followers seem to regard it as a barrier to knowledge of past intentions.[60] Some phenomenological sceptics define our presuppositions in terms of individual prejudices, others define them in terms of social traditions, but they all make the same point. They argue that accounts of the past are necessarily corrupted by the subjective biases of those who tell them. Perhaps they are right. But this need not worry us. Whereas logical empiricists typically abhor presuppositions, semantic holism encourages us to look upon them as a necessary part of all human experience. The influence of the subjective biases of historians on the histories they tell does not affect anthropological epistemology. Because our account of objectivity relies on criteria of comparison, we can accept that the presuppositions of historians necessarily influence the stories they tell, and still defend the possibility of objective knowledge of the past. Historians do not have to eliminate all biases from within themselves: rather, we deal with subjective influences when we evaluate their accounts of the past. Objectivity rests on the possibility of our comparing rival accounts of historical meanings. Neither postmodern nor phenomenological sceptics give us any good reason to suppose we cannot make such comparisons.

CONCLUSION

Earlier we found that historians of ideas recreate historical objects from relics available to them in the present. Now I have outlined a form of justification appropriate to the history of ideas so understood. I began by arguing that no method was either necessary or sufficient to ensure that historians of ideas successfully reconstructed historical objects. This argument was deductive: our conception of coming to understand an utterance incorporates a distinction between passing theories and prior theories, and this distinction implies that there cannot be a logic of discovery for the history of ideas. Historians of ideas cannot justify their theories by reference to the procedures they adopt for arriving at them. They can recreate historical objects on the basis of the relics available to them by whatever means they choose. They can focus on a particular type of context, they can undertake a painstaking investigation of one or more relics, or they can sit around waiting for inspiration. We may prefer a special procedure to all others, and we may do so because we have good reason to think it more likely to bring success than all others,

---

[60] For the invocation of Gadamer's arguments to deny we can have knowledge of past intentions, see Gunnell, *Political Theory*, pp. 96–116.

but no procedure inevitably brings either success or failure, so any such preference must be a matter for heuristics, not logic. Next I argued that historians could not justify their theories by reference to pure facts. This argument, too, was deductive: the place of theories within all experience implies that there are no pure facts, so there cannot be a logic of vindication or refutation. More generally, a rejection of the distinction between the analytic and the synthetic as types of knowledge should leave one suspicious of all given truths. Because theories infuse all perception, there are no given empirical facts, and because we cannot sustain a rigid distinction between the synthetic and the analytic, the absence of given empirical facts implies that there are no given logical truths. We are led, therefore, to an anti-foundationalism in which 'justification is not a matter of a special relation between ideas (or words) and objects, but of conversation, of social practice'.[61] The justification of knowledge cannot depend on its relationship to things as they are. It must depend instead on our identifying a practice by which we can select some beliefs as objective for us.

In analysing justified knowledge, we must take an anthropological turn. We must move away from attempts to establish a secure link between individual ideas or words and things as they are. We must proceed instead to defend a whole body of knowledge produced by a reasonable epistemological practice. Moreover, the reasonableness of this practice must come from its being defined in terms of the very considerations that make us reject foundationalism. Thus, I used deductive arguments to construct a concept of intellectual honesty from the implications of semantic holism. Historians should justify their theories by comparing them with their rivals by reference to criteria of accuracy, comprehensiveness, consistency, progressiveness, fruitfulness, and openness. Historians should relate their theories to a wide range of accepted facts and show how their theories cohere with others. When their theories depart from accepted facts, they should offer alternative accounts of the facts, and show how these alternatives suggest new theories that receive support from the facts. When they do so, their justification of their theories will be reasonable, but not decisive. Other historians could legitimately stick with an alternative theory if they expected thereby to resolve fruitfully the problems confronting it.

Because historical theories cannot be justified decisively, they might seem to be divorced from the truth, or even to be incommensurable with

---

[61] Rorty, *Philosophy and the Mirror of Nature*, p. 170.

one another. All too often post-modernists and their critics assume that a rejection of foundationalism must lead to an irrationalist relativism. In contrast, I have defended both truth and commensurability as deductions from the nature of our being in the world. Anti-foundationalism requires one to avoid appeals to given truths, but there are other ways of justifying knowledge. Truth can act as a regulative ideal in that our interactions with our environment give us a good reason to take the theories we select using our criteria of comparison as successive approximations to the truth. What is more, the way our interactions with our environment push us towards truth underpins the possibility of our comparing rival worldviews even when they are radically different. We can conclude, therefore, without fear of falling into the pitfalls of an irrationalist relativism, that historians of ideas should adopt a form of justification under which they defend their theories by means of a comparison with the alternatives on offer. They should show how their theories are more accurate and comprehensive in relation to the agreed facts, and more consistent in their use of standards of evidence and reasoning; and they should show how their theories are developing in a progressive and fruitful way while remaining open to criticism.

CHAPTER 4

On belief

INTRODUCTION

Our analysis of historical meanings showed that they were intentions or individual viewpoints. The current unpopularity of intentionalist analyses of historical meaning owes much to a sceptical opposition to the possibility of our recovering the intentions of people from the past. Phenomenological sceptics, in particular, argue that historians cannot reproduce the past as it was, but rather must be engaged in a continuous dialogue, a fusion of horizons. Historians cannot return to a primal past: they necessarily appropriate a text that already bears the traces of previous appropriations, and they do so from their present perspective. Much of what these sceptics say makes excellent sense as a phenomenological account of historical understanding. To argue that historians cannot have unmediated access to the past, to argue that historians play a creative role when they read a text, to argue these things is to explicate some of the consequences that flow from a rejection of the very idea of given empirical facts. None the less, the fact that historians do not have unmediated access to the past does not imply that they cannot have objective knowledge of the past. Scholars can reach a sceptical rejection of intentionalism only if they adopt an additional premise, namely, that we cannot have objective knowledge of things of which we do not have pure experiences. To reject intentionalism, therefore, the sceptics must equate objective knowledge with an unmediated access to pure facts. Only by doing so can they provide themselves with a yardstick by which to dismiss the idea of historians having objective knowledge of past viewpoints.

An anti-foundational, anthropological epistemology undermines such scepticism by denying that we can have pure experiences of anything. Given that we cannot have pure experiences of anything, we will reach one of two conclusions. Either we will conclude that any attempt to know anything is doomed to fail, in which case to study the objects postulated by the sceptics is just as pointless and irrational as to study individual viewpoints. Or we will conclude that we can, and should, defend an analysis of objective knowledge that does not rely on pure experience, in which case the sceptics' phenomenological analysis of historical understanding cannot actually sustain their sceptical conclusions. We can avoid an irrationalist post-modernism by defending an analysis of objective knowledge in terms of a fallible human practice, rather than an unquestionable relationship between ideas or words and the objects to which they refer. Because objective knowledge arises from a comparison of rival histories, not an unmediated experience of reality, the fact that historians cannot have direct access to past intentions cannot be a reason to renounce an intentional theory of historical meaning. No doubt the historian always approaches the past with subjective prejudices, and no doubt there must always be a distance between a text and the viewpoint of its author; but neither of these negates the possibility of historians obtaining objective knowledge of past viewpoints. On the contrary, historians can still have objective knowledge of past viewpoints since objectivity does not depend on our having direct access to things in themselves. Once we define objectivity in terms of a comparison between rival bodies of knowledge, we remove the last objection to an intentional theory of historical meaning.

We can return now, therefore, to the task of analysing the objects studied by historians of ideas. Earlier we found that historical meanings are equivalent to the individual viewpoints held by people in the past. Individual viewpoints, or weak intentions, differ from strong intentions in that they need not be conscious and they are embodied in the relevant utterance rather than being a prior commitment to make that utterance. Next we will find that these individual viewpoints consist of expressed beliefs. Historians of ideas extrapolate from the relics available to them to the beliefs people expressed at some time in the past. In addition, we will find that the grammar of our concepts commits us to logical presumptions in favour of sincere, conscious, and rational beliefs. Sincerity is conceptually prior to deception because the very possibility of deception presupposes a norm of sincerity. The conscious is conceptually prior to the unconscious because the only access we have to hidden beliefs and pro-attitudes is our inability to make sense of things in terms of open ones. The rational is conceptually prior to the irrational because the existence of any language presupposes a norm of consistency governing its use. The conceptual priority of sincere, conscious, and rational beliefs establishes presumptions in their favour. Because these presumptions, unlike expectations, are given to us by the grammar of our concepts, they are conceptually prior to our actual investigations of the past. Historians should presume that the expressed beliefs they study were held sincerely, consciously, and rationally by the people to whom they ascribe them. They should try initially to explain why an individual expressed a given viewpoint by treating it as a set of sincere, conscious, and rational beliefs.

INDIVIDUAL VIEWPOINTS AS BELIEFS

The viewpoints of authors consist of the beliefs they hope to express by saying what they say. Both our phenomenological conception of ourselves and our habitual treatment of others suggest that people generally use language to express thoughts that they hope others will understand. Hermeneutic meanings come from the thoughts people intend to convey by making the utterances they do. Besides, hermeneutic meanings must be related to thoughts because if authors assigned to utterances meanings that were not thoughts, they would assign to utterances meanings they might not have cognitive access to, which would be ridiculous. Individual viewpoints must consist, therefore, of thoughts or beliefs. To say this is not to postulate a causal relationship between beliefs and individual viewpoints. It is to suggest that we take individual viewpoints to be the beliefs authors express in their utterances.

How exactly we conceive of beliefs will depend on the metaphysical status we ascribe to the concepts we use to denote psychological states. This is something I want to leave as open as I can: as far as I am concerned, historians may legitimately take belief, pro-attitude, and the like to be concepts denoting genuine mental states, or purely functional concepts, or concepts defined exclusively by reference to behaviour. None the less, I want to say a little more about the concept of belief while continuing to avoid metaphysical issues in philosophical psychology. I want to do so by discussing the way in which we attribute beliefs to people. A belief is a psychological state we attribute to someone in an attempt to explain and predict behaviour. It is the psychological state in which one holds a proposition true. Here too there are numerous debates about how we should analyse the concept of an attitude to a proposition, most of which I also want to leave open.[1] I can safely do so because intentionalism has almost nothing to say about how we should

---

[1] See the wide variety of issues discussed, and viewpoints adopted, in N. Salmon and S. Soames (eds.), *Propositions and Attitudes* (New York: Oxford University Press, 1988).

attribute beliefs to people. Certainly a rejection of contextualism, conventionalism, and hermeneutic occasionalism does not preclude a view of the attribution of beliefs as a contextually sensitive process. We can accept, if we wish, that 'to believe' is a contextually sensitive verb in that to say 'X believes Y' is to say 'Y renders X's belief reasonably well', where what constitutes a reasonable rendition of a belief varies with the relevant context.[2] Crucially, however, we must accept that we cannot derive beliefs from behaviour without also invoking pro-attitudes, and this means that we cannot equate beliefs with what people avow. How people act, including what they avow, depends on their pro-attitudes as well as their beliefs, so we can deduce their beliefs from their behaviour only if we know about their pro-attitudes; but because how they act depends on their beliefs as well as their pro-attitudes, we can know about their pro-attitudes only if we know about their beliefs. Clearly, therefore, we must make sense of actions by reference to both beliefs and pro-attitudes in a single, holistic, interpretative process. Even if our concern is with people's beliefs alone, we can attribute beliefs to them only through an interpretative process in which we also attribute pro-attitudes to them. Thus, the strictest behaviourist definition we can allow is: beliefs are what people would avow if their only preference was for expressing the propositions they take to be true. It is because pro-attitudes can prompt people to avow beliefs they do not hold that we must identify historical meanings with expressed beliefs rather than actual beliefs. Imagine, for example, that John believes he is a poor runner but in order to impress Jane he says he is a good runner. The meaning of his utterance is obviously the belief he expresses, that he is a good runner, not the belief he actually holds, that he is a poor runner. Historical meanings derive from the viewpoints people intend to convey in their utterances, and these viewpoints are the beliefs they express, not those they hold true.

Perhaps critics will object to our equating individual viewpoints with expressed beliefs. One possible reason for doing so is that our language contains concepts which describe different activities of consciousness – concepts such as thinking, preferring, and feeling. Our use of these concepts might seem to imply that we should divide consciousness up into various parts, where one part might consist of beliefs and another of individual viewpoints. Actually, however, because a single entity can perform many different activities, the existence of various concepts

---

[2] Compare M. Richard, *Propositional Attitudes: An Essay on Thoughts and How We Ascribe Them* (Cambridge: Cambridge University Press, 1990).

describing different activities of consciousness need not point to divisions within consciousness itself. Indeed, if our distinctions between the different activities of consciousness did undermine the unity of consciousness, we would have to conclude that the distinctions were spurious, not that consciousness was divided. We have a strong commitment to a belief in the unity of consciousness because it establishes the possibility of our being aware of our own beliefs; it underwrites our sense of personal identity. Our sense of personal identity depends on our conceiving of ourselves as psychological unities capable of making coherent plans in the light of our beliefs and pro-attitudes. If, for instance, I did not have a preference for going to the cinema, and if I did not think the cinema was open on Tuesday, there would be little sense in my planning to go to the cinema next Tuesday.

Although we cannot distinguish between different parts of consciousness, we can distinguish between different ways in which a unified consciousness relates to the external world. The varied activities of consciousness are differentiated by their respective relationships to the world, not their locations in consciousness. Thus, critics might object to our equating individual viewpoints with expressed beliefs by arguing that the two have different relationships to the world. Some of these critics might define individual viewpoints in terms of pro-attitudes as well as beliefs. An individual viewpoint might include the activity of preferring something to be true of reality as well as, or even instead of, the activity of thinking something to be true of reality. Others might try to define individual viewpoints in terms of intended illocutionary force as well as beliefs. An individual viewpoint might include the activity of giving point to an utterance as well as, or even instead of, the activity of thinking something to be true. I will consider these two possibilities in turn.

To begin, consider the possibility of individual viewpoints including pro-attitudes as well as, or even instead of, beliefs. Philosophers often follow Hume in distinguishing motives or strong intentions from beliefs by including desires in the former but not the latter.[3] Indeed, if they, like me, believe that desires are only one of several possible bases for preferences, and so motives, they typically include all sorts of pro-attitudes in their analysis of motives or strong intentions but not in their analysis of beliefs. Motives can incorporate pro-attitudes in a way beliefs cannot. Thus, whereas beliefs always consist solely of attempts to reflect

---

[3] Hume, *Treatise of Human Nature.*

the world, motives can incorporate preferences for imaginary worlds. Motives and beliefs have different directions of fit to the world. People want the world to correspond to the pro-attitudes that motivate them, but they want their beliefs to correspond to the world as it is. Although some philosophers reject a Humean analysis of motives by assimilating desires to beliefs, I will not follow them.[4] Instead, I will defend an analysis of individual viewpoints as expressed beliefs by arguing that the distinction between the individual viewpoints of concern to historians and the motives analysed by Humeans is such that we should exclude pro-attitudes, including desires, from the former even if they are part of the latter. Pro-attitudes might be relevant to motives, but they are still not relevant to individual viewpoints. The distinction between motives and individual viewpoints appears in their different relationships to utterances. A motive gives the reason why someone made an utterance: to say Besant's motive in writing on religious unity was to attain fame and fortune is to say she wrote in order to attain fame and fortune. In contrast, an individual viewpoint gives the hermeneutic meaning of an utterance: to say Besant's viewpoint in writing was to illustrate the fundamental unity of the great religions is to describe the meaning of her work. Thus, because pro-attitudes can be a reason for doing something, they enter into motives, but equally, because pro-attitudes cannot be part of the meaning of a work, they do not enter into individual viewpoints. Imagine, for example, that Besant wrote about the unity of the great religions simply because she wanted fame and fortune. Because her preference for fame and fortune was an integral part of her motive, historians would have to refer to this preference to explain why she wrote the work she did. None the less, because her preference for fame and fortune still would not be relevant to her individual viewpoint, historians could understand her work as a defence of religious tolerance based on a claim about the unity of all religions even if they knew nothing of her preference for fame and fortune. Thus, because pro-attitudes are irrelevant to individual viewpoints, we can continue to equate individual viewpoints with expressed beliefs. Besant's viewpoint, for example, consisted of her expressed belief that all religions teach the same essential truths so that the devotees of the various religions should tolerate one another. It did so, moreover, irrespective of the particular motives she had for writing what she did. No doubt pro-attitudes enter

[4] For a defence of the Humean analysis that fits well with my arguments, see M. Smith, 'The humean theory of motivation', *Mind* 96 (1987), 36–61.

into motives or strong intentions, but this does not mean that they enter into individual viewpoints or weak intentions.

Perhaps critics might argue that individual viewpoints are just overt motives. For instance, they might say, if Besant's viewpoint was that people should exhibit religious tolerance because all religions teach the same basic truths, then she had a preference for religious tolerance, and even if her other pro-attitudes did not enter into her viewpoint, this preference was constitutive of it. Thus, they might conclude, individual viewpoints include at least some of the pro-attitudes that motivate authors. Really, however, the example here proffered on behalf of our critics demonstrates only that individual viewpoints can coincide with pro-attitudes. It does not show that individual viewpoints can incorporate pro-attitudes. No individual viewpoint ever includes any pro-attitude because all pro-attitudes are extraneous to the meaning of a work. For example, Besant might have hoped to promote religious unity, or she might have been indifferent to religious unity and, say, merely interested in her own fame and fortune. In either case, the meaning of her work still would consist solely of her argument for religious unity, that is, the beliefs she expressed in her utterance. Our critics have fallen victim to a confusion that arises because individual viewpoints can coincide with pro-attitudes. The coincidence of some beliefs with some pro-attitudes follows from the unity of consciousness. The unity of consciousness implies that our pro-attitudes can be the subject of our beliefs. Thus, whenever we act to fulfil pro-attitudes we know we have, we believe we have the relevant pro-attitudes, so our beliefs coincide with our pro-attitudes. Sometimes people explicitly say why they are making an utterance, and sometimes their motive is clear from the content of their utterance, and in both of these cases, their viewpoints will include their knowledge of their motives. Imagine, for example, that Besant wrote about the unity of different religions simply because she hoped to promote religious tolerance. In this case, she would have had a pro-attitude to religious unity, and she would have expressed a belief that she had a pro-attitude to religious unity, so her pro-attitude would have coincided with her individual viewpoint. No doubt there are numerous similar occasions when the difference between an individual viewpoint and a motive slips away to become little more than a different description of a single attitude we attribute to someone. None the less, although the distinction between motives and individual viewpoints sometimes seems to dissolve, this does not mean that individual viewpoints are a type of motive. On the contrary, there are numerous other occasions when we can distinguish individual viewpoints from motives, and these occasions underpin the validity of a similar distinction in cases when the two happen to coincide.

Consider now the possibility of individual viewpoints including intended illocutionary forces as well as, or even instead of, beliefs. This possibility seems to be raised by the way conventionalists such as Skinner deploy speech-act theory in their analysis of historical meaning. Speech-act theory itself arises from the insight that to make an utterance is to perform an action.[5] To speak or to write is to perform an illocutionary action such as to warn, command, or teach. However, to recognise that to make an utterance is to perform an action is not to commit oneself to any particular analysis of hermeneutic meaning. All actions are the products of beliefs as well as pro-attitudes, and this leaves open the possibility of the meaning of actions being a product of beliefs alone. Again, speech-act theorists identify the illocutionary force of an utterance with its point, and this leaves open the possibility of the meaning of utterances being a product of beliefs alone. The point of an utterance might be either irrelevant to its meaning or itself an expression of belief. Imagine, for example, that a policeman shouts out to a skater 'the ice over there is very thin'. Clearly his utterance has the intended illocutionary force of a warning in that the point of his utterance is to warn the skater of danger. However, to recognise this is not to conclude that his concern to warn the skater constitutes a part of the meaning of his utterance, let alone a part of its meaning that is not a belief. Before we can judge the reasonableness of this conclusion, we have to map the concept of intended illocutionary force back on to the concepts of belief and pro-attitude with which we explain human actions. Skinner seems to analyse speech-acts in a way which leaves open the possibility of historical meanings or individual viewpoints deriving exclusively from beliefs.[6] Although he argues that to understand an utterance we must recover its intended illocutionary force, he does not define the meaning of an utterance to include this force. Instead he equates the meaning of an utterance solely with the sense and reference of its terms. Clearly, moreover, there is nothing to stop us going on to analyse sense and reference solely in terms of the beliefs an author expresses in making an utterance. Skinner's own perspective allows us, therefore, to map meaning exclusively on to belief, with intended illocutionary force mapping on to the pro-attitudes that motivate expressions of belief. We can say

---

[5] J. Austin, *How to Do Things with Words*, ed. J. Urmson and M. Sbisa (Oxford: Clarendon Press, 1975).   [6] See, in particular, Skinner, "'Social meaning'", pp. 79–96.

that speech-acts, being actions, embody not only beliefs or meanings but also pro-attitudes or intended illocutionary forces. If we want to study a speech-act – as Skinner generally does – we must concern ourselves with its meaning and its intended illocutionary force.[7] But if we want to study only the meaning of the action – the task of the historian of ideas – we need concern ourselves only with the beliefs it expresses.

Although Skinner analyses speech-acts in a way which leaves open the possibility of individual viewpoints deriving exclusively from beliefs, it is not clear that this is what he intends to do. Indeed, some of his followers, including Tully, suggest that his use of speech-act theory commits us to a theory of historical meaning as including something other than belief.[8] They imply that the meaning of an utterance comes not only from its locutionary meaning but also its intended illocutionary force. They argue that the intended illocutionary force of an utterance constitutes a special part of its meaning directed at the state of affairs the author wants to bring about. The policeman, for example, intends his utterance as a warning – he has a pro-attitude to alerting the skater to a danger, and because this pro-attitude is part of his viewpoint, the meaning of his utterance cannot derive solely from the beliefs he expresses in it. Part of the problem here seems to be a failure to understand Wittgenstein's dictum that 'meaning is use'.[9] All too often Skinner's followers take this dictum to imply that meaning is action in context. They argue that when Wittgenstein analyses meaning as use, he shows that meaning derives from action, so that meanings, like actions, must embody not only beliefs but also something such as pro-attitudes or intended illocutionary forces. Really, however, Wittgenstein's analysis of meaning as use represents a reduction of all forms of meaning to hermeneutic ones. It represents, first, a rejection of his earlier picture theory of language in favour of the belief that use underlies the semantic relationship of language to the world, and, second, a rejection of his earlier view of use as being governed by strict linguistic conventions in favour of the belief that hermeneutic meanings arise through the creative deployment of words within an open linguistic

---

[7] Skinner says his principal concern has been with actions not meanings in Skinner, 'Reply to my critics', p. 270.
[8] For example, Tully, 'Pen is a mighty sword', p. 9.
[9] Tully uses Wittgenstein's dictum 'words are deeds' as a motto for his collection of Skinner's writings. The confusion here is to take this dictum to imply that meanings are deeds, rather than that meanings appear only in words that are deeds. The same confusion appears in a tendency among Skinner's followers to say 'meaning is action in context', rather than 'meaning is something that appears only in action in context'.

practice.[10] When Wittgenstein analyses meaning as use, he implies that meanings only appear in actions: semantic and linguistic meanings are abstractions based on hermeneutic meanings as they appear in particular utterances. He does not imply that meanings are actions, and so, like actions, must incorporate something other than belief.

In any case, no matter how we should unpack Wittgenstein's dictum that 'meaning is use', speech-act theorists definitely go astray whenever they equate meaning with intended illocutionary force understood as a sort of pro-attitude. They do so because intended illocutionary forces arise only when individual viewpoints understood as expressed beliefs happen to point back to plausible motives. On these occasions, a part of the viewpoint expressed in an utterance provides evidence of a motive of the author in making it – we will call this the illocutionary viewpoint.[11] On these occasions, a plausible motive of the author in making an utterance is also indicated by the individual viewpoint expressed in it – we will call this the illocutionary motive. For example, the viewpoint of the policeman is that the skater should be wary because the ice is thin, and so dangerous, and this viewpoint points back to his motive being to warn the skater. Because his viewpoint provides evidence of his motive, we can describe it as an illocutionary viewpoint, and we can describe his motive as an illocutionary motive. Speech-act theorists are sometimes tempted to include pro-attitudes in the meanings of utterances only because they fail to analyse the concept of intended illocutionary force into those of illocutionary viewpoint and illocutionary motive. When the meaning of an utterance incorporates an illocutionary viewpoint, they are tempted to redescribe this viewpoint in terms of the related illocutionary motive. Thus, they wrongly see the illocutionary motive as part of the meaning of the utterance, when really the meaning of the utterance derives solely from the beliefs it expresses. Consider the example of the policeman. Speech-act theorists might redescribe his view that the skater should be wary of the thin ice in terms of his motive to warn the skater. If they did so, however, they would wrongly identify his motive as part of the meaning of his utterance, when really the meaning of his utterance derives solely from his belief that the skater should be wary because the ice is thin. The illocutionary force of an

[10] Compare J. Bogen, *Wittgenstein's Philosophy of Language: Some Aspects of Its Development* (London: Routledge & Kegan Paul, 1972), particularly p. 199.
[11] If one equates illocutionary forces exclusively with illocutionary viewpoints, one will conclude the former do not exist other than as part of meaning. Compare L. Cohen, 'Do illocutionary forces exist?', *Philosophical Quarterly* 14 (1964), 118–37.

utterance gives its mood, or more accurately, its point – to warn, to command, to teach, and so on. In so far as the point of an utterance contributes to its meaning, intended illocutionary forces are part of the beliefs expressed by the author. Thus, the meaning of the policeman's utterance includes his belief that the skater should be wary because the ice is thin. But in so far as we include the motives of authors in the point of their utterances, intended illocutionary forces do not contribute to the meanings of utterances. Thus, the meaning of the policeman's utterance does not include his pro-attitude to warning the skater.

Critics might make the following objection. Although our analysis of intended illocutionary force enables us to equate individual viewpoints exclusively with beliefs, we have given them no reason to accept this complex analysis in preference to its simpler rivals. The justification for our analysis of intended illocutionary force rests, however, on those cases in which viewpoints and motives do not coincide. Only our analysis fits these cases. Although intended illocutionary forces might appear to introduce pro-attitudes into meaning whenever individual viewpoints point back to plausible motives, those occasions when viewpoints do not point back to motives show that this is just an illusion produced by the conjunction of viewpoints and motives. Imagine, for example, that a policeman who is walking past a lake says 'the ice over there is very thin' with the sole aim of indicating his local knowledge to his companion. The viewpoint expressed in his utterance does not point to any particular motive, so his utterance has no obvious intended illocutionary force. Intended illocutionary forces arise only when the viewpoint expressed in an utterance points back to a motive for making it. When the viewpoint expressed in an utterance does not point back to a motive for making it, there is no intended illocutionary force.

Next critics might try to reject our analysis of intended illocutionary forces by saying they never vanish in the way we have suggested. The critics might argue that the meaning of the policeman's utterance to his companion includes the intended illocutionary force of a description. Yet this argument does not work. On the one hand, suppose 'X' and 'I tell you X' convey the same meaning. In this case, because speech-act theorists argue that intended illocutionary forces constitute a special part of the meaning of utterances, telling or describing cannot be an example of an intended illocutionary force. On the other hand, suppose 'X' and 'I tell you X' do not convey the same meaning because performative clauses alter the meaning of utterances. This leads to several unacceptable conclusions. For a start, if performative clauses

alter the meaning of utterances, we cannot make the intended illocutionary force of an utterance explicit without changing its meaning.
Imagine a policeman shouts to a skater 'the ice over there is very thin',
the skater calls back 'pardon', and the policeman replies 'I warn you the
ice over there is very thin'. The critics have no option but to say that the
policeman means something different in his two utterances. More
importantly, if performative clauses alter the meaning of utterances,
intended illocutionary forces can become part of the normal meaning of
an utterance, so they cannot constitute a special sort of meaning. If 'X'
and 'I tell you X' have different meanings, the meaning of the latter
surely includes the idea of telling. But if the idea of telling constitutes
part of the meaning of 'I tell you X', what is the illocutionary force of 'I
tell you X'? It cannot have the illocutionary force of telling because the
idea of telling is a part of its normal meaning, and illocutionary forces
supposedly constitute a special sort of meaning.

As a last resort, critics might try to reject our analysis of intended
illocutionary force by identifying performative clauses that alter individual viewpoints without thereby bringing the intended illocutionary force
into the viewpoint expressed in the utterance.[12] In these cases, the critics
might argue, intended illocutionary forces really do constitute a special
part of the meaning of utterances. Imagine, for example, a policeman
says 'the ice over there is very thin' so as to taunt a skater who is stuck in
the middle of the lake. If the policeman said 'I am taunting you by
saying the ice over there is very thin', he would undermine his effort to
taunt the skater since he would make the intended illocutionary force of
his utterance explicit. If he makes his taunt explicit, he alters the
meaning of his utterance, but he also ceases to taunt. Actually, however,
this argument merely reworks the confusion between viewpoints and
motives. When the policeman makes his taunting explicit, he undermines his action by making it almost impossible for him to bring about
the state of affairs he prefers, but he does not alter the meaning of his
utterance. If a passer-by heard him say 'the ice over there is very thin',
and understood him to mean 'I am taunting you (the skater) by saying
the ice over there is very thin', the passer-by would have grasped his
meaning correctly. The policeman means the same thing whether he
says 'the ice over there is very thin' or 'I am taunting you by saying the

---

[12] Compare Skinner, 'Conventions and the understanding of speech-acts', where he deploys this
argument against Cohen, 'Do illocutionary forces exist?' Clearly Skinner can rebut Cohen, but
he can do so only because illocutionary viewpoints sometimes point back to illocutionary
motives, not because illocutionary motives enter into the meaning of utterances.

ice over there is very thin'. It is just his belief that saying 'the ice over there is very thin' will exasperate the skater points back to his motive being to taunt the skater, so that if he makes this belief explicit, he thereby makes his motive explicit, and if he makes his motive explicit, he ensures it will be frustrated because taunts must be implicit if they are to succeed.

We can conclude, therefore, that intended illocutionary force does not exist as a special component of the meaning of utterances. Speech-act theorists who suggest the contrary have fallen for an illusion created by the way the viewpoints expressed in utterances often point back to plausible motives for making utterances. Really we should analyse an intended illocutionary force as a conjunction of an individual viewpoint pointing back to a motive and a motive evidenced by an individual viewpoint. Thus, because we can regard intended illocutionary forces as part of individual viewpoints, they can enter into the meaning of utterances; but they can do so only in so far as they are expressed beliefs. Similarly, because we can regard intended illocutionary forces as motives, they can be other than expressed beliefs, but they are so only in so far as they do not enter into the meaning of utterances. In either case, we can continue to equate individual viewpoints exclusively with expressed beliefs.

Actually we can be more ambitious in our attempt to show that individual viewpoints are expressed beliefs. We can show that this conclusion follows as a deductive inference from the existence of a genuine distinction between the history of ideas and history in general. No doubt scholars can legitimately define the history of ideas in a wide variety of ways. For example, within a broad account of the history of ideas defined in contrast to actions, they might distinguish a narrower account of the history of ideas from intellectual history, the history of philosophy, and the like; or within a broad account of the history of action, they might distinguish a history of speech-acts from a history of various other types of action.[13] None the less, we must analyse the history of ideas in contrast to a general history of action if only because our current concern is to clarify the nature of individual viewpoints by contrasting them with actions. It is as uninteresting as it is obvious, however, to say that historians of ideas concentrate on ideas whereas other historians also consider things such as actions and events. We need to know what

[13] Compare M. Mandelbaum, 'The history of ideas, intellectual history, and the history of philosophy', *History and Theory* 4 (1965), Beiheft 5: *The Historiography of the History of Philosophy*, 31–66.

we mean by an idea, and how we should distinguish ideas from things such as actions and events. Problems arise here not only because actions typically embody ideas, but also because to express an idea is to perform an action. Thus, historians of ideas might study actions as expressions of ideas, and other historians might refer to expressions of ideas as actions. When we say that historians of ideas study works, we do not imply that there exists a particular type of thing called a work. Historians of ideas can treat numerous different things, including books, paintings, and actions, as works expressing human intelligence. Thus, the identity of the history of ideas must rest on the way in which we treat some things as expressions of meaning; but because these things can be the subject matter of other forms of historical investigation, we must also be able to treat them as something other, or more, than expressions of meaning, although when we do so, we will be doing something other, or more, than the history of ideas. All historians study the same things. Historians of ideas concern themselves with these things as expressions of meaning. Other historians treat them as something other, or more, than expressions of meaning.

The history of ideas postulates a component of certain things that allows us to treat them as expressions of meaning, but this component cannot be all there is to them because we also can treat them in other ways. If we reverse the direction of this statement, we discover the following: there must be a component of certain things that is of no relevance to historians of ideas and against which we define the component that is relevant to historians of ideas. Some things must possess two components: one makes them an expression of meaning, and so objects for study by historians of ideas; the other might convey a meaning to us, but it cannot be an expression of meaning since it does not enter into the history of ideas. Consider the example of human actions. Because actions can legitimately be studied by both historians of ideas and other historians, they must have two components, one of which identifies them as expressions of meaning and the other of which identifies them as more than expressions of meaning. What are these two components? Someone might suggest we contrast the ideas expressed in an action with the related physical movements. There are, however, two problems with this proposal. The first is that bodily movements can express ideas so they cannot be the component of actions of no interest to historians of ideas. For example, because Petrarch's bodily movements in climbing Mount Ventoux expressed his idea that beautiful views have value, we can treat his bodily movements as a work possessing meaning.

Bodily movements are themselves actions that must instantiate our two components. The second problem is that to express an idea can be to act in a way which does not depend on a bodily movement. For example, if Jane shouts 'watch out', she might perform the act of warning, but we would not describe her act of warning in terms of, say, the movements of her vocal cords. Bodily movements are not an essential feature of all actions. More generally, because we can treat any behavioural component of an action as an expression of intelligence, and because an action can be purely verbal, therefore, the two components of actions that make them expressions of meaning and other than expressions of meaning must be psychological, not behavioural. They must be psychological even though behaviourists will want to define the relevant psychological components in suitably behavioural terms. The obvious psychological components of an action are a belief and a pro-attitude. Actions clearly express meaning by virtue of the beliefs they embody. We take Petrarch's climb to have a meaning, for example, because it embodies a belief in the value of beautiful views. Likewise, actions do more than express meaning by virtue of the pro-attitudes they embody. We do not treat Petrarch's climb as meaningful, for example, if we consider whether he climbed Mount Ventoux because he wanted to see the view or because he wanted to attain fame and fortune by dramatising the idea that beautiful views have value.

The distinctiveness of the history of ideas as a subset of the discipline of history requires us to identify two psychological components of things such as human actions. One of these components, belief, is constitutive of their meaning. The other, pro-attitude, is irrelevant to their meaning. Thus, we can define individual viewpoints as the beliefs authors express in works as opposed to the pro-attitudes that motivate them to produce works. Because historians of ideas study things as expressions of meaning, they focus exclusively on the beliefs from which meanings derive. Because other historians study things both as expressions of meaning and as more than this, they focus on both the beliefs from which meanings derive and the pro-attitudes that make the relevant things more than expressions of meaning. All historians study the same things. It is just that historians of ideas ask questions exclusively about the beliefs these things express, whereas other historians also ask questions about the pro-attitudes that motivated these things. Historians have recourse to a wide range of relics from which to reconstruct the past. The relics are the products of human activity, and historians approach them as such. Historians reconstruct the past by deploying the key concepts we use to make sense of all human activity, namely, belief and pro-attitude. The relevant beliefs identify the intentional, or meaningful, content of the activity. The relevant pro-attitudes explain why someone engaged in it.

Many of the arguments I have made so far have been pushing us towards the important conclusion that the objects studied by historians of ideas are expressed beliefs. Historians of ideas study meanings, but to say this is to make the central issue the nature of the meanings they study. I have argued that they study hermeneutic meanings, understood as individual viewpoints, not semantic or linguistic meanings. The meanings studied by historians of ideas are products of the creative activity of individuals, not linguistic contexts or social conventions. Now I have tried to show that the activity by which individuals produce hermeneutic meanings is that of expressing beliefs. When people make an utterance, they express ideas or beliefs, and it is these ideas or beliefs that constitute the objects studied by historians of ideas. Historical meanings consist of expressed beliefs that convey the individual viewpoints of individuals. What, though, is a belief? So far, we have equated belief only with the psychological state of holding a proposition to be true.

Philosophers will approach the analysis of belief in different ways depending on their different concerns. Some will focus on the contrasts between belief, opinion, and knowledge. We will not do so, however, since our concern is with any belief expressed in an utterance no matter how strongly or justifiably it is held. Others will focus on what counts as a justified belief. We will not do so, however, since we dealt with this issue when we analysed the nature of objectivity. Yet others will focus on the nature of belief as a psychological state. We will not do so, however, since I want to leave this metaphysical issue of philosophical psychology as open as I can. Our concern in analysing the nature of belief is to explore the nature of the objects studied by historians of ideas. Although we cannot give any more content to the concept of belief as such, we can establish logical presumptions in favour of sincere, conscious, and rational belief. We can draw on the grammar of our concepts to show that historians of ideas should presume that the meanings they study consist of sincere, conscious, and rational beliefs.

Before we do this, however, we must clarify the nature of a presumption as it differs from an expectation. A presumption exists when X is conceptually prior to Y. To say that X is conceptually prior to Y is to make a logical claim based on a study of our concepts, not a factual one based on a study of the world. It is to say that the grammar of our concepts shows that Y depends on X. Presumptions belong, therefore, to the logic of a discipline; they underpin our studies of the world; they are logically or conceptually prior to any concrete information or specific theory we might have about a particular thing or set of things. Because they arise out of the categories structuring our beliefs, they cannot be overturned without our adopting a new set of beliefs. Expectations, in contrast, belong to the substantive content of a discipline. They are products of our studies of the world; they arise out of the concrete information or specific theories we acquire about a particular thing or set of things. Because they rest on particular beliefs about specific objects, they could be overturned if we decided the relevant beliefs were wrong. Whereas presumptions are given to us by our concepts in a way which makes them logically prior to all specific historical studies, expectations arise as a result of the specific historical studies we undertake against the background of our presumptions. Because we have rejected a distinction between the analytic and synthetic conceived as different types of knowledge, we cannot say that presumptions are self-evident tautologies or logically necessary truths. Equally, however, because we have adopted a distinction between the analytic and synthetic conceived as different ways of coming to know things, we can say that presumptions are given to us as a result of our drawing out the implications of the concepts with which we make sense of the world. Presumptions are analytic in the sense of being true for us simply by virtue of meaning. They belong to the grammar of our concepts.

Presumptions arise out of a relationship of conceptual priority, not conceptual identity. When we analyse belief as the psychological state of holding a proposition true, we evoke a relationship of identity such that X is Y or Y constitutes X. In contrast, when we analyse deception to establish the conceptual priority of sincerity over insincerity, we will say only that X logically precedes Y, or Y logically presupposes X, and we will thereby point to a presumption in favour of X. Crucially, because presumptions embody a relationship of logical priority, not identity, to defend presumptions in favour of sincere, conscious, and rational belief is not to preclude historians interpreting a work in terms of insincere, unconscious, or irrational beliefs. Our presumptions will establish only that the process of ascribing beliefs to people is one governed by norms in favour of the sincere, conscious, and rational. The purpose of our presumptions is not to fix the sort of beliefs historians can ascribe to people. It is rather to identify the norms governing the process by which they ascribe beliefs to people. No doubt some critics will argue that if presumptions are logically prior to concrete studies of the world, we should have nothing to do with them. Such critics would have us avoid all commitments that are not warranted by the evidence. They would have us rely solely on 'genuinely empirical criteria' to evaluate the evidence and perhaps thereby to arrive at expectations.[14] They would dismiss all presumptions as unjustified *a priori* assumptions. Clearly, however, these critics assume that we can have pure experiences, which, as we have seen, we cannot. Because all facts are theory laden, we cannot have purely empirical criteria, so the way we understand and treat the evidence must be governed in part by the categories infusing our experience. Because we cannot but describe the world in terms of a particular set of theories, the way we treat things must depend on a conceptually prior commitment to the categories, and so presumptions, implied by that set of theories. The debate here, therefore, cannot be one of *a priori* assumptions against empirical studies. Rather, it must be one about the nature of the presumptions we should bring to our empirical studies. Historians of ideas must approach their studies with some presumptions. The only question is what presumptions these should be.

In cases of deception, people do not believe the ideas they intend to convey through their utterance, so their expressed beliefs necessarily differ from their actual ones. If, for instance, Besant had wanted to promote religious tolerance but had not believed that all religions taught the same fundamental truths, if she had advanced her argument not out of genuine conviction but because she thought doing so would promote her aims, then her expressed beliefs would not have been her actual beliefs, so her work would have been an instance of deception. Although we cannot rule out the possibility of deception, we can establish the conceptual priority of sincerity. Although deception occurs, and although we expect it to occur in some circumstances, its occurrence, and

---

[14] Skinner, 'Meaning and understanding', pp. 42–3. Skinner is criticising Strauss's presumption that philosophers practise deception. The problem is that Skinner assumes that historians can approach works without presumptions, and he offers no argument to support this assumption. In contrast, I have argued that historians cannot approach works without presumptions, so to rebut Strauss one must argue that historians should adopt presumptions other than those he advocates. Later I will reject his esoteric thesis by arguing for a presumption of sincerity.

our expectation of its occurrence, always presuppose a logical presumption of sincerity. Thus, historians who want to explain why someone held a belief should start by assuming that it was an actual, sincere belief. There are, of course, two types of deception: deception of others and deception of oneself. I will consider them in turn, starting with deception of others.

Without doubt people sometimes practise deception on others. Such acts of deception, however, always presuppose a norm of sincerity. We can deceive people only because they generally assume we are sincere in what we say; after all, if they did not assume we were sincere in what we said, we could not deceive them by saying something we did not sincerely believe. Logically, perhaps, there might be a norm of insincerity as a background to acts of deception in which people spoke sincerely, but this inverted world is hard to conceive of and certainly not one we can recognise as our own.[15] In our world, there exists a presumption of sincerity which acts as an essential prerequisite for the possibility of deception. Again, without doubt we do expect some people in some situations to engage in deception. We only ever do so, however, as a result of previous, specific investigations that themselves rested on a prior, logical presumption of sincerity. We expect people to hide their actual beliefs in some situations only because we know something about the sort of people they are and the sort of situation they are in. We have this knowledge, moreover, only as a result of our having had previous dealings with people, and these dealings ultimately must have occurred against the background of a presumption of sincerity. We come to expect people to practise deception in some circumstances only because we know things about them, so any expectation of deception must be part of the actual development of our knowledge, not part of its logical underpinnings. Sincerity is conceptually prior to insincerity.

The presence of a general presumption of sincerity in our world might not appear to establish that this presumption operates throughout our world. Perhaps one or more special areas within our world are governed by a presumption of insincerity. Leo Strauss has defended a particularly influential version of such an esoteric thesis.[16] Strauss argues that philosophers always hide their actual beliefs behind an exoteric

---

[15] It can be argued that we cannot even conceive of such an inverted world because any language must embody a presumption of truthfulness. D. Lewis, *Convention* (Cambridge, Mass.: Harvard University Press, 1969), pp. 148–52.

[16] L. Strauss, 'Persecution and the art of writing', in *Persecution and the Art of Writing* (Glencoe, Ill.: Free Press, 1952), pp. 22–37. On the place of an esoteric thesis in Strauss's thought, see S. Drury, *The Political Ideas of Leo Strauss* (New York: St Martin's Press, 1988).

veneer in order to make them accessible to worthy and responsible initiates but not the vulgar and dangerous rabble. It is true that he sometimes appears to claim only that historians should allow for some philosophers having hidden their true beliefs to avoid persecution in illiberal societies. He says, for example, 'the book in question must have been composed in an era of persecution, that is, at a time when some political or other orthodoxy was enforced by law or custom'.[17] Actually, however, he adopts a much stronger esoteric thesis than this reasonable one. For a start, Strauss defines persecution incredibly broadly to include 'all writers who hold heterodox opinions', and, even more incredibly, he defines philosophy as inherently heterodox on the grounds that 'there is a necessary conflict between philosophy and politics'.[18] All philosophers, therefore, live in societies in which they hold heterodox opinions that make them liable to persecution. In addition, Strauss argues that we should define persecution in relation to an appropriate view of 'popular education and its limits'; we should recognise that all philosophers believe that 'the gulf separating "the wise" and "the vulgar" was a basic fact of human nature which could not be influenced by any progress of popular education . . . [so] public communication of the philosophic or scientific truth was impossible or undesirable, not only for the time being but for all times'.[19] All philosophers, therefore, live in societies in which the vulgar would persecute them if they made their beliefs public.

Strauss's esoteric thesis leads him to conclude that if historians want to uncover the true beliefs of philosophers, they have to read between the lines. Historians have to use a variety of special techniques to peel away the exoteric skin and reach the esoteric core of a philosopher's writing. Some of Strauss's special techniques are heuristic devices that historians might use on various occasions even if they were not convinced by his esoteric thesis: these include considering what authors do not say as well as what they say, and paying particular attention to any apparent contradictions in a work. But some of his special techniques appear strange, and it is unlikely historians who did not accept something akin to his theory would use them under normal circumstances: these include focusing on the middle of the text understood as metaphorically, as well as literally, its core, and studying the number of chapters and paragraphs in a text. Strauss's arguments for adopting his

---

[17] Strauss, 'Persecution and the art of writing', p. 32.
[18] *Ibid.*, p. 24; L. Strauss, 'On a forgotten kind of writing', in *What is Political Philosophy?* (Glencoe, Ill.: Free Press, 1959), p. 229.   [19] Strauss, 'Persecution and the art of writing', pp. 33 and 34.

esoteric thesis fail for reasons that apply equally to all attempts to defend any such thesis no matter what area of society it purports to concern. I will begin, therefore, by developing general arguments against the very possibility of there being a satisfactory defence of any esoteric thesis. Only later will I apply these arguments to the particular case of Strauss.

Because a general presumption of sincerity operates in our world, proponents of an esoteric thesis must give us reasons to assume people in a particular area of our world habitually practise deception. The reasons they could give us could be either factual or theoretical. Either they could point to our shared understanding of a number of actual instances and say 'look this person really does practise deception an awful lot'; or they could say 'such and such a theory should lead us to expect this person to practise deception an awful lot'. However, both of these sorts of reasons can apply only to the substantive development of the history of ideas, not its logical underpinnings. They can sustain only an expectation, not a presumption, of deception. Proponents of an esoteric thesis in effect mistake an expectation for a presumption.[20] Any conceivable argument for thinking someone will practise deception could support only a concrete expectation of deception. It could support nothing more than this because it would have to depend on specific investigations, which, in turn, would have to embody a prior, logical presumption of sincerity. All of this is fairly obvious with respect to arguments based on facts. An esoteric thesis commends a logical presumption to us prior to any investigation into actual instances, so we could not defend it by pointing to actual instances because to do so we would have to have investigated these instances prior to adopting it. Our investigations of the actual instances would have to precede our adoption of the esoteric thesis, so they would have to deploy our normal presumption of sincerity. Thus, any esoteric thesis based on a factual argument would be a mere expectation, itself parasitic on a logical presumption of sincerity. We cannot justify a presumption of deception with respect to philosophers, politicians, or any other group simply by pointing out how often members of the group practise deception. We cannot do so because we could not know how often they practise deception except through prior investigations of their utterances, and these prior investigations would have to be made using our normal presumption of sincerity.

Exactly the same difficulty undermines the possibility of a satisfactory theoretical defence of an esoteric thesis. Any theoretical argument for

---

[20] For the claim that we should expect insincerity in past philosophers, see F. Nietzsche, *Beyond Good and Evil*, trans. W. Kaufman (New York: Vintage, 1960), p. 30.

thinking that someone or some group will generally practise deception must rest on one (or both) of the following positions: either it must point to a characteristic of the group other than the beliefs they adopt, or it must point to the beliefs they adopt; either it must show that the members of the group have greater reason than others do to hide their beliefs no matter what the nature of their beliefs might be, or it must show that the members of the group are more likely to adopt beliefs they need to hide than are others. Both of these positions, however, can sustain only a concrete expectation, not a logical presumption, of deception. On the one hand, we cannot adopt a logical presumption that the members of a group have a special reason to hide beliefs they hold in common with other members of their society. Although there might have been societies in which a given group had a particular reason to hide commonly held beliefs, there might equally have been societies in which they did not do so. We could conclude that the former had dominated in history only through a concrete investigation, which would have to embody a presumption of sincerity because it would be prior to our adoption of the esoteric thesis. No esoteric thesis can rest on a theory that a group are especially likely to hide their beliefs simply because they are that group. On the other hand, we cannot adopt a logical presumption that the members of a group are particularly likely to adopt beliefs that need to be hidden. The initial argument against such a presumption should be clear by now. To discover what beliefs the group held, and what beliefs other people held, would require a concrete investigation prior to our adoption of the esoteric thesis, and any such investigation would have to incorporate a presumption of sincerity. Esotericists might try to undermine this initial argument, however, by defining the group in a way which would lead us to expect its members to hold certain beliefs. The follow-up argument countering this objection is as follows. If we introduce such a definition of the group, we make the question of whether someone was or was not a member of it dependent on the factual matter of the beliefs he held. To discover whether or not we should apply the esoteric thesis to any given author, we would have to investigate his beliefs to find out whether or not he belonged to the group, and this investigation would have to incorporate a logical presumption of sincerity. An esoteric thesis cannot rest on a theory that a group are especially liable to hold beliefs that need to be hidden. Clearly, therefore, there can be only concrete expectations of deception, not a logical presumption of it.

The preceding argument against the possibility of an esoteric thesis can be illustrated by reference to Strauss. Suppose we think of Strauss's esoteric thesis as a product of his historical studies. In this case, we will want to say that his esoteric thesis cannot be antecedent to his historical studies, so that the latter must incorporate a logical presumption of sincerity. Suppose we now think of Strauss's esoteric thesis as a product of his political theory. After all, he often defends the application of a presumption of deception to philosophers on the grounds that they have to hide their actual beliefs to avoid persecution. As yet, however, we have no reason to believe that philosophers are more liable to persecution than other people. There may have been societies which persecuted philosophers for being philosophers, but equally there may have been societies which did not do so. Strauss could show that the former had dominated only by pursuing a concrete study of past societies; but because this study would be prior to his esoteric thesis, it would have to incorporate a prior, logical presumption of sincerity. Strauss actually suggests that philosophers are peculiarly liable to persecution because of the nature of their beliefs. He says: 'philosophy or science, the highest activity of man, is the attempt to replace opinion about "all things" by knowledge of "all things"; but opinion is the element of society; philosophy or science is therefore the attempt to dissolve the element in which society breathes, and thus it endangers society'.[21] There are two arguments here. The first is that philosophy is a questioning activity, so we should expect philosophers to question orthodox beliefs more often than do other people. The second is that philosophers discover the truth, and that truth is inimical to social order, so we should expect them to keep the truth from the vulgar. Clearly, however, if philosophers are people who question orthodox beliefs; or who uncover dangerous truths, Strauss can decide whether Plato, Aristotle, or anyone else was or was not a philosopher only through a concrete study of their beliefs, but because this study would be prior to his esoteric thesis, it would have to incorporate a prior, logical presumption of sincerity.

Any esoteric thesis must rest on an unacceptable assumption. To conclude that a given group have a special reason for hiding their beliefs, an esotericist must assume, prior to any concrete investigation, that its members are especially likely to hold certain beliefs. But such an assumption must be illegitimate since we cannot know what sort of beliefs the members of a group are likely to hold except as a result of concrete investigations. Strauss, for example, suggests that philosophers

---

[21] Strauss, 'On a forgotten kind of writing', p. 221.

have a special reason to hide their beliefs because they know things which, if widely known, would lead to the disintegration of society. He argues that philosophers accept 'basic truths which would not be pronounced in public by any decent man, because they would do harm to many people who, having been hurt, would naturally be inclined to hurt in turn him who pronounces the unpleasant truths'.[22] This argument assumes, however, that philosophers know the truth, and the truth is dangerous, so philosophers hide the truth, where all of these assumptions are, to say the least, highly dubious. For a start, the assumption that philosophers know the truth contradicts Strauss's own commendable ambition of understanding authors as they understood themselves. If we assume that people knew such and such before we read their works, we cannot be said properly to concentrate on what they thought. Moreover, the assumption that the truth philosophers know is dangerous implies that they always reach more or less the same conclusion. If we assume that philosophers all knew the same thing, we must present disagreements between them as superficial and cosmetic. Finally, the assumption that philosophers hide a truth they know to be dangerous suggests they always intend to convey highly sanitised ideas. If we assume that philosophers intend to hide dangerous truths from the vulgar, we must regard those whom the vulgar took to be attacking the social order as remarkably incompetent in realising their intentions.

The conceptual priority of sincerity implies that expressed beliefs constitute the presumed object for explanation in the history of ideas. Historians should assume that people meant what they said unless there is evidence to the contrary. Besides, the parasitic nature of deception suggests that what people said will be important even if they did not sincerely believe it. People will fail to convince others that they sincerely believe something they do not unless they act in a way the others regard as compatible with their expressed beliefs. If their actions diverge from their expressed beliefs, the others will say that their actions belie their expressed beliefs, and because the others will convict them of insincerity, their attempts at deception will fail. Thus, expressed beliefs restrict the range of actions people can undertake even when they are not sincerely held.[23]

---

[22] Strauss, 'Persecution and the art of writing', p. 36.
[23] Compare the discussion of opposition in Q. Skinner, 'The principles and practice of opposition: the case of Bolingbroke versus Walpole', in N. McKendrick (ed.), *Historical Perspectives: Essays in Honour of J. H. Plumb* (London: Europa Publications, 1974), pp. 93–128.

THE PRIORITY OF THE CONSCIOUS

Self-deception is more complicated than deception. The possibility of people deceiving themselves presupposes that they can express beliefs contrary to their actual beliefs without realising they are doing so. Self-deception presupposes a distinction between the expressed beliefs, which are conscious, and the actual beliefs, which are unconscious. I will argue that conscious beliefs are conceptually prior to unconscious ones in that we define the unconscious as a deviation from the conscious. Before I do so, however, I want to emphasise that because the conceptual priority of the conscious derives from the grammar of our concepts, it restricts the range we can ascribe to any concept of the unconscious, not just the one developed by Sigmund Freud.[24] Unless we are to reject folk psychology, which we will later find we cannot do, we must restrict the range of the unconscious irrespective of the precise content we give to it. At the moment, therefore, I am trying to establish limits to the ways in which historians can use any concept of the unconscious. Only later will I try to specify the content they should give to the concept of the unconscious.

We can reveal the priority of the conscious most easily by considering the way we discuss human actions. Our usual account of our actions suggests they are under our conscious control, in that we act voluntarily. When we say that people went to the café because they were hungry, for example, we imply that they chose to go to the café because they were conscious of their hunger. In contrast, our usual account of unconscious actions suggests that they are beyond our control, not matters of choice. Unconscious behaviour appears to be compulsive. When we say that people went to the café for unconscious reasons, for example, we imply they could not help but go to the café. The significant point here is that when we identify unconscious behaviour as compulsive we contrast it with voluntary behaviour postulated as the norm. Because the idea of compulsive behaviour presupposes a background of voluntary action, and because the converse is not true, therefore, the conscious must be conceptually prior to the unconscious. Conscious beliefs must be conceptually prior to unconscious ones. The conceptual priority of the

[24] The extent of Freud's influence on later psycho-historians is brought out by P. Pomper, *The Structure of Mind in History: Five Major Figures in Psycho-history* (New York: Columbia University, 1985). On different analytic approaches to psycho-history, see P. Loewenberg, 'Psychoanalytic models of history: Freud and after', in W. Runyan (ed.), *Psychology and Historical Interpretation* (New York: Oxford University Press, 1980), pp. 126–56. On non-analytic approaches, see W. Runyan, 'Alternatives to psychoanalytic psychobiography', in *ibid.*, pp. 219–44.

conscious appears in two special features of the way we talk about the unconscious. The first is that we invoke the unconscious only when we cannot make sense of human activity in terms of the conscious. For example, if people thought they went to the café because they were hungry, we would usually accept their conscious assessment of their action. We would look for unconscious beliefs only if, say, someone who constantly went to the café ten minutes after eating a three-course meal thought he did so because of hunger. The conscious is prior to the unconscious in that the unconscious enters our accounts of human activity only on occasions when the conscious fails us. The second derivative aspect of the way we talk about the unconscious is that we do so in terms which mirror our account of the conscious. We try to explain compulsive behaviour in terms of beliefs, desires, and other concepts whose meanings derive from our understanding of the conscious. We do not discuss the unconscious in the mechanical or physical terms we use to describe the workings of a watch or the movements of the planets. For example, while an explanation of compulsive eating in terms of the unconscious might refer to unconscious beliefs that thin is beautiful and beautiful people are happy people, it could not refer to a chemical imbalance in the brain. Indeed, if we could explain compulsive behaviour in physical terms, we would talk of the physiological basis of such behaviour, not its unconscious roots. If we could not find an intelligible pattern to people's actions, if we could not account for their actions in terms of beliefs, desires, and other such concepts, we would talk of their actions being senseless, not of their actions having unconscious springs. The conscious is prior to the unconscious in that our understanding of the unconscious rests on an analogy with the conscious.

The conceptual priority of the conscious over the unconscious can be brought out in a somewhat different way. If we are to be consistent, we must try to reconcile the way we discuss the beliefs and actions of other people with the assumptions we hold about ourselves as people whose beliefs and actions are themselves open to such explanations. Here we typically treat our actions as things we consciously decide to do, and we treat our beliefs as things we consciously consider to be true. Indeed, it is hard to see how we could regard ourselves in any other way. If I did not think my beliefs were things I held to be true, and my actions were things I decided to do, I could not conceive of myself as a human being since I could not make sense of the idea that I had a personality. Thus, as a rule, historians should endeavour to treat others as people who choose to act in certain ways and who consider certain things to be true. As a rule, historians should treat the beliefs and actions of other people as products of conscious minds.

Because the conscious is conceptually prior to the unconscious, conscious beliefs constitute the presumed object of explanation in the history of ideas. To say that we refer to the unconscious only when we cannot make sense of something in terms of the conscious is to say that historians should take a belief to be conscious unless they find doing so unsatisfactory. Besides, the parasitic nature of the unconscious is such that conscious beliefs will be important even when unconscious beliefs are at work. What people consciously believe they believe is itself a conscious belief of theirs, and historians who want to recover the beliefs of an author must consider what he believed he believed. Thus, the conscious always constitutes a part of the webs of belief that historians of ideas seek to explain.

Having established the conceptual priority of conscious beliefs over unconscious ones, we now can go on to consider how we ought to define a conscious belief. To start, we should distinguish the three ways in which someone might hold a belief at any given moment. First, people have self-conscious beliefs – beliefs they are aware of at that particular moment. We are self-consciously aware of a belief only when we are thinking about it: when we stop thinking about it, it ceases to be a part of our self-conscious mind. Although self-conscious beliefs are by definition things people are thinking about, they need not be especially reasonable or measured. They constitute the object of our attention, but our attention might be biased, reckless, or both. Second, people have pre-conscious beliefs – beliefs they hold even though they are not self-consciously aware of them at that particular moment. Pre-conscious beliefs must exist if only because we cannot think about all our beliefs at any single moment in time. The pre-conscious includes both beliefs people have held self-consciously at some time and beliefs we reasonably can ascribe to them even though they never have held them self-consciously. It is even possible for a pre-conscious belief to remain implicit throughout its whole career: think, for example, of the belief that there are more than a hundred trees in the world. Third, people might have unconscious beliefs – beliefs that they are unaware they hold and that contradict their self-conscious beliefs, their pre-conscious beliefs, or both. Our unconscious beliefs are not only implicit, as are our pre-conscious ones, they are also contrary to at least one of our conscious or pre-conscious ones. Conflict or contradiction is an integral feature of the unconscious.

There are a number of good reasons why we should classify pre-conscious beliefs along with self-conscious ones as part of the conscious mind. For a start, some pre-conscious beliefs clearly resemble self-conscious ones, and we cannot distinguish them from our other pre-conscious beliefs, so all pre-conscious beliefs must resemble self-conscious ones. Consider the pre-conscious beliefs that move in and out of the self-conscious mind. Surely these beliefs are beliefs of which we are conscious. Imagine, for example, a time when Besant was thinking about Christian ethics. Surely we do not want to say that her belief that all religions teach the same fundamental truths became unconscious whenever her awareness thus turned towards something else. Surely we want to say rather that her belief in the unity of all religions was a conscious belief even when she was thinking about something else. At any given moment, however, the pre-conscious beliefs of which we have never been aware stand in exactly the same relationship to our consciousness as do those which have moved in and out of our self-consciousness. Thus, because the latter are conscious beliefs, all our pre-conscious beliefs must be conscious beliefs. Consider, for example, ecumenical Christians who would accept that all religions teach the same basic truths although they have never self-consciously thought about such things. These ecumenical Christians have the same attitude as does Besant to the proposition 'all religions teach the same fundamental truths'. They are not thinking about it, but if we asked them about it, they would assent to it. Thus, if Besant holds a conscious belief in religious unity, presumably they do as well. Perhaps critics might try to distinguish Besant from the ecumenical Christians by saying she was once self-consciously aware of her belief whereas they never were. But this distinction fails because it uses past psychological states to define current ones, and we cannot do this without undermining our account of things such as losing one's memory or simply changing one's mind. Imagine, for example, that Besant banged her head, developed total amnesia, read religious books, and thus came to share the beliefs of the ecumenical Christians. Surely we would not want to say Besant believed in religious unity consciously whereas the Christians did so only unconsciously. Surely we would not want to say Besant held a conscious belief the Christians did not merely because of something she had believed prior to her amnesia.

Semantic holism provides us with another good reason for taking pre-conscious beliefs to be part of the conscious, not the unconscious, mind. Because our beliefs map on to reality only as an interconnected web, what we believe to be true of reality by a particular self-conscious belief must depend on our other beliefs. Thus, assuming we cannot be aware of all the relevant beliefs at the same time, what we believe by a self-conscious belief must depend on a number of our pre-conscious beliefs. Our self-conscious beliefs represent the tip of an iceberg which can exist only in conjunction with the submerged beliefs of our pre-conscious. We can think self-consciously about a belief only by taking various pre-conscious beliefs for granted, although, of course, which beliefs we think about and which we take for granted can change from moment to moment. Semantic holism suggests, therefore, that we cannot separate self-conscious beliefs from a background of pre-conscious ones. Indeed, we can show that self-conscious beliefs rely on a background of pre-conscious ones without relying on semantic holism. Earlier I pointed out that our self-conscious beliefs need not be especially reasonable or measured. Most of our self-conscious awareness is in fact spontaneous and immediate rather than reflective; we rarely think about what our beliefs entail or how they link up with one another. Crucially, we can act in accord with such unreflective, self-conscious beliefs only because we also possess a suitable set of pre-conscious beliefs. If we had to think self-consciously about every belief entailed by every action we performed, we would hardly ever be able to act. When soccer players head the ball, for instance, they do not pause to think consciously about the possibility of catching it: rather, their self-conscious mind focuses on where they should direct it while their pre-conscious deals with things such as the rule forbidding them to handle it. Our very ability to act in accord with our self-conscious beliefs typically requires us to take a bundle of pre-conscious beliefs for granted. This implies, moreover, that we cannot separate our self-conscious beliefs from their pre-conscious background. The pre-conscious must be an integral part of the conscious mind.

Not only are our pre-conscious beliefs bound indissolubly to our self-conscious ones, they are also clearly distinct from our unconscious beliefs. Whereas pre-conscious beliefs support conscious ones, unconscious beliefs are in conflict with conscious ones. It is true that some scholars want to defend a broader concept of the unconscious than the one we are adopting. They want to define the unconscious to include any belief we would not acknowledge we hold even though we do. These scholars might be unhappy at our stipulation that unconscious beliefs must contradict other beliefs. Moreover, their broader concept of the unconscious might seem to open up the possibility of assimilating at least part of the pre-conscious to the unconscious. Actually, however, there is little difference between their broad concept of the unconscious and our more restricted one since theirs, too, in effect makes conflict central to the unconscious. After all, if people will not acknowledge that they hold a belief that they do, they will presumably affirm the belief that they do not believe it, so presumably their belief in it contradicts their belief that they do not believe it. Besides, even if there are some occasions when a broader account of the unconscious would differ from our more restricted one, we still must stick with ours. We must define the unconscious in terms of contradiction because our concern lies with cases of self-deception and these always entail contradiction. We have introduced the idea of unconscious beliefs as a logical corollary of self-deception, so the nature of self-deception must provide the context in which we define the unconscious. Thus, unconscious beliefs must not only be beliefs the believer does not accept, but also beliefs that are in some way contrary to the conscious beliefs of the believer. Just as deception occurs when one person persuades another of something he believes to be false, so self-deception occurs when people consciously believe something they unconsciously believe to be false. To deceive oneself is to tell oneself something one does not believe. Because we equate the unconscious with self-deception, unconscious beliefs must be contrary to conscious ones. Yet we ascribe pre-conscious beliefs to people when we take their actions to imply they hold these beliefs, so pre-conscious beliefs must be implicit within, or at least compatible with, the conscious beliefs guiding their actions. Thus, because unconscious beliefs are contrary to conscious ones, whereas pre-conscious beliefs are compatible with conscious ones, pre-conscious beliefs cannot belong in the unconscious mind.

The conceptual priority of the conscious, defined to include the pre-conscious as well as the self-conscious, directs us to a hermeneutics of recovery. Historians of ideas set out initially to recover the conscious beliefs of authors. Some critics complain that a hermeneutics of recovery forces historians to accept the accounts authors give of their works. They say that it denies historians any way of making sense of occasions in which the meaning of a work differs from the understanding its author has of it.[25] This criticism does not apply to the position we have adopted, since our position allows historians to go beyond the accounts

[25] J. Habermas, 'The hermeneutic claim to universality', in J. Bleicher (ed.), *Contemporary Hermeneutics: Hermeneutics and Method, Philosophy and Critique* (London: Routledge & Kegan Paul, 1980), pp. 181–211. Also see C. Olsen, 'Knowledge of one's own intentional actions', *Philosophical Quarterly* 19 (1969), 324–36.

authors give of their own works in two ways. For a start, the conceptual priority of the conscious does not imply that historians can never refer to the unconscious. On the contrary, when historians cannot make sense of their material in terms of the conscious mind, they can legitimately invoke the unconscious. When they thus introduce the unconscious, they not only go beyond the account an author gives of his work, they also reject this account. They must do so because people's unconscious beliefs necessarily contradict their conscious ones. The second way in which historians can go beyond the accounts authors give of their works is by referring to pre-conscious beliefs authors were not aware they held. Whereas authors cannot describe their works in terms of beliefs they do not realise they hold, historians will want to refer to such beliefs whenever they think these beliefs influenced the meaning of a work. None the less, because pre-conscious beliefs are still the beliefs of the author, an understanding of a work as expressing such beliefs still must have a certain relationship to the self-understanding of its author. Pre-conscious beliefs are implicit within, or at least compatible with, self-conscious beliefs. Ideally, therefore, authors should acknowledge that such beliefs are implicit in their work, and they must at least recognise that an account based on such beliefs represents a plausible account of their work. In practice, of course, historians rarely have the opportunity to check their account of a work with its author, but the absence of such an opportunity does not affect the underlying principle. Historians can sidestep the principle that their account of a work must be one the author could have found plausible only by ascribing unconscious beliefs to the author.

Other critics complain that a hermeneutics of recovery requires historians to seek psychic identification with their subjects. Yet our arguments do not demand that historians possess any special facility for re-enacting the lives of others. In our view, historians ascribe beliefs and pro-attitudes to people, but they do not do so on the grounds that they have relived the mental lives of the people concerned. Indeed, too great a concern with empathy rests on a mistaken analysis of objectivity. The problem is that even the most scrupulous proponents of history as re-enactment, such as R. G. Collingwood, slide from a weak to a strong account of empathy. A correct, weak concern with empathy asserts only that historians should not attempt to 'emulate the scientist in searching for causes or laws of events' since to understand any action we have to discover 'the thought expressed in it'.[26] An erroneous, strong concern

---

[26] Collingwood, *Idea of History*, p. 214.

with empathy asserts that to discover the thoughts expressed in past actions we have to 're-enact the past' in our own mind, we have to 'go through the process the [actor] did in deciding on this particular [action]'.[27] Now, if objectivity depended on pure perceptions, historians of ideas might have to re-enact the mental processes of the authors they study in order to have a pure experience of the viewpoints of these authors. Actually, however, because objectivity rests on a practice of comparison, the worth of the histories we tell does not depend on our successfully having identified with our subjects. Indeed, as with most logics of discovery, a preoccupation with empathy would be a useless hindrance to the historian. If a historian succeeded in entering into the psyche of his subjects so as to go through their mental processes, he would find he could not refer to their pre-conscious and unconscious beliefs, so he would be unable to transcend the limits of the accounts his subjects would give of their own works. Thus, because pre-conscious and unconscious beliefs sometimes do constitute part of the meaning of a work, successful psychic identification would be a barrier to our understanding the past.

Although there cannot be a logic of discovery for the history of ideas, we can offer heuristic hints to historians. Because historians of ideas hope to recover the self-conscious and pre-conscious beliefs of people from the past, they should be aware of the pitfalls of abstraction and jargon. When they explicate a work using a language the author would not have used, they should remember that the language they adopt must convey the beliefs of the author. The further they move from the concepts of the author, the harder they will have to labour to show how these concepts illuminate the beliefs of the author. One of the roles of historians of ideas is to act as translators explaining the people of the past to us today. Generally they will find it difficult to perform this role adequately if they pay insufficient attention to the way the people of the past understood themselves. We should be quite clear, therefore, that to allow historians to go beyond the self-understanding of their subjects is not to license insensitivity to unfamiliar cultures.

THE PRIORITY OF THE RATIONAL

It might appear that we can ascribe conceptual priority to rational beliefs along with conscious ones. Because we regard both unconscious

[27] *Ibid.*, pp. 282–3. On the metaphysical and spiritual themes lurking in the concept of re-enactment, see D. Bates, 'Rediscovering Collingwood's spiritual history (in and out of context)', *History and Theory* 35 (1996), 29–55.

and irrational beliefs as somewhat pathological, we might be tempted, without further reflection, to treat the latter as part of the former defined in contrast to normal beliefs. Actually, however, we can imagine an unconscious set of beliefs being rational in the substantive sense of being objectively valid let alone in the broad sense of being consistent. Indeed, we can also imagine a conscious set of beliefs being irrational in the broad sense of being inconsistent let alone in the substantive sense of not being objectively valid. Although these imagined possibilities might strike us as improbable, they are not logically incoherent. Further reflection, however, will lead us to conclude there are good reasons for ascribing conceptual priority to rational, consistent beliefs as well as conscious ones. A critic might complain at the outset that a restricted concept of rationality, understood as consistency, has no real content since everyone can meet its requirements.[28] Maybe the critic would be right if we were hoping to use rationality as a category for evaluating the beliefs of others. But even if a restricted concept of rationality cannot play an evaluative role, we still must use it as a category for understanding the beliefs of others. We must do so because our folk psychology gives such a role to such a category.

Although we cannot rule out the possibility of irrationality, we can establish the conceptual priority of rational beliefs defined in terms of consistency. We can do so using an argument parallel to the one we gave to establish a norm of sincerity. Crucially, there could not be a language at all unless saying one thing ruled out saying something else. Our ability to ascribe a meaning to innumerable utterances depends on the fact that to assert them is to deny the contrary.[29] If, for instance, saying something was somewhere did not rule out saying it was not there, the statement that it was there would have no meaning. (Of course, some objects might have special properties enabling them to be somewhere and not to be there at the same time, but in this case to say something without these properties was somewhere would have to be to rule out saying it was not there.) The very existence of a language presupposes a norm of consistency governing its use in particular utterances. Thus, even if a language could exist without an identifiable concept akin to our idea of rationality, it still would have to embody attributes akin to those we equate with rationality, notably, a concern with consistency. What is

---

[28] A view suggested perhaps by Rorty, *Philosophy and the Mirror of Nature*, p. 174.

[29] Compare D. Dennett, 'Intentional systems', in *Brainstorms: Philosophical Essays on Mind and Psychology* (Brighton, Sussex: Harvester Press, 1981), pp. 3–22. As we have seen, even philosophers who reject the traditional notion of analyticity accept that a concern with consistency must be a feature of all webs of belief. Quine, *Word and Object*, p. 59.

more, these attributes would have to constitute a norm within the language because if its users did not presume consistency, they would not be able to ascribe meanings to utterances. The place of a norm of consistency in language entails at least a tacit acceptance of the conceptual priority of rational beliefs. We could not treat people's use of language as governed by a norm of consistency unless we presumed they held consistent beliefs. If, for example, someone said something was somewhere, we could not take this to rule out him saying it was not there unless we presumed he did not believe it to be both there and not there. Our ability to ascribe meanings to utterances depends, therefore, on our ascribing conceptual priority to rational beliefs.

Once again, we can highlight the conceptual priority of rationality by emphasising the need to reconcile the way we propose to explain the beliefs of others with the assumptions we hold about ourselves as people who hold beliefs amenable to explanation. We should treat the beliefs of others as consistent because we treat our own beliefs as consistent. Indeed, it is difficult to imagine how we could avoid treating our own beliefs in terms of a presumption of rational consistency. After all, if I did not think my beliefs were more or less consistent, I could not conceive of myself as someone who could adopt reasons for action in the light of my beliefs, so I would have to conclude I lacked any stable identity. Because we presume we have rational beliefs, and because we should try to reconcile the way we treat other people with the view we have of ourselves as such a person, we should initially presume that others too have rational beliefs.

We can even ascribe to rational beliefs an absolute, as well as a conceptual, priority. Consider the implications of our characteristically having reasons for acting as we do. Because we cannot act in incompatible ways at the same time, our beliefs must exhibit a fairly high degree of consistency at any given moment in time since they inform our actions. Because we act as we do, we must have a set of beliefs capable of sustaining such actions, so our beliefs must be fairly rational. Successfully to go to the delicatessen and buy food, for example, I have to believe it exists, is open, and sells food. I cannot believe, say, that it is open but does not exist. Likewise, because our behaviour does not consist of a series of unconnected actions but rather a series of linked actions sometimes organised according to complex plans, our beliefs must exhibit some stability through time. Because we can perform a series of actions in accord with an overall plan, we must have a set of beliefs capable of sustaining such actions, so our beliefs must be fairly stable. Successfully to plan a skiing holiday, for example, I have to believe I am going to a place where there will be snow and where I will ski, and I have to do so while I book the hotel, buy the tickets, pack, and so on. I cannot change my beliefs so that, say, when I pack I do so in accord with the belief that I am going to a tropical beach. Our beliefs must cohere to the extent necessary to enable us to act in the world, and, indeed, to act over time in accord with complex plans. Our beliefs must be fairly consistent and fairly stable. They must be fairly rational. Of course, because the actual priority of rational belief is far from absolute, people can adopt inconsistent beliefs: they can make mistakes in reasoning, or their pro-attitudes can influence their beliefs illegitimately. Moreover, because the particular set of consistent beliefs someone holds depends on the actions he performs, and because we cannot identify a set of actions people must perform, therefore, the actual priority of rational belief does not enable us to identify even a minimal way in which people's beliefs must be consistent. All we can say is that because X performs the set of actions Y, he must hold beliefs possessing a minimal consistency Z, where the content we give to Z depends on the nature of Y. Fortunately, however, the limits to any detailed analysis of the actual priority of rational beliefs does not affect my arguments as these arguments will draw only on the conceptual priority of such beliefs.

The conceptual priority of the rational means that rational beliefs constitute the presumed object for explanation in the history of ideas. For a start, because rationality is actually prior to irrationality, historians who want to explain a belief will usually be considering a rational one, unless they have deliberately selected an irrational one. In addition, because rationality is conceptually prior to irrationality, historians who want to explain a belief should presume it is rational unless they have a special reason to expect it not to be so. Historians should describe beliefs as irrational only when they fail to make sense of them in rational terms. If, for example, they find that someone believed both that something was somewhere and that it was not there, they should look for another belief to reconcile these beliefs, before they leap to the conclusion that the beliefs were irrational.

The priority of rational belief applies only to a limited concept of rationality understood as internal consistency. There are, however, philosophers who would have us adopt different concepts of rationality.[30] Some of them suggest we should restrict the idea of rational belief

---

[30] On the different issues raised by different concepts of rationality, see S. Lukes, 'Some problems about rationality', in B. Wilson (ed.), *Rationality* (Oxford: Basil Blackwell, 1970), pp. 194–213.

to objectively valid beliefs. Others suggest we should stretch it to include any belief serving any given end. Consider first the claims of objective rationality. The argument we deployed to defend a presumption of consistency bears a clear resemblance to the one used to support a principle of charity by philosophers such as Donald Davidson. Davidson's principle of charity would have us presume that others hold beliefs we hold true. He argues that semantic holism implies that if most of the others' beliefs were ones we did not hold true, we could not grasp what objects they were talking about.[31] There are two points to be made about Davidson's principle of charity. The first is that even if he were right, his position would not sustain a presumption of objective rationality. It would not do so because the same belief can be objective in one context but not in another. It is possible we and those we interpret might share a belief that is objective for us given a comparison between the rival webs of belief available in our culture but not objective for them given a comparison between the rival webs of belief available in their culture. Because the objective status of a belief varies with the intellectual context, Davidson's principle of charity does not constitute a presumption of objective rationality. The second point to make about Davidson's argument is that it is flawed. To know what objects others are talking about we need to share very few beliefs with them since we can pick out the objects we believe they are talking about using concepts we do not ascribe to them.[32] Consider, for instance, people from another time or culture who conceive of the moon very differently from us because they hold very different beliefs from us. We still can pick out the object about which they hold the relevant beliefs using our concept of the moon. The open nature of language and thought means we need hold very few shared beliefs in common with those whom we wish to understand.

The following argument also might seem to establish the viability of extending the priority of rationality from consistent belief to objective belief defined in terms of our anthropological epistemology. Human actions are generally successful, so human perceptions must be generally accurate, so we can presume that human beliefs generally are objectively rational. We should presume that human beliefs usually rest on valid evidence and valid reasoning because the broad accuracy of human perceptions gives us good reason to think things usually are as we

---

[31] Davidson, 'Radical interpretation' and 'Thought and talk', in *Inquiries into Truth and Interpretation*, pp. 125–39 and 155–70.

[32] Compare C. McGinn, 'Charity, interpretation, and belief', *Journal of Philosophy* 74 (1977), 521–35.

perceive them to be. Although we used a related argument to rebut the charge of relativism, we cannot defend a presumption of objective rationality in this way. We cannot do so because objectivity depends not only on the broad accuracy of our perceptions, but also, and more importantly, on a comparison between different webs of belief. Thus, a presumption in favour of accurate perception by itself cannot sustain a presumption in favour of objective belief. Consider, for example, two scientists who believe the universe is in no sense probabilistic, and who justify this belief by reference to a given set of perceptions. For a scientist who lived in the nineteenth century, this belief would have been objective because it would have been part of the best web of beliefs then available. For a scientist who lives today, in contrast, this belief is not objective because it is contrary to the Born interpretation of quantum mechanics, which is part of the best web of beliefs now available. Both scientists generally have accurate perceptions, which is why we can reject relativism, but whereas one scientist reaches an objective belief from these perceptions, the other does not, which is why we cannot move from the general accuracy of our perceptions to a presumption in favour of objective belief. Although our regulative ideal of truth postulates a corresponding account of objective rationality, objective rationality so understood has no conceptual priority in individual cases and so no explanatory power.

Most accounts of objective rationality still suggest that we should regard an individual belief as rational provided the believer has valid grounds for holding it to be true. For example, a belief in quantum mechanics is objectively rational because we can ground it on various inter-subjective observations, whereas a belief in voodoo is not because we cannot so ground it. Clearly, however, all such accounts of objective rationality fail together with the possibility of establishing a logic of justification. They fail because they presuppose a procedure, or set of criteria, by which we can reach, or identify, rational beliefs. Proponents of an objective concept of rationality, like proponents of a logic of discovery, hope to define particular beliefs as objectively rational, or as objectively true, independently of the webs of belief to which they belong. They postulate a test such that if a belief passes, it is objective or true, and if it fails, it is irrational or false. In contrast, we have seen that we cannot test individual beliefs without assuming the validity of other beliefs, so that no single test can determine the status of an individual belief. Thus, just as there cannot be a logic of justification, so we cannot define objective rationality in terms of valid grounds for holding a

particular belief. Any viable account of objective rationality must portray objectivity as a property of a web of beliefs, not individual beliefs.

We can pronounce a web of beliefs to be objectively rational only as a
result of a comparison with its rivals. Anyone who wants to do so is, of
course, free to use the term rational to pick out objective beliefs defined
in this way, but if people do this, they thereby deprive the concept of
rationality of its explanatory power.[33] The problem is that we must allow
a legitimate role to dogmatism. We must allow people to hold on to
theories that appear to be on the wane while they try to resolve, in a
positive and fruitful manner, the particular problems those theories
confront. We must allow them to do so because they might succeed, in
which case they would revive the fortunes of those theories. Thus,
having beliefs that are not objective cannot be a compelling reason to
reject those beliefs. On the contrary, because theories can make come-
backs, we might do better if we sometimes stick with our beliefs when
they are under pressure, rather than always swaying with the prevailing
wind. Moreover, because people do not have a compelling reason to
reject beliefs that are not objective, we do not have any reason to
presume they do so, which means that objective beliefs do not have the
conceptual, explanatory priority over other beliefs that consistent beliefs
do. To identify rational belief with objective belief is, therefore, to
deprive it of its explanatory power. (Of course, despite their lack of
explanatory power, concepts of objective rationality might be useful as
predictive tools: thus, scholars who use concepts of objective rationality
to build models of human action would be well advised to describe their
conclusions as ideal types, not explanations of actual behaviour.) Perhaps, however, critics might argue that more and more people will
generally reject a theory if it goes on and on failing to make a comeback,
so in the long run people will generally convert to objective beliefs.
These critics might be right, but their argument shows only that we must
distinguish objectivity as a feature of human beliefs from rationality as a
means of explaining human beliefs. In so far as individuals as a collective
generally convert to webs of belief that are objective, objectivity will be a
feature of the changing composition of human belief. But because
individuals as individuals do not have a compelling reason to convert to
webs of belief that are objective, objectivity cannot act as an explanatory

---

[33] Concepts of objective rationality typically lack explanatory power because they are normative:
they tell us how we ought to go about forming beliefs, not how we do so. For an attempt to use
evolutionary theory to bridge this gap, see R. Nozick, *The Nature of Rationality* (Princeton:
Princeton University Press, 1993).

concept. Perhaps people generally do convert to objective beliefs, but this does not mean that they do so for compelling reasons. The concept of rational belief has explanatory power only when we restrict its content to consistency.

Let us turn now to the claims of instrumental rationality, that is, rational belief defined as any belief serving a given end. Although instrumental concepts of rationality usually appear in works on rational action, some philosophers have developed a related concept of rational belief, perhaps without being aware of doing so. A number of philosophers inspired by Wittgenstein chafe at the restraints imposed by an insistence that all our beliefs must aim at an understanding of the world. D. Z. Philips, Peter Winch, and others try to use Wittgenstein's later work to locate religious beliefs in a conceptual space where they would become more or less invulnerable to charges of cognitive irrationality.[34] They invoke Wittgenstein in defence of the idea that the meaning of religious terms derives from their place in a specific language game, or way of life, so that we cannot condemn religious beliefs from outside religious discourse, or religious life. They argue that religious beliefs can be evaluated only from within the religious life of which they are part. Within this religious life, moreover, many key beliefs serve emotional or symbolic functions rather than cognitive ones. The rationality of religious beliefs depends, therefore, solely on their performing an emotional or symbolic role, not on their cognitive value in relation to other beliefs. The thrust of my objection to their argument will be that we cannot isolate different language games played by any one individual in the decisive way they propose. Because our beliefs form a single, inter-linked web, any belief must stand in a cognitive relationship to other beliefs, so no belief can be isolated in an allegedly distinct part of our life to which we ascribe purely emotional or symbolic functions. Indeed, I think Wittgenstein used the idea of a language game to repudiate a traditional objectivism, according to which we can decide issues of objectivity or rationality from outside all human practices, not to suggest we should deconstruct individuals by allowing them to operate with incompatible criteria of objectivity or rationality in different areas of their lives.

In any case, no matter how we should make sense of Wittgenstein's later philosophy, we confront the difficulty that some of his followers challenge the validity of historians working with a concept of rationality

[34] See, in particular, D. Philips, 'Philosophy, theology, and the reality of God', *Philosophical Quarterly* 13 (1963), 344–50; and P. Winch, 'Understanding a primitive society', in *Ethics and Action* (London: Routledge & Kegan Paul, 1972), particularly pp. 38–40.

as consistency. Although the proponents of an instrumental concept of rational belief, such as Philips and Winch, typically want only to fend off the threat that over-ambitious analyses of objective rationality pose to religious and ethical beliefs, their arguments also challenge our more moderate analysis of rationality as consistency. Their arguments imply that people can have contradictory beliefs that are none the less rational since they fulfil emotional or symbolic functions.[35] Some beliefs, Philips and Winch suggest, enable people to make sense of things of great importance to them. Beliefs can help people to distance themselves from things of great value to them in a way which enables them emotionally to come to terms with what happens if these things fail them. Christians, for example, might comprehend a dreadful tragedy in terms of God's will, and doing so might help them to cope with the tragedy. Similarly, other beliefs act as symbols of things people value greatly such as ethical standards. A belief in Christ, for example, might stand less for a belief in the actual incarnation of God than for a commitment to Jesus as the symbol of an ideal, moral life.

Much of the appeal of an instrumental concept of rational belief rests on a muddle between symbolic beliefs and symbolic statements. A statement can be either a literal one expressing certain beliefs or a symbolic one indicating certain beliefs. In both cases, however, the beliefs themselves are literal ones. If people say they believe in Christ, they might be either literally asserting a belief in the incarnation of God or symbolically asserting a belief in Jesus's life as a moral ideal. In both cases, however, the belief they hold is a literal one: either they believe that Christ was the incarnation of God or they believe that the life of Jesus provides us with a moral ideal. Moreover, in both cases, because the belief itself is a literal belief, we should ponder its consistency with the other beliefs of the author. A symbolic statement symbolises a literal belief, so although we should treat symbolic statements as things to be decoded, we should approach the decoded, literal beliefs with a pre-sumption of consistency. The mere existence of symbolic statements does not require us, therefore, to retreat to an instrumental concept of rational belief. Sophisticated proponents of an instrumental concept of rational belief argue that some beliefs fulfil emotional functions we cannot decode into literal beliefs. Some beliefs are expressive: they express an emotional attitude instead of indicating a literal belief about something.[36] A belief in the will of God, for example, could be a way of

[35] As is suggested by Winch, 'Understanding a primitive Society', particularly pp. 38–40.
[36] This is a central theme of D. Philips, *The Concept of Prayer* (London: Routledge & Kegan Paul, 1967).

finding meaning in life or of accepting things being as they are. Crucially, however, expressive beliefs are not purely expressive since they always entail other literal beliefs. A belief in the will of God, for example, assumes there is a God who in some sense wills things to happen on earth. Thus, because expressive beliefs imply actual beliefs, and because these actual beliefs must be consistent with other actual beliefs, we should approach expressive beliefs with a suitable presumption of consistency. Indeed, the preceding argument suggests that all instrumental beliefs are likely to be self-defeating. Semantic holism implies that the adoption of an instrumental belief will have a ripple effect on one's other beliefs as one modifies them to accommodate it, and we should expect this effect to result in false beliefs which will then do one more damage, sadness, or whatever, than one avoids by holding the instrumental belief.[37] As a last resort, proponents of an instrumental concept of rational belief might argue that although most expressive beliefs imply literal ones, some do not. Surely, however, any belief that fulfils an emotional function must be a belief in a thing or a state of affairs, where to believe in a thing or a state of affairs must be, at the very least, to put one's faith in it, and to put one's faith in it, one must believe in either its existence or its desirability, so one must hold a literal belief. All expressive beliefs presuppose a belief in the existence or desirability of a thing or a state of affairs, even if they are not reducible to such a belief. No belief stands outside of a larger web of beliefs in the way it would have to if it were to avoid being implicated in our cognitive aims. All beliefs presuppose some actual beliefs which we should approach with a presumption of consistency.

We have found that historians should accept the conceptual priority of rational beliefs, where rationality is defined as inner consistency. Two well-known dangers await any such proposal that historians of ideas treat their material in rational terms: the dangers are ethnocentrism and relativism. Can we plot a course between a concept of rationality that excludes so much that it falls into ethnocentrism and one that includes so much that it falls into relativism? Consider first the danger that to portray beliefs as rational will be to translate them into the discourse of modern Western culture and thereby invalidate the self-understanding of other times and cultures. Most people who worry about such ethnocentrism seem to have in mind the following: it would be ethnocentric to assume that all attempts to understand the world are self-critical in the sense of, say, looking for falsifying evidence. They need not worry

---

[37] Compare, Nozick, *Nature of Rationality*, pp. 69–71.

that we will make this mistake. Our approach does not entail a presumption in favour of a self-critical stance towards one's beliefs. Indeed, a rejection of the conceptual priority of objective rationality requires us to steer clear of any such presumption. To be rational, a set of beliefs must be consistent, but there is no reason to suppose that it need be especially reflective, self-critical, or concerned with the evidence. We should be clear about this because if we equated rational belief with a self-critical stance, we would also invite a charge of intellectualism and so irrelevance. Most people accept a large number of beliefs on the authority of others. They do so because to check and validate all their beliefs would require an inordinate amount of time and energy. Thus, if we identified rationality with a self-critical disposition, we would restrict the applicability of our concept of rationality to a small proportion of beliefs. A concept of rationality as consistency, in contrast, allows us to avoid intellectualism. By equating rationality with consistency, we make it a feature of webs of belief rather than a type of action or a disposition. By ensuring that rationality does not depend on a type of action or a disposition, we make it possible for beliefs to be rational no matter how they are reached and no matter how unreflectively they are held.

Some people who worry about ethnocentrism, however, seem to have in mind the following: it would be ethnocentric to insist that beliefs must represent an attempt to understand the world. We cannot agree with this because our analysis of expressive beliefs showed that all beliefs are entangled in webs of belief that represent attempts to understand the world. Of course, if something is ethnocentric and true, we still should accept it. Indeed, an innocent form of ethnocentrism is inevitable since we do not have pure perceptions and so are bound to approach others from within our own cultural perspective.[38] What concerns us, however, is not the charge that we have fallen for this innocent ethnocentrism, but that we have fallen for a pernicious ethnocentrism which will make us inflexible during our encounter with others. The charge is that we are committed to the universality, or superiority, of our own perspective. Fortunately, however, we need not accept that our concept of rationality is ethnocentric in a pernicious sense. For a start, our concept of rationality implies that beliefs in other cultures are equally rational to beliefs in our culture provided only they are equally consistent. This means that we cannot say we are more rational or that we think more logically than do members of other cultures. Moreover, our concept of

[38] R. Rorty, 'On ethnocentrism: a reply to Clifford Geertz', *Michigan Quarterly Review* 25 (1986), 525–34.

rationality requires us to understand beliefs in other cultures in terms of the other beliefs of these cultures. We must try to make sense of other beliefs by knitting them together in consistent webs. In contrast, critics who would insist on our treating beliefs in other cultures as expressive ones will be patronising to these other cultures. When people talk about things such as the will of God, they typically think they are making literal statements, not expressive ones. Thus, critics who took such utterances to be expressive would fail to take them as their authors would wish. Indeed, if critics took a belief to be expressive when the believer thought it was literal, the priority of the conscious implies that the critics would thereby suggest that the belief was so bizarre they had to introduce the unconscious to make sense of it. Clearly, therefore, we show most respect for people from other cultures when we treat their beliefs as genuine attempts to understand the world.

The second danger to confront any proposal that historians of ideas treat their material in rational terms is relativism. The problem is that if what counts as a rational belief depends on the other beliefs of the believer, then rationality is relative. Worse still, a relative concept of rationality seems to cover just about everything and so be vacuous. Most people who worry about relativism seem to have in mind a traditional, anthropological idea. Anthropological relativism suggests that almost all our beliefs, including apparently irrational ones such as those associated with magic, are rational in their own terms. Beliefs we think of as irrational are in fact rational.[39] Our position requires us to accept this traditional, anthropological idea. Beliefs such as those associated with magic are indeed rational provided only they are consistent. To adopt an anthropological relativism with respect to rationality is not, however, to adopt a thesis of incommensurability which would make objectivity relative.[40] On the contrary, it is to admit, albeit tacitly, that the thesis of incommensurability is false. The anthropological practice of showing other beliefs to be rational in their own terms presupposes that they possess some features in common with ours. Before we can make a web of beliefs appear internally consistent, we must find it intelligible, so we must be able to translate it into our terms, so it must have some features in common with ours, notably a concern with

---

[39] As is suggested by Winch, 'Understanding a primitive society'.
[40] Although Winch draws on Wittgenstein to argue that anthropological relativism leads to a scepticism grounded on the problem of the incommensurability of different concepts of rationality, other philosophers have argued powerfully that Wittgenstein should not be used in this way. See, in particular, J. Lear, 'Leaving the world alone', *Journal of Philosophy* 79 (1982), 382–403.

consistency.[41] What all of this suggests is, first, that we can rebut the thesis of incommensurability underlying relativist views of objectivity by insisting on the possibility of our comparing rival webs of belief; and, second, that an insistence on the possibility of our comparing rival webs of belief does not entail a concept of objective rationality. A relativist view of objectivity is false because we can compare various webs of belief in terms of our criteria of comparison; but people who do not hold objectively valid beliefs do not necessarily hold irrational ones. The possibility of our being rational without being objective does not rule out the possibility of our being objective.

Some people who worry about relativism, however, seem to have in mind a modern, nihilistic idea. Nihilistic relativism suggests that all beliefs, including apparently rational ones such as those associated with science, have an irrational origin epitomised above all by the will to power. Beliefs we think of as rational are in fact irrational.[42] Our position enables us to reject this modern, nihilistic idea. We have avoided a descent into nihilistic relativism by divorcing the rationality of beliefs from the nature of their origins. Our concept of rationality as consistency frees rationality from a dependence on any particular account of the formation of beliefs; it allows for beliefs being rational even if they derive from something like the will to power. Whatever the source of webs of belief, some of them might be consistent and so rational, and others might be inconsistent and so irrational. It is important thus to avoid nihilistic relativism because such relativism is vacuous. The vacuity of nihilistic relativism appears in the way it refutes itself. If all beliefs are equally irrational, the belief that all beliefs are equally irrational must be irrational, so to hold it, let alone propound it, makes no sense. If people think all beliefs are absurd, they think their beliefs are absurd, so they should stop propagating such nonsense. The self-refutation of nihilistic relativism shows that its advocates cannot make sense of their own arguments, as numerous philosophers have pointed out. In addition, the self-refutation of nihilistic relativism has another often unrecognised implication. It shows that we must reject relativism because of the very nature of our being in the world. The very idea of having beliefs presupposes that something is true and something is false,

---

[41] It is a genuine requirement of interpretation, in a way Davidson's stronger principle of charity is not, that we must share some beliefs with the appropriate others. See D. Lewis, 'Radical interpretation', in *Philosophical Papers*, vol. 1 (New York: Oxford University Press, 1983), pp. 108–18.

[42] See the essays collected in M. Foucault, *Power/Knowledge: Selected Interviews and Other Writings 1972–77*, ed. C. Gordon. (Brighton, Sussex: Harvester Press, 1980).

so relativism is false. Again, either we must accept relativism is false or we must deny we hold beliefs, but to deny we hold beliefs would be to deny we could act on them in the world, so we must accept that relativism is false.

I have completed my analysis of the objects studied by historians of ideas. Earlier I argued that historians of ideas use relics from the past to obtain knowledge of historical meanings understood as individual viewpoints. Scholars attack such intentionalist analyses of historical meaning as implausible for two main reasons. The first source of opposition to intentionalism is a rejection of atomistic individualism. Contextualists and conventionalists often appear to reject intentionalism because they want to stress the way individuals are embedded in social contexts. They want to give due weight to the influence of a social inheritance on the language and ideas of the individual. In contrast, we found that to reject atomistic individualism is not to oppose intentionalism. Historical meanings consist of individual viewpoints; it is just that individuals reach the viewpoints they do only from within, and under the influence of, particular social contexts. The second source of opposition to intentionalism is a rejection of the possibility of our having pure experiences of past intentions. Reception theorists and others reject intentionalism because they want to stress the way the presuppositions of a reader always influence his reading of a work. They want to give due weight to the influence of the relevant social and historical context on the language and ideas of the historian. In contrast, we found that to reject the possibility of pure experiences of past intentions is not to oppose intentionalism. Because we cannot have pure experiences of anything, objective knowledge cannot depend on pure experiences. Historians can have knowledge of past intentions, therefore, even though their presuppositions always influence their reading of a work. Unless we wish to defend either the idea that our social inheritance determines what we say or the idea that we have pure experiences, we should stick with an intentionalist analysis of historical meaning. Intentionalists, however, have not been clear enough about their own position. In particular, I argued earlier that historical meanings did not consist of strong intentions defined as the conscious prior purposes of authors and authors alone, but rather of individual viewpoints defined as the meaning an utterance had for its author or a later reader whether consciously or unconsciously. Now I have filled out this analysis of the historical objects postulated by the history of ideas by analysing the concept of an individual viewpoint. An individual viewpoint consists of expressed beliefs. This analysis of an individual viewpoint relied principally on inductive arguments to draw out the similarities and differences among concepts such as belief, pro-attitude, motive, and illocutionary force. The meaning of an object was shown to consist solely of the beliefs it expressed.

A fuller analysis of the objects studied by historians of ideas requires us to unpack our concept of belief. One way of doing this would be to enter the domain of philosophical psychology, asking what metaphysical status we should ascribe to psychological states. Instead of asking this, however, I deployed a series of deductive arguments to establish the conceptual priority of sincere, conscious, and rational beliefs. The priority of the sincere follows from the dependence of deceit on a general expectation of truthfulness. The priority of the conscious follows from the way in which we model our account of the unconscious on the conscious. The priority of the rational follows from the very fact that we perform actions, hold beliefs, and have the abilities we do. These three conceptual priorities show that our concept of a belief carries with it presumptions in favour of the sincere, conscious, and rational. A presumption is a matter of logic given to us by the grammar of our concepts, not an expectation set up for us by our actual studies. Because all experiences are theory laden, we necessarily approach the world through a set of concepts, and these concepts require us to approach the world with certain presumptions. It is important, moreover, to recognise how presumptions play a different role from heuristic techniques. Heuristic techniques tell historians how they might set about arriving at a suitable understanding of a work. Because heuristic techniques provide advice on how to understand works, they are sensitive to all sorts of information about the work to be approached, so they typically vary according to the nature of the work being studied. Consider, for example, the heuristic maxim 'try to make authors appear as rational as possible'.[43] Sensible historians will apply this maxim more forcefully to renowned philosophers than to popularisers. They will be prepared, for example, to ascribe unexpressed beliefs of greater complexity to Thomas Hobbes than to Besant.[44] They will be prepared to do so because we hold theories such as that philosophers tend to be more

---

[43] On the need for rationality as a heuristic category, see Skinner, 'Reply to my critics', particularly pp. 246–8. In addition, rationality can act as an appraisive category by which to judge the merit of a work.   [44] Compare Pocock, 'History of political thought'.

concerned than popularisers with the consistency of their work. Presumptions, in contrast, tell us about the logical structure of a discipline. They distinguish the dominant and subsidiary objects postulated by a discipline in a way which enables us to identify the dominant and subsidiary forms of reasoning appropriate to it. Because presumptions form part of the logic of a discipline, they apply with equal force throughout the whole of it. A presumption in favour of rational belief, for example, plays the same role in a study of Besant as in one of Hobbes. Whenever we interpret a work as expressive of insincere, unconscious, or irrational beliefs, or whenever we expect a work to express such beliefs, we necessarily do so against the background of a prior, logical presumption against such beliefs.

Presumptions tell us what properties we can legitimately predicate of objects when we consider the dominant form of reasoning appropriate to them. Thus, the main significance of the conceptual priority of sincere, conscious, and rational beliefs lies in the implication that historians, as a matter of logic, should start by seeking to explain expressed beliefs as if they are sincere, conscious, and rational. Their historical studies might lead them to reject this initial assumption in other cases, and even to expect this initial assumption not to apply, or to apply only to a limited extent, in some cases. But the logic of their discipline remains such that they should invoke insincerity, the unconscious, or the irrational only if they cannot make sense of their material without doing so. Explanation in the history of ideas exhibits a layered structure. First historians describe an idealised history composed purely of sincere, conscious, rational beliefs – they explain their material in the language we use to account for such beliefs. Then they account for discrepancies from this idealised story in terms of deceit, the unconscious, and the irrational – they have recourse to other languages only when the language we use to account for normal beliefs proves inadequate for their purposes. I will proceed now to examine the precise nature of these different forms of explanation.

CHAPTER 5

On synchronic explanation

INTRODUCTION

Once historians have reconstructed historical objects by studying the relics available to them, they usually want to explain why the past was as it was. Ultimately historians hope to do more than describe a mere succession of events: they hope to explain these events to show us why things happened as they did. After historians have used various relics to reconstruct the past, they typically try to explain why the past was as it was, and they do so in a process that itself can lead them to modify their understanding of the past. Historians usually combine several of the historical objects they have recovered in a single narrative. After historians of ideas have reconstructed beliefs, they typically try to explain why people held those beliefs. Historians of ideas usually make sense of the meanings they have ascribed to works by relating them to their historical antecedents. Imagine, for example, a historian who discovers that Besant wrote about her intention to highlight the unity of the religions of the world, and rightly takes her sincerely to have meant what she said. Surely the historian will want to know why Besant believed the religions of the world were fundamentally similar. How should the historian set about satisfying his curiosity?

Questions of understanding ask what a work means or what beliefs an individual expressed in a work. Questions of explanation ask why a work has the meaning it does or why an individual believed what he did. Sometimes philosophers define understanding and explanation in a different way from this. They adopt a narrower concept of explanation defined as the form of explanation incorporating the scientific notion of causation, and they do so in contrast to a concept of understanding, or narrative, defined as the form of explanation appropriate to history conceived as a discipline in which the scientific notion of causation does not operate.[1] Given these latter definitions, to insist on a role for explanation as well as understanding in history is to commit oneself to the view that the scientific notion of causation should appear in studies of the past. In contrast, my broader concept of explanation covers all attempts to say why an object or event is or was as it is or was irrespective of whether or not one does so in terms of a scientific notion of causation.[2] This broader concept of explanation does not tie explanation to a particular type of connection between objects. Thus, when I insist on a role for explanation in history, I do not commit myself to the view that history instantiates the scientific notion of causation. Explanation is a legitimate part of history irrespective of whether or not beliefs, actions, and the like have causes.[3]

My distinction between understanding and explanation serves its own purpose. It signals a concern to question the order of priorities found in most studies of the history of ideas. Contextualists, conventionalists, the New Critics, hermeneutic theorists, and others emphasise the way in which we should come to understand a work. They focus almost exclusively on the nature of meaning and the process of understanding. They seem to address historians who sit in archives or libraries with a work before them, struggling to grasp its meaning. Perhaps the historians concentrate solely on the one work, or perhaps they read other works as well, but they seek to understand the work before them. How, the contextualists and others ask, can such historians come to know the meaning of the work before them? Our analysis of objective knowledge suggests, however, that something is amiss with all of this. We found that objective knowledge of the meaning of a work depends on a comparison between whole webs of belief. Historians can come to know what a work means only by comparing rival webs of belief, each of which presumably includes not only an understanding of the work and various other works but also explanatory theories linking these understandings to one another. Whether or not historians should take an understanding of a work to be valid depends in part, therefore, on the adequacy of the explanation they would give for its having that meaning. We cannot isolate understanding from explanation in the way many writers on the history

[1] G. von Wright, *Explanation and Understanding* (London: Routledge & Kegan Paul, 1971); A. Megill, 'Recounting the past: "description", explanation, and narrative in historiography', *American Historical Review* 94 (1989), 627–53.
[2] For a measured attempt to relate something akin to this distinction between explanation and understanding to that between the natural and human sciences, see Ricœur, *Interpretation Theory*, pp. 71–80.
[3] Compare P. Roth, 'Narrative explanation: the case of history', *History and Theory* 27 (1988), 1–13.

of ideas seem to do. Rather, an anthropological epistemology requires us to give questions of explanation a weight at least equal to that of questions of understanding.

The order of priorities found in most works on the history of ideas points to a faith in a logic of discovery or of justification. A faith in our ability to know things outside the context of a web of beliefs would lead one to conclude that historians can justify their understanding of a work without postulating explanatory theories. An anthropological epistemology, in contrast, implies that there is little point in asking 'how should historians come to understand a work?' After all, the way they do so does not determine the validity of their understanding. Historians can have objective knowledge of a work's meaning only in the context of a suitable web of beliefs, an important part of which will typically be the explanation they give of that meaning. No doubt some scholars will try to collapse this distinction between understanding a work and explaining it. They will argue that to grasp the inter-subjective meaning of a work is to explain it. Certainly, because contextualists and conventionalists believe that the meaning of a work comes from a paradigm or ruling set of conventions, they are likely to argue that to show that a work means such and such because it belongs in a particular paradigm is to explain its appearance as a social fact. They are likely to say that to understand a work is to explain it as a manifestation of a paradigm understood as a set of social meanings. Our procedural individualism, in contrast, requires us to reject the somewhat mystical idea of works as social facts. Thus, we must continue to distinguish between understanding and explanation.

Let me turn now, therefore, to the form of explanation appropriate to the history of ideas. Because historical meanings are expressed beliefs, historians can explain the appearance of meanings by explaining why the individuals concerned expressed the beliefs they did. Moreover, the conceptual priority of the sincere, conscious, and rational means that historians should treat works as expressions of such beliefs. To begin, therefore, we should ask what form of explanation is appropriate to such beliefs. I will argue that the grammar of folk psychology precludes the possibility of historians explaining beliefs in scientific or pseudo-scientific terms. Historians cannot reduce facts about beliefs to matters of physiology or to sociological or psychological laws.

Historians should explain beliefs by reference to traditions and dilemmas. One way of seeing why they should do so is to reflect on the implications of adopting an anthropological epistemology. Our theory of objective knowledge consists of an analysis of a practice, not a defence of the possibility of pure experiences or purely logical constructions. Thus, our epistemology must contain within it a description of a practice by which people might come to hold beliefs. It is true, of course, that our anthropological epistemology constitutes a normative account of belief. None the less, this does not prevent it from telling us how we should explain beliefs. On the contrary, because an anthropological epistemology describes the way rational people come to hold beliefs, and because an argument for the priority of the rational implies that historians should treat beliefs initially as rational, our epistemology therefore, applies to the very beliefs we are currently considering. It is also true, of course, that our argument for the priority of rational beliefs applies only to consistency, not objectivity. None the less, this does not matter provided we look only at the account our epistemology gives of the way a single individual should develop a consistent web of beliefs, and not at the account it gives of the way various individuals should compare their webs to arrive at an objective point of view. Our analysis of objectivity points the way, therefore, towards an analysis of the initial form of explanation historians should use to say why people held the beliefs they did. The webs of belief we compare in our epistemological practice are rival bundles of theories referring to generally accepted facts. Thus, just as semantic holism implies that objectivity is a property of a bundle of theories, not a single theory, so historians should explain a belief by showing how it fits into a larger web of beliefs, not by examining it in isolation. Explanations of belief should refer to intellectual traditions. Similarly, just as objectivity depends on our criticising bundles of theories by reference to generally accepted facts, so historians should explain beliefs by showing how they represent responses to a clash between perceived facts and established convictions. Explanations of belief should refer to dilemmas.

AGAINST SCIENTISM

The Grail of a unified science has tempted numerous scholars to reduce questions of belief to questions of physiology. A faith in the universal applicability of the scientific form of explanation has tempted even more scholars to reduce matters of belief to psychological or sociological laws. At least for the moment, however, historians of ideas should not treat their discipline as a branch of a universal science. The nature of belief is such that they must adopt a form of explanation quite different from that of natural science. A web of beliefs constitutes a human understanding of the world, so historians who consider webs of belief necessarily deal with products of intelligence. Historians of ideas want to make intelligible the way someone else has made the world intelligible; they want to understand how someone else has understood things; they want to explain the way someone else has explained things. The natural sciences, in contrast, offer us explanations of physical phenomena which are not products of intelligence, say, an apple falling to the ground, a lake freezing over, or a person perspiring. Scientific explanation, therefore, does not have the same double-layered nature as explanation in the history of ideas. Natural scientists seek only to make things intelligible or to explain things: they do not seek to make intelligible attempts to make things intelligible or to explain explanations. Whereas the history of ideas deploys a set of concepts appropriate to things considered as aspects or products of mind, the natural sciences deploy one appropriate to things considered as purely physical objects. It seems reasonable to suppose, moreover, that the language appropriate to mental phenomena is categorically distinct from that appropriate to purely physical phenomena.[4] If this is so, the history of ideas and the natural sciences must instantiate different forms of explanation. Although historians and scientists may study the same things, they do so using different languages, which commit them to different forms of explanation. Consider, for example, scholars who study the cave paintings at Ajanta in India. When historians approach the paintings as products of mind, they explain them by reference to things such as the religious culture of ancient India, a culture which itself was an attempt to make the world intelligible. In contrast, when scientists approach the paintings as physical objects, they explain them by reference to things such as the process of erosion in the Deccan hills, a process which is not itself an attempt to make things intelligible. Although the historians and scientists study the same paintings, the former use a language applicable to the paintings considered as products of mind, whereas the latter use one applicable to the paintings considered as physical objects.

We discuss aspects, and products, of mind using the language of folk psychology.[5] Folk psychology consists of a cluster of concepts that refer

[4] Compare Collingwood, *The Idea of History*, particularly pp. 285–8; M. Oakeshott, *On Human Conduct* (Oxford: Clarendon Press, 1975), pp. 1–107; and P. Winch, *The Idea of a Social Science* (London: Routledge & Kegan Paul, 1958).
[5] On the ineliminable and sufficient nature of folk psychology, see L. Rudder, *Saving Belief: A Critique of Physicalism* (Princeton: Princeton University Press, 1987).

to human attitudes, perhaps attitudes to states of affairs, or perhaps attitudes to propositions. It consists of concepts such as fear, belief, desire, and pleasure. No doubt we are capable of having the psychological attitudes we can, and of doing the things we can, only because we have certain physiological characteristics. Just as we can see colour only because our eyes have a certain physiological structure, so perhaps we can hold beliefs only because we have a linguistic faculty, and perhaps we can have a linguistic faculty only because of the physiology of the brain.[6] None the less, although our capacities to believe, to prefer, and the like, undoubtedly depend in part on our physiology, the way in which we exercise these capacities clearly depends on a range of personal, cultural, educational, and social factors, none of which is properly physiological. The fact that our capacities to believe, to prefer, and the like have physiological prerequisites does not imply that the content of our beliefs, preferences, and the like derive from specific physiological states. Even if we should discuss our capacity for holding attitudes and for performing actions in physiological terms, we must still discuss the specific attitudes we hold and the specific actions we perform using folk psychology. Thus, although the concepts of folk psychology have no place in our accounts of purely physical objects, they are vital to our accounts of objects that are aspects or products of mind. Indeed, whereas we can understand and respond to physical objects without invoking concepts such as belief and pro-attitude, not only our understanding of other people but also our interactions with them depend on our ability to use folk psychology. Time after time we move from our perceptions of how people behaved in certain situations to inferences about the beliefs and pro-attitudes that led them so to behave, and then we move from these inferences to conjectures about how they might behave in the future in rather different situations, and finally we decide upon our own behaviour in the light of these conjectures about how others will behave. What is more, the success of folk psychology in enabling us to make fairly successful, if far from infallible, predictions about how others will behave surely gives us a good reason to stick with this way of discussing aspects and products of mind. After all, if the concepts of folk psychology bore no relation to things as they are, our frequent successes in understanding and predicting the behaviour of other people would presumably be down to mere chance, which seems highly unlikely. The utility of folk psychology gives us a good reason to

---

[6] That our linguistic faculty has a physiological origin is argued by N. Chomsky, *Reflections on Language* (London: Temple Smith, 1976), pp. 3–35.

assume that we cannot explain beliefs, actions, and the like in purely physical terms.

The worshippers of science who assimilate the history of ideas to the natural sciences deny that mental objects require a different form of explanation from their physical counterparts. They typically rest their scientism on one of two arguments. If they are physicalists, they argue that mental objects are at most manifestations of physical ones. If they are social positivists, they argue that mental objects are in principle no different from physical ones. According to physicalists, we can explain mental phenomena in purely physical terms. An obvious difficulty with their position is that we do not do so. On the contrary, we discuss aspects and products of mind using the language of folk psychology, a language with no place in our descriptions and accounts of physical objects. Physicalists respond to this difficulty by adopting either a confrontational or a conciliatory position. Confrontational physicalists reject folk psychology as utterly false. Conciliatory physicalists accept the accuracy of folk psychology only to argue that we can reduce propositions referring to objects such as beliefs to propositions referring exclusively to physical objects.

Conciliatory physicalists do not claim that folk psychology is wrong. Instead, they defend an identity theory of the mind. They say that all psychological states correspond to physiological ones, so that we can reduce folk psychology to the natural sciences. Conciliatory physicalists would have us translate our talk of beliefs and the like into talk of physiological states in a way which would presumably enable us to explain mental phenomena in purely physical terms. Clearly we do talk about mind in both mental and physical terms. We talk both of people having such and such a preference, and of their having such and such a chemical imbalance in the brain. The question we now have to answer, however, is how these two ways of talking about mind relate to one another. Conciliatory physicalists argue that at least in principle we can reduce the language of folk psychology to that of cognitive science. Actually, however, we cannot do so for the sufficient reason that the two languages instantiate incompatible categories. We apply the concepts of folk psychology using criteria of rationality, and these criteria have no place in the application of concepts in the natural sciences. We have seen already how the relationship of beliefs to behaviour requires us to begin by trying to identify beliefs as rational. We ascribe beliefs, pro-attitudes, and the like to people in accord with a presumption of rationality. We bring out the consistency in their beliefs and actions.

Thus, the criteria governing the application of the concepts of folk psychology centre on a normative notion of rationality. Natural scientists, in contrast, ascribe various properties to physical objects without reference to criteria of rationality. They apply the concepts of their disciplines using non-normative criteria such as mass, velocity, and concentration. Crucially, because the application of the concepts of folk psychology depends on normative criteria, and because we cannot express these criteria in the language of the natural sciences, therefore, we cannot reduce the concepts of folk psychology to those of the natural sciences. When two sets of concepts have incompatible criteria of application, we cannot express one in terms of the other.

Perhaps a critic will point out that this rebuttal of conciliatory physicalism does not apply to its non-reductionist form as exemplified by the anomalous monism of Davidson.[7] Davidson is a monist because he believes that every mental event is a physical event. His monism is anomalous because he does not believe that physical predicates can have the same extensions as mental ones. He does not believe that we can reduce the concepts of folk psychology to those of the natural sciences. Clearly, therefore, our argument against conciliatory physicalism need not cover its non-reductionist forms simply because they do not threaten the historian's attachment to folk psychology. If non-reductive physicalism is correct, mental objects are also physical objects that we can describe using physiological concepts; but the possibility of our describing these physical objects in physiological terms neither invalidates nor supplants our use of folk psychology to describe the equivalent mental objects. On the contrary, non-reductive physicalism implies that when we approach a thing as a mental object, we must describe it using the concepts of folk psychology, not those of the natural sciences. What is more, non-reductive physicalism implies that the appropriate physiological description of a physical object is neither more complete nor more fundamental than the appropriate description of it considered as a mental object. Because neither type of description is reducible to the other, they are different but equal. The appropriate physiological description is a part of the natural sciences, not history, and the appropriate psychological description is a part of history, not the natural sciences. We can conclude, therefore, that if non-reductive physicalism is correct historians should continue to approach the past using the concepts of folk psychology.

[7] D. Davidson, 'Mental events', in *Essays on Actions and Events*, pp. 207–27.

Some philosophers might regard our inability to reduce folk psychology to physiology as indicative of the incompatibility of the two, and so as evidence in favour of confrontational physicalism. Confrontational physicalists would not have us explain mental phenomena in physical terms.[8] They would have us stop using concepts such as belief altogether. They argue that folk psychology conflicts with a cognitive science concerned to give purely physiological descriptions of the aspects and products of mind. The epistemic authority of science, they continue, means we should reject folk psychology, not cognitive science. One can undermine confrontational physicalism by showing that natural science is compatible with folk psychology, and, more dramatically still, by suggesting that it is extremely unlikely it will ever contradict folk psychology. Although I want to avoid a commitment to any particular view of the metaphysical status of psychological concepts, I will begin by assuming the truth of a functionalist theory of mind. A functionalist theory of mind defines the concepts of folk psychology by their collective role in explaining a move from certain types of input to certain types of output.[9] It defines concepts such as belief and pro-attitude in terms of their role in explaining why people in a given situation behave as they do. Functionalism enables us to reconcile folk psychology with the natural sciences. Indeed, it enables us to do so even if we grant the unlikely assumption that the natural sciences require us to describe cognitive states in exclusively physiological terms. We can say, first, that people are made up of the physiological states which constitute the subject matter of cognitive science, and, second, that these states fulfil the roles which provide the content of functional definitions of the concepts of folk psychology. We do not need to worry about a modularity principle, according to which we would have to correlate distinct, isolable physiological states with distinct, isolable folk roles. The mere fact that the folk roles can be filled by physiological states, however this happens, is sufficient to reconcile folk psychology with cognitive science. Indeed, a functional analysis of the concepts of folk psychology renders it almost impervious to any future assault from cognitive science. If the concepts of folk psychology refer to functional roles that determine

[8] S. Stich, *From Folk Psychology to Cognitive Science* (Cambridge, Mass.: MIT Press, 1983). Stich rejects folk psychology in part because experiments show the beliefs and desires we invoke in connection with equivalent verbal and non-verbal behaviour do not always tally with one another. Later I will argue that folk psychology enables us to explain such discrepancies by representing them as distortions associated with deception, the unconscious, and the irrational.
[9] The classic statement of functionalism remains H. Putnam, 'The nature of mental states', in *Philosophical Papers*, vol. II: *Mind, Language and Reality*, pp. 429–40.

when we should apply these concepts but do not give them any positive
metaphysical content, our use of these concepts will be wrong only if we
are wrong about these functional roles. But we are very unlikely to be
wrong about these functional roles since they are purely functional.
They relate inputs to outputs, where the relevant inputs and outputs are
about as close to basic observations as we can get. Again, if we define
belief, pro-attitude, and the like in terms of a move from certain types of
input to certain types of output, we are right to use these folk concepts
provided only that this move really does take place, and surely we are
unlikely ever to conclude that people do not move from being in certain
situations to behaving in certain ways. Thus, the functionalist theory of
mind leaves folk psychology remarkably secure against any possible
assault launched in the name of natural science.

Although functionalism continues to attract a substantial following, it
is open to a number of objections. These objections are so telling that
even its leading progenitor, Hilary Putnam, now rejects it as false.[10] The
main objection to functionalism is that we can imagine objects which
neither understand a language nor have beliefs and pro-attitudes but
still satisfy functionalist definitions of meaning and mind.[11] Given the
vulnerability of functionalism, and my preference for leaving open the
metaphysical status of psychological states, I want to see how well we
can defend folk psychology against confrontational physicalism if we
forsake our appeal to functionalism. Even if we rejected the functionalist
theory of mind, folk psychology would remain fairly secure. Although
we could no longer be sure that the natural sciences would not overturn
our non-functionalist interpretation of folk psychology sometime in the
future, we could still defend folk psychology as the best understanding of
mental objects currently available to us. Even confrontational physicalists do not argue that cognitive science already offers us a usable
alternative to folk psychology. They argue only that cognitive scientists
will come up with a purely physical understanding of beliefs, pro-
attitudes, and the like sometime in the future. We can reasonably ask
them, therefore, what we should do while we wait for cognitive scientists
to tell us how we should comprehend mental phenomena. We cannot
replace folk psychology with a physicalist language because a physicalist
language is what we are waiting for. And we cannot replace folk
psychology with some other language because confrontational physical-

[10] H. Putnam, *Representation and Reality* (Cambridge, Mass.: MIT Press, 1988).
[11] See the parable of the Chinese Room in J. Searle, *Minds, Brains and Science* (Cambridge, Mass.:
Harvard University Press, 1984), pp. 28–38.

ists do not champion another language. Even if folk psychology contradicted natural science, therefore, we would still have to stick with it until
natural scientists successfully developed an alternative account of beliefs, pro-attitudes, and the like.

We can now counter all possible physicalist objections to constructing
the logic of the history of ideas out of the grammar of folk psychology.
Because our adherence to folk psychology depends on a categorical gap
between it and the language of natural science, we can neither reduce
nor replace folk psychology until cognitive scientists bridge this gap by
developing a purely physical account of mental objects. At the moment,
however, natural scientists have not bridged this gap, so historians
cannot renounce folk psychology. Physicalism embodies an aspiration;
it is a research programme based on a faith in science. No doubt, if the
aspiration became a reality, historians would have to rethink their
discipline. But until it becomes a reality – if it ever does – historians must
continue to work with folk psychology.

Let us turn now to the form of scientism associated with social
positivism. Social positivists, including many Marxists, argue that the
language of folk psychology is analogous to that of the natural sciences.[12]
They are reductionists who seek to install the scientific concept of
causation into folk psychology. They argue that causal laws determine
the nature of beliefs, actions, and the like: just as gravity causes apples to
fall, so sociological or psychological forces cause people to believe what
they do. No doubt social positivists sometimes fudge the issue by adding
a rider to the effect that sociological or psychological forces determine
beliefs only in the last instance. No doubt, moreover, this rider often
enables them to introduce worthy subtleties into their historical studies.
But this rider still misses the philosophical point. Either social positivists
want to install the scientific concept of causation into folk psychology or
they do not. If they do not, they should stop talking in quasi-scientific
terms of forces determining beliefs, and instead join the search for a
concept of causation appropriate to folk psychology. If they do, they can
continue to talk of social or psychological forces determining beliefs; but
equally we can challenge the appropriateness of their concept of causation for the history or ideas. Social positivism attracts scholars for two

---

[12] Marx's clearest statement of his own views is K. Marx, 'Preface to *A Critique of Political Economy*',
in *Karl Marx: Selected Writings*, ed. D. McLellan (Oxford: Oxford University Press, 1977), pp.
388–91. Of course, some Marxists have read him as a historicist, not a determinist. On these two
readings and their roots in Marx's own views, see von Wright, *Explanation and Understanding*, pp.
7–8 and 31–2.

main reasons. Sometimes it represents an attempt to claim the prestige of the natural sciences for a favoured approach; after all, talk of explaining beliefs by causal laws can sound impressively rigorous compared to avowedly unscientific, hermeneutic approaches. At other times, social positivism springs from lax thinking: scholars rightly recognise there is a universal feature of explanation in that to explain something is to relate it to other things, and this leads them wrongly to assume that the relationship between something and its explanation must also be universal, where the prestige of the natural sciences ensures that they identify this universal relationship with the scientific concept of causation. The two main attractions of social positivism derive, therefore, from the prestige of natural science. Surely, however, we should not take the successes of natural science to preclude other forms of explanation? The undoubted power of natural science does not mean that we should model disciplines deploying other languages on it. On the contrary, because these disciplines rely on other languages, we can unpack the categories which operate in these disciplines only by studying the implications of the concepts operating therein. Scholars should not legislate to other disciplines from the case of natural science.

We cannot explain the existence or nature of beliefs by presenting them as the determined outcome of law-like relations. We cannot do so because a scientific concept of causation has no place in folk psychology. When we discuss a belief we deploy a folk psychology which commits us to seeing it as a product of reason, a folk psychology whose criteria of application centre on a normative notion of rationality. To say that someone believes something is to say that some sort of being fashioned it in accord with his reason. Thus, to explain a meaningful object, we must refer to the reasons someone had for fashioning it in the way he did. Folk psychology requires us to explain meaningful objects as products of reason. Furthermore, when we explain an object as a product of reason, we suggest that the person concerned, in some sense, could have reasoned differently, and had he done so, that the object would not have come into being as it did. If an object depends on the reasoned decision, or choice, of a person, we must explain it as the product of that decision, so we cannot explain it as a determined outcome of a law-like process; after all, choices would not be choices if they were fixed by a causal law. We can conclude, therefore, that folk psychology instantiates a concept of rationality which precludes our explaining meaningful objects using the scientific concept of causation.

Critics might propose that we look upon the reasons why people came to believe or do a thing as the cause of their so doing. Here, too, they might point out that we have not repudiated Davidson's anomalous monism – a non-reductionist physicalism in which reasons cause actions.[13] Actually, however, Davidson's position does not conflict with ours here. Anomalous monism allows a reason to be the cause of an action only under an alternative, physical description. It implies that there could be physical descriptions of reasons and actions under which the relationship between them would be a causal one. When Davidson made his argument, philosophers were debating whether or not we could relate psychological descriptions of actions back to reasons for actions by way of causal laws. Davidson argued that they were wrong to assume that this debate alone could decide whether or not reasons caused actions. He pointed out that even if there were no causal laws of the sort then being discussed, there might still be alternative, physical descriptions of actions and reasons under which reasons might indeed cause actions. Non-reductive physicalism implies that reasons can cause actions only if we describe the reason and action as other than aspects or products of mind. Indeed, Davidson's anomalous monism leads him to conclude that the scientific notion of causation does not belong in folk psychology. He argues that events relate to one another as cause and effect only if they are subsumed under a strict law; and we cannot subsume psychological events under strict laws because folk psychology is neither a closed language nor reducible to a closed language. Once again, therefore, we can conclude that non-reductive physicalism has no significance for historians of ideas since they study reasons and actions as meaningful objects, not physical ones.

The inapplicability of the scientific concept of causation to meaningful objects appears in the self-defeating nature of all reductionist attempts to explain beliefs in terms of psychological or sociological laws. Any law-like statement of the form 'all beliefs are products of X' must be an expression of belief. Thus, if it were true, it would be a product of X. For example, if economic conditions determined all beliefs, the belief that economic conditions determined all beliefs would be a product of economic conditions. But this is absurd. Reductionism seems straightforward only if we take the proposition 'X determines all beliefs' to be an insight, and not itself a belief to be reduced to X. Clearly the true reductionist must say 'X determines my belief that X determines all beliefs'. Yet this proposition too seems straightforward only if we take it as an insight, and not itself a belief to be reduced to X. The true reductionist must say 'X determines my belief that X determines my belief that X determines all beliefs'. Yet this proposition – but perhaps the point is clear. Reductionism is self-defeating because we cannot make sense of a statement of reductionism unless we take it to be an insight, in which case we tacitly admit that it is false. We cannot make sense of the belief that we should discuss beliefs in terms of the scientific concept of causation unless we discuss it in terms of a psychological language that implies it is false.

Historians of ideas study meaningful objects, not physical ones, and they have to do so using the language of folk psychology, not natural science. Historians cannot repudiate folk psychology because we cannot reduce the concepts within it to physiological ones, and, at least at the moment, we do not have an adequate, physical alternative to it. What is more, they cannot transplant the language of natural science into folk psychology because the two are strictly incompatible. The categories of folk psychology revolve around the concepts of reason, decision, and choice, concepts which rule out the determinism of the natural sciences. Consequently, historians of ideas have to adopt a form of explanation appropriate to folk psychology. They must explain beliefs in a way which instantiates a normative concept of rationality rather than the scientific concept of causation. The grammar of folk psychology requires us to explain beliefs by elucidating the reasons people have for adopting them, not by pointing to the physiological states of the believer or sociological or psychological laws. No doubt the reasons people have for adopting a belief sometimes derive from their experiences and so indirectly their social location, and sometimes from the influence of their emotional make up on their process of belief-formation. Even in these cases, however, sociological and psychological facts are relevant only because they inform the reasons people have for adopting a given belief. They are not relevant because of a law-like generalisation of the form 'people in social location X or with psychological make-up Y adopt belief Z'.

SYNCHRONIC EXPLANATION

Numerous scholars would accept that to explain beliefs historians must elucidate the reasons people have for adopting them. How exactly they should do this, however, remains unclear. When philosophers insist that historians explain beliefs by reference to reasons, they raise complex questions about why individuals have the reasons they do. Fortunately our presumptions in favour of sincere, conscious, and rational beliefs help to narrow the initial scope of such questions. They imply that to ask why individuals have the reasons they do is initially to ask about the intellectual, as opposed to the emotional, background to their reasoning. The key issues here revolve around two sets of concepts. The first set includes concepts such as tradition, paradigm, language, and episteme. These concepts embody attempts both to specify how we should analyse the social context in which individuals exercise their power of reasoning, and to indicate how much weight we should give to the social context as a factor in their reasoning. The second set includes concepts such as anomaly, problem, reason, and agency. These concepts embody attempts to specify how we should analyse the process by which beliefs change, and, more especially, the role of the individual in this process. Most historians of ideas would recognise these two sets of concepts as those that do the explanatory work in their discipline. A historian explains why people adopted the beliefs they did by reference to their reasoning, or speech, in relation to an already existing set of ideas, or language. Different historians and philosophers, however, ascribe a different content and explanatory weight to the individual and social factors here evoked. To devise a form of explanation appropriate to the history of ideas, therefore, we need to analyse, first, the nature of the social background to individual reasoning, and, second, the process of individual reasoning.

An analysis of the social and individual factors involved in human reasoning typically consists largely of an analysis of their relationship to each other. Analyses of the relationship of social structure to individual agency sometimes seems to have generated two hostile camps akin to the irrationalist sceptics and foundationalist objectivists. The similarity of the two disputes is no coincidence. Just as foundationalist objectivism appeals to our ability to grasp given truths, so an undue stress on agency often rests on a faith in the ability of the individual to exercise his reason unaffected by his social context. Individuals allegedly reach the beliefs they do by exercising a pure, objective reason. Similarly, just as irrationalist scepticism appeals to our inability to grasp given truths, so an undue stress on social structures often rests on a belief in the impossibility of the individual exercising his reason apart from as determined by his social context. Individuals allegedly reach the beliefs they do by reasoning in a way that is fixed by irrational presuppositions given to them by their social contexts. Once again, I will avoid the two extreme positions entrenched in these hostile camps. I will draw on semantic holism to defend a form of explanation that avoids both an undue emphasis on agency and an equally undue emphasis on social structure.

Historians of ideas should explain the objects they postulate by undertaking rational reconstructions, not scientific investigations, of the past. But whose concept of rationality should they adopt? Should they reconstruct a web of beliefs using their concept of rationality or the believer's concept of rationality? If we phrase these questions in this way, as philosophers are inclined to do, we risk obscuring what is at stake here.[14] If we phrase them in this way, we suggest that there are entirely different concepts of rationality between which historians have to choose. In contrast, we found earlier that although people may not share a substantive, objective concept of rationality, they do share a limited concept of rationality defined in terms of consistency. Again, philosophers who argue that historians must adopt the concept of rationality of those they study typically do so on the grounds that social practices are constituted at least in part by the language and under-standing of the participants. They argue that the concept of rationality held by those we study defines the very objects we are studying.[15] Even if this were so, we found earlier that languages overlap in a way that undermines the apparent dichotomy between different rationalities.[16] Our language must share some formal features with those we study, notably a concern with consistency, and these features are enough to enable us to apprehend the language embodied in their social practices through our language. Thus, because people share a limited concept of rationality as consistency, the principal aim of historians of ideas must be to reveal the consistency of the webs of belief they recover. Whenever they do this, they deploy a universal, not a particular, concept of rationality.

Certainly, other webs of belief might incorporate substantive con-cepts of rationality different from ours. These substantive concepts of rationality specify different views of things such as what should count as evidence for a particular proposition. However, once we accept the primacy of rational consistency, these different substantive views of rationality cease to pose a philosophical difficulty. Obviously if histor-ians are to reveal the inner consistency of a web of beliefs, they must do

---

[14] Contrast Winch, 'Understanding a primitive society', pp. 30–1.
[15] Gadamer, *Truth and Method*, pp. 345–431; Winch, *The Idea of a Social Science*.
[16] In addition, language might not be constitutive of social practices in quite the way Gadamer and Winch suggest. See Rorty, *Philosophy and the Mirror of Nature*, pp. 343–56.

so in terms of the substantive concept of rationality internal to it. Consider, for example, people who believe in the law of karma because their substantive concept of rationality tells them that an experience they have had provides conclusive evidence for this belief. A historian who wants to describe the inner consistency of their beliefs must show how their belief in the law of karma hangs together with their understanding of the relevant experience and their substantive concept of rationality. Again, the conceptual priority of conscious, rational beliefs reinforces the foregoing account of the historian's relationship to various concepts of rationality. It implies that historians should begin by approaching webs of belief as though they are internally consistent: it implies that historians should approach beliefs as though they are held for reasons that make sense to the believer. Historians of ideas try to make intelligible to us the way other people have made the world intelligible. They do so by presenting people's beliefs as internally consistent webs which incorporate particular, substantive concepts of rationality. We find their historical descriptions intelligible because we share a limited concept of rationality, defined as internal consistency, not only with them, but also with the subjects of their histories.

Explanation in the history of ideas begins with an attempt to explicate a particular belief in terms of the believer's reasons for holding it. Historians who want to explain a sincere, conscious, and rational belief must begin by reconstructing the relevant individual's beliefs as a fairly consistent web. Let us consider two extreme views of what such a reconstruction might entail. On the one hand, logical empiricists generally argue that we have pure observations capable of giving us factual beliefs, where our theoretical beliefs are attempts to find significant patterns among such facts. They might suggest, therefore, that historians can reveal the internal logic of a web of beliefs by relating its first-order beliefs to specific experiences, and by portraying its second-order beliefs as attempts to account for patterns among its first-order beliefs. On the other hand, irrationalists and idealists sometimes argue that basic categories construct the nature and content of the experiences out of which our beliefs arise. They might suggest, therefore, that historians can reveal the internal logic of a web of beliefs by relating its constituent beliefs to fundamental categories, which, in some sense, are given as *a priori* truths.

Semantic holism ascribes a task to the historian of ideas different from both of these extremes. It implies that the objectivity of a belief depends on its relationship to various other beliefs. There cannot be any self-supporting beliefs. No belief can be rational either by reference to an experience or *a priori*. Certainly some beliefs refer to reality; it is just that they are not pure but rather embody theoretical assumptions. Thus, the logical empiricists must be wrong: historians cannot reveal the inner consistency of a web of beliefs by portraying it as a pyramid founded upon pure observations. Certainly also our theoretical assumptions inform our understanding of our experiences; it is just that they are not given *a priori* but rather derive from our earlier interactions with the world. Thus, the irrationalists and idealists must be wrong: historians cannot reveal the inner consistency of a web of beliefs by portraying it as an inverted pyramid resting on given *a priori* truths. Historians cannot uncover the inner consistency of a web of beliefs by describing it as a pyramid based on either experiences or basic categories. Indeed, the hierarchical metaphor of a pyramid is totally inappropriate here. A web of beliefs resembles a network that maps on to reality at various points, where these points are defined by the way in which the relevant beliefs relate to one another. Webs of belief constitute networks of interconnected concepts, with the concepts, and the connections between them, being defined in part by beliefs about external reality. Sometimes historians will want to elucidate a belief that is a long way from points in the web that map on to external reality in terms of beliefs that are close to such points. At other times historians will want to elucidate beliefs that are close to points that map on to external reality in terms of beliefs that are far from such points. In neither case, however, does the fact that a historian chooses to start from a particular point in a web of beliefs imply that that particular point constitutes an epistemic foundation for the web of beliefs. Webs of belief are boundless, spherical networks, not hierarchical pyramids. Thus, historians who want to produce a rational reconstruction of a web of beliefs resemble puzzlers who want to piece together a spherical jigsaw. Each piece of the jigsaw, each belief, belongs where it does by virtue of the pieces around it. The puzzler completes the jigsaw by joining all the pieces together to form a single picture which then makes sense of each individual piece. None the less, the jigsaw has no obvious starting point since each piece stands in an essentially similar relationship to those around it. The puzzler has no corners or edges from which to build inwards. Because a web of beliefs does not have a hierarchical structure, historians can start with equal legitimacy from any point within it. They can select the starting point best suited to their particular inquiry.

Historians of ideas can explain why someone held a particular belief by locating it in the context of his web of beliefs. Because webs of belief are spherical networks, there is no foundational type of belief in them to which the explanation of a particular belief must refer. Imagine that historians follow this form of explanation and thereby show that someone believed in the law of karma because he believed in theories such as reincarnation. Next the historians probably will want to know why he believed in the particular web of beliefs he did. Let us look now, therefore, at the question of how a historian can explain why people held the webs of belief they did. Once again we can distinguish between two extreme views of the historian's task. On the one hand, logical empiricists generally argue that people hold webs of belief as a result of pure experiences. They might suggest, therefore, that the historian can explain why people held the webs of belief they did by reference to their experiences alone. The historian needs to consider only the circumstances people find themselves in, not the way they construct or interpret their circumstances through the traditions they inherit. Here logical empiricism can inspire an atomistic individualism, according to which individuals reach rational beliefs through pure observations and pure reasoning free from all undue social influence.[17] On the other hand, irrationalists and idealists often argue that people hold their webs of belief as a result of inheriting a certain way of making sense of the world. They might suggest, therefore, that the historian can explain why people held the webs of belief they did solely by reference to the traditions and theories that informed, or even constructed, their perceptions. The historian needs to consider only the general concepts people inherit, not the way they respond to their circumstances. Here irrationalism and idealism can inspire a strong structuralism, according to which the social context determines the beliefs any given individual comes to hold.[18]

Semantic holism shows both of these extreme views to be mistaken. It requires us to reject both atomistic individualism and strong structuralism. Consider first the atomistic individualism associated with logical empiricism. Certainly, people come to believe the things they do only in the context of their own life-histories: my web of beliefs is my web of beliefs precisely because I have come to accept certain beliefs as mine.

---

[17] Think, for example, of those classical empiricists (Locke), and their forerunners (Hobbes), who appealed to atomistic individuals in a state of nature.
[18] See, in particular, Foucault, *Order of Things*. Think also, however, of a tendency apparent in much Hegelian idealism.

What interests us, however, is why a particular web of beliefs should become part of a particular life-history: why I hold the particular web of beliefs I do. Because we cannot have pure experiences, we necessarily construe our personal experiences in terms of a prior bundle of theories. We cannot arrive at beliefs through experiences unless we already have a prior web of beliefs. Experiences can generate beliefs only where there is already is a web of beliefs in terms of which to make sense of the experiences. Thus, the logical empiricists are wrong: we cannot explain webs of belief by reference to the pure experiences of the relevant individuals. Our experiences can lead us to beliefs only because we already have access to webs of belief in the form of the traditions of our community. Individuals necessarily arrive at their webs of belief by way of their participation in the intellectual traditions of their communities.[19]

Critics might object to such a stress on inherited traditions on the grounds that there must have been a moment of origin – a state of nature.[20] Their argument would run as follows. Clearly traditions exist only as emergent entities dependent on the webs of belief of individuals. Thus, if individuals really could hold webs of belief only against the background of inherited traditions, neither individuals who hold beliefs nor traditions could ever have come into being at all. Individuals who hold beliefs could not have come into being because they could have done so only against the background of a tradition, and yet no tradition could exist prior to an individual who holds beliefs. Traditions could not have come into being because they could have done so only as a result of an individual who holds beliefs, and yet no individual could hold beliefs prior to the existence of a tradition. Thus, because individuals do hold beliefs, and because traditions do exist, there must have been a moment of origin. What is more, because traditions surely cannot exist prior to an individual who holds beliefs, this moment of origin must have consisted of an individual who came to hold beliefs in the absence of any tradition. Finally, because an original individual must have come to hold beliefs in the absence of any tradition, we must accept that other individuals can do so too. People must be able to hold webs of belief in isolation from others on the basis of their experiences alone.

To rebut this criticism, I want to investigate sorites terms. The sorites

---

[19] Phenomenological and hermeneutic studies often emphasise the ineluctable role played by tradition in human understanding. See Collingwood, *The Idea of History*; and Gadamer, *Truth and Method*, particularly pp. 245–74.

[20] Because my concerns are logical, I cannot allow even for an original position that acts as a purely hypothetical device, as in J. Rawls, *A Theory of Justice* (Oxford: Clarendon Press, 1972). See M. Bevir, 'The individual and society', *Political Studies* 44 (1996), 102–14.

paradox arises because we can start from true premises, follow a series of apparently valid arguments – arguments that affirm the antecedent – and yet arrive at a false conclusion. For instance, people with one more hair on their head than a bald person presumably are bald; thus, if X is bald, Y who has one more hair than X is bald, so Z who has one more hair than Y is bald, and so we might go on in a manner that would appear to enable us eventually to show anyone to be bald no matter how hairy they happened to be. Although the semantic importance of sorites terms remains a moot point, their paradoxical nature clearly derives from their being vague predicates. We cannot specify exactly the circumstances in which we may rightly describe something using a sorites term. We cannot say exactly what constitutes baldness. Moreover, the vagueness of the relevant predicates clearly reflects the existence of borderline cases that we are uncertain whether or not to describe using a given sorites term. There are some people we would be unsure whether or not to call bald even if we knew exactly how many hairs they had on their heads. The existence of these borderline cases means that we cannot accept without some qualification statements such as 'people with one more hair on their head than a bald person are themselves bald'. The crucial point here is that the qualification means that we cannot talk of moments of origin in relation to sorites terms. Imagine, for example, that Peter has gone bald over the last five years. Today, at time T, he is entirely bald. We might suppose that at time T* when he had one more hair than he does now he was also bald, and at time T** when he had one more hair than at time T* he was also bald, and so on. But if we accepted this supposition without any qualification, we would have to conclude Peter was bald five years ago, which is false *ex hypothesi*. Because bald is a sorites term, we cannot pinpoint the exact moment when Peter went bald. We can say only that during the last five years Peter has passed through a number of borderline states so that he was hairy then but is bald now. Peter's being bald has no moment of origin.

Let me turn now to the application of this analysis of sorites terms to our discussion of how historians should explain why people held the webs of belief they did. The fact is: both 'an individual who holds beliefs' and 'an inherited tradition' are akin to sorites terms in a way that undermines the need for a moment of origin lying behind explanations of webs of belief. The theory of evolution even suggests that 'an individual' is a vague predicate since humans evolved from creatures who were a bit less human-like and so on. More importantly, we definitely cannot say what exactly constitutes the holding of a web of beliefs. The holding of beliefs does not become a reality at any definite point on a spectrum of cases running from, say, purposive behaviour without language, through the use of single words, and the use of whole sentences tied to particular nouns, to elementary forms of abstract theorising. Numerous borderline cases separate cases in which beliefs are clearly not held from cases in which they clearly are held. Likewise, inherited traditions do not become a reality at any definite point on a spectrum of cases running from, say, birds who migrate along established routes, through chimpanzees who co-operate strategically to capture monkeys, and a family of hunter-gathers who follow the rains, to a tribe that plants its crops at a particular time of year. Numerous borderline cases separate cases in which inherited traditions clearly are not present from cases in which they clearly are present. Crucially, because both 'an individual who holds beliefs' and 'an inherited tradition' are vague predicates, we cannot talk of a moment of origin when either people came to hold beliefs or inherited traditions came into being. We must talk instead of individuals necessarily holding their webs of belief against a background of inherited traditions, and of inherited traditions necessarily arising out of the beliefs of individuals. The grammar of our concepts shows that individuals with beliefs and inherited traditions came into being together, not successively. The concept of individuals who hold beliefs depends on the concept of an inherited tradition, and the concept of an inherited tradition depends on the concept of individuals who hold beliefs. Neither makes sense without the other.

We can conclude, therefore, that historians study people who held webs of belief against the background of traditions, where these traditions themselves must have derived from people holding webs of belief against the background of earlier traditions, and so on. Historians must deploy this idea of a cycle of inherited traditions and individuals who hold beliefs because it is part of the grammar of the concepts governing their discipline. If scholars wanted to investigate the origins of the historical cycle of inherited traditions and individuals who hold beliefs, they would have to develop a different set of concepts from that currently used by historians. They would have to devise a set of concepts in which traditions and individuals were not conceived in terms of one another. If they succeeded in devising such concepts, they might be able to ask about the origins of the cyclical relationship between traditions and individuals, but they would do so in a way that would be radically different from history as we now understand it.

Consider now the strong structuralism associated with idealism and irrationalism. Idealists and irrationalists often argue that semantic meanings and beliefs are the products of the internal relations of self-sufficient languages or traditions. They might conclude, therefore, that historians can explain why someone holds a particular web of beliefs exclusively by reference to the tradition to which it belongs. They might adopt a strong structuralism leaving little, if any, room for human agency. Certainly, people adopt their webs of belief against a background of traditions which already exist as a common heritage: I come to formulate my beliefs in a world where other people already have expressed their beliefs. What interests us, however, is how the webs of belief of particular individuals relate to the traditions they inherit: how I develop my web of beliefs in relation to the beliefs other people have already expressed. Because structural meanings are abstractions based on hermeneutic meanings, traditions must be emergent entities. Moreover, traditions cannot be self-sufficient because they are based on the webs of belief of individuals, who therefore must be able to adopt beliefs that extend or modify them. Thus, the idealists and irrationalists are wrong: we cannot explain webs of belief as the products of self-sufficient traditions. Traditions arise, develop, and wither only because individuals come to hold the beliefs they do for reasons of their own.

Idealists and irrationalists might object to my denying the self-sufficiency of traditions after I have already accepted that individuals always reach their webs of belief against the background of inherited traditions. They might argue that if people always reach their beliefs through traditions, we must be able to explain webs of belief exclusively by reference to the appropriate traditions. Actually, however, my arguments for invoking inherited traditions to explain historical objects do not commit me to the view that inherited traditions are sufficient to explain these objects. On the contrary, my account of tradition allows for human agency in a way that undermines any attempt to explain a web of beliefs without reference to the individual believer. The variety of agency that survives my appeal to tradition is the ability of individuals to extend and modify the traditions they inherit. Just because individuals start out from an inherited tradition this does not imply that they cannot go on to adjust it. Indeed, traditions change over time, and we cannot explain these changes unless we accept that individuals are capable of altering the traditions they inherit. The easiest way to make this point is counter-factually. Traditions arise from the beliefs of numerous individuals, so that if they determined the beliefs of individuals, we would have a closed circle that would preclude change. Imagine that the totality of beliefs held by individuals in a society is as it is, so that the traditions therein are as they are. Because traditions are emergent entities, they cannot alter unless the totality of the beliefs held by individuals changes. But if traditions really determined beliefs, the totality of the beliefs held by individuals could not alter unless the traditions did so. In order to explain change, therefore, we must summon up individuals who can extend and modify the traditions that provide the starting points from which they arrive at their webs of belief. The possiblity of agency even extends to the ability of individuals to reflect on different traditions and thus decide to migrate from one to another. Just because individuals start out against the background of an inherited tradition this does not imply that they cannot end up within a very different one. Indeed, people do migrate from, say, Christianity to Islam, and we can explain their doing so only by accepting that individuals are capable of moving across any boundaries allegedly dividing traditions. Some scholars appear to cast doubt on the possibility of such boundary crossings by arguing that individuals who adhere to one tradition cannot grasp the meaning of the concepts constitutive of another.[21] Doing so, however, requires them to embrace the thesis of incommensurability we have already found to be false. For a start, even when two traditions make use of different concepts, they can still overlap in ways that might provide people who subscribe to one with points of entry into another. Indeed, we have seen how our being in the world guarantees the broad accuracy of perception in a way that suggests that different traditions will overlap in just this way. Moreover, even if two traditions did not overlap at all, the adherents of one could observe the practices of the adherents of the other and so learn the meaning of the concepts embodied in these practices. We have seen how our being in the world requires us to act to certain effect, and how this encourages people from different cultures to come to terms with each other's worldview. Individuals are agents capable both of modifying traditions and of migrating across traditions.

Critics might respond to this stress on human agency by arguing that traditions themselves determine which choices are, and are not, available to individuals therein. They might say that a tradition defines the set of options available to its adherents. Although its adherents are free to choose from among these options, they are not free to go beyond boundaries determined by the tradition itself. Foucault, for example, allows for the presence of competing outlooks in his epistemes in a way

---

[21] On the incommensurability of paradigms, see especially Kuhn, *Structure of Scientific Revolutions*. A similar position is defended in MacIntyre, *Whose Justice? Which Rationality?*

that suggests that he gives to epistemes the role of a limiting framework. He describes competing views of the nature of species, for example, as 'simultaneous requirements in the archaeological network that defines the knowledge of nature in the classical age'.[22] Elsewhere he has even written of 'historical rules, always specific to time and place, and which, for a given period and within a social and, economic, geographic, or linguistic zone, define the framework within which the enunciative functions are expressed'.[23] Several other philosophers, moreover, have described the thought of an epoch as governed by something akin to 'absolute presuppositions'.[24] Whenever they do so, they imply that an episteme, epoch, or tradition prescribes boundaries beyond which its adherents cannot go. They suggest that the social context sets limits to the beliefs individuals can come to hold. Properly to defend agency, therefore, we must challenge the idea of traditions as limiting frameworks. We must show that traditions do not prescribe limits to the choices available to the individuals who set out from within them. Nobody can say that traditions impose limits on agents, however, unless in principle we could recognise such a limit if it existed: clearly if we could not have knowledge of something even if it did exist, we could not have any conceivable grounds for asserting it did exist. What is more, we could not recognise such a limit even in principle unless we could have criteria by which to distinguish a necessary limit imposed on agency by a tradition from a conditional limit that agents could go beyond although they happened not yet to have done so. Thus, we can prove that traditions do not set limits to agency by showing that in principle we could not identify any such limit since we could not have criteria to distinguish it from a purely conditional one.

Imagine that we could identify limits that a tradition imposed on the choices open to its adherents. Because these limits would be imposed by the tradition itself, they could not be natural limits transcending all traditions, as, for instance, there is a natural limit to how fast someone can run. Moreover, because we could identify the limits, we could describe them to the people who adhered to the tradition in question, so that assuming they could understand us, they too could come to recognise the limits. Finally, because they too could come to recognise the limits, and because the limits could not be natural limits, therefore, they could transcend the limits, so really the limits could not be limits at all.

---

[22] Foucault, *Order of Things*, p. 150.   [23] Foucault, *Archaeology of Knowledge*, pp. 153–4.
[24] See R. Collingwood, *An Essay on Metaphysics* (Oxford: Clarendon Press, 1940), particularly pp. 21–48.

The fact is that any limit we could identify could not be a real limit, so traditions cannot impose limits on the beliefs individuals can adopt. A critic might object that although we could describe the limits imposed by a tradition to its adherents, they could not come to understand us. But this objection rests on the thesis of incommensurability we have found to be false. Because all worldviews are commensurable, the adherents of any tradition whatsoever could come to understand what we tell them. Another critic might allow that people can transcend the limits imposed by a tradition only to insist that if they do so they destroy it. But this is irrelevant. We are ruling out limits on human agency, not limits to what we might include within a tradition. The fact that agents who made certain choices would thereby transform the tradition they adhered to in no way suggests that there are limits to the choices they might make. No doubt certain choices would entail a decisive departure from a given tradition, but this does not mean that the tradition prevents its adherents from making these choices. We can conclude, therefore, that we could not identify any necessary limits imposed by traditions on the choices available to their adherents. If we could do so, we could describe the limits to the adherents who could then transgress the limits, so the limits would be conditional, not necessary. What is more, because we could not identify any limit imposed on agency by any tradition, we must conclude that the very idea of such a limit rests on a conceptual confusion.

Historians cannot explain why people held the webs of belief they did exclusively in terms of either inherited traditions or pure experience and reason. They must eschew both strong structuralism and atomistic individualism. Instead, they need to explore how tradition and agency interact with one another. The grammar of our concepts shows both that traditions underlie the possibility of agency and that agency decides the development, and so content, of traditions. People reach the webs of belief they do against the background of traditions, but they are agents who can extend, modify, or even reject the traditions that provided the background to their initial webs of belief. Historians can explain why someone held the web of beliefs he did by reference to the way he reasoned against the background of an inherited tradition. To fill out this form of explanation, however, we must analyse our concepts of tradition and reasoning.

THE NATURE OF TRADITIONS

The foregoing analysis of the relationship of tradition to agency suggests an account of the nature of intellectual traditions and of their role in explaining webs of belief. Because people necessarily reach their initial webs of belief by way of an inherited tradition, we can start by defining a tradition as a set of understandings someone acquires as an initial web of beliefs during a process of socialisation. The new born infant develops into a mature adult with beliefs; and because these beliefs cannot come exclusively from its experience and its reason alone, they must embody a tradition transmitted to it during a process of socialisation. The new born infant learns to find his way in the world by being taught to recognise objects, identify their characteristics, name them, and speak about them, where the objects he thus picks out and discusses are made available to him by a tradition. The infant learns to recognise, to identify, to name, and to speak about objects through contact with others whose theories give them, and so the infant, experience of one set of objects rather than another. The infant learns to pick out objects as a result of being shown them and told their names, but what he can be shown and taught to name depends on the objects of which his teachers have experiences, and so on the theories with which these teachers already make sense of the world. A tradition provides the theories that construct the objects the infant initially finds in the world.

It is important to recognise that this analysis of the process of socialisation stands as a philosophical deduction from the grammar of our concepts, not an empirical induction from our theory-laden experience. The empirical claim could be only that as a contingent fact people are embedded in social contexts. The philosophical claim, in contrast, is that we cannot conceive of anyone ever holding beliefs apart from in a social context. The categories governing our concepts show that people come to hold beliefs only as a result of a process in which they are initiated into a tradition. Thus, there cannot have been a time when traditions did not operate in this way. Strauss must be wrong when he says, 'classical philosophy originally acquired the fundamental concepts of political philosophy by starting from political phenomena as they present themselves to "the natural consciousness"'.[25] Similarly, there could not be supermen capable of transcending the influence of tradition. Strauss also must be wrong when he implies that we might overcome tradition so as to perceive political phenomena in their

---

[25] L. Strauss, 'Political philosophy and history', in *What is Political Philosophy?*, p. 75.

natural appearance.[26] Nobody could conceivably escape the hold of tradition, neither someone from the past nor someone in the future. All people at all times set out from an inherited set of shared understandings they acquired during a process of socialisation. We necessarily acquire a way of seeing the world along with the values, concerns, and assumptions others impart to us. There are values, concerns, and assumptions lurking in the very way our language divides up the world by deploying concepts embodying one set of distinctions rather than another.

Although tradition is unavoidable, it is so as a starting point, not as something that determines, or even limits, later performances. We should be cautious, therefore, of representing tradition as an inevitable presence within all we do in case we thereby leave too slight a role for agency. Certainly, because traditions do not determine or even limit later performances, we should not imply that they are in some way constitutive of the webs of belief people later come to hold. Although individuals must set out from within a tradition, they later can extend, modify, or even reject it in a way that might make it anything but constitutive of the web of beliefs they come to hold. Philosophers indebted to the hermeneutic tradition are particularly prone to talk of tradition, a social language, or something else of the sort, as if it were integral to everything one ever does. They represent tradition as an impersonal force immanent within, even definitive of, performances.[27] Really, however, we should conceive of a tradition primarily as an initial influence on people. The content of the tradition will appear in their later performances only in so far as their agency has not led them to change it, where every part of it is in principle open to change. Moreover, when the content of the tradition does not appear in their later performances, it influences them only by virtue of being the initial background against which they set out. Tradition is an influence that works through individuals on individuals. It is a necessary part of the background to everything anyone believes or does, but not a necessary presence in all they believe and do.

Tradition is unavoidable as a starting point, not as a final destination. This means that we need not define a tradition in essentialist terms. Indeed, we should be extremely wary of ever doing so. The essentialist fallacy is exemplified by A. O. Lovejoy's project of studying unit ideas as they change their outer form and enter into various shifting relation-

---

[26] *Ibid.*, p. 77.
[27] See, for example, Collingwood, *The Idea of History*; Gadamer, *Truth and Method*; MacIntyre, *Whose Justice? Which Rationality?*; and Winch, *The Idea of a Social Science*.

ships with one another over time. Lovejoy himself, of course, did not
describe his unit ideas as traditions. He seems, rather, to have thought of
unit ideas as appearing within traditions composed of clusters of such
unit ideas. None the less, whether we choose to talk of traditions, clusters
of unit ideas, or unit ideas does not matter. What matters is that we
should eschew essentialism: we should be wary of any talk of 'primary
and persistent' objects in the history of ideas.[28] Essentialists equate
traditions with fixed essences to which they ascribe variations. They
define traditions in terms of an unchanging core, which appears in
different outer garbs from time to time and even from person to person.
No doubt there are occasions when historians can legitimately point to
the persistence through time of a core idea; or, rather, because the
clarity of a tradition depends on the links between its constituent ideas,
they can point to the persistence through time of a cluster of core ideas.
Equally, however, historians can choose to concentrate on a tradition
with no essential core. They might identify a tradition with a group of
ideas widely shared by a number of individuals although no one idea
was held by all of them. Or they might identify a tradition with a group
of ideas passed down from generation to generation, changing a little
each time, so that no single idea persisted from start to finish. More
significantly, because individuals are agents who play an active role in
the learning process, and because we cannot identify limits to the
changes they can introduce to the webs of belief they inherit, historians
will usually encounter difficulties if they try to define a tradition in terms
of a fixed core. Individuals who take a given idea from their teachers do
not also have to take the other ideas their teachers associate with it.
Rather, they can modify or reject any particular idea in any group of
ideas while holding steady any of the other ideas in that group. The
bearer of a tradition might think of it as a unified whole possessing an
essential core. In fact, however, it will be composed of a variety of parts,
each of which can be reflected upon, and so accepted, modified, or
rejected, by itself. Individuals can respond selectively to the different
parts of the webs of belief they acquire as an inheritance. Indeed,
because people usually want to improve their heritage by making it
more coherent, more accurate, and more relevant to contemporary
issues, they often do respond selectively to it. They accept some parts of
it, modify others, and reject others. Traditions change as they are

---

[28] A. Lovejoy, *The Great Chain of Being: A Study of the History of an Idea* (Cambridge, Mass.: Harvard
University Press, 1936), p. 7. Also see A. Lovejoy, 'The historiography of ideas', in *Essays in the
History of Ideas* (Baltimore: Johns Hopkins University Press, 1948), pp. 1–13.

transmitted from person to person.[29] Essentialism typically results, therefore, either in a tradition whose range is severely restricted because agents rapidly depart from its fixed core, or in a tradition composed of beliefs that are defined so broadly that it lacks clarity and so merit.

Tradition is an influence that works through others on one, rather than a defining presence in all one believes and does. The relationship of teacher to pupil provides a useful metaphor for the way others impart a tradition to one; although we must not take this metaphor to refer exclusively to a formal, face to face relationship. The learning process requires teachers who initiate and pupils who learn. Individuals acquire their initial webs of belief by listening to other people, including their parents, educators, the authors they read, and their fellows. Typically each individual will fulfil both of these roles at some point in time. The teachers will once have been pupils who acquired their initial webs of belief from earlier teachers, and the pupils will later become teachers who provide future pupils with initial webs of belief. It is because beliefs thus pass from generation to generation that we can talk of teachers initiating pupils into intellectual traditions that persist and develop through time. Although pupils receive their initial webs of belief from teachers during fairly brief moments in time, these moments always represent the culmination of a larger historical process. The teacher who transmits the beliefs is just the most recent link in a long chain of people who began as pupils and ended as teachers, passing an always changing set of beliefs down to each other. A long historical sequence lies behind the comparatively brief moment when a new pupil is initiated into a tradition.

Because traditions persist only through teachers initiating pupils into shared understandings, we must avoid hypostatising them. We must not ascribe to traditions an occult or Platonic existence independent of the beliefs of specific individuals. Traditions are not fixed entities people happen to discover. They are contingent entities people produce by their own activities. The exponents of a tradition bring it into being and determine its progress by developing their webs of belief in the ways they do. A defence of procedural individualism clearly implies that traditions arise only out of the beliefs of specific individuals, and a defence of agency implies that traditions do not determine the beliefs of their exponents. Consequently, we can identify the beliefs that make up a

---

[29] Although Lovejoy allows for change, he immediately adds the qualification that 'increments of absolute novelty seem to me a good deal rarer than is sometimes supposed'. See Lovejoy, *Great Chain of Being*, p. 4.

tradition only by reference to the shared understandings and temporal links that allow us to associate its exponents with one another. Pupils learn what they do from individual teachers, not a social tradition: they listen to lectures by individuals, not society; they discuss affairs with individuals, not society; they read books written by individuals, not society; they watch television programmes made by individuals, not society; and they reflect on beliefs held by individuals, not society. Intellectual traditions exist only as the sum of the beliefs of their individual exponents in their relations with one another.

Because structural meanings are abstractions derived from her-meneutic meanings, traditions must be emergent entities based on the beliefs of individuals. Specific webs of belief do not partake of traditions conceived as ideal forms. Rather, traditions emerge out of specific webs of belief and the relations between them. Individuals hold webs of belief, and traditions are composed of the webs of belief of various individuals who are related to one another as teachers and pupils. Let us examine more closely the nature of the relationship that must exist between beliefs if they are to constitute a tradition. For a start, the beliefs that make up a tradition must have passed from generation to generation. They must embody a series of temporal relationships in which they provided the starting point for each of their later exemplars. Indeed, traditions can play an explanatory role in the history of ideas only because the webs of belief of which they are composed have an appro-priate temporal relationship to one another. Traditions must be com-posed of beliefs that were relayed from teacher to pupil to pupil's pupil and so on. The beliefs must have provided a starting point for each of their successive exponents. The existence of the appropriate temporal connections, however, need not have been a result of any deliberate design. Nobody need have intended to pass on the relevant set of beliefs, nor even have been conscious of doing so. Typically the temporal continuity between the beliefs within a tradition appears as a series of developments of transmitted themes. As beliefs pass from teacher to pupil, so the pupil modifies and extends the themes, or conceptual connections, that linked the beliefs to each other. Thus, although we must be able to trace a historical line from the start of a tradition to its finish, the developments introduced by its successive adherents might be such that the start and finish have nothing in common apart from their temporal link. The beliefs of the most recent exponent of a tradition might be utterly different from those of earlier exponents of the same tradition. An abstract web of beliefs that was not passed on in this way, however, would be a mere snapshot. It would be a summary of one or more moments in time, rather than a tradition capable of relating moments in time to one another by exhibiting their historical continuity. If, for example, historians discovered that Chinese Buddhists and American Indians had held beliefs resembling those of modern anarchists, they could not talk legitimately of a tradition of anarchism incorporating all these beliefs. A tradition must consist of more than a series of instances that happen to resemble each other, or that resemble each other because they arose in similar situations or for similar reasons. A tradition must consist of a series of instances that resemble one another precisely because they exercised a formative influence on one another in a definite, historical chain.

As well as suitable temporal connections, traditions must embody suitable conceptual connections. The beliefs a teacher passed on to a pupil must form a fairly coherent set. They must form an intelligible whole so that we can see why they went along together. Traditions have to embody appropriate conceptual connections because their explanatory value in the history of ideas derives from the fact that they provided someone with an initial web of beliefs, where any web of beliefs must exhibit a degree of consistency. The beliefs within a tradition could not have provided someone with an initial starting point unless they coalesced to form a moderately coherent web. Similar reasoning implies that the inner consistency of the beliefs in a tradition must appear in the substantive content of those beliefs, although it also might appear in a number of its other features, including an approach to certain objects, a mode of presentation, or just an expression of allegiance. Only beliefs whose content cohered to some degree could provide the infant with an initial understanding of the world. Thus, the beliefs in a tradition must exhibit a degree of conceptual coherence, although, of course, this need not be absolute and the beliefs certainly need not be logically deducible from each other. Traditions cannot be made up of purely random beliefs that successive individuals happen to have held in common. If, for example, historians discovered that various people believed both that God came to earth and that our souls survived death, they could not talk of a tradition composed of these beliefs alone. If, however, they found that these two beliefs went along with others such as that Christ, the Son of God, came to earth and taught his followers to have faith in an afterlife, they could then talk of a Christian tradition composed of this fairly coherent set of beliefs.

We can conclude, therefore, that traditions consist of various webs of belief linked to one another both temporally and conceptually. Beyond this conclusion, however, we cannot define any clear limits to what counts as a tradition. Certainly we cannot specify necessary or sufficient conditions for asserting that the appropriate temporal and conceptual links really did exist. We cannot do so because an anthropological epistemology shows that the reasonableness of any such assertion rests on a comparison with rival histories, not on fixed conditions.[30] All we can say is that if historians want to evoke a tradition, the evidence they use to show the tradition existed must be evidence of appropriate temporal and conceptual links between the relevant webs of belief.

Although the beliefs in a tradition must relate to one another both temporally and conceptually, their substantive content is unimportant. Because tradition is unavoidable, all webs of belief must have their roots in traditions. They must do so whether they are aesthetic or practical, sacred or secular, legendary or factual, pre-modern or scientific, valued because of their lineage or their reasonableness. It does not matter whether they are transmitted orally or in a written form. It does not matter whether pupils are meant to accept them on another's authority or through being shown how to derive them from first principles. All beliefs must arise against the background of tradition. The concept of tradition that historians deploy to explain beliefs differs, therefore, from the one that other scholars associate exclusively with the customary ways of pre-modern peoples. The concept of tradition that we have been developing does not refer specifically to pre-industrial, rural communities governed by prescriptive authority and customary laws inspired by religious values. It applies equally cogently to modern communities with their greater concern for legal authority and rational laws ostensibly grounded on scientific knowledge. Perhaps there is a useful distinction to be made between pre-modern and scientific authorities, between beliefs adopted as part of an entrenched folklore and those adopted as a result of methodical procedures and controlled reasoning. Even if there is, however, it must occur within an explanatory concept of tradition.[31] Even we moderns cannot have pure experiences; we too must arrive at our beliefs by way of the traditions found in our commu-

---

[30] Contrast the analysis of influence in Q. Skinner, 'The limits of historical explanation', *Philosophy* 41 (1966), 199–215. Skinner now accepts that his criteria for asserting influence were too strict, but he still does not see that we cannot have any such criteria. Skinner, 'Meaning and understanding', pp. 45–6.

[31] We certainly cannot distinguish modern and traditional beliefs using criteria akin to those of the logical positivists, notably verifiability by pure evidence. Contrast H. Acton, 'Tradition and some other forms of order', *Proceedings of the Aristotelian Society* 53 (1952–53), 1–28.

nities. Novices in science do not work out appropriate procedures, reasoning, and accepted truths by themselves.[32] They are initiated into a tradition of science by their teachers, and only after they have been thus initiated do they proceed to advance science through their own work. Even when they later go back to check or repudiate the received scientific wisdom, they do so against the background of a tradition into which they already have been initiated. Traditions are emergent entities composed of webs of belief that possess the appropriate temporal and conceptual links to one another. The content of beliefs does not decide whether or not they constitute a tradition.

Historians have before them both individuals who hold webs of belief and traditions composed of webs of belief related to one another in the manner just specified. How should they decide which tradition helps to explain why a particular individual holds the web of beliefs he does? Many of the problems attendant on the concept of tradition arise because historians try to decide this issue by comparing the beliefs of the individual with a hypostatised tradition. In contrast, just as we rejected an essentialist analysis of tradition, so we must eschew the temptation to locate an individual in a tradition by comparing his beliefs with a checklist of core ideas or a suitable philosophical move. For a start, because traditions are not fixed entities of which specific webs of belief partake, we cannot locate a person in one by comparing his beliefs with its allegedly key features. Rather, because traditions are the contingent products of the ways in which people develop their specific beliefs, we must identify the tradition against the background against which someone comes to hold the beliefs he does by tracing appropriate temporal connections back through time. Philosophers are far too inclined to reify traditions, as if the question to ask were 'Does this individual express the ideas constitutive of this fixed tradition?' or 'Does this individual make the required philosophical move in the development of this tradition?' rather than 'What temporal connections do we need to trace back to explain why this individual had these beliefs as his starting point?'[33] In addition, philosophers should not regard a tradition as 'a concrete manner of behaviour' as if there were some authentic set of experiences its exponents could attempt to articulate as constitutive of it.[34] Tradi-

---

[32] Compare Kuhn, *Structure of Scientific Revolutions*.

[33] Contrast respectively MacIntyre, *Whose Justice? Which Rationality?* and L. Strauss, *Natural Right and History* (Chicago: University of Chicago Press, 1953).

[34] M. Oakeshott, 'Political education', in *Rationalism in Politics and Other Essays* (Oxford: Oxford University Press, 1962), p. 128.

tions are not fixed entities that play a judicial role in our understanding. They do not enable us to evaluate particular webs of belief against an allegedly privileged web of beliefs or an allegedly authentic set of experiences. Rather, they are evolving entities that play an instrumental role in our understanding. They help us to explain the content of particular webs of belief by relating them to the relevant prior webs of belief.

No particular web of beliefs or set of experiences has a privileged, automatic, or natural role in defining any tradition. Even if Marx himself somehow told us that he meant such and such, this would not mean that such and such constituted a privileged, defining web of beliefs for a hypostatised Marxist tradition. The Marxist tradition in which we locate someone must consist of whatever webs of belief we come across as we trace the temporal connections back from that person's beliefs in our attempt to explain them. Marx's new statement would be just one more that we might or might not arrive at while tracing these connections. There is no single, authentic Marxist tradition, just numerous Marxist traditions each of which helps to explain a different web of beliefs. Likewise, no particular set of logical relationships has a privileged, automatic, or natural role in defining any tradition. Historians must define traditions in terms of webs of belief that were related to one another in an appropriate manner. They cannot do so in terms of the logical relationships they believe relate various beliefs to one another. Even if Locke held beliefs we can read as responses to, or elucidations of, Hobbes's beliefs, Hobbes would not necessarily belong in the tradition in which we locate Locke. The tradition in which we locate Locke must consist of the webs of belief we come across as we trace the temporal connections back from his beliefs in our attempt to explain them. The logical links between Locke and Hobbes become relevant only if they are reinforced by appropriate temporal links. Traditions are not hypostatised entities. They do not consist of either a privileged web of beliefs or an authentic set of philosophically significant relationships. Historians must define traditions by reference to historical facts about webs of belief and the links between them. They can identify a tradition only through a study of the webs of belief of the individuals within it. Only the beliefs of individuals can acquaint them with traditions; only inference from the beliefs of individuals can enable them to explore the nature of traditions; and only checks against the beliefs of individuals can provide them with tests of their claims about traditions.

Because traditions are not hypostatised entities, a historian can decide which individuals belong in a tradition only by tracing the temporal connections that bind a web of beliefs back to its predecessors. A historian cannot decide whether individuals belong in a tradition by comparing their beliefs with an abstract moment in a logical argument or with a privileged set of beliefs or experiences. Even if people want to identify themselves with a tradition, they cannot do so by saying that their beliefs share key features with, or address questions raised by, those they see as their predecessors. People can identify themselves with a tradition only by showing that their beliefs are linked to those they see as their predecessors by a series of appropriate, temporal connections. Whenever people locate themselves in a tradition, therefore, they make a historical argument with which others might disagree. To locate themselves in a tradition, they have to defend a particular account of the conceptual and temporal relationships between the beliefs of those they see as their predecessors. Moreover, this account will usually conflict with the accounts other people give of these relationships when locating themselves in a similar or different tradition. This is why conflicts over how to interpret traditions are a more or less permanent feature of social life. Such conflicts arise because people offer incompatible views of the past in their attempts to locate themselves in traditions. Such conflicts do not imply that there is an authentic tradition over which to struggle. Nor do such conflicts, together with the developments they produce, constitute the defining characteristic of traditions.[35]

A rejection of all hypostatised views of tradition should lead us to conclude that historians can locate an individual in a wide variety of traditions for different purposes. Because there are no hypostatised traditions, the historian's task cannot be to locate the individual in one of a finite set of fixed traditions. Rather, because historians identify the tradition against which someone came to hold the beliefs they did by tracing the relevant temporal connections back through time, the pre-cise content they give to the tradition will depend on the beliefs they thereby hope to explain. If they want to explain someone's web of beliefs as a whole, they will define the relevant tradition in one way: if they want to explain only part of his web of beliefs, they might define the relevant tradition differently: and if they want to explain another part of his beliefs, they might define the relevant tradition differently again. Because historians identify a tradition by tracing temporal and concep-tual links back through time starting with the beliefs they wish to

---

[35] Contrast MacIntyre, *Whose Justice? Which Rationality?*, pp. 349–69.

explain, the content of the tradition they identify typically varies with the beliefs they wish to explain. Different features of a web of beliefs typically have somewhat different temporal and conceptual connections to earlier webs of belief. Thus, when two historians set out to explain different features of a single web of beliefs, they typically trace back different temporal and conceptual connections in a way that quite properly leads them to identify different traditions as appropriate explanations for the different objects of interest to them. There is a very real sense, therefore, in which historians define traditions according to their own purposes. Historians do not pigeonhole each individual in one of a fixed number of reified traditions. They select one tradition from among the many in which they could locate an individual because it best explains the particular beliefs they are studying.

Once we recognise that historians can select traditions to suit their different purposes, we will dismiss as besides the point several heated debates about how exactly historians should make sense of particular individuals. Consider, for example, the complaints made by contextualists and conventionalists about the failure of epic theorists to locate authors in a proper historical context. Consider, more particularly, Dunn's complaint about Strauss's failure to locate Locke in the Puritan tradition. We will say that what counts as a proper historical context depends on what one hopes to explain. Moreover, this suggests that the interpretations of the epic theorists and their critics often are more compatible than either group appears to think. For example, if, like Dunn, historians want to explain Locke's political thought, then no doubt Locke's debt to the Puritan tradition will be of much greater import than his debt to Hobbes, but if, like Strauss, historians want to explain features of modern political philosophy found in Hobbes and Locke, then no doubt they should construct a tradition rather different from the Puritan one evoked by Dunn.[36] Even if the tradition Strauss describes does not provide the best context for Locke's thought as a whole, it might still be the right one to explain the features of Locke's thought in which he is interested. Dunn's complaint that Strauss ignores Locke's debt to the religious ideas of the Puritans misses the point. Properly to repudiate the traditions constructed by epic theorists such as Strauss, contextualists and conventionalists cannot show only that we can best make sense of the thought of a particular author by locating him in a different tradition. They must show that the traditions con-

---

[36] Dunn, *Political Thought of John Locke*; and Strauss, *Natural Right and History*.

structed by the epic theorists do not embody appropriate temporal and conceptual connections. They should condemn Strauss not by arguing that he misinterprets certain authors, but, as Pocock, Skinner, and others have done, by arguing that the tradition he postulates lacks suitable temporal connections.[37] All too often epic theorists evoke an alleged tradition of classic works running from Plato onwards without bothering to demonstrate the historical existence of genuine temporal links between the works they include in this tradition.

Once we recognise that historians can select traditions to suit their different purposes, we will also deny that historians always must postulate a single tradition, episteme, or whatever governing the thought of a given epoch. To reject the hypostatisation of traditions is to accept that we cannot say of traditions what Foucault does of epistemes, namely, that 'in any given culture and at any given moment, there is always only one *episteme*'.[38] Earlier we found that traditions do not structure thought because pupils are agents who play an active part in the learning process. Now we have found that historians select traditions to fit the beliefs they wish to explain. Clearly, therefore, there is no reason why historians should have to select traditions covering all of the thought of an epoch. Individuals disagree as well as agree, so historians can always pick out a plurality of traditions that were present at any given time. Moreover, because individuals disagree at various levels of generality, historians can choose how broadly they want to define their traditions. No doubt historians can pick out very general themes characteristic of the whole thought of an epoch, and, moreover, they might then describe the result as a sort of episteme, though not one that precludes agency. Equally, however, historians can pick out themes found only in this group, or only in that group, and, moreover, they can then describe the result as a number of overlapping, competing traditions. We can conclude, therefore, that the thought of an epoch cannot possess a monolithic character which precludes historians talking of there being more than one tradition at work therein.

Indeed, if historians identify a single tradition or episteme governing the thought of an epoch, it will be of little interest since it will have little explanatory power. The thought of an epoch is made up of the webs of belief of numerous individuals complete with all their agreements and

---

[37] J. Pocock, 'Prophet and inquisitor', *Political Theory* 3 (1975), 385–401; Skinner, 'Meaning and understanding'; and, more gently, J. Gunnell, 'The myth of the tradition', *American Political Science Review* 72 (1978), 122–34; and Gunnell, *Political Theory*, particularly pp. 34–93.

[38] Foucault, *Order of Things*, p. 168.

disagreements. Historians select a tradition from within this medley of beliefs in order to explain a web of beliefs held by an individual. The explanatory value of traditions lies in the way they illustrate the process by which individuals inherited beliefs from their communities. Thus, the more widely historians define a tradition, the weaker its explanatory power will be. If historians select monolithic epistemes, they will have to define them solely in terms of the beliefs held by everyone in the given epoch, so that when they try to explain the web of beliefs of a particular individual, they will be able to explain only why he held these universal beliefs, not why he held numerous other, more specific beliefs. Although the concept of an episteme is associated with Foucault, he is not the only scholar guilty of ignoring the explanatory weakness of too broadly defined a tradition. While scholars indebted to ontological hermeneutics and phenomenology correctly emphasise the ineluctable role played by tradition in human understanding, they all too rarely recognise that because the tradition they thus evoke covers the past as a whole, it is too broad a concept to play any useful explanatory role in the history of ideas.[39] Once again, therefore, we should distinguish between the legitimate ontological hermeneutics exemplified by Gadamer, and the mistaken methodological hermeneutics others often adopt in his name. Historians benefit from approaching the thought of an epoch not as a monolithic tradition, but rather as a number of overlapping, competing traditions. When they do so, they will define each tradition to include both beliefs that were universally accepted at the time and also some other beliefs. Thus, they will be able to use each tradition to explain why an individual held all of the beliefs therein, not just those universally accepted at the time. The more narrowly historians define a tradition, the greater its explanatory power.

The concept of tradition reminds us that the grammar of our concepts implies that we necessarily inherit our initial web of beliefs from our social context. Historians pick out specific historical traditions from the general tradition in which we all have our being in order to show how this process of inheritance worked with respect to specific beliefs. They select traditions out of tradition, conceived as the general background of human life, in order to explain specific features of that life. The value of the traditions they select derives from the explanatory power of the conceptual and temporal links between the beliefs of which they are composed. Indeed, the clarity and precision with which histor-

[39] Gunnell, *Political Theory*; and A. Lockyer, '"Traditions" as context in the history of political theory', *Political Studies* 27 (1979), 201–17.

ians analyse these links fixes the intelligibility and relevance of the tradition they select. The more exact their account of these links, the more fully we will be able to grasp the nature and location of the tradition, so the more explanatory work it will be able to do. Temporal links reveal a movement from the beliefs of teachers to those of pupils. They show how the relevant beliefs passed from one generation to another, thereby explaining why the beliefs persisted through time. Conceptual links reveal a pattern in beliefs that persisted together through time. They show us how the relevant beliefs form a fairly coherent set, thereby explaining why the beliefs persisted together as a loose knit whole, rather than as isolated units or units brought together by mere chance.

WHAT TRADITIONS EXPLAIN

What role exactly do traditions play in explaining why individuals held the webs of belief they did? Tradition is the unavoidable background to all we say and do, but not a constitutive presence in all we say and do. Individuals can come to hold beliefs, and so act, only against the background of a social inheritance; but this inheritance does not limit the beliefs they later can go on to hold, or the actions they can go on to perform. Traditions are not hypostatised entities which appear in various guises at different times. They are contingent and evolving entities that operate through teachers as influences on pupils, where the pupils can extend and modify them in unlimited ways. The role of traditions, therefore, must be to explain why people set out with the initial webs of belief they do, not to explain why they go on to change these initial webs in the ways they do. For a start, because pupils sometimes remain faithful to the beliefs they acquired during the process of socialisation, they sometimes hold a web of beliefs that corresponds to a tradition imparted to them by others. Whenever pupils learn something from a teacher, one way of explaining the belief of the pupils is to say they learnt it from a teacher. Thus, historians can sometimes explain why an individual holds the web of beliefs he does simply by saying he learnt it from teachers who imparted a tradition to him. More importantly, because beliefs only map on to reality as inter-connected webs, because no belief can be self-supporting, therefore, individuals must always locate their particular beliefs in a larger web. Pupils must acquire a web of beliefs in an initial process of socialisation before they can modify this web as and when they learn new beliefs or renounce old ones. Whenever pupils depart from the beliefs they learnt from their teachers, they do so against a background composed of the tradition their teachers imparted to them. Thus, historians who want to explain the intellectual development of an individual must set out from the tradition from which he began. Traditions provide the essential starting point for all explanations of why an individual held a given web of beliefs.

People always arrive at their webs of belief against the background of numerous prior webs of belief which overlap in all sorts of complex ways. When historians identify a tradition as a starting point for an individual, they describe his beliefs in relation to various other webs of belief that they have selected from among this complexity. They associate the imagery, syntax, phraseology, and conceptual content of his beliefs with those of an identifiable set of prior webs of belief. When they do so, they show that he subscribed to a tradition composed of this set of prior webs of belief, where, of course, to subscribe to a tradition is not to follow it slavishly but rather to set out from it. Moreover, when historians show that a tradition was the point of departure for an individual, they identify it as a suitable point of departure for their explanation of why he later arrived at the web of beliefs he did. To say traditions provide historians with points of departure from which to explain why someone held the web of beliefs he did is, however, to recognise that traditions are not sufficient for such explanations. Traditions provide only a synchronic explanation of people's beliefs. Because traditions evolve as a result of human agency, they cannot explain the ways in which people develop their beliefs. Historians cannot invoke traditions to explain why someone modified the beliefs he inherited in the way he did. They cannot do so because the modification of inherited beliefs is an act of agency performed against the background of a tradition but not decided by it. Historians cannot explain why someone held a particular web of beliefs solely by reference to a social structure, and this is so whether they call that structure an episteme, paradigm, or tradition. Fully to explain why people held the particular webs of belief they did, historians must supplement synchronic explanations with suitable diachronic ones. They cannot just relate beliefs to webs of belief, and webs of belief to traditions. They must also refer to the reasons people had for modifying the traditions they inherited in the ways they did.

Historians can explain why someone held a belief by placing it in the context of his whole web of beliefs. In addition, they can begin to explain why he held that web of beliefs by placing it in the context of the tradition from which he set out. None the less, if they are fully to explain why he held that web of beliefs, they must also provide a diachronic account of any departures he made from this inherited tradition. Critics might object that this synchronic form of explanation comes perilously close to the contextualist theory of meaning we rejected earlier.[40] Actually, however, our proposed use of webs of belief and intellectual traditions differs significantly from the use contextualists make of concepts such as paradigms and epistemes. Crucially, whereas contextualists are concerned with historical understanding, we are concerned with historical explanation. Whereas contextualists argue that paradigms and epistemes enable historians to understand the meaning of utterances, we have argued that webs of belief and traditions enable historians to provide the beginnings of an explanation of beliefs. Moreover, because we have argued that webs of belief and traditions enter into explanations, rather than underlying meanings, we can accept that historians might grasp the meaning of an utterance without studying the appropriate web of beliefs or tradition. Consider, for instance, the proposition 'values determine prices'. Semantic holists deny that this proposition has any semantic meaning on the grounds that the term 'value' does not have a fixed reference: they say the semantic meaning of 'value' depends on one's theoretical perspective. Imagine that historians discover that W. S. Jevons said 'values determine prices'. Because contextualists extend semantic holism illegitimately to hermeneutics, they will argue that Jevons's utterance has no meaning outside of a particular paradigm or episteme. They will say the meaning of Jevons's utterance depends on a social paradigm or episteme, so that historians cannot understand it unless they place it in this context. In contrast, we will allow for historians concluding that Jevons believed that values determine prices while leaving open the question of what exactly he thought about the nature of economic value. Webs of belief and traditions help historians to explain beliefs. They are not part of the meaning of works.

The critics might object next that the distinction between understanding utterances and explaining beliefs does not amount to much. They might argue as follows: people necessarily express their beliefs using language, so if paradigms or webs of belief explain individual beliefs, surely these paradigms must also explain the meaning of utteran-

---

[40] For an explicit appeal to tradition as the context in which historians understand a text, rather than explain beliefs, see Lockyer, '"Traditions" as context'. Pocock discusses tradition as a theoretical term in Pocock, 'History of political thought'; and J. Pocock, 'Time, institutions and action: an essay on traditions and their understanding', in *Politics, Language and Time*, pp. 233–72.

ces, and if these paradigms explain the meaning of utterances, surely we
can say that knowledge of the relevant paradigms enriches our appreciation of particular utterances. This argument contains a valid point. We
must accept that to show X believed A because X also believed B, C,
and D is to increase our understanding of X's beliefs as well as to start to
explain X's belief A by locating it in the appropriate web of beliefs.
Because beliefs exist as inter-connected webs; to locate a belief in its web
is to fill out its content and thus to aid our understanding of it. None the
less, when the critics equate our concept of a web of beliefs with the
paradigms and epistemes of the contextualists, they ignore the reasoning
behind our distinction between understanding utterances and explaining beliefs. We turned our attention to expressed beliefs because we
identified hermeneutic meanings with individual viewpoints as opposed
to the linguistic structures of the contextualists. Thus, whereas we focus
on webs of belief conceived as individual viewpoints, contextualists
focus on paradigms conceived as social structures. Whereas our synchronic form of explanation relates a belief to the web of beliefs of the
individual believer, the contextualists relate an utterance to a social
structure. This is why historians inspired by contextualism tend either to
assimilate diverse individuals to a mythical time-spirit or to pull an
individual apart. If, like Foucault, they believe that each epoch possesses
a single dominant episteme, they will tend to ride roughshod over the
differences within an epoch. When they tell the history of their putative
epistemes, they will tend to downplay the particularities of the thought
of individuals, or groups of individuals, by representing differences of
opinion as logically necessary products of underlying themes to which
their subjects had a common allegiance. Foucault, for example, accepts
that there was a debate among classical thinkers about the nature of
money, but he plays down their differences on the grounds that 'if we
investigate the knowledge that made all those various opinions simultaneously possible, we perceive that the opposition between them is
superficial; and that, though it is logically necessary, it is so on the basis
of a single arrangement that simply creates, at any given point, the
alternatives of an indispensable choice'.[41] Similarly, if, like Pocock,
contextualists believe in various coexisting and overlapping paradigms,
they will tend to crush out personal identity. When they tell the history
of their putative social languages, they will tend to introduce some
utterances by an individual in the story of one language, and other

---

[41] Foucault, *Order of Things*, p. 181.

utterances by the same individual in the story of another language, but at no point will they feel a proper need to bring these different utterances together to show the individual held a coherent web of beliefs. Pocock, for example, has argued that Burke's study of the French Revolution belongs in both the language of the common law and the language of political economy; but instead of trying to show how Burke reconciled these two languages, he says 'it seems more important to establish that Burke can be read in both of these contexts than to inquire whether he can be read in both of them simultaneously'.[42]

Our focus on individual viewpoints leads to a different approach to history from that inspired by contextualism. Because we will locate a belief in the web of beliefs of the individual believer, we will not assimilate individuals to things such as social epistemes, paradigms, or languages. Imagine, for example, that historians want to enrich their appreciation of Jevons's utterance 'values determine prices' by putting it in the relevant context. Contextualists define the relevant context as a social paradigm, so presumably they will scurry off to study works by Jevons's predecessors, such as J. S. Mill, or people who influenced him, such as Jeremy Bentham. They will tell us that his utterance belongs in the context of classical economics or utilitarianism. They will try to increase our understanding of his utterance by defining its terms by reference to classical economics or utilitarianism. Unfortunately for them, however, Jevons did not conceive of economic value in the same way as did either the classical economists or the utilitarians. In contrast, we have defined the relevant context as the web of beliefs of the individual concerned, so we will look at Jevons's other utterances to see what he thought about economic value. We will discover that Jevons held a marginal utility theory of value. For Jevons, the proposition 'values determine prices' implied that 'the ratio of exchange of any two commodities will be the reciprocal of the final degrees of utility of the quantities of commodity available for consumption after the exchange is completed'.[43] The context of interest to historians of ideas consists of the web of beliefs of the individual they are studying. It does not consist of a social episteme, paradigm, or language.

The critics might finally object that if we explain beliefs by reference

[42] J. Pocock, 'The political economy of Burke's analysis of a the French Revolution', in *Virtue, Commerce and History*, p. 194. For his study of Burke in relation to the common law, see J. Pocock, 'Burke and the Ancient Constitution: a problem in the history of ideas', in *Politics, Language and Time*, pp. 193–212.

[43] W. Jevons, *The Theory of Political Economy*, ed. R. Collison Black (Harmondsworth, Middlesex: Penguin, 1970), p. 139.

to webs of belief, and webs of belief by reference to traditions, then the relevant contexts for beliefs must ultimately be traditions understood as social epistemes or paradigms. This objection ignores the limitations our defence of human agency led us to place on the explanatory role of traditions. We found that pupils can extend and modify the traditions of their teachers in an unlimited number of ways. Traditions influence our beliefs, but they are not constitutive of them. Thus, traditions can provide no more than a starting point for an explanation of a web of beliefs, and certainly not a full explanation of the beliefs a given individual holds at a given moment. People develop their beliefs against the background of an inherited tradition, so we can begin to give an account of their intellectual development by describing the relevant tradition. But people go on to adjust their beliefs, or at least to internalise their inheritance, so we must continue our account of their intellectual development by discussing why they adjusted their beliefs as they did. Moreover, because people extend and modify traditions, we cannot fill out the content of their beliefs by appealing to the traditions from which they set out. We cannot do so because they might no longer believe in the beliefs we would thereby ascribe to them. Imagine, for example, that historians want to explain why Jevons held the web of beliefs he did after he had developed his marginal utility theory of value. Although they probably will start by locating his beliefs against the background of the tradition of classical economics, this tradition cannot explain why he went on to modify it in the way he did. To explain the way in which Jevons's beliefs developed, historians must have recourse to a diachronic form of explanation. Moreover, because Jevons departed from classical economics, historians would misunderstand his utterance 'values determine prices' if they tried to unpack it by appealing to a concept of value found in the tradition of classical economics. Traditions provide only a starting point from which to explain why people held the beliefs they did. They do not provide a context that adds to our understanding of people's beliefs.

CONCLUSION

Scholars who write on the nature of the history of ideas typically focus on the nature of meaning and the process of understanding. They define the task of historians of ideas as being to understand the meaning of a work. Then they explore the nature of this task without giving much consideration to the question of how historians should explain why a work had the meaning it did. They typically neglect this latter question because at best they see understanding as prior to explanation and at worst they regard explanation as unimportant. In contrast, our anthropological epistemology implies that the validity of an understanding of a work cannot be decided in isolation but only by comparing rival bodies of theories including explanations. The explanation we give of why a work had the meaning it did is not only important in its own right, it also affects the validity of our ascription of that meaning to that work. Our anthropological epistemology requires us to give a new prominence to questions of explanation.

I have gone some way towards uncovering the forms of explanation appropriate to the history of ideas by drawing on the rejection of pure perception that inspired our anthropological epistemology. To begin, I rejected all forms of scientism by deploying deductive arguments to show that mental phenomena require different forms of explanation from physical phenomena. We talk about beliefs using the language of folk psychology, and this language can be neither reduced to physical statements nor made to incorporate the scientific concept of causation. Folk psychology encapsulates normative criteria of rationality in a way that accords with our presumptions in favour of sincere, conscious, and rational beliefs. Indeed, it is because we ascribe beliefs to people in accord with criteria of rationality that an anthropological epistemology plays an important role in prescribing the forms of explanation appropriate to the history of ideas. Because there are no given truths, what it is rational for people to believe must depend on their webs of belief, not pure perceptions or given categories. Because there are no given truths, because objectivity depends on a human practice, therefore, historians have to work with a weak concept of rationality as consistency. Thus, historians can begin to give a rational explanation of a belief by showing how it fits into the broader web of beliefs of the believer. What is more, because there are no given truths, because experience and ratiocination can occur only within a prior web of beliefs, therefore, people must always reach the webs of belief they do against the background of inherited traditions. Because there are no self-evident truths, people must acquire their initial web of beliefs from their communities. Thus, historians can begin to explain why someone held a given web of beliefs by situating it in an appropriate tradition.

The concept of tradition invoked here is a universal one. It expresses a logical conclusion implied by the grammar of our concepts, namely, that individuals always set out from a social inheritance but this social inheritance does not place limits on where they might end up. Within this concept of tradition, therefore, one might distinguish various, more precisely defined types of tradition. For example, one might define a discipline as any tradition that pursues cognitive goals in accord with an objective principle of rationality, and one might define a science as any discipline characterised in addition by a commitment to solving shared problems using shared techniques.[44] Once one had made such distinctions, one might try to devise sociological theories to explain why disciplines, sciences, and the like come into being, develop, and decline in the ways they do. Ultimately one might aspire to provide a general theory of tradition composed of a classification covering all traditions together with sociological theories specifying the circumstances in which the various types of tradition appear, develop, and decline. Instead of trying to devise such a theory, however, I want to point out only that any distinctive type of tradition, and any special form of explanation appropriate to it, would have to fit within the framework of the logic I have outlined. Any particular type of tradition would have to possess the properties I have described as characteristic of all traditions.

One of the properties common to all traditions is that although individuals set out from them, they do not limit the ways individuals might develop them. No doubt some traditions discourage agency whereas others encourage it. But all traditions leave open the ways in which their adherents will develop the webs of belief they inherit. This is why traditions are not sufficient to explain why someone held the web of beliefs he did. Individuals are agents who can extend, modify, and even reject the traditions they inherit. Whenever a teacher imparts a tradition to a pupil, there remain several possible outcomes: the pupil might adopt the tradition, or modify it in a way unforeseen by the teacher, or even renounce it altogether. Thus, historians cannot explain why people held the webs of belief they did simply by associating these webs with traditions. They cannot do so because to come to hold beliefs people must internalise them, and when they internalise them, they make them their own in a way that enables them to transform them. What we now need, therefore, is a form of explanation applicable to the way people develop their webs of belief. How should historians explain why people modify, extend, and depart from traditions in the way they do? So far I have identified a synchronic form of explanation that relates single beliefs to webs of belief, and webs of belief to traditions. Next I must identify a diachronic form of explanation appropriate to departures from tradition and changes of belief.

[44] Something like disciplines and sciences so understood are the focus respectively of Toulmin, *Human Understanding*; and Kuhn, *Structure of Scientific Revolutions*.

CHAPTER 6

On diachronic explanation

INTRODUCTION

We need to consider now how historians should account for departures from tradition and so changes in belief. Although individuals always reach the beliefs they do against the background of inherited traditions, the traditions cannot explain how they go on to develop the beliefs they inherit. Because humans possess a capacity for agency, a logic for the history of ideas must incorporate both diachronic and synchronic forms of explanation. Because humans are capable of exercising their individual reason against a social background, a logic of the history of ideas must incorporate an analysis of thought as well as tradition. Next, therefore, I will consider why and how people reflect on the webs of belief they inherit so as to extend, modify, or even reject them. I will analyse the nature of individual reasoning as it takes place against the background of an inherited tradition.

Clearly, when historians consider changes of belief, they should continue to presume the beliefs they study are sincere, conscious, and rational. Likewise, they should continue to work with a folk psychology they apply using criteria of rationality. I will continue, therefore, to concentrate on the forms of explanation appropriate to sincere, conscious, and rational beliefs. A historian should explain departures from traditions by reference to the reasons people had for extending, modifying, or even rejecting the traditions that provided them with their initial inheritances. Our anthropological epistemology shows that people approach objective knowledge by adjusting bundles of theories in response to generally accepted facts. Thus, if people behave rationally, they will change their beliefs whenever they accept a new understanding, whether it be a fact or a powerful theory. People develop, adjust, and transform traditions in response to dilemmas, where dilemmas are authoritative understandings that put into question their existing webs

221

of belief. Dilemmas prompt changes of belief because they consist of new beliefs and any new belief necessarily poses a question of the agent's web of beliefs. Historians can explain a change of belief, therefore, by referring to the relevant dilemma. They can explain why someone reached a particular web of beliefs by representing it as a product of a series of modifications made to an inherited tradition in response to a series of dilemmas.

While dilemmas play a vital role in diachronic explanations in the history of ideas, we will find we cannot reduce the concept of a dilemma any further. The failure of reductionist approaches to things akin to dilemmas follows from semantic holism. Because beliefs form webs, not hierarchic structures, there is neither one foundational type of belief nor one basic type of dilemma. For a start, because no belief is immune from revision, dilemmas can afflict any of our moral, philosophical, religious, scientific, historical, or other subsets of belief. In addition, because the authority and content of an experience must depend on the individual's prior set of theories, we cannot say that only one area of life produces dilemmas. All areas of our experience can lead us to adopt a new belief, so dilemmas can arise out of all areas of our experience. Dilemmas can arise from an experience of the relationships of production, an acquaintance with a philosophical argument or scientific theory, a mystical experience, an encounter with a different culture, and so on. Although our experiences influence the beliefs we come to hold by posing dilemmas for the traditions we inherit, no one type of experience is basic to all others. Thus, any experience can potentially generate a new belief and so a dilemma. All experiences, moreover, are theory laden. Thus, no experience or dilemma can require people to change their beliefs in any one way.

A historian can explain why people changed their beliefs in the ways they did by pointing to the dilemmas they faced. This diachronic form of explanation, like its synchronic counterpart, draws on a folk psychology we apply using criteria of rationality. The dominant forms of explanation in the history of ideas are rational ones, and, as such, they work by pointing to the conditional connections linking the beliefs with which they deal. Conditional connections differ from both arbitrary ones, which cannot explain anything, and physically necessary ones, which appear in explanations in the natural sciences. They arise from themes that are immanent within and given immediately by the beliefs they connect.

WHY BELIEFS CHANGE

People only believe ideas they make their own. Although traditions provide the necessary starting point for intellectual biographies, traditions cannot explain the way people develop the beliefs they inherit. The human capacity for agency implies that change originates in decisions made by individuals, not in the inner logic of various traditions. The ability of people to revise traditions illustrates the facile nature of any supposed contrast between the traditional and the rational.[1] Traditions would deny the free play of reason only if they fixed our responses to things – surely we must accept this point irrespective of whether we want to promote a rational enlightenment so as to question traditional forms of authority, or save traditional ways of life from a technocratic and soulless rationalism, or even if we are unmoved by all such issues. Thus, because traditions do not fix our responses for us, they do not stand in contrast to reason. Our earlier analysis of structure and agency points rather to the interpenetration of authority and freedom. Because people always start out against the background of a tradition, traditions necessarily provide the authoritative contexts within which we exercise our reason. Equally, however, because traditions never fix limits to the conclusions people can reach, the free exercise of our reason is not undermined by the presence of an authoritative tradition. Individuals initiate change by exercising their reason in the local context of their existing beliefs. They exercise their reason to depart from the traditions they inherited in one way rather than another.

Developments in people's beliefs, and so in traditions, occur because of their particular reflections. Clearly, therefore, historians must refer to the reflections of the individual whom they are studying if they are to explain why he came to hold the web of beliefs he did. A historian can explain why people did or did not continue to believe certain things only by going beyond the traditions from which they started on their journeys to explain why they later internalised some beliefs and not others so as to depart from their traditions in the ways they did. To explain changes in the beliefs of individuals, and so in the content of traditions, historians must turn from a synchronic perspective to a diachronic one. They must turn from the impact of traditions on individuals to the impact of individuals on traditions.

Because the power of agency is a universal human faculty, historians

[1] Contrast Acton, 'Tradition'.

must deploy diachronic explanations whenever they study anyone's intellectual biography. Not only the great philosophers, but all people at all times are capable of reasoning against an inherited background so as to reach a novel web of beliefs. This simple fact renders irrelevant not only the attempts by the structuralists and their successors to explain conceptual change without evoking agency, but also the call for historians to provide evidence of people intending to exercise their reason in a certain way.[2] The ubiquity of change follows from the fact that as humans we possess a faculty of agency. For a start, people always confront slightly novel circumstances that require them to apply anew the traditional beliefs they inherited. Moreover, because the beliefs people inherit cannot fix the criteria of their own application, when people thus confront novel circumstances, they necessarily develop the tradition they inherited in what is a continual process of conceptual change.[3] Whenever people confront a new situation, they have to extend the tradition they have inherited in order to encompass it. Even if a tradition appears to tell people how they should extend it, it can actually provide them at most with a guide to what they might do, not a rule deciding what they must do. A tradition can point people in a given direction, but the only way they have of checking whether they have been true to the tradition is by asking whether they and their fellow adherents are content with what they eventually decide to do. How one might legitimately extend a tradition to cover novel circumstances depends on one's practice in doing so. It is not fixed by the tradition itself. Thus, change occurs even on those occasions when people think they are adhering strictly to a tradition they regard as sacrosanct. Traditions could be static only if we never encountered novel circumstances.

The ubiquity of change also reflects the fact that people always think about, and perhaps try to improve upon, their inheritance. Every time people reflect on the beliefs they inherited from their teachers, they are liable to become aware of a difficulty in their understanding of the beliefs. Their concern to resolve the difficulty will typically prompt them to modify the beliefs. Even if people think they are trying only to understand correctly a tradition they regard as sacrosanct, their effort to do so will generally involve their exercising their reason, which, in turn,

[2] See respectively Foucault, *Order of Things*; and Pocock, 'State of the art', pp. 24–5.
[3] Compare the discussion of what is involved in following a rule in Wittgenstein, *Philosophical Investigations*, ## 143–242.

will entail their developing the tradition they are trying to understand. No doubt some traditions, such as one based on a single divine revelation, encourage their adherents to describe the results of their reasoning as mere elucidations, not innovations. No doubt, moreover, some traditions, such as modern science, encourage their adherents actively to seek innovations as a source of intellectual progress. In both cases, however, innovation necessarily occurs if only as a result of the humble effort to understand what has gone before. Conceptual change does not occur as a series of random fluctuations totally unrelated to human agency. Nor is it exclusively the result of the self-conscious attempts of a few thinkers to devise a more coherent set of beliefs. Rather, conceptual change occurs because all of us are individual agents who reflect on the traditions we inherit in the light of our own experiences and thereby alter these traditions in accord with our own reasoning.

How can a historian explain why people develop and revise their webs of belief in the particular ways they do? The conceptual priority of sincere, conscious, and rational beliefs commits us to folk psychology with its criteria of rationality. The form of explanation appropriate to a change of belief begins, therefore, with the task of providing a rational reconstruction of the reasons the people concerned had for changing their beliefs in the ways they did. Consider, once again, two extreme views of what such a task might entail. On the one hand, logical empiricists might argue that rational people test their theoretical beliefs against pure observations, modifying any beliefs in conflict with these observations. They might conclude that historians can provide us with a rational explanation of a change of belief by showing how certain observations falsified the old beliefs while providing support for the new.[4] On the other hand, idealists might argue that rational people try to make their beliefs comprehensive and logically consistent, modifying beliefs in conflict with one another. They might conclude that historians can provide us with a rational explanation of a change of belief by showing how the old web of beliefs contained two contradictory propositions which the new web reconciles or deals with in some other appropriate way.[5] Irrationalists, of course, typically deny that changes of belief are rational at all: they argue that rationality is relative to a

---

[4] This view is suggested by Popper, *Objective Knowledge*.
[5] The classic example of such idealism is, of course, G. Hegel, *The Philosophy of History*, trans. J. Sibree, intro. C. Friedrich (New York: Dover Publications, 1956).

paradigm, or web of beliefs, so that no change of paradigm properly can be described as rational.[6]

Semantic holism suggests that the form of explanation appropriate to a rational change of belief differs from those prescribed by both logical empiricists and idealists. Because there are neither pure observations nor self-supporting beliefs, no single observation or belief can provide a sufficient explanation of any change of belief. Certainly people want their webs of belief to coincide with their experience of reality, but their experience of reality is not pure, so an observation alone cannot require them to change their beliefs. Thus, the logical empiricists are wrong: historians cannot explain changes of beliefs solely by reference to observations or experiences. Certainly people also try to make their webs of belief internally consistent, but their beliefs refer to an external world, so the consistency they seek must be consistency in terms of their understanding of the world. Thus, the idealists are wrong: historians cannot explain changes of belief solely by reference to the inner logic of a tradition or web of beliefs. Historians can never explain a change of belief simply by pointing to some sort of certainty that allegedly compelled an individual to modify a web of beliefs as he did. Perceptions entail theories, so no pure observation can compel people to reject a belief with strong theoretical support. Similarly, theories attempt to make sense of an external reality, so no supposition can compel people to reject a belief with strong experiential support. Because webs of belief are networks of interconnected concepts mapping on to reality at various points, historians can explain changes of belief only by exploring the multiple ways in which a new understanding interacts with an old web of beliefs. Sometimes they will have to show how a new experience promoted a new view of old theories. At other times they will have to show how a new theory promoted a new interpretation of old experiences. No single starting point underlies all changes of belief. Rather, beliefs develop in a fluctuating process with all sorts of beliefs pushing and pulling one another in all sorts of ways. Semantic holism suggests, therefore, that people modify their beliefs in response to dilemmas, but that no dilemma requires any particular modification. Imagine, for instance, that Peter refers to an understanding in support of his views and against Paul's. If Paul accepts the understanding, it provides him

---

[6] Foucault, *Order of Things*. Any belief in paradigms or absolute presuppositions surely pushes one towards an irrationalist relativism akin to that of Foucault. See Kuhn, *Structure of Scientific Revolutions*; and Collingwood, *Essay on Metaphysics*. For a discussion of the problem, focusing on Collingwood, see Toulmin, *Human Understanding*, pp. 65–80.

with a dilemma to which he ought to respond. But although Paul should change his beliefs to respond to the dilemma, there is no unique way in which he must respond and so no unique way in which he must change his beliefs. He can adjust his beliefs so as to reject the understanding, he can introduce a new speculative theory to reconcile it with his beliefs, he can modify his beliefs to accommodate it, or he can say that Peter is right.

We can fill out this brief account of the way people change their beliefs by analysing the concept of a dilemma. Numerous philosophers, especially philosophers of science who have rejected logical positivism, ascribe a prominent role to concepts akin to that of a dilemma. The most prominent examples are no doubt the idea of an anomaly in the work of Kuhn and of a problem in the work of Sir Karl Popper, while others include the idea of a problem in the work of Larry Laudan and of a problem again in the work of Stephen Toulmin.[7] The concept of a dilemma has much in common with these alternatives because they too represent attempts to conceptualise the way in which individuals reason against the background of an inherited body of knowledge so as to develop that body of knowledge. They too represent attempts to analyse thought conceived as a form of rational agency, and, moreover, to do so in the wake of logical positivism and often also atomistic individualism. (The concept that most clearly represents such an attempt is Kuhn's 'anomaly', while the one that least does so is Popper's 'problem'.) The rise of these concepts follows a recognisable pattern. Once philosophers accept that no experience can prove conclusively the truth of any given proposition, they generally conclude that what we accept as true depends on our background theories.[8] Moreover, once they grant that what we accept as true depends on our background theories, they generally avoid analysing rational thought in objective terms that do not refer to background theories. Finally, once they thus reject verificationism, they generally either dismiss rational thought altogether by suggesting that background theories determine what we take as true, or, more plausibly, they equate rational thought with the attempt to improve our background theories by reflecting on the difficulties we find in them and in their relationship to our experience. It is this chain of reasoning that

---

[7] Kuhn, *Structure of Scientific Revolutions*; Popper, *Objective Knowledge*; L. Laudan, *Progress and Its Problems* (Berkeley: University of California Press, 1977); and Toulmin, *Human Understanding*.

[8] The only significant alternative seems to be the strict falsificationism of Popper's early work. On the varieties of falsificationism, and the distinction between Popper's early and later work, see Lakatos, 'Falsification and the methodology of scientific research programmes', particularly pp. 10–47.

explains why the demise of logical positivism has led in the philosophy of science to the rise of concepts akin to ours of a dilemma.

Despite the overlap between the concept of a dilemma and various concepts in the philosophy of science, there are important differences here. Often, though by no means always, the differences reflect the fact that philosophers of science typically take for granted things such as the predominantly empirical nature of beliefs, a high level of agreement about background theories, and a shared commitment to the advancement of knowledge through experimentation. (It is no coincidence that these assumptions are again most clear in Kuhn's work and least clear in Popper's work.) Perhaps such assumptions are reasonable when one explores the sociology of individual reasoning in science. Clearly, however, they have no place in a philosophical study of individual reasoning as such. Not everyone reasons in the ways which characterise the scientific community, so we cannot explain all changes in all webs of belief in the ways we might explain the changing content of scientific knowledge. Much of our analysis of the concept of a dilemma, therefore, will consist of an emphasis on the need to ensure that it remains broader than the alternatives deployed by philosophers of science.

A dilemma is a new belief which merely by virtue of the fact that one accepts it as true poses a question of one's existing beliefs. It is important to recognise that we cannot identify dilemmas exclusively with facts understood as exemplary perceptions. Philosophers of science are inclined to discuss anomalies and problems as if they are almost always factual beliefs generated by experiments.[9] Even if we reasonably can do so in so far as we restrict our attention to the case of science, once we look beyond science we no longer can do so. Of course, a fact can constitute a dilemma: for example, the discovery by Victorian geologists that many rocks were far too old to fit into the cosmology theologians had derived from the Bible constituted a clear dilemma for Christians who believed that Genesis required the world to be about 5,000 years old. However, theories that are quite distant from observations also can constitute dilemmas: for example, the theory of evolution proved an even greater stumbling block than geology for many Victorian Christians. Even moral beliefs with little descriptive content can be dilemmas: for example, Victorian Christians often reacted strongly against talk of hell-fire and eternal damnation precisely because they believed these

---

[9] Contrast, in particular, Kuhn's admirable concern to allow for 'inventions, or novelties of theory', as well as 'discoveries of fact', and his equally admirable recognition of the 'exceedingly artificial' nature of the distinction between the two. Kuhn, *Structure of Scientific Revolutions*, p. 52.

theological doctrines to be immoral. All we can say, therefore, is that a dilemma is any understanding that requires someone to modify his existing web of beliefs if only by accepting it as true. The relevant understanding can lie anywhere on an unbroken spectrum passing from exemplary perceptions with little theoretical content to complex theoretical constructions with only a distant basis in perceptions. What turns an understanding into a dilemma is the authority it has for the person for whom it constitutes a dilemma. It acquires this authority, moreover, simply because that person accepts it as true. When people accept an understanding as true, they come to believe it, so they must incorporate it into their existing webs of belief. When they incorporate it into their existing webs of belief, they necessarily extend or modify their beliefs to accommodate it.

A dilemma is an authoritative understanding that poses a question for one's existing web of beliefs. Whenever we come to believe something new, we ask our current web of beliefs how it is going to accommodate the new arrival. Here too we have a contrast between the concept of a dilemma and similar concepts found in the philosophy of science. The stability of science – the fact that most changes in scientific beliefs extend existing theories rather than overturning them – encourages philosophers of science, notably Kuhn, to focus on the rare anomalies that lead scientists to renounce a number of entrenched theories. Anomalies are the rare pieces of factual evidence or theoretical innovations in conflict with an established paradigm. From Kuhn's perspective, therefore, most conceptual change occurs as scientists extend a ruling paradigm, with anomalies being responsible only for the occasional, revolutionary change. He believes that 'resistance guarantees that scientists will not be lightly distracted and that the anomalies that lead to paradigm change will penetrate existing knowledge to the core'.[10] Dilemmas, in contrast, arise all the time. The concept of a dilemma includes not only rare anomalies prompting scientists to make drastic changes to their webs of belief, but also the concerns that prompt scientists to extend prevailing theories during a period of normal science, and even the trivial puzzles that lead all of us to adopt new beliefs all the time in our everyday existence. Whenever people accept a new understanding, they recognise that the world is not as they had previously thought. This recognition entails their asking themselves what the world is really like. Any time people come to accept a new belief, that belief will constitute a dilemma

---

[10] *Ibid.*, p. 65.

for them no matter how mundane or trivial it or its effects may be. All new beliefs open up an existing web of beliefs for reconsideration in a process that leads to the extension, and typically modification, of that web of beliefs. Whenever we take a new understanding to be authoritative, we ask ourselves a question – we present ourselves with a dilemma. When we resolve the dilemma, we answer the question by changing our beliefs to incorporate the new understanding.

Changes of belief come about as a result of an inner, Socratic dialogue of question and answer. The new webs of belief people adopt stand as answers to the dilemmas they pose for their old webs of belief when they take a new understanding to be true. In a sense, therefore, the diachronic development of human belief consists of a series of particular responses to particular dilemmas.[11] After all, dilemmas exist only for individuals in the context of their particular webs of belief. An understanding becomes a dilemma only because specific individuals take it to be both true and outside of, and so in a weak sense contrary to, their existing beliefs. The theory of evolution, for example, does not constitute a dilemma merely by virtue of its character. Rather, it represented a dilemma for some Victorians because they as individuals ascribed authority to it. If they had rejected evolution as false or unscientific, they would not have needed to modify their beliefs to accommodate it. Similarly, a dilemma exists only in the context of the webs of belief of the individuals for whom it exists. It does so because whether or not people ascribe the requisite authority to an understanding depends primarily on their existing webs of belief. Their existing webs of belief contain substantive concepts of rationality that indicate when exactly they should take an understanding to be true. Victorian Christians typically ascribed authority to the theory of evolution, for example, because they took it to be a scientific theory and they took science to be authoritative. Indeed, the character of a dilemma derives largely from the existing webs of belief of those for whom it exists. Whether a new belief requires people to modify or merely extend their existing web of beliefs depends on the nature of that web of beliefs. People need to modify their existing beliefs if they conflict with the new belief. For example, because the theory of evolution contradicted the biblical account of the origin of species, Christians who were committed biblical literalists had either to modify their beliefs or reject the theory of evolution. People need only to extend their existing beliefs if

[11] Compare R. Collingwood, *An Autobiography*, intro. S. Toulmin (Oxford: Oxford University Press, 1978), pp. 29–43.

the new one is compatible with, but also external to, them. For example, Christians who rejected biblical literalism merely had to extend their beliefs to include, say, the idea of a God working through the process of evolution.

The foregoing analysis of dilemmas in relation to the webs of belief of particular individuals distinguishes them from the more objectivist concept of a problem associated with Popper. Although other philosophers of science, including Kuhn, sometimes appear to ascribe to anomalies an existence independent of individuals, we can generally unpack their concepts as inter-subjective dilemmas.[12] We can say that the strong consensus among scientists means that a dilemma in science usually afflicts a substantial number of scientists who share the beliefs that give the dilemma its character. Popper, in contrast, explicitly rejects any such inter-subjective account of problems in favour of an extreme objectivism. He insists that problems exist independently of the beliefs of every individual subject. He writes, for example, that problems 'need not have their conscious counterpart' and even 'where they have their conscious counterpart, the conscious problem need not coincide with the objective problem'.[13] Popper reaches this objectivist view of problems because he regards them as difficulties in theories that themselves exist independently of every individual subject. Because the theories exist objectively, the problems within them must also do so. Popper's objectivist analysis of problems arises, therefore, out of his commitment to a world 3 composed of theories existing independently of individual subjects. According to Popper, world 1 is the physical world of particles, waves, and the like; world 2 is the mental world of states of consciousness, including beliefs, emotions, and the like; and world 3 is the world of the objective products of consciousness, including theoretical systems, critical arguments, and problems. World 3 consists of objective thoughts that possess an autonomous existence quite apart from the actual beliefs of individuals. More concretely, Popper identifies world 3 with the intended and unintended products of individual minds, where these products persist independently of all minds in objects such as biological organs, language, and books.

A recognition of the place of procedural individualism in the history

---

[12] Kuhn, for example, rather surprisingly talks of anomalies appearing because of a 'recognition that nature has somehow violated the paradigm-induced expectations that govern normal science'. Kuhn, *Structure of Scientific Revolutions*, pp. 52–3. Surely, however, it is people's inter-subjective beliefs about nature, not nature itself, which challenge paradigms.

[13] Popper, *Objective Knowledge*, p. 242.

of ideas undermines Popper's theory of world 3. Procedural individualism implies that hermeneutic meanings exist only for individuals: they
do not exist autonomously in a world 3. Thus, the objects Popper takes
to be constitutive of world 3 can have historical meaning only for
knowing subjects. They can exist only either outside of history as some
sort of Platonic form or within history in so far as individual subjects
really do conceive of them. If there is a world 3, therefore, it must be
composed of Platonic forms and so of no interest to historians. The
theories, arguments, and problems in such a world 3 would interest
historians only if they became objects in world 2 as a result of being
entertained by particular individuals. Indeed, the theories, arguments,
and problems published in journals and books remain mere marks on
pages apart from when particular individuals attach meanings to them.
As mere marks on pages, moreover, they are meaningless, and so do not
constitute theories, arguments, and problems at all. A theory is a theory
only if it is held by someone. What is more, because there can be no
theories in a Popperian world 3, there cannot be objective problems
afflicting such theories. Because any theory that exists in time must be a
subjective theory held by particular individuals, any problem that exists
in time must be a subjective dilemma afflicting the webs of belief of
specific individuals. The historian has no business, therefore, with a
world 3 composed of objective theories and problems. Besides, a historian who focused on Popper's alleged world 3 would almost certainly go
astray. Imagine that Popper reconstructs an objective world 3 problem-
situation as X, where X makes it rational for scientists to believe Y.
Popper can thus explain why the scientist believed Y by saying it was
rational for him to do so in his situation X. Imagine now, however, the
scientist's subjective understanding of the problem-situation in world 2
was Z, not X. Surely historians cannot accept Popper's explanation that
the scientist believed Y because of the nature of the problem-situation
X. Surely historians must explain why the scientist believed Y in terms
of his subjective understanding Z. Historians of ideas study a world 2
that is composed of the webs of belief and the dilemmas held and
confronted by particular individuals.

   Clearly we can reject Popper's world 3 in this way while allowing that
dilemmas can be inter-subjective, in that they afflict more than one
person. If a group of people who hold similar webs of belief all accept as
true an understanding previously excluded from these beliefs, they will
face a common dilemma. Much depends here, of course, on the level of
abstraction at which historians decide to discuss the dilemma of interest

to them. The broader historians make their definition of a dilemma, the greater the number of people the dilemma will have affected. For instance, when historians talk in general terms of the Victorian crisis of faith, they refer to a dilemma confronted by all those who worried about the compatibility of faith with any number of scientific and ethical doctrines; whereas if they talk more narrowly of the impact of the theory of evolution on religion, they refer to a dilemma confronted by those who worried about the compatibility of faith with this one doctrine; and if they talk more narrowly still of the impact of Darwin's account of the descent of human beings on religion, they refer to a dilemma confronted only by those people who worried about the compatibility of the doctrine of the divine creation of species with the theory of evolution. No matter how broadly historians define a dilemma, however, it will have existed historically only in so far as it had a place in the actual beliefs of specific people. Historians can identify dilemmas only through a study of the beliefs of particular individuals.

Dilemmas arise from beliefs that people accept as true when previously they had not done so. This analysis of a dilemma is much broader than that which philosophers of science typically give of related concepts such as anomalies or problems. The concept of a dilemma includes every new belief no matter how one arrives at it and no matter how insignificant it and its consequences may be. The introduction of any new belief into a web of beliefs necessarily entails some change in that web. At a minimum, the new belief will require an extension of the old ones, and to extend the old ones will be to modify them. Let me now summarise briefly the implications of this analysis of a dilemma for practising historians. Our analysis of a dilemma suggests that historians should treat dilemmas in much the same way as they should any other belief. Because a dilemma arises from a belief held as true by specific people, historians can understand and explain dilemmas in much the same way as they do any other belief. For a start, although there is neither a logic of discovery nor a logic of justification by which they can be certain they have recovered a dilemma correctly, they can arrive at objective knowledge of a dilemma by criticising and comparing rival accounts of the past. They can explain the nature and salience of a dilemma, moreover, by reference to the webs of belief to which it belongs. They can show why a new understanding posed the questions it did by exhibiting its relationship to the other beliefs in the relevant webs of belief. However, historians cannot explain the presence of dilemmas, as they do webs of belief, by referring to an inherited tradition. They cannot do so because dilemmas are beliefs that people reach by exercising their reason to make sense of their experiences against the background of a tradition they inherited. Instead, therefore, historians must explain the appearance of a dilemma by reference to the process of reflection by which people made sense of their experiences.

HOW BELIEFS CHANGE

Let us turn now from the dilemmas that inspire changes of belief to the nature of the changes they inspire. Because we have defined a dilemma broadly to include every occasion on which someone adopts a new belief, we must allow that dilemmas can inspire changes of belief of very different magnitudes. On the one hand, our analysis of a dilemma incorporates much more than the rare anomalies that prompt scientists to make drastic changes to accepted wisdom. We cannot restrict our analysis of changes of belief, therefore, to the cataclysmic dramas that Kuhn considers in his theory of scientific revolutions.[14] On the other hand, however, although we have ruled out the very possibility of the incommensurability Kuhn associates with a paradigm shift, our analysis of changes of belief must clearly cover revolutionary transformations as well as more minor ones.[15] A logical analysis of the way people change their beliefs must be a broad one applicable to all such changes. Sometimes people incorporate a new understanding into their webs of belief without making many changes to it, but at other times they do so only by making vast changes. We must allow for both cases.

The way people respond to any given dilemma reflects both the character of the dilemma and the content of their existing webs of belief. Consider first the influence of the character of a dilemma on the changes people make in response to it. When confronted with a new understanding, people must either reject it or develop their existing beliefs to accommodate it. If they reject it, their beliefs will remain unchanged. If they develop their beliefs to accommodate it, they must do so in a way which makes room for it, so the modifications they make to their beliefs must reflect its character. To face a dilemma is to ask oneself what an authoritative understanding says about how the world

---

[14] Kuhn, *Structure of Scientific Revolutions*. Also see A. MacIntyre, 'Epistemological crises, dramatic narrative, and the philosophy of science', *The Monist* 60 (1977), 453–72; and MacIntyre, *Whose Justice? Which Rationality?*, pp. 361–6.

[15] For a rejection of the very idea of dramatic, revolutionary transformations, see Toulmin, *Human Understanding*, pp. 96–130.

is, and, of course, to ask oneself a question is always to adopt a perspective from which to look for an answer. Every dilemma points us, therefore, to ways in which we might resolve it. Certainly a number of Victorians resolved the conflict they perceived between faith and the theory of evolution by modifying their religious beliefs in a way that reflected the character of the dilemma they faced. They argued that God was immanent in the evolutionary process. God worked through natural processes in the world, rather than intervening miraculously from beyond. The character of the dilemma they faced pointed to the solution they devised in a way which made themes in the dilemma integral to the modified web of beliefs they adopted. They reconciled the theory of evolution with a belief in God by presenting the evolutionary process as itself a manifestation of God's will. Their new web of beliefs included a religious rendition of the new understanding that had posed them a dilemma.

Consider now the influence of people's existing webs of belief on the nature of the changes they make in response to a dilemma. If people are to accommodate a new understanding, they must hook it on to aspects of their existing beliefs. The content of their existing beliefs, moreover, will make certain hooks available to them. To find a home for a new belief among their old ones, they must make intelligible connections between it and them. The connections they can make will obviously depend on the nature of their old beliefs. People can integrate a new belief into their existing beliefs only by relating themes in the former to some already present in the latter. Thus, our existing web of beliefs provides a litany to which we offer a series of responses as we come to terms with any given dilemma. Our existing web of beliefs gives us resources upon which to draw in our attempt to accommodate a new understanding in our view of the world. When we react to a dilemma, we do so by drawing on themes already present in our beliefs, and this means that these themes necessarily influence the way in which our beliefs change. Certainly the pantheistic beliefs associated with the romantics provided some Victorians with a hook on which to hang a theory of evolution. Some Victorians moved from a pantheistic faith in nature as a mode of God's being by way of the theory of evolution to an immanentist faith according to which God worked his will through natural processes in the world. Their existing web of beliefs provided them with a resource with which they responded to the dilemma posed by the theory of evolution. They reconciled the theory of evolution with faith in God by hooking the former on to pantheistic themes in their existing beliefs. Their new web of beliefs incorporated an evolutionary rendition of themes drawn from their old one.

After people find hooks in their existing webs of belief on which to hang the understanding constitutive of a dilemma, they have to go on to modify several more of their existing beliefs. To see why this is so, we need to remember that semantic holism implies that our beliefs map on to reality only as coherent webs. Thus, a change in any one belief requires some compensating and corresponding changes to be made to other related beliefs. A new understanding affects a web of beliefs somewhat as a stone does a pool of water into which it falls. A dramatic disturbance occurs at the place where the stone enters the water, and from there ripples spread out, gradually fading away as they recede from the centre of the disturbance. As people alter one belief, so they almost necessarily have to modify the beliefs connected with it, and then the beliefs connected with these others, and so on. Once again the additional changes people thus make to their existing beliefs will reflect both the character of the dilemma and the content of the beliefs themselves. As people modify beliefs further and further away from the centre of the disturbance, so they strengthen the hooks that pull the new understanding into their beliefs. They adjust more and more of their existing beliefs the better to accommodate the new arrival. Each adjustment they make relates the new understanding to additional beliefs in ways mediated by previous adjustments. Each adjustment they make enriches the themes that bring the new understanding into a coherent relationship with their existing beliefs.

To summarise the above analysis of the process by which people change their beliefs to accommodate a new one, we might say that it consists of their pushing and pulling at both their existing webs of belief and the new one so as to bring them into a coherent relationship with one another. People accommodate a new belief by hooking it on to themes found in some of their existing beliefs and adjusting the rest of their beliefs accordingly. It is important to emphasise that presumptions in favour of sincere, conscious, and rational beliefs apply to this process. When people change their beliefs in the way just described, they do so in an effort to improve them by embracing a new belief they take to be true. They change their beliefs to improve their knowledge of the world. Themes and hooks, therefore, always link the conceptual content of the relevant beliefs to one another. Indeed, a logical analysis of changes of belief differs from psychologistic accounts of belief-formation principally in thus insisting on the conceptual nature of the process. Proponents of psychologism argue that people change their beliefs for arational reasons that have nothing to do with a quest for a better understanding of the world. They suggest that people develop their webs of belief in ways which have little to do with the conceptual content of those beliefs. Cognitive dissonance theorists, for example, investigate the mechanisms by which people reassert the validity of a belief after they accept vital evidence against it. People adopt these mechanisms, the theorists tell us, not because of a concern to hold valid beliefs, but because of an unconscious desire to avoid the pain they would feel if they relinquished the relevant belief.[16] We need not deny that such psychologistic accounts of belief-formation have a role in historical explanation; indeed, we will later explore the appropriate form of such accounts. None the less, our presumptions in favour of sincere, conscious, and rational beliefs imply that the dominant form of explanation for changes of belief must refer to a rational process, not a psychologistic one. Psychologism focuses on the ways in which the unconscious and irrational workings of the mind can prompt people to form new beliefs. Our logic, in contrast, must start by analysing the rational process by which people develop their webs of belief in pursuit of a better understanding of the world.

Although the form of explanation outlined above deals with rational changes of belief, this does not mean that it applies only to cases when people clearly strove over a period of time to devise a rational response to a dilemma. People often change their beliefs in a flash; the resolution of a dilemma, the answer to a question, comes to them in a moment. When this happens they might not seem to have arrived at their new beliefs as a result of a process of rational deliberation. This does not mean, however, that rational forms of explanation are inappropriate to such changes of belief. Crucially, we cannot explain any change of belief by following the actual psychological process by which the individual concerned made the change. Whenever we unpack such a psychological process, we do so by describing a series of intermediate psychological states – beliefs, pro-attitudes, and the like. No matter how many intermediate states we thus identify, we always come up against the moment when one psychological state gives way to another. Ultimately we always run up against the questions of why and how an initial psychological state gave rise to a later one. Clearly, therefore, any attempt to explain a change of belief solely in terms of psychological states necessarily runs aground on the rock of the nature of the connections between

---

[16] L. Festinger, *A Theory of Cognitive Dissonance* (Stanford: Stanford University Press, 1957).

such states. Rational forms of explanation come into their own in providing us with a means of avoiding this rock. The conceptual priority of rationality enables historians to presume that the connections between psychological states are rational ones: it enables them to traverse the moment when people actually change their beliefs. The concept of rationality provides us with an account of how the mind works, and this account explains how one psychological state can arise out of another. One set of beliefs arises out of another because the believer exercises his reason.

Although the foregoing analysis of the way in which people change their beliefs unpacks a rational process, the process remains an open-ended one. People always resolve a dilemma by creatively using their current webs of belief, rather than passively following them. Passively to follow a web of beliefs would be to draw out consequences already contained within it. The existing web of beliefs would fix the way one resolved the dilemma. But, as we have seen, people cannot follow webs of belief in this way. They cannot do so because webs of belief are able to act only as guides to their own application. Just as traditions cannot determine the way one extends them to embrace novel circumstances, so webs of belief cannot fix the way one extends them to accommodate new beliefs. Whenever people confront a dilemma, they necessarily apply their existing beliefs to it; but this does not mean that their existing beliefs fix the criteria of their own application. Any existing web of beliefs provides hints as to how one might proceed, but it is always possible for one to ignore any given hint. Whenever a person uses a web of beliefs to respond to a dilemma, he draws on its resources to guide him as he modifies his beliefs to accommodate the understanding constitutive of the dilemma. None the less, people's existing beliefs will suggest several ways of resolving any dilemma, and the only way they have of checking the adequacy of the particular way in which they happen to use their existing beliefs is to ask if they and their fellows are content with the way they do so. No doubt some changes of belief seem to entail nothing more than the passive following of an existing web of beliefs or tradition. Actually, however, these cases are merely those when we happen to accept the adequacy of the way the people concerned used their beliefs to resolve the relevant dilemma. Whenever we think that people applied their beliefs in the way they should have done, we will be inclined to say they were true to their beliefs – they followed tradition. We will say such things, however, simply because we judge it is so, not because their application of their old beliefs corresponds to criteria fixed by those beliefs.

To confront a dilemma is to ask oneself a question, where the very idea of asking oneself a question presupposes there is no settled answer. Questions are open invitations to a dialogue, not resolutions of a dialogue, so when we ask a question, we cannot already have settled on the answer. The exact way in which people deploy their existing web of beliefs to resolve a given dilemma must remain indeterminate for as long as the dilemma remains a dilemma for them. Similarly, because the process of responding to a dilemma is always a creative one in which people creatively use their existing beliefs, people's old beliefs never set identifiable limits to the new beliefs at which they might arrive. Webs of belief, like traditions, do not circumscribe the ways in which people might develop them. There are no limits to the ways in which people might modify their beliefs in response to a dilemma. This suggests, moreover, that we cannot properly predict how a person will respond to a dilemma. We cannot do so even if we have perfect information about his old web of beliefs and the dilemma. Whatever parameters we built into our predictions, people might always arrive at a new web of beliefs that fell outside those parameters. We cannot make assured predictions about future beliefs. All we can offer is an informed conjecture.[17] The impossibility of predicting future beliefs also follows from a counter-factual argument. Imagine that our knowledge of changes of belief did enable us to predict how people would modify their beliefs in response to a dilemma. If this were so, we could predict future beliefs that did not yet exist. But this conclusion is absurd; after all, if we could predict future beliefs, we could possess these beliefs, so we could know future knowledge, which we obviously cannot do. Clearly, therefore, the ability of historians to explain changes of belief does not entail a corresponding ability to predict them. Explanations of the content of new webs of belief are always reconstructions based on the advantage of hindsight.

People change their beliefs by hooking a new understanding on to themes already present therein. We cannot specify this process in any greater detail precisely because it is a creative, indeterminate one. People's old webs of belief provide them with resources with which they can accommodate a new belief, and a new belief provides them with hints as to how they might locate it in their old web of beliefs; but these

---

[17] It has been argued that folk psychology provides us with a means of living together rather than a means of making such conjectures. See A. Morton, 'Folk psychology is not a predictive device', *Mind* 105 (1996), 119–37. Surely, however, folk psychology enables us to live together only because it provides us with a means of making such conjectures.

resources and hints do not determine, or even place identifiable limits on, the new webs of belief they finally adopt. Let me now summarise briefly the implications of this analysis of changes of belief for practising historians. Our analysis suggests that historians can explain how people respond to a given dilemma by referring to both the dilemma and the webs of belief it affected. They can use the advantages of hindsight to devise rational reconstructions of the processes by which people brought new understandings into coherent relationships with their existing beliefs. They can make intelligible the content of a new web of beliefs by portraying it as a product of the use of an earlier web of beliefs to resolve a specific dilemma.

Historians can explain why people changed their beliefs in the ways they did by presenting the new webs of belief as responses to dilemmas that confronted the old ones. Critics might object that this diachronic form of explanation closely resembles a logic of discovery when we earlier dismissed such a logic as inappropriate to the history of ideas. The critics might say that if historians can explain a new web of beliefs by portraying it as a response to a dilemma faced by the old one, surely they can recover the new beliefs by studying the relevant dilemma, or, at the very least, surely they cannot recover the new beliefs without studying the relevant dilemma. Actually, however, our diachronic form of explanation does not lead to a logic of discovery. Crucially, whereas a logic of discovery entails an unswerving adherence to a method, our diachronic form of explanation does not do so. Whereas any logic of discovery would require historians to arrive at their explanations of changes of belief in a special way, our arguments allow historians to light upon an explanation in any way they like provided only that they express their explanation in a particular form. Suppose, for instance, that Jevons adopted a marginal utility theory of value in response to a dilemma confronting classical economics. We have here the outline of an explanation of Jevons's new beliefs couched in the terms of our diachronic form of explanation, but we have still not said anything to indicate the need for a special method. Historians might recover the dilemma, Jevons's old web of beliefs, and Jevons's new web of beliefs by any method they happen to hit upon. They might do so by reading his works, by investigating the social context, by studying the linguistic context, or by guesswork. We will insist only that once they have recovered the relevant historical objects using whatever method they do, they must explain Jevons's change of belief using our diachronic form of explanation. They must explain his new web of beliefs by showing how it represents a response to a dilemma that confronted his old beliefs.

Critics might object that the distinction between a method and a form of explanation lacks the content it would need to prevent our approach collapsing into a logic of discovery. They might argue that although our insistence on a particular form of explanation does not imply that a given method is necessary to produce good history, it does imply that a given method is sufficient to produce good history. After all, they might say, if the impact of dilemmas on webs of belief explains changes of belief, surely historians can be certain of recovering a change of belief if they recover the old web of beliefs and the dilemma? We can respond to this objection in general terms as well as with special reference to the history of ideas. In general terms, forms of explanation set up empty schemas, whereas logics of discovery purport to tell people how to set about filling in these schemas on any given occasion. Thus, because an explanatory schema need not tell people how to fill it in on particular occasions, a form of explanation need not lead to a logic of discovery. A form of explanation appropriate to the natural sciences, for example, might include, as a bare minimum, the idea of an initial state of affairs causing a later one to come into being in such and such a way. Clearly, however, this schema does not provide scientists with a logic of discovery. It does not tell them how to set about filling it in on any given occasion. It does not do so because the nature of the link between two states of affairs, and so how one causes the other, is itself a vital part of what scientists try to discover. Certainly, once scientists know how a causal connection relates two states of affairs, they can use knowledge of one term and of the relevant causal connection to discover the other term. But when scientists thereby tell people that a later state of affairs will follow from an initial state of affairs because of such and such a causal relationship, they are announcing the results of a scientific investigation, not undertaking a scientific investigation. Thus, although a particular form of explanation operates in science, it does not provide scientists with a logic of discovery.

In the case of the history of ideas, the relevant explanatory schema is as follows: an old web of beliefs changes into a new web of beliefs because of a dilemma. Critics might point out that in the history of ideas a concept of rationality establishes the link between the two terms of this explanatory schema. They might argue that because historians do not need to discover the nature of this link, our explanatory schema entails a logic of discovery. Surely, they might say, if historians know the nature of the initial state of affairs, then because they know the nature of the link between the two terms, they must be able to discover the later state of affairs. This criticism suggests that the place of a presumption of rationality in the history of ideas means our diachronic form of explanation leads to a logic of discovery. Actually, however, we cannot thus derive a logic of discovery from our explanatory schema. The critics must accept that the link between the two states of affairs is a rational one or else their argument fails because the nature of the link is no longer fixed. But if the link between the two states of affairs is a rational, not causal, one, there is no possibility of historians deducing the later state of affairs from the earlier one. Indeed, because the link between two states of affairs is a rational one, historians can reconstruct the movement from the earlier one to the later only with the benefit of hindsight. Nobody could have predicted the movement no matter what prior knowledge they had. Historians cannot deduce one state of beliefs from another, and this means that they cannot be certain of discovering a new web of beliefs from prior knowledge of the relevant old web of beliefs and the dilemma effecting it. Thus, our diachronic form of explanation does not entail a logic of discovery.

Explanatory schemas give rise to logics of discovery only when both of the following conditions are met. First, scholars have prior knowledge of the mechanism by which an earlier state of affairs brings a later one into being. Second, the nature of this mechanism is such that scholars can predict a later state of affairs provided they have knowledge of the earlier state of affairs. The first condition might be met in the history of ideas, but the second is not. Historians of ideas can presume that the link between two states of belief is a rational one, but the nature of a rational link precludes their predicting later webs of belief from their knowledge of earlier ones. Thus, because our explanatory schema does not allow for prediction, it does not lead to a logic of discovery.

Consider, once again, the example of Jevons. Jevons's initial beliefs were those of a utilitarian committed to classical economics. The main dilemma he faced was that the classical theory of distribution seemed to be disproved by contemporary statistics. The classical theory of distribution consisted of the wages-fund doctrine and the Malthusian law of population. The statistics suggested that the 1850s and 1860s had witnessed the emergence of trade unions, a rapid growth in population, and a rise in real wages. Jevons, and many of his contemporaries, were perplexed by the gap between their economic theory and the statistical evidence. If trade unions could raise wages, how could economists accept a wages-fund doctrine, according to which there was, in the short term, a fixed amount of savings to pay wages? Similarly, if living standards and population could rise simultaneously, how could economists accept Malthusianism, according to which population growth responded to wage rates so as to bring wages back down to subsistence level? Even if we know all about Jevons's initial web of beliefs and the dilemma he faced, however, we still cannot deduce therefrom that he would adopt a marginalist approach to economics. We cannot do so because his adoption of marginalism was a creative reaction, not a fixed response, to the dilemmas he faced. This is why even if contemporaries of Jevons had had perfect knowledge of his beliefs and the dilemmas he faced, they still could not have predicted that he would develop the marginalist theory. It is also why other economists with similar beliefs who faced similar dilemmas did not go on to equate value with marginal utility. Once we know that Jevons turned to marginalism, we can give a retrospective explanation of his later beliefs by locating them against the background of his earlier beliefs and the dilemmas he faced. But this does not mean that we can follow some putative logic of discovery so as to deduce his later beliefs from prior knowledge of his earlier ones and the dilemmas he faced.

THE IRREDUCIBILITY OF DILEMMAS

A dilemma is a new belief, where any new belief, merely by virtue of being adopted, poses a question of the web of beliefs into which it is inserted. A dilemma arises for individuals, therefore, whenever their reflections in relation to their experiences lead them to adopt a new understanding as authoritative. We have to say that experiences thus lead people to adopt new beliefs only in relation to a process of reflection simply because all experiences are theory laden. The belief which an experience prompts always depends in part on the theories by which one makes sense of the experience – although, as we have seen, the theorising invoked here need not be especially conscious or prolonged. None the less, while our theories always enter into our experiences, our experiences affect the beliefs we eventually come to hold; they do so because they pose questions for the beliefs we inherit as a tradition. The concept of a dilemma signifies, therefore, the importance of social life as an influence on consciousness. Two questions are raised by any such attempt to relate beliefs back to experiences. The first asks about the exact relationship of experiences to the beliefs they inspire. Do experiences cause, set limits to, or just influence beliefs? Our previous arguments for the unconstrained nature of individual reasoning show that experiences only influence beliefs rather than determining them or setting limits to them. The second question asks about the reciprocity of the relationship between beliefs and experiences. Do beliefs cause, limit, or influence experiences in much the same way as experiences do beliefs, or is the relationship all one way? Our previous arguments for the theory-laden nature of all experience show that the relationship is a reciprocal one since beliefs necessarily enter into experiences.

There is a third, equally important question associated with the influence of life on consciousness. It asks whether we can privilege one type of experience, or understanding thereof, as the exclusive or primary source of all changes of belief. Do economic, political, or some other set of experiences, or epistemological, semiotic, or some other set of understandings, have a special role as a source of new beliefs? The generality of our analysis of a dilemma as any new belief certainly suggests that we might ask whether we can reduce dilemmas to a specific type of experience or understanding. The most popular form of reductionism remains perhaps the Marxist one of reducing beliefs or social consciousness to economic experiences or material life.[18] Others would include Foucault's attempt to explain the nature of his epistemes by reference to semiotic theories, as though an understanding of language were authoritative for all beliefs; and Sir Lewis Namier's epiphenomenalism, according to which ideas, especially moral principles, 'are a mere libretto' to the emotions and interests, as though the quest for power and office were authoritative for all beliefs.[19]

Our repudiation of foundationalism, in both its traditional or absolute form and its structuralist or historicised form, requires us to reject all such reductionisms. If we could reduce dilemmas to a single type of understanding, all our beliefs would take their validity from that type of understanding. Yet our criticisms of logical empiricism, idealism, and irrationalism have shown that this is not so. Semantic holism implies that our beliefs resemble a spherical web, not a pyramid. Our beliefs do not follow from one another in a chain secured at a single point to a particular type of understanding or a particular type of theory-laden experience. Rather, our beliefs all draw support from one another as they map on to reality as a complex whole. Again, no one type of experience can fix the

---

[18] Marx, 'Preface to *A Critique of Political Economy*'.
[19] See Foucault, *Order of Things*; and L. Namier, 'Human nature in politics', in *Personalities and Powers* (London: Hamish Hamilton, 1955), p. 4.

beliefs we come to hold simply because we play an active role in constructing our experiences in terms of our current webs of belief, and these webs of belief incorporate beliefs about things other than any one type of experience. Similar considerations explain why anti-foundationalism has led to a renewed emphasis on the autonomy of the history of ideas. As philosophers and historians have recognised how 'the creative interpretation of experience also shapes experience', so they have become increasingly suspicious of attempts to reduce the beliefs someone adopts to any one facet of his social location, whether that be his social class, race, sex, or something else.[20] Historians such as Dominick LaCapra certainly emphasise the importance and variety of the groups to which individuals belong, and thereby undermine any hegemony social history once might have exercised over intellectual history.[21]

Surely, however, the lesson thus brought home by anti-foundationalism merely reinforces what our common sense, or rather folk psychology, has already taught us? Consider for a moment what a strong programme of reducing dilemmas to one type of understanding or experience would entail. If every dilemma arose from the one area of life, human nature would have to be such that all our ideas derived their validity from one type of understanding and experience. Humans would have to be economic animals, political animals, religious animals, or whatever, in a very strong sense indeed. In contrast, we have found that folk psychology commends to us a view of humans as characterised by endowments such as a linguistic faculty, a capacity for agency, and an ability to exercise their reason in local contexts. All of these abilities, moreover, apply to life as a whole, not just a privileged area thereof. People encounter an idea of God mainly in their religious lives, not their political or economic ones; they encounter an idea of a republic mainly in their political lives, not their economic or religious ones; and they encounter an idea of wages mainly in their economic lives, not their religious or political ones. Thus, explanations of people's conception of God in terms of their political experiences, or their political values by reference to their economic experiences, or their beliefs about wage structures in terms of their religious experiences all seem inherently implausible. The most important area of life for the formation of a type of beliefs is usually that which the beliefs conceptualise. Attempts to

---

[20] W. Bouwsma, 'Intellectual history in the 1980s: from history of ideas to history of meaning', *Journal of Interdisciplinary History* 12 (1981), 283.
[21] See the essays collected in LaCapra, *Rethinking Intellectual History*; and D. LaCapra, *History and Criticism* (Ithaca, N.Y.: Cornell University Press, 1985).

reduce any group of beliefs to some other area of life always tend, therefore, to become extremely convoluted and so unconvincing to anyone not already committed to the reductionist programme. Besides, because we can trust the broad accuracy of our perceptions, we have good reason to accept the beliefs inspired by our experiences in general. Almost all our experiences, not just those in one special area of life, provide us with valid grounds for adopting a new belief as true. Dilemmas can arise in all areas of our lives because our acceptance of the broad accuracy of our perceptions enables us to treat our experiences as authoritative. We simply cannot reduce the beliefs people come to hold to a single area of life. Our analysis of a dilemma must remain a very general one.

All our experiences and all our beliefs link up with one another. They constitute a seamless, holistic web. Thus, although we can categorise a specific set of experiences and beliefs as such and such an area of life, the categories we thus use do not demarcate an isolated, self-sufficient area. Moreover, because all areas of life thus depend on others, we cannot identify any area of life as authoritative over all others. Most individuals, for example, have experiences of work and God, and these experiences are saturated respectively with their existing economic and religious beliefs, which, in turn, interpenetrate with the rest of their webs of belief. This means, first, that their understanding of work and of faith interact with each other since they exist as parts of a single worldview, and, second, that we cannot reduce either type of understanding to the other because their interaction is one of reciprocal influence. A religious belief can influence one's political views: a spiritual belief in the importance of detaching oneself from the world might lead someone to political quietism. Equally, however, an understanding associated with work can influence one's religious views: a belief that a denomination favours an economic group might lead someone to worship elsewhere. The different areas of life are neither independent of one another nor reducible to one another.

Because the concept of a dilemma is irreducible, we can do no more than provide a list of the different types of understanding people can take as authoritative. We might categorise dilemmas according to the topic of the understanding they embody: a dilemma might be a new belief about religion, politics, economics, or history. Alternatively we might categorise dilemmas according to the sort of encounter from which they arise: a dilemma might arise as people reflect on their existing beliefs in an attempt to make them more rational, as people try to extend their existing beliefs to apply them to a new sort of experience, or as people encounter an alternative tradition or culture in which they discern things of merit. No doubt lists of this sort can play a valuable heuristic role. None the less, they are of no logical significance and so need not concern us. Because every type of experience and every type of belief can be authoritative, a full list would have to consist of a set of headings defined so that collectively they covered the whole range of human life. Any such list would have to be constructed especially for this purpose, and even then it would be of no use to historians. When historians want to explain a change of beliefs, they must refer to the relevant dilemma in specific terms. How a philosopher might categorise the dilemma using an arbitrarily selected set of headings will not alter the way in which historians describe it. We can conclude, therefore, that although the concept of a dilemma plays a vital role in diachronic explanations in the history of ideas, we cannot reduce it any further, and there is little point in our constructing a typology of different types of dilemma.

The irreducible diversity of the dilemmas people face also follows from the very nature of thought. When people think, they reflect on one or more of the beliefs they hold, and they do so from within the context of their whole web of beliefs. More importantly, the open and creative nature of thought suggests that there are no special types of belief people can hold but not reflect on in this way; and because people can reflect on every belief they hold, every type of belief must be capable of standing as a dilemma. It is by exercising their faculty for thought that people first accept a new belief as authoritative and then modify their existing webs of belief so as to make room for it. It is by exercising their faculty for thought that they change their webs of belief so as both to incorporate the new beliefs they come to accept as true and to reject the old beliefs they come to regard as false. If people ever stopped thinking, they would continue with the same set of beliefs for the rest of their lives; but perhaps we should rather say, if they ever stopped thinking, they would cease to hold beliefs.

Because beliefs change only as a result of reflection or thought, never as a result of a brute experience, a diachronic form of explanation for the history of ideas must fit in with a suitable analysis of the process of thinking. We must be able, in other words, to analyse the process of thinking in a way which parallels our analysis of how dilemmas lead people to change their beliefs. The process of thinking resembles an inner dialogue in which individuals examine some of their beliefs critically. When people think, they discuss something with another part of themselves; they reflect on some of their beliefs from another perspective which they have adopted precisely in order so to do. The inherently critical nature of this inner dialogue explains why some scholars have looked upon thought, or at least some modes of thought, as inherently destructive of established beliefs and practices.[22] Because thought is a critical process, it typically ends in a change of beliefs, and so in a rejection, or at least modification, of what was previously taken to be true. None the less, the critical nature of all thought arises in relation to the web of beliefs of the individual concerned, rather than the prevailing outlook in society. The process of thinking, therefore, might lead individuals to adopt beliefs that are more sympathetic to the prevailing outlook in their societies than were those with which they set out. Thought can reinforce social norms as well as undermine them.

To analyse the process of thinking as an inner dialogue is to postulate two components to it. The first is the part of our web of beliefs on which we reflect. This is always, at least in part, an understanding of the way things are. When we think, we think about an object; we try to grasp the nature of an object so as to arrive at true beliefs about it. The object we think about might be either one we have been aware of for some time or one we only just have conceived of. In either case, however, it will be one we construct using our existing theories as well as our sensations of the world. Our grasp of an object always incorporates a theoretical component. None the less, the theory-laden nature of our understanding of an object does not prevent it taking over so as to lead us to modify our beliefs, including perhaps the theoretical component within it. When we think about an object, we focus upon it, and this process can end in our modifying our web of beliefs, including our view of the object itself. The second component to thought is the perspective from which we reflect on an object. Because this perspective is part of our existing web of beliefs, to say we reflect on some beliefs is not to postulate a higher or neutral standpoint from which we do so. Rather, we do so by bringing one part of our web of beliefs to bear on another part. We encourage a particular belief of ours to step forward so that we can consider it from the perspective of our other beliefs. We investigate the accuracy of a belief by inspecting it in the sometimes harsh light of the

[22] Various suggestions along these lines appear throughout E. Burke, *Reflections on the Revolution in France*, ed. C. O'Brien (Harmondsworth, Middlesex: Penguin Books, 1968). For the argument that rationalism, viewed as one mode of thought, destroys established practices, see M. Oakeshott, 'Rationalism in politics', in *Rationalism in Politics and Other Essays*, pp. 1–36.

rest of our beliefs. Of course, the process of thinking can recur time and time again, and, moreover, it can do so with respect to a series of related objects. If the process of thinking leads us to change our understanding of an object, we can bring our modified understanding of that object to the fore so as to reflect on it in the light of our other beliefs and perhaps modify it again. Similarly, our creative and imaginative faculties enable us to think something through in a tentative, provisional manner. We can adopt a belief hypothetically and explore its adequacy. By doing so, moreover, we can reflect on, and so compare, rival views of the world.

It is important to see how well this analysis of thinking ties in with the diachronic form of explanation appropriate to the history of ideas. The key point is that dilemmas arise whenever the process of thinking produces a tension between the object one thinks about and the perspective from which one does so. People face a dilemma whenever they bring to the fore an understanding that appears inadequate in the light of the other beliefs they bring to bear on it. If they take as authoritative their view of the object they are thinking about, it will pose a dilemma for the perspective from which they are thinking about it. If they take as authoritative the beliefs they bring to bear on the object they are thinking about, these beliefs will pose a dilemma for their view of the object. In either case, the fact that they confront a dilemma gives them a reason to change some of their beliefs. The fact that their view of an object is inadequate in the light of their other beliefs constitutes a good reason for them to modify one or the other so as to render them consonant with each other.

Although the process of thinking consists of the examination of a particular belief from the perspective of the rest of one's beliefs, no method or set of procedural rules fixes the way in which we perform this examination. We explore the belief we bring to the fore in a fluid and creative fashion. We juxtapose a belief or hypothesis with the rest of our beliefs or various hypotheses in the hope that we will thereby recognise, or perhaps construct, either new connections to link it to them or new obstacles to divorce it from them. We play around with ideas, perhaps more or less at random, or perhaps in a fairly controlled way relying on tried and trusted techniques; we play around with ideas, waiting for new insights and flashes of inspiration. What all of this suggests is that thought is a faculty; it is a skill we exercise, not a procedure we follow. Thought is a creative faculty that enables us to devise new ideas. It is a skill we can exercise on novel content and in novel circumstances to arrive at novel conclusions. As thinking beings, we are not restricted to a set of ideas which others could derive from our existing stock of ideas using clearly defined conventions, procedures, or rules. This is why historians cannot identify limits to the beliefs someone might reach against the background of a given tradition. This also is why historians can explain changes of belief only retrospectively. Historians cannot predict how someone will react to a dilemma no matter what information they possess. They cannot do so because the way people react to dilemmas depends on a creative process. None the less, once historians know how someone did react, they can give a rational account of the creative process by which he did so. They can do so because the creative process of thinking is not a random one. Indeed, because people think about a belief by bringing their other beliefs to bear on it, the content of their thought reflects both the thing they think about and the perspective they adopt to do so. When we think about a belief, we bring it to the fore, so that it informs the content of our thought. Moreover, because we consider it from the perspective of our other beliefs, not a neutral standpoint, these other beliefs also inform the content of our thought. Thus, although the process of examining a belief is an open and creative one containing any number of possibilities, it is not uncontrolled, or arbitrary, lacking guiding themes or concerns.

It is important to see once again how well this analysis of thinking ties in with the diachronic form of explanation appropriate to the history of ideas. Just as the content of thought reflects the object being considered and the perspective from which one considers it, so people respond to dilemmas in ways which reflect the dilemma itself and their existing webs of belief. People change their beliefs as they respond to dilemmas through a process of thinking that is informed by both the understanding they reflect on and the beliefs from which they do so.

Several philosophers have argued against a unified analysis of thought such as the one we have adopted. The best-known attempt to show that we think about different things in different ways is probably that of Kant.[23] Kant distinguished between understanding, which apprehends our perceptions so as to give us knowledge, and reason, which seeks a meaning in things so as to give us reflections on the unknowable. Our understanding comprehends what is given to the senses: it sustains knowledge of what we perceive. Our reason ponders metaphysical questions whose answers are unknowable; it sustains reflections on the meaning of things. Various philosophers have drawn distinctions akin to

---

[23] I. Kant, *Critique of Pure Reason*, trans. N. Kemp Smith (London: Macmillan, 1964).

Kant's in an attempt to isolate metaphysical thinking as uniquely unconcerned with knowledge of the world of experience.[24] Yet other philosophers have distinguished scientific thinking from common sense, typically by arguing that scientists withdraw from the world of everyday experience to undertake controlled experiments.[25] All such distinctions challenge the unified analysis of thought we have adopted. Surely, however, any distinction between types of thinking must occur in the context of a unified analysis of thought? Surely because our beliefs form a holistic web, the way we think must be fundamentally the same irrespective of whether our thoughts concern metaphysics, science, or common sense? Surely the process of thinking always entails our bringing our whole web of beliefs to bear on a given understanding? When philosophers reflect on metaphysical issues, they examine certain sorts of ideas from the perspective of their other beliefs, including those they derive from their experiences of the world, and, what is more, the conclusions they reach react on their other beliefs, again including those they derive from their experiences of the world. Similarly, when scientists appear to withdraw from the world of everyday experience, they actually do so in accord with their beliefs in order to find a suitable perspective from which to reflect on a given hypothesis. All thinking aims at knowledge of the world as we experience it. Kant opposed this view because he wrongly thought the nature of mind fixed basic theories that infused all our perceptions. He did not think of these theories as part of a contingent, holistic web of beliefs constructed by an individual mind against the background of an inherited tradition. Thus, he wrongly argued that because the world of experience had to occur within the bounds of these theories, attempts to think beyond these theories could not possibly aim at knowledge of the world of experience.

Yet again we can see how this analysis of thinking ties in with the diachronic form of explanation appropriate to the history of ideas. Just as our analysis of thinking embraces metaphysics, science, and common sense, so our analysis of a dilemma had to be broader than alternatives such as Kuhn's concept of an anomaly. Thinking is not a special skill exercised by special people, or on special topics, or in special conditions. It is something we all do whenever we reflect on anything, no matter how transitory our attention, and no matter how trivial the topic.

---

[24] H. Arendt, *The Life of the Mind*, 2 vols., ed. M. McCarthy (New York: Harcourt Brace Jovanovich, 1978), vol. I: *Thinking*.   [25] *Ibid.*, particularly pp. 53–65.

RATIONAL EXPLANATION

Having analysed the synchronic and diachronic forms of explanation appropriate to sincere, conscious, and rational beliefs, we should examine how such explanations work. Every form of explanation works by postulating pertinent connections between certain objects. Although I have argued that rational forms of explanation do not embody the scientific concept of causation, I have said little about the nature of the connections they do embody.[26] Rational explanations work by revealing conditional connections between beliefs. Synchronic rational explanations uncover the conditional connections between the beliefs that hang together in a given web of beliefs. Diachronic rational explanations uncover the conditional connections between a tradition, an initial web of beliefs, a dilemma, and a later web of beliefs. Because every form of explanation works by showing how the objects connect with one another, what distinguishes rational explanations from others is the precise nature of the conditional connections that hold together the beliefs with which they deal. Crucially, conditional connections are neither necessary nor arbitrary. It is because they are not necessary that we cannot express them as physical or logical laws; and it is because they are not arbitrary that we can none the less use them to explain the beliefs they connect to one another.

Scholars from all sorts of disciplines use the word cause to describe the relationship between the objects they study. When they do so, however, they rarely tell us anything about the actual nature of the connections between these objects. Typically they use the word cause to indicate the presence of a significant relationship of the sort that characterises explanation in their discipline, not to convey a philosophical view of the nature of this relationship.[27] When, for example, historians identify Darwinism was a cause of the Victorian crisis of faith, they suggest that Darwinism stood in a significant relationship to the crisis of faith, but they do not tell us whether this relationship is one of necessity, function, teleology, or accident. In contrast, when we analyse as conditional those connections that characterise the dominant forms of explanation in the history of ideas, we do so specifically in order to convey a

---

[26] On the rational nature of historical explanation, compare Collingwood, *Idea of History*, pp. 205–31; and W. Dray, *Laws and Explanation in History* (Oxford: Oxford University Press, 1957). On the differences between rational explanation and other forms of explanation, compare M. Oakeshott, 'Historical events', in *On History and Other Essays* (Oxford: Basil Blackwell, 1983), pp. 45–96; and von Wright, *Explanation and Understanding*.

[27] One might try, however, to provide a logico-historical analysis of the different senses of the word cause. See, for example, Collingwood, *Essay on Metaphysics*, pp. 285–343.

view of their nature. The idea of a conditional connection gives content to a concept of causation appropriate to the history of ideas.

When we deny that the scientific concept of causation has any place in explanations in the history of ideas, we contrast conditional connections with the physically necessary ones characteristic of natural science. Earlier I excluded the scientific concept of causation from explanations in the history of ideas because folk psychology entails a concept of human agency which implies that people could have chosen to do other than they did. Explanations in natural science, in contrast, work by pointing to physical connections that are necessary precisely because they do not include the idea of objects being able to choose to do other than they do do. Some philosophers, of course, follow Hume in analysing the scientific concept of causation in terms of regularity, not necessity.[28] A Humean view of causation still leads, however, to a distinction between explanation in the history of ideas and in natural sciences closely resembling the one just made. It suggests that the regularities explored by historians of ideas, but not those explored by natural scientists, arise because people choose to do what they do. Imagine, for example, that historians of ideas uncovered a regularity to the effect that the emergence of liberal beliefs always leads on to the emergence of socialist beliefs. The explanation of this regularity would have to lie in an account of what it was about liberal beliefs that made the agents who held them tend to go on to adopt socialist beliefs. Historians would have to point to the reasons people had for moving from the former state to the latter one. They would have to refer to people's choices in a way natural scientists do not. Perhaps some philosophers would reject not only the idea of necessity, but also the distinction between different regularities. Perhaps they would do so on the grounds that this distinction, like the idea of necessity, has no basis in experience. Surely, however, if they did so, they would commit themselves to a rigid empiricism we have found to be false. Given our rejection of pure experience, we must allow that we can postulate different types of regularities, where one such difference will surely mirror the distinction between physically necessary connections and those postulated by folk psychology. Thus, even if the connections scientists study are regularities, not necessities, these regularities must be unaffected by

---

[28] Hume argued that our idea of necessity was a mistaken one which arose because we projected back on to the world habitual associations derived from our experience of regularities. Hume, *Treatise of Human Nature*, pp. 400–1.

agency in a way which distinguishes them from the connections studied by historians of ideas.

We should contrast conditional connections with physical ones irrespective of whether we see the latter as necessities or regularities. Whereas physical connections lie entirely outside the control of human agency, conditional ones are in some way a product of people choosing to believe and do the things they do.[29] Whereas natural scientists explain things using law-like generalisations, historians of ideas must explain things in terms that allow for the presence of free will and so eschew law-like generalisations. It is true, of course, that if we adopt anomalous monism, we will allow that people could describe the beliefs historians study in a language other than folk psychology and thereby explain beliefs by reference to law-like generalisations. If people explained beliefs in this way, however, they would be natural scientists, not historians, precisely because they would be using a physical language, not folk psychology. Human agency prevents us assimilating conditional connections to physical ones no matter what gloss we put on the latter. The real objection to assimilating explanation in the history of ideas to explanation in the natural sciences is not a pragmatic one such as that historians cannot isolate the variables they consider important, or that historians cannot conduct experiments. Nor is it a matter of there being a convenient division of labour between social scientists who concern themselves with law-like generalisations about human affairs and historians who concern themselves with the details of particular beliefs and actions. The real objection to assimilating explanation in the history of ideas to explanation in the natural sciences is rather that the two disciplines rely on categorically distinct connections. Natural scientists explain things using law-like generalisations which postulate physical connections. Historians of ideas explain things primarily in rational terms by highlighting conditional connections.

Once we grasp the real basis of the contrast between explanation in the history of ideas and in the natural sciences, we can distinguish conditional connections from various other connections, all of which point to, or at least can point to, physical necessity. For a start, conditional connections are not the same as unique ones.[30] An object can be

---

[29] It has been argued that psychological explanation treats phenomena as the manifestation of a capacity explicable by analysis. R. Cummins, *The Nature of Psychological Explanation* (Cambridge, Mass.: MIT Press, 1983). The problem with this argument is that our capacity for agency does not seem to be susceptible to the required type of analysis precisely because the capacity to choose precludes suitable physical connections.

[30] Contrast K. Popper, *The Poverty of Historicism* (London: Routledge & Kegan Paul, 1957), pp. 143–4.

entirely unique, or have unique features, and as such it can give rise to another unique object, or one with unique features. In these cases, the connections between the two objects are also unique so they cannot be ones we experience as regularities. None the less, the consequent might be a physically necessary result of the antecedent from which it derives: we might have good reason to postulate a physically necessary connection between two unique objects. The consequent certainly need not be a product of human agency. Conditional connections are not like this. Although conditional connections can be unique, they need not be; after all, people can share some beliefs connected in similar ways, even if their webs of belief differ in other respects. Besides, irrespective of whether conditional connections are unique, they cannot be physically necessary. They always arise from human agency.

In addition, conditional connections are not the same as statistical or probabilistic ones. An object can be one we relate to various outcomes to each of which we assign a definite probability. In these cases, we cannot say that the initial object necessarily leads to any one other. None the less, the various consequents, as and when they occur, might still be physically necessary results of the earlier object: we might have good reason to postulate physically necessary connections between an object and several possible outcomes each of a given probability. The outcome need not depend on human agency. Conditional connections are not like this either. Perhaps historians could construct a statistical table to tell us how often a belief did or did not appear in conjunction with another belief. If they did so, however, the table would merely record how things happened to have been; it would not give us any insight into why things were as they were.[31] To explain why things were as they were, historians would have to show us why the relevant beliefs went along together in the ways they did. To add explanatory power to their statistical correlations, they would have to make them intelligible in terms of human agency by putting conditional connections in the spaces suggested by the table. A statistical correlation between a belief in karma and a belief in reincarnation, for example, would have no explanatory significance unless one could unpack it by reference to the reasons people have for holding the two together. To explain why a belief in karma has often gone along with one in reincarnation, historians must recover the reasons people have had for linking the two beliefs to one another.

Finally, conditional connections differ from the functional or teleo-

---

[31] Perhaps the table also might have some predictive power, but to be able to predict something will happen is not necessarily to understand why it will happen.

logical connections often investigated by biologists. Biologists might appear to explain things by showing how they fulfil a function: for example, they might say that giraffes have long necks in order to reach food high up from the ground. Actually, however, functional explanations in biology work only because theories of genetics and natural selection allow biologists to take for granted a set of physically necessary connections: for example, genetic theories allow biologists to postulate a physical process of mutation leading to the birth of an animal with a long neck somewhat akin to a giraffe, and the theory of natural selection allows them to postulate a physical process such that this quasi-giraffe flourishes and has offspring with long necks. Thus, although biological characteristics often fulfil definite functions, the functions explain the phenomena only by virtue of theories that postulate a series of physically necessary connections between two objects. Conditional connections are not like this since they unpack the workings of human agency in a way which precludes the idea of physical necessity. If a historian insists on saying that a belief fulfilled some function, the functional relationship must embody things such as our conditional connections rather than the physically necessary ones instanced in biology. The functional relationship must be one we unpack in terms of the reasons and choices of the people concerned, not theories of genetics and natural selection. Thus, we cannot locate history in a larger set of life sciences based on the theory of evolution.[32]

When we deny that conditional connections are necessary, we contrast them with logical ones as well as physical ones. We do so because logical connections, like physical ones, preclude the idea of things being able to choose to do other than they do do. If X is a logical corollary of Y, nobody is in a position to choose to have Y but not X. They cannot choose to do so because the mere fact of Y brings X with it – Y makes X logically necessary. The contrast between conditional connections and logical ones implies that rational explanations in the history of ideas must differ from both explanations from first principles and explanations from consequences.[33] Explanations from first principles work by uncovering relations of logical entailment: one starts from a given set of axioms and explains further principles by deducing them from these axioms; one shows how the further principles are entailed by the

[32] Contrast P. van Parijs, *Evolutionary Explanation in the Social Sciences: An Emerging Paradigm* (London: Tavistock, 1981).
[33] Hegel's dialectic postulates the Absolute or Spirit as a final cause in a way which lead him to analyse historical explanation as a type of logical necessity. Hegel, *Philosophy of History*, pp. 8–79.

axioms. Explanations from consequences work by uncovering relations of logical requirement: one starts from an end state, and explains previous events by deducing them from that end state; one shows how the previous events are required by the end state. In both cases, the form of explanation relies on the presence of logically necessary connections as opposed to the conditional ones that relate sincere, rational, and conscious beliefs to each other.

All too often, scholars contrast the necessary with the arbitrary as if there were no intermediary position. They seek to assimilate explanation in the history of ideas to either scientific or logical explanation in the mistaken belief that the only alternative is to renounce the very possibility of explanation in the history of ideas. I want to insist, in contrast, that conditional connections are neither necessary nor arbitrary; after all, if they were arbitrary, we would be unable to explain anything by referring to them. An arbitrary connection is not one that does not exist, but rather one of no explanatory significance. It has no significance because the things it links tell us nothing about one another. The model of such a connection is chance. We describe two situations as being connected by chance when we recognise that they are related but cannot see any significant reason for their being so. No doubt relationships of chance do occur among the objects studied by historians of ideas: that Peter held beliefs X at the time Paul changed his beliefs in a way Y need be of no explanatory significance at all. Crucially, however, the conditional connections informing rational explanations are logically distinct from arbitrary ones. We do not describe beliefs as conditionally connected when we cannot see any significant reason for their being connected. Rather, we describe them as conditionally connected when we can see a significant reason for their being connected but this reason does not make their being connected necessary. We postulate a conditional connection between beliefs whenever their relationship is a product of rational, human agency. To reject the assimilation of explanation in the history of ideas to arbitrary occurrences is not to reject the very idea of things such as fate, chance, and the inexplicable: it is to insist only that rational explanations rely on conditional connections, not arbitrary ones. Similarly, to insist that rational explanations do not embody arbitrary connections is not to define the task of the historian as the discovery of things of lasting value from among a mêlée of objects; it is to say only that whenever historians of ideas explain an object they do so by postulating conditional connections, not arbitrary ones.

Once we grasp the real basis of the contrast between explanation in the history of ideas and the description of arbitrary occurrences, we can distinguish conditional connections from various other types of connection, all of which represent, or at least can represent, mere chance. For a start, conditional connections are not the same as symbolic ones. A symbol is tied to what it symbolises in a relationship of representation. An image of a cigarette with a red line through it, for example, can represent the command 'do not smoke'.[34] Although we can often see why someone might choose a particular symbol to represent something, this need not be the case. We could decide entirely arbitrarily, for example, to use a capped asterisk to symbolise a purely symbolic relationship. Conditional connections are not like this since beliefs provide a context of intelligibility for one another rather than representing one another. We uncover a conditional connection when we see why certain beliefs went together. We do not decide to introduce one in a purely arbitrary way. In addition, conditional connections are not the same as resembling connections. When objects resemble one another, they are related by their similarities, and because objects that resemble one another have characteristics in common, we can always find similarities that place them together. None the less, it is sometimes a matter of chance that objects resemble one another, and in these cases the presence of similarities between the objects does not mean they give us any insight into one another. A number of football teams, for example, resemble one another in having blue strips, but this similarity has no explanatory significance. It tells us only that they wear blue strips without giving us any insight into why they do so. Conditional connections are not like this either. Beliefs do not resemble one another by virtue of having some similar characteristics. They make one another intelligible by virtue of providing the appropriate context for each other.

I want to turn now to a more positive analysis of the conditional connections that sustain the rational forms of explanation appropriate to the history of ideas. To begin, I should emphasise that conditionality is just as real and significant a mode of existence as necessity. Beliefs are connected conditionally in that they need not have been brought together as they were. They could have been related differently or even kept separate from one another. Any web of beliefs, any tradition, is a

---

[34] Many post-structuralists argue that the only connections available to us are imperfect symbolic ones. They do so because their anti-rationalist scepticism leads them to ignore the way our concepts enable us to postulate other types of connections. See, for example, Derrida, 'Differance'.

product of human creativity, so a different web of beliefs, or tradition, could have arisen in its place. Although the connections between beliefs are in this sense conditional, they are not conditional in the entirely different sense of being provisional or incidental. On the contrary, after a web of beliefs has been brought into being by human creativity, it is just as real as anything else. Once beliefs have been brought into being, the connections between them are a given feature of the world. Because the connections between beliefs are conditional, something else could have come into being when they did. Once they have come into being, however, they are just as real as the rest of our world. Indeed, conditional connections often seem to be necessary precisely because they are a real part of the world of experience. Once they have come into being, they present themselves to us as given features of the world in a way which can mislead us into assuming that their coming into the world was necessary. None the less, their existence as given features of the world establishes only that their coming into being was possible, not that it was inevitable. They might not have come into being, but now they have, they are real. Conditionality and necessity are, therefore, different but equally important modes of existence.

Conditional connections exist when the nature of one object draws on the nature of another. The former is conditioned by the latter, so they do not have an arbitrary relationship to one another. Equally, however, the former does not follow from the latter, so they do not have a necessary relationship to one another. Again, conditional connections exist when beliefs reflect, develop, or modify themes that occur in others. It is not inevitable that a belief should pick up themes in the way it does, which is why conditional connections are not necessary ones. Equally, however, the themes really do abide in the beliefs concerned, which is why conditional connections are not arbitrary ones. A theme is an idea suggested by the specific character of several beliefs. It is an idea of which we find hints in various beliefs. Any belief will give us intimations of associated ideas which might or might not have been picked up as beliefs by the holder of the original belief. When they are picked up, they become themes linking the relevant beliefs. The idea of the divine creation of species, for example, suggests the idea of a God capable of intervening in this world, which, in turn, hints at the idea of miracles, and so one might go on. These religious ideas are not linked indissolubly to one another, but nor are they an arbitrary set. Rather, they go together in that they take up, elucidate, and develop intimations found in one another. They go together in that themes running through them relate them to one another in a conditional manner.

I can fill out the concept of a theme by returning to the contrasts between conditional connections and arbitrary and necessary ones. Because conditional connections are not arbitrary ones, themes must be immanent within the beliefs they bring together. Conditional connections differ from symbolic and resembling ones because we find the former in the world whereas we construct the latter two for ourselves. We find that X picks up themes in Y whereas we decide to use X as a symbol for Y or to relate X to Y in terms of a particular resemblance. What is more, symbolical and resembling connections are arbitrary precisely because our ability to construct them means there need be no significance in X symbolising or resembling Y. Thus, if we constructed themes, the connections between beliefs would be arbitrary, but the connections between beliefs are not arbitrary, so themes must be immanent within beliefs. Historians uncover themes that really do exist in the beliefs they study. The presence of the themes shows that the beliefs really do belong together. Because themes are immanent in the beliefs they connect, historians should concern themselves only with themes that actually did link beliefs in the past. Imagine, for example, that historians unpack themes linking the idea of species developing in an evolutionary process to that of God being immanent in the world. The themes must be present in the ideas as they are understood by the historians or else the historians could not link the ideas to one another. Yet the existence of the themes in the ideas as they are understood by the historian does not entail their existence in the ideas as they were understood by others. Thus, the mere existence of the themes does not allow historians to explain the appearance of immanentism in Victorian Britain by reference to the theory of evolution. The validity of this explanation depends on the Victorians having made the same conditional connections identified by the historians. A rational explanation of past beliefs must rest on conditional connections that really were immanent in the consciousness of the relevant historical figures.

Because conditional connections are not necessary, themes must be given immediately by the content of the beliefs they bring together. Conditional connections differ from unique, statistical, and functional ones in that we express them solely in terms of the relevant beliefs, whereas we can express the latter three as fixed, universal laws. Historians describe the connections they find between particular beliefs whereas natural scientists deploy laws of the form 'Y will occur in a set proportion of cases in which X occurs even if X occurs only once'. What is more, unique, statistical, and functional connections are necessary precisely because they rely on general laws to fix the relationship between X and Y. Thus, if the themes linking beliefs were fixed by abstract laws, the connections between beliefs would be necessary ones, but the connections between beliefs are not necessary, so themes must be given immediately by the content of the beliefs they bring together. Historians do not identify a theme as an instance of a general law defining a fixed relationship between the beliefs they are considering. Rather, they describe a theme solely in terms of the content of the particular beliefs it relates to one another. Because themes are given immediately by the beliefs they connect, when people cannot see the conditional connection between two beliefs, historians can bring them to do so only by describing other beliefs that fill it out. Imagine, for example, someone who can see no connection between the idea of species evolving and the idea of an immanent God. Historians could not show him the connection by appealing to some general law. All they could do would be to describe various other ideas that act as intermediate stages between the two principal ones. They might say, for instance, that the theory of evolution implies that developments in the world occur gradually through natural processes, which suggests that any God who influences events in the world must work gradually through natural processes, which, in turn, points to God being immanent in the world. Here too, of course, when historians fill out an account of the connection between two principal beliefs by pointing to other, intermediate ones, the validity of their account will depend on the relevant people really having held the intermediate beliefs they ascribe to them.

The foregoing analysis of a theme allows for some conditional connections being both many sided and multi-directional. Conditional connections can be many sided because themes are not exhausted by the beliefs in which they appear. Themes are not consumed by any one, two, or more beliefs. Rather, they can cover any number of beliefs, bringing them together around a hint found in all of them, and, what is more, they can be extended to yet more beliefs which also pick up on this hint. Conditional connections can be multi-directional because themes are things of which several beliefs partake, not things one belief gives to another. Themes do not link a belief to one that goes naturally or logically before it. Rather, they link two or more beliefs that go along together in a reciprocal relationship. When a conditional connection is diachronic, however, the temporal aspect of the relationship will be such that one web of beliefs resolves a dilemma in an earlier one, so the former must come before the latter, so the conditional connection must be a uni-directional one.

Conditional connections arise from themes that are both immanent within and given immediately by the beliefs they connect. It is these connections that relate beliefs to one another in webs, traditions, and also dilemmas. A web of beliefs consists of various beliefs connected conditionally to one another by suitable themes. A tradition consists of various webs of belief related to one another not only temporally but also conceptually: each web of beliefs in a tradition picks up on themes found in its immediate predecessors, before perhaps going on to modify these themes, and then hand them down to a later web of beliefs. A dilemma consists of a new belief that poses a question for an existing web of beliefs, where the new belief is connected conditionally to both the existing web of beliefs and the new one it inspires: people take a new belief to be authoritative in part because it picks up on significant themes in their existing web of beliefs, and they solve dilemmas in part by picking up on themes in the new belief itself. Rational explanations in the history of ideas work, therefore, by uncovering conditional connections between beliefs as they appear in webs, traditions, and dilemmas.

CONCLUSION

I have completed my analysis of the synchronic and diachronic forms of explanation historians should adopt for sincere, conscious, and rational beliefs. To begin, I argued that historians cannot explain beliefs in scientific terms because folk psychology can neither be reduced to physical statements nor made to incorporate the scientific idea of causation. I proceeded, therefore, to outline alternative, rational forms of explanation for the history of ideas. An initial focus on rational beliefs meant that the forms of explanation I outlined reflected our anthropological epistemology. Indeed, I constructed the forms of explanation largely through an analysis of human reasoning relying on deductive arguments to draw out the implications of semantic holism and a more general, anti-foundational suspicion of self-evident truths. The synchronic form of explanation I reached requires historians, first, to make sense of a particular belief by relating it to the web of beliefs in which it belongs, and, second, to make sense of a web of beliefs by relating it to the tradition from which it emerged. Here semantic holism implies, first, that the rationality of a belief must depend on the web of beliefs in which it belongs, and, second, that people cannot acquire a web of beliefs through pure experience or pure reason but only in a process of socialisation. The diachronic form of explanation I reached requires historians to make sense of the way people modify their webs of belief by portraying the new beliefs as responses to dilemmas confronting the old ones. Here semantic holism implies that dilemmas cannot be the result of pure experience or pure reason, but rather must arise because people adopt a new belief as authoritative within their existing web of beliefs. The character of a dilemma must reflect, therefore, both the new belief and the web of beliefs it impacts upon. Similarly, semantic holism implies that dilemmas do not require people to respond to them in any given way, but rather to push and pull at their webs of belief so as to accommodate the new belief. Although the changes people make in response to a dilemma reflect the character of both their existing beliefs and the dilemma itself, the process of change must remain an open, creative one. Finally, semantic holism implies that we cannot reduce dilemmas to any one type of belief or experience since our beliefs form an inter-connected web, not a hierarchy. Although people's experiences influence their beliefs by posing dilemmas for them, historians cannot privilege any one type of experience because people play an active role in constructing their experiences using their existing webs of belief which already incorporate beliefs about things other than the one type of experience. To conclude my analysis of the dominant synchronic and diachronic forms of explanation in the history of ideas, I examined the nature of the conditional connections on which they rely. Rational explanations uncover conditional connections, not necessary or arbitrary ones. These conditional connections arise as a result of beliefs picking up and developing themes found in one another.

The concept of a dilemma, like that of a tradition, is a universal one. It expresses a logical conclusion implied by the grammar of our concepts, namely that when individuals adopt a new belief they have to modify, or at least extend, their existing beliefs to accommodate it, and their existing beliefs cannot fix the way they do so. The universality of the concept of a dilemma underlies many of the differences between it and similar concepts found in the philosophy of science. Within our very general concept of a dilemma, however, one might try to distinguish between several more precisely defined such concepts. For example, one might define an anomaly as an inter-subjective dilemma in a scientific discipline, or one might define as counter-hegemonic any dilemma

confronting beliefs that legitimise authority.[35] Similarly, one might distinguish between traditions according to how they encourage one to
react to dilemmas. For example, one might define as open any tradition
that encourages its adherents to seek out dilemmas and to respond
innovatively to them, and one might define as closed any tradition that
does the opposite.[36] Once one had made distinctions of these types, one
could try to devise sociological theories to explain things such as the
nature and development of open and closed traditions by reference to
the ways in which they cope with dilemmas, anomalies, and counter-
hegemonies. Instead of trying to devise such theories, however, I want
only to point out that any analysis of a distinctive type of dilemma or
way of responding to a dilemma must fit within the framework of our
logic. Any distinctive type of dilemma must have the properties I have
ascribed to dilemmas in general as well as any more specific to it. And
any distinctive way of responding to dilemmas must have the properties
I have ascribed to the general process of change as well as any more
specific to it.

One of the properties common to all dilemmas is that they prompt
people to change their webs of belief so as to ensure the beliefs remain
sincere, conscious, and rational. Indeed, I invoked the concept of a
dilemma as part of an attempt to uncover the dominant forms of
explanation for the history of ideas, forms of explanation that apply only
to sincere, conscious, and rational beliefs. Thus, a history of ideas
couched exclusively in terms of these forms of explanation would
neglect the distortions that arise as a result of deception, the unconscious, and irrationality. Next, therefore, we must examine the nature of
these distortions, and ask what forms of explanation are appropriate to
them. We must uncover the subsidiary forms of explanation appropriate
to the history of ideas.

[35] Compare respectively Kuhn, *Structure of Scientific Revolutions*; and A. Gramsci, *Selections from the Prison Notebooks*, ed. and trans. Q. Hoare and G. Smith (London: Lawrence & Wishart, 1971).
[36] A highly polemical attempt to do something akin to this is K. Popper, *The Open Society and Its Enemies*, 2 vols. (London: Routledge & Kegan Paul, 1966). My anthropological epistemology contains a more moderate attempt to do so, as does Lakatos, 'Falsification and the methodology of scientific research programmes'.

CHAPTER 7

On distortions

The synchronic and diachronic forms of explanation I have outlined apply only to sincere, conscious, and rational beliefs. Historians can explain these beliefs by locating them in webs of belief, which, in turn, they can explain by showing them to be the products of the way individuals extended and modified intellectual traditions in response to specific dilemmas. Earlier I justified an initial focus on these beliefs by showing how the grammar of our concepts requires us to ascribe beliefs to people in a process governed by norms in favour of the sincere, conscious, and rational. Clearly, however, not all beliefs are of this type. A presumption in favour of a type of belief certainly does not imply that all beliefs are of that type. Historians can legitimately ascribe insincere, unconscious, and irrational beliefs to people. Our analysis of objectivity as a product of a comparison between rival webs of belief precludes our identifying necessary or sufficient conditions for postulating such distorted beliefs as historical objects. None the less, we can say that historians sometimes find inconsistencies between the beliefs someone overtly attributes to himself and the way he behaves, and, moreover, they can often make sense of these inconsistencies by postulating distorted beliefs. Whenever historians thus postulate distorted beliefs, they invoke historical objects to which our synchronic and diachronic forms of explanation are inapplicable. To complete a logic for the history of ideas, therefore, we must identify the forms of explanation appropriate to distorted beliefs. We must specify how historians should explain insincere, unconscious, and irrational beliefs.

Our three presumptions generate three corresponding types of distortion, namely, deception, self-deception, and irrationality. Next I will analyse each of these three types of distortion to identify the somewhat different forms of explanation appropriate to them. To begin, we will find that deception is an action performed for a definite motive. Deception occurs because pro-attitudes can lead people to express beliefs other than the ones they actually hold in attempts to bring about a state of affairs they would prefer. Thus, historians who want to explain a case of deception must refer to the pro-attitude that constituted the relevant motive. Next we will find self-deception is analogous to deception in that it too is performed with a clear motive. Self-deception occurs because pro-attitudes sometimes lead people to repress their actual beliefs in their unconscious while expressing different beliefs in accord with their preferences. Thus, historians who want to explain a case of self-deception must also refer to the pro-attitude that constituted the relevant motive. Finally we will find that cases of irrationality either resemble cases of self-deception or else are inexplicable: if an irrationality is motivated, it arises because of a pro-attitude; if it is not motivated, we cannot explain it properly but can only assimilate it to a pattern. Thus, historians who want to explain a case of irrational belief once again must do so by referring to the pro-attitude that motivated it.

We will conclude, therefore, that pro-attitudes provide the core component of the forms of explanation appropriate to all three types of distortion. Not all pro-attitudes, however, produce distortions. A pro-attitude produces a distortion only if it plays an illegitimate role, that is, if it acts as a reason for adopting or expressing a belief instead of a reason for performing some other type of action. When we form or express beliefs, we should do so in an attempt to reach or convey true or objective beliefs. Distortions arise whenever other, illegitimate preferences influence the process of belief-formation so as to lead someone to hold or express insincere, unconscious, or irrational beliefs. A pro-attitude can rest on any one of a need, desire, or reason, each of which requires a somewhat different form of explanation. A need is a physiological requirement of the body, so it is explicable in the physical terms appropriate to the natural sciences. A desire is an emotion, so it is explicable as a product of the passions. A reason is a conviction produced by thought, so it is explicable using the form of explanation we have found to be appropriate for rational beliefs. To accept that any one of a need, desire, or reason can inspire a pro-attitude, and so act as the motive for an action, is to reject various forms of reductionism. It is to reject a physicalism that reduces all motives and pro-attitudes to needs or drives, an emotionalism that argues the passions alone can move us to act, and a rationalism that insists that our reason always can trump our other motives. Whether a pro-attitude is based on a need, a desire, or a reason, however, the connection between it and the beliefs or actions it inspires is always volitional. Volitional connections arise whenever our will takes us from a pro-attitude to an action.

DECEPTION

People depart from the norm of sincere belief whenever they express beliefs other than their actual beliefs in acts of deception. When someone attempts to deceive other people, he tries to make them believe something he believes to be false. This definition of deception concentrates on someone trying to bring people to believe something, as opposed to succeeding in doing so. It does so because our interest in deception derives from a distinction between actual and expressed beliefs. When people's actual beliefs differ from their expressed ones, historians have to go beyond the expressed beliefs if they are to recover the actual ones, and they have to do so irrespective of whether or not the people concerned did or did not succeed in deceiving anyone. Similarly, this definition of deception requires deceivers only to believe, not to know, that what they tell others is false. Perhaps successful deception requires a deceiver to impart an actual falsehood, but once again our interest is in all cases in which expressed beliefs differ from actual ones, irrespective of where the truth lies. Finally, this definition of deception makes lying one type of deception rather than a synonym for deception. When people lie, they try to make others believe something they believe to be false, but people can try to make others believe something they believe to be false without actually lying. People can engage in deception not only by expressing beliefs contrary to those they hold, but also by subtly misrepresenting their beliefs: they can put a particular gloss on a statement they believe to be basically true, they can answer a question so as to side step an issue, or they can express only one aspect of their beliefs on a subject. Imagine, for example, that a politician believes that a worldwide trade cycle and government incompetence have combined to create an economic depression. If the politician told an interviewer a worldwide trade cycle had caused the depression, he might not be lying, but he still would be deceiving the interviewer by implying that the depression was in no way the fault of the government. Deception occurs whenever people attempt to mislead others by expressing beliefs other than those they actually hold.

All instances of deception involve some disjunction between actual and expressed beliefs. How can historians explain these two sets of beliefs and also the disjunction between them? Consider first the actual beliefs of the deceiver. The fact that someone practises deception does not imply that his actual beliefs are unconscious or irrational. Thus, historians can explain the actual beliefs of deceivers in the same way they explain all conscious, rational beliefs. No doubt the evidence historians have of the actual beliefs of deceivers will generally differ from the evidence they have of the actual beliefs of sincere people. No doubt, moreover, the difference between these types of evidence suggests that historians will usually have more trouble identifying the beliefs of deceivers than of sincere people. None the less, the greater difficulty associated with attributing beliefs to deceivers does not alter the way historians should explain the beliefs they do attribute to them. Because the beliefs deceivers hide are like other actual beliefs, the form of explanation appropriate to them is the same as for other actual beliefs. A historian can explain the actual beliefs of deceivers by relating any particular belief to the appropriate web of beliefs, and by portraying the web of beliefs as a product of the development of a tradition in response to dilemmas.

Consider next the disjunction between actual and expressed beliefs. When historians approach such a disjunction, they seek to explain an action, not just beliefs. They ask why someone performed the act of deception he did. Earlier we found that when historians focus on actions, they have to consider pro-attitudes as well as beliefs. To explain a disjunction between actual and expressed beliefs, therefore, historians must refer to the pro-attitudes that motivated the deceiver. Imagine, for example, that a politician tries to absolve the government of blame for a depression by saying it is a result of a worldwide trade cycle when he actually believes the government is at least partly responsible for it. Historians might explain the gap between his expressed and actual beliefs by referring to his pro-attitude towards enhancing the popularity of the government. The relevant pro-attitude explains why he performed an act of deception, that is, why he expressed beliefs other than those he actually held. Although the pro-attitude behind any given act of deception will usually be a hidden preference for a definite outcome, this need not be so. Sometimes deceivers act as they do because of an open preference for a definite outcome. If they want to prick pomposity or to expose folly, they may well tell other people about the outcome they hope to bring about. In these cases, historians might be able to justify their claim that a particular pro-attitude motivated an act of deception by reference to statements in which the deceiver openly acknowledged this was so. Moreover, sometimes deceivers act as they do because of an open pro-attitude that does not even point to a definite outcome: Shakespearean comedy certainly provides several examples of deception motivated by a simple delight in fun and mischief. In these cases, historians will have to explain the act of deception in terms of a vague pro-attitude possessing little positive content.

Consider finally the expressed beliefs of the deceiver. Deceivers express beliefs other than their actual ones in order to mislead others about something. Typically, therefore, they choose to express the beliefs they do because they think other people will understand or react to these beliefs in a certain way. Deceivers express the beliefs they do because they believe that social conventions will lead others to understand them in a way that will promote a state of affairs towards which they hold a pro-attitude. Thus, historians can explain why a deceiver expressed the beliefs he did by referring to his actual beliefs about how others would react to the beliefs he expressed. Historians can explain the expressed beliefs of a deceiver by showing that he thought expressing these beliefs would promote a state of affairs for which he had a preference. When, for example, a politician says that a worldwide trade cycle caused a depression he actually believes to be in part a result of the mismanagement of the economy by the government, he does so because he thinks other people will take him to be absolving the government of blame for the depression; he does so because he expects thereby to enhance the popularity of the government. The actual beliefs deceivers hold about how others will react to the beliefs they express are typically conscious, rational beliefs. Thus, historians can explain the ways in which a deceiver believed other people would understand the beliefs he expressed in the same way they explain all conscious, rational beliefs. They can explain why a deceiver believed his expressed beliefs would promote a state of affairs for which he had a preference by reference to the relevant web of beliefs, tradition, and dilemmas.

Now we are in a position to summarise the form of explanation appropriate to acts of deception. A full explanation of an act of deception should combine the following three moments. First, historians can explain the actual beliefs of the deceiver in the same way that they explain all conscious, rational beliefs. Second, historians can explain the expressed beliefs of the deceiver by relating them to the deceiver's actual beliefs about how other people would respond to these expressed beliefs, and by explaining these actual beliefs in the same way that they explain

all conscious, rational beliefs. Finally, historians can explain the disjunction between the actual and expressed beliefs of the deceiver in terms of
a pro-attitude held by the deceiver.

SELF-DECEPTION

People depart from the norm of conscious belief when they deceive
themselves. The concept of the unconscious enables us to account for
expressed beliefs differing from actual beliefs in cases of self-deception.
Consider, for example, a cancer patient, George, whom the doctors say
has a year to live. Imagine George asserts that he will soon be well, while
acting as though he will be dead within a year by, say, sorting out his
financial affairs, making a will, and looking into arrangements for his
funeral. Imagine also that, as far as we can tell, he sincerely believes he
will be well before too long. Such self-deception seems to present us with
a paradox. Deception occurs whenever someone tries, perhaps successfully, to make others believe something he believes to be false. The
paradox of self-deception arises because of the difficulty of conceiving
how someone could try to make himself believe something he believes to
be false. An act of deception clearly requires the deceiver to acknowledge the belief he attempts to hide from others, and surely someone
cannot try to hide from himself a belief he must acknowledge. Surely, for
example, George cannot sincerely believe he soon will be well if he
knows full well he will die within the year. The obvious solution to the
paradox of self-deception is to split the consciousness of self-deceivers
into two parts, with one part deceiving the other, and with a censor
effectively keeping the two parts separate. Self-deceivers block out a part
of their mind, so when this part deceives the other, no single, undivided
consciousness lies to itself. We can analyse self-deception, therefore, in
terms of expressed or conscious beliefs, actual or unconscious beliefs,
and a censor that stops the unconscious beliefs entering into the conscious mind. George, for example, may unconsciously believe he will be
dead in a year, while a censor keeps this actual belief out of his
conscious, and his unconscious fear of death leads him consciously to
believe he will be well before too long.

Some philosophers, notably Jean-Paul Sartre, argue that not even the
concept of the unconscious can resolve the paradox of self-deception.[1]

---

[1] J. P. Sartre, *Being and Nothingness: An Essay on Phenomenological Ontology*, trans. H. Barnes (London: Methuen, 1981), pp. 47–54.

They argue that any censor keeping unconscious beliefs out of the conscious must itself be conscious of both the conscious and the unconscious. The proposed censor must be an undivided unity that lies to itself. Thus, the paradox of self-deception reappears, only now it confronts the censor rather than the individual consciousness as a whole. How, these philosophers ask, can a censor allow itself to block out beliefs it believes to be true? This argument has a more general form: one part of the mind, no matter how defined, cannot deceive another part of the mind unless it is conscious of the content of this other part, in which case it will be deceiving itself in a way which reintroduces the initial paradox of self-deception. The Sartrean argument, in both its specific and general forms, actually rests on a confusion. To be conscious of the existence of certain beliefs is not necessarily to believe them. Thus, the censor does not have to share the beliefs of either the conscious or the unconscious mind. It has only to be aware of their existence in respectively the conscious and the unconscious. It needs to recognise that there is a conflict between the beliefs in the conscious and those in the unconscious, but it does not have to make a judgement about the truth or falsity of any of the beliefs involved. Thus, the censor can allow itself to block out beliefs because it needs only to know they are contrary to certain other beliefs, not to believe they are true. The censor need neither adopt contradictory beliefs nor lie to itself. It simply has to be aware of the existence of contradictory beliefs and so of the way one part of the mind deceives another. This argument too has a more general form: any one part of the mind can deceive any other part by making it believe something, and to do this it must be conscious of the other part believing this thing, but it itself need not believe this thing – it must lie to the other part of the mind, but it need not lie to itself. Just as deceivers know that those they successfully deceive believe something without themselves believing it, so one part of the mind can know that another part of the mind believes something without itself believing it. Thus, just as deceivers can lie to others without thereby lying to themselves, so one part of the mind can lie to another without thereby lying to itself. We can resolve the paradox of self-deception, therefore, by using the concept of the unconscious to postulate a split in the mind.[2]

The next question to ask is whether or not we can resolve the paradox of self-deception without postulating the unconscious. It seems unlikely

---

[2] Of course, the existence of splits in a mind would mean we would have to conceive of that mind not as a single seamless web but rather as several such webs linked to each other in the specific way to be described.

that we can do so. However we approach the paradox of self-deception, we must preserve the disjunction between expressed and actual beliefs since this is what makes self-deception relevant to historians of ideas. Crucially, if people are not unconscious of the disjunctions dividing their expressed beliefs from their actual beliefs, these disjunctions must be either conscious or pre-conscious. If people are conscious of the disjunction between the beliefs they express and the beliefs they hold, they cannot really be said to believe the beliefs they express, so they cannot be deceiving themselves. They might deceive others, but they cannot be deceiving themselves simply because they know that what they are saying is not what they believe. Likewise, if people have a pre-conscious awareness of the disjunction between their expressed and actual beliefs, they will acknowledge this disjunction if someone points it out to them, so once again they cannot be deceiving themselves. Although we could define self-deception to incorporate cases in which people have a pre-conscious awareness of the disjunction between their expressed and actual beliefs, I will consider such cases as examples of irrationality, not self-deception. I will restrict the concept of self-deception to cases in which people would not acknowledge the disjunction between their expressed and actual beliefs even if someone pointed it out to them. This means that I cannot resolve the paradox of self-deception without postulating a split between the conscious and the unconscious mind of the self-deceiver.

Clearly we should now analyse the concept of the unconscious. Earlier we defined the unconscious in opposition to the pre-conscious as well as the conscious. The conscious consists of the beliefs we are aware of holding at any given time. The pre-conscious consists of other beliefs we hold that are consistent with our conscious ones. Pre-conscious beliefs can usually be brought into the conscious by the normal processes of introspection, so that people would usually acknowledge they held them if asked. The unconscious consists of the beliefs we hold that are not consistent with our conscious ones. Unconscious beliefs usually cannot be brought into the conscious by the normal processes of introspection, so people usually would not acknowledge they held them if asked. In addition, we have identified a need for an unconscious censor to keep unconscious beliefs separate from the conscious. A minimalist definition of the unconscious would have to refer to this censor as well as to our analysis of unconscious beliefs.

More extensive accounts of the unconscious typically incorporate a particular view of its development. Easily the best known of these accounts is that of Freud. According to Freud, the unconscious develops from instincts that are repressed as a consequence of childhood experiences which thus exercise a hidden influence on almost all aspects of adult behaviour.[3] There are a number of difficulties with Freud's account of the development of the unconscious. Unpacking these difficulties will enable us to reach a more satisfactory alternative. Many of the difficulties with Freud's account of the unconscious stem from his initial commitment to physicalism and his continuing faith in various forms of quasi-physicalist reductionism.[4] Criticisms of psycho-history usually focus on either the lack of evidence for its central claims or the methodological problems confronting historians who seek to recreate the conditions of the clinic.[5] Our concern, in contrast, lies with the conceptual or logical relationship between two ways of describing human affairs. Just as earlier we found that the folk psychology deployed by historians excludes a physicalist reductionism, so now we must recognise that this implies that historians cannot adopt a concept of the unconscious based on physicalist assumptions. We have reached here a position akin to that of Wittgenstein when he encouraged us to describe psychoanalysis as an interpretation of meanings, not a diagnosis of causes.[6] Historians cannot deploy any formal psychology that relies on physicalist premises. If they did do so, they would imply that physicalism was true, so they would undermine the categories on which their discipline relies. Historians cannot adopt a physicalist concept of the unconscious, whether Freud's or not, because all such concepts rest on premises that are incompatible with those governing the rest of their discipline. As I consider Freud's account of the way the unconscious develops, I will do so, therefore, in terms of the logical requirements that folk psychology places on any concept of the unconscious historians might deploy. Although I will use Freud as a stalking-horse, the logical

---

[3] Freud's views changed significantly during his lifetime, and there are a number of debates about how important his earlier commitments – including his physicalism – remained for his later ones. Provided we bear in mind the problems of extending his views of one period to another, we can see clearly his concept of the unconscious and his general project in respectively S. Freud, *The Unconscious, Introductory Lectures on Psychoanalysis*, vols. XV and XVI, both in *The Standard Edition of The Complete Psychological Works of Sigmund Freud*, ed. and trans. J. Strachey, 24 vols. (London: Hogarth, 1953–74).

[4] For his physicalism, see especially S. Freud, *Project for a Scientific Psychology*, *Works*, vol. I, pp. 283–397. On its continuing influence, see P. Amacher, *Freud's Neurological Education and Its Influence on Psychoanalytic Theory* (New York: International Universities Press, 1965).

[5] D. Stannard, *Shrinking History: On Freud and the Failure of Psychohistory* (Oxford: Oxford University Press, 1980). For a more general assessment of Freudianism, see S. Fisher and R. Greenberg, *The Scientific Credibility of Freud's Theories and Therapy* (Hassocks, Sussex: Harvester Press, 1977).

[6] Wittgenstein, 'Conversations on Freud'.

requirements I identify will apply to the deployment as a historical tool of any formal psychology, whether analytic or non-analytic.[7]

Freud related the unconscious back to biological drives or instincts, as opposed to pro-attitudes, beliefs, or something else of the sort, because he believed that human behaviour had a physiological basis.[8] He argued that humans had innate instincts, which, if repressed, either remained blocked awaiting a suitable outlet or transferred themselves from the emotion originally expressing them to another substitute emotion. Repressed instincts constituted much of the unconscious conceived as an object capable of explaining neurotic behaviour. In contrast, we have found physicalism to be a mere research programme based on a faith in the potential of the natural sciences. This means that we must avoid any account of the unconscious that presupposes a quasi-physicalist reductionism. We must replace Freud's account of an unconscious based on biological instincts with one based on pro-attitudes that may or may not have their origins in drives or instincts. Once we thus move beyond Freud's concept of the instincts, we necessarily begin to question his theory of repression.[9] Because people cannot bring unconscious beliefs into their conscious mind through the usual processes of introspection, there must be a censor blocking access to them. Freud used his theory of repression to account for such censorship. He argued that traumatic events cause people to repress the emotions through which they originally expressed their instincts. In contrast, because we must avoid a commitment to instincts which must be either expressed or repressed, we cannot identify the process of censorship with such a theory of repression. Instead, we will leave open the issue of how people censor their unconscious beliefs. We will allow, for example, that self-deceivers may sometimes be conscious of the pro-attitude motivating their self-deception, although they can never be aware of the way it influences their beliefs. Once we thus move away from Freud's theory of repression, we also begin to question his emphasis on childhood experiences.[10]

[7] On different formal psychologies that have been used in historical studies, see Loewenberg, 'Psychoanalytic models of history', and Runyan, 'Alternatives to psychoanalytic psychobiography'.
[8] His early physicalism is clear in Freud, 'Project'. During his middle period he turned to innate instincts or drives towards pleasure and death. See S. Freud, *Beyond the Pleasure Principle, Works*, vol. XVIII, pp. 1–64. His mature, structural theory of the mind defined the Id in terms of these instincts, the Ego in terms of a desexualised libido, and the Superego in terms of a part of the death instinct we project on to our parents. See S. Freud, 'The Ego and the Id', *Works*, vol. XIX, pp. 1–66.   [9] S. Freud, 'Repression', *Works*, vol. XIV, pp. 141–58.
[10] Freud first suggested that the traumatic experience was always a sexual one during childhood in S. Freud, 'Further remarks on the neuro-psychoses of defence', *Works*, vol. III, pp. 157–86.

Because Freud saw all repressions as responses to childhood traumas, he argued that ultimately childhood experiences explain the nature of adult neuroses. Although we too need some way of making sense of the results of the action of the unconscious, we have rejected Freud's theory of repression, so we cannot reduce the action of the unconscious to childhood traumas that allegedly cause people to repress their emotions. We cannot privilege the experiences associated with childhood and sexuality in the way Freud does. Instead, we will leave unspecified the source of the content of the unconscious. Finally, once we thus move away from both Freud's quasi-physicalism and his stress on childhood experiences, we no longer have any reason to adopt his belief that the unconscious influences almost all aspects of adult behaviour. Freud believed the experiences of the child determined the way in which the instincts developed to produce the emotional make up of the adult. In contrast, we have eschewed any particular view of the formation of people's emotional make-up, so we must avoid the temptation to reduce the behaviour of the adult to any single determining factor.

We need an account of the unconscious that avoids the problems attendant on Freud's. This does not mean our account will negate Freud's. Rather, it will offer a broad framework encompassing much of his theory without endorsing the questionable commitments inspired by his quasi-physicalist reductionism. If physicalism ever became more than a research project, we might want to narrow our account of the unconscious to coincide precisely with Freud's. To recognise this possibility is to reject a criticism often levelled at psychoanalysis, namely, that it is unfalsifiable and so inherently illegitimate.[11] We must reject this criticism because we defined objective knowledge by reference to criteria of comparison, not the possibility of falsification. All we can say, therefore, is that the current limitations of the physicalist research programme undermine Freud's account of the unconscious. If these limitations are ever overcome, we might adopt Freudianism or something like it. In the meantime, however, we must adopt a broader account of the unconscious suited to our analysis of self-deception. Because our interest in the unconscious arises out of an attempt to conceptualise self-deception as a form of distorted belief, we must eschew any reductionist attempt to portray the unconscious as an influence on normal beliefs and actions. The nature of self-deception as a distortion provides the context for our analysis of the unconscious.

[11] K. Popper, 'Science: conjectures and refutations', in *Conjectures and Refutations: The Growth of Scientific Knowledge* (London: Routledge & Kegan Paul, 1972), pp. 33–65.

Self-deception, like deception, represents a difference between expressed and actual beliefs. Consider first the actual beliefs of self-deceivers. These beliefs are exactly like normal beliefs except that they have been barred from the conscious mind, or, in Freud's terms, repressed. Thus, historians can explain unconscious beliefs in the same way as they explain normal beliefs, that is, by relating them to webs of belief, traditions, and dilemmas. George, the cancer patient, for example, might believe unconsciously that he will die because doctors have told him so, and he thinks doctors generally know what they are talking about, and anyway he thinks cancer often does end in death. Moreover, he may believe – consciously or perhaps unconsciously – that doctors know what they are talking about and cancer often ends in death because these beliefs were conveyed to him as part of an intellectual tradition during a process of socialisation.

Consider next the disjunction between actual and expressed beliefs in cases of self-deception. The disjunction arises because of the operation of a censor as well as a pro-attitude. After all, self-deception, unlike deception, involves people hiding their unconscious beliefs from themselves, and this means there must be a censor to prevent them consciously acknowledging their actual beliefs. Historians must appeal to a censor to explain how acts of self-deception occur. In addition, self-deception, like deception, is an action, not a belief, so there must be a pro-attitude to motivate it: historians must refer to the pro-attitude that motivated a given case of self-deception if they are to explain the disjunction between actual and expressed beliefs. Crucially, a pro-attitude and the action of a censor are sufficient to explain the action of the unconscious as the source of self-deception so we have no reason to ascribe a physiological or instinctual basis to the unconscious. Yet once we eschew the idea of an instinctual basis for the unconscious, we leave the nature of the censor unclear, and this means that historians must explain the disjunction between expressed and actual beliefs in cases of self-deception mainly by reference to the productive effect of the relevant pro-attitudes. The pro-attitudes that inspire acts of self-deception, unlike those that inspire acts of deception, must be hidden. Self-deceivers cannot be conscious of the way in which their pro-attitudes influence their beliefs. Although the relevant pro-attitudes can be part of the conscious as well as the unconscious, when this is so, their operation must be hidden from the conscious. Moreover, because self-deceivers cannot know of the operation of the pro-attitude, they cannot tell others about it. Historians, therefore, can never justify a claim that a certain pro-attitude underlay a given instance of self-deception by reference to the utterances of the self-deceiver. They can justify such a claim only by showing the actions of the self-deceiver embody unacknowledged beliefs. Furthermore, the pro-attitudes that underlie self-deception, unlike those that underlie deception, must be preferences for a definite outcome. People always have some sort of a preference for true beliefs, so only a rival preference for a definite state of affairs can lead them to act so as to prevent their having true beliefs. People cannot deceive themselves out of sheer mischief. They must want their beliefs to be true unless they have a particular reason not to do so. Thus, historians must always give quite specific content to a pro-attitude that inspired an act of self-deception. They can explain the disjunction between actual and expressed beliefs in cases of self-deception only by reference to hidden pro-attitudes to quite specific states of affairs. George, for example, might repress beliefs about the general accuracy of what doctors say and the terminal nature of many cancers because of a preference for being alive. If he does so, he may still be conscious of his preference for living, but he cannot be conscious of its influence on his beliefs.

Consider finally the expressed beliefs of self-deceivers. Although these beliefs belong in the conscious mind, not the unconscious, historians must explain them if they are to explain the precise nature of an instance of self-deception. Self-deceivers almost always rationalise the beliefs they adopt at the prompting of a pro-attitude. Because people have a preference for true beliefs, they almost always try to make the beliefs with which they deceive themselves as convincing as they can. At the very least, they try to make the conscious beliefs they express more or less internally coherent. Thus, historians can begin to explain the expressed beliefs of a self-deceiver by presenting them as a coherent web. None the less, historians cannot explain the emergence and nature of such webs of belief by showing how self-deceivers modify intellectual traditions to respond to dilemmas. They cannot do so because self-deceivers adopt the conscious beliefs they do as a result of the action of their unconscious, not a process of socialisation. Indeed, because the expressed beliefs of self-deceivers always represent an attempt to realise an aim other than truth, an explanation of them must refer to this aim. Because a self-deceiver expresses the web of beliefs he does in an attempt to satisfy a pro-attitude, historians can explain the expressed beliefs of the self-deceiver by reference to the unconscious operation of the appropriate pro-attitude. Crucially, because historians can make sense of the expressed beliefs of a self-deceiver simply by portraying them as a web of beliefs centred on an unconscious pro-attitude, they need not relate the content and result of the unconscious back to childhood experiences. Imagine, for example, that George justifies the belief he will be well soon by saying that doctors often seem unduly pessimistic, that techniques for treating cancer have improved greatly in recent years, and that anyway he already feels better. We could explain the web of beliefs he thereby expresses by showing how it centres on the unconscious operation of his preference for staying alive. We could say he expresses all these beliefs because they lend plausibility to his belief that he will recover.

Now we are in a position to summarise both our concept of the unconscious and the form of explanation appropriate to it. The unconscious consists of, first, pro-attitudes that exercise an illegitimate influence on beliefs, and, second, the actual beliefs that are excluded from the conscious by the action of these pro-attitudes. Unconscious pro-attitudes are in harmony with conscious beliefs, not unconscious ones. There are three parts to the form of explanation appropriate to the unconscious so conceived. First, historians should explain the unconscious, actual beliefs as they do normal beliefs, although to explain why these beliefs are kept out of the conscious they must show they run contrary to the pro-attitude motivating their repression. Second, historians should explain the conscious, expressed beliefs by showing how they form a coherent web centred on the pro-attitude motivating them. Third, historians should explain the disjunction of the unconscious and conscious beliefs by referring to the illegitimate action of the pro-attitude motivating the conscious ones and also by invoking a censor that keeps the two apart.

IRRATIONALITY

Irrationality is the final type of distortion for which we must identify a suitable form of explanation. The content of our presumption in favour of the rational gives us a weak concept of irrationality as inconsistency. As yet, however, we have said little about why it is irrational to believe two things that are inconsistent with one another. When people believe two contradictory beliefs X and Y, they might have good reasons for believing X, so believing X cannot be the source of their irrationality. Moreover, they may have good reasons for believing Y, so believing Y cannot be the source of their irrationality. Their irrationality consists solely in their believing both X and Y when X and Y conflict with each other.

Critics might object that a concern with consistency is culturally specific, so that our definition of irrationality applies only to people from certain cultures.[12] To consider this criticism, we need to unpack an ambiguity in the concept of consistency. In a strong sense, a concern with consistency suggests an attempt to adhere to all the varied logical operations we today in our culture take to be valid. Perhaps the validity of some of these logical operations is indeed specific to particular cultures, though equally perhaps the validity of others is not. In a weak sense, however, a concern with consistency suggests nothing more than an attempt to adhere to whatever logical operations one considers to be valid. Weak consistency consists merely in following the logical maxims one accepts for oneself, not the particular logical maxims we today in our culture take to be valid. Thus, if we ground our definition of irrational belief on a weak concept of consistency, we thereby meet the scruples of our critics. Besides, a weak concept of consistency has the added advantage of allowing for the possibility of people willingly accepting the presence of some contradictions in their webs of belief. We need to allow for this possibility because a shift from a static to a dynamic concept of objectivity detracts somewhat from the overwhelming importance philosophers often place on the elimination of contradictions from beliefs. Our anthropological epistemology implies that inconsistent beliefs can be objective provided they are part of the web of beliefs that best meets the criteria of comparison we specified.[13] Irrationality in belief consists, therefore, of a failure to relate one's beliefs to each other in accord with one's own second-order beliefs about the nature of best belief. Perhaps, however, critics will respond to even this weak concept of consistency by condemning the idea of second-order beliefs about the nature of best belief as culturally specific. If someone had no second-order beliefs about the nature of best belief, however, they would have no way of deciding what to believe and what not to believe, so they would be unable to hold any beliefs whatsoever. Thus, because anyone who has beliefs must have second-order beliefs about the nature of best belief, our definition of irrationality is not culturally specific.

---

[12] Some philosophers indebted to Wittgenstein would clearly say we have no reason to apply a concern with consistency across language games to other cultures. Indeed, they say this even about our own culture. See, for example, Philips, 'Philosophy, theology, and the reality of god'.

[13] Compare Lakatos, 'Falsification and the methodology of scientific research programmes'; and Toulmin, *Human Understanding*.

Irrationality consists in holding beliefs that do not coalesce with one another in the way prescribed by one's own beliefs about the nature of best belief.

Philosophers distinguish between hot and cold cases of irrationality according to whether or not the irrationality is motivated by a pro-attitude. Cases of hot irrationality resemble the distortions that arise when the operation of an unconscious pro-attitude results in expressed and actual beliefs that not only differ but actually contradict each other. No doubt some cases of hot irrationality could not occur if the people concerned had either conscious or pre-conscious knowledge of all of their beliefs. None the less, we cannot reduce hot irrationality to a subcategory of the unconscious because in cases of hot irrationality the person concerned can be aware of all the relevant beliefs, perhaps consciously, but more plausibly pre-consciously. Imagine, for instance, that Peter believes in God solely because of a pro-attitude to the existence of God. Because consciousness that a given belief derives from a pro-attitude is not sufficient to prevent the formation of the belief, we can also imagine that he knows he believes in God solely because of this pro-attitude. Thus, if we imagine finally that Peter believes that pro-attitudes are an inadequate basis for the formation of beliefs, we have a description of Peter consciously holding irrational beliefs. Hot irrationality can be conscious or pre-conscious as well as unconscious.

How can we make sense of those motivated irrationalities that are pre-conscious or even conscious? One of the most influential analyses of hot irrationality comes from Davidson. Davidson follows Freud's account of the unconscious in that he postulates splits in the mind.[14] He unpacks hot irrationality in terms of a main system of beliefs and a subsystem organised around a pro-attitude. Irrationality arises because the subsystem interferes with the normal functioning of the main system. Peter, for example, has a main system of beliefs including both a belief that pro-attitudes are not an adequate basis for belief and also a belief that the evidence does not warrant faith in God. He has a subsystem of beliefs organised around his preference for the existence of God. His irrationality arises because the subsystem leads him to believe in God despite the main system implying he should not do so. Davidson's account of splits in the mind differs from Freud's principally in that it does not require the subsystem to be unconscious, but also in that it neither identifies any particular number of subsystems nor insists on any

---

[14] D. Davidson, 'Paradoxes of irrationality', in Wollheim and Hopkins (eds.), *Philosophical Essays on Freud*, pp. 289–305.

particular beliefs belonging exclusively to one part of the mind. We might ask, however, whether postulating splits in the mind adds anything of substance to an analysis of hot irrationality couched in terms of a main system of beliefs, a subsystem of beliefs, and a pro-attitude. Postulating splits in the mind does not enhance our understanding of the beliefs in the main system since they are not distortions but rather are explicable in the same way as normal beliefs. Similarly, postulating splits in the mind does not enhance our understanding of the rogue beliefs in the subsystem since they are explicable solely in terms of their inner coherence and the pro-attitude on which they are centred. Finally, the idea of splits in the mind does not enhance our understanding of that which produces the conflict between the main system and subsystem of beliefs since the relevant pro-attitude fills this role. It seems, therefore, the only reason one could have for postulating splits in the mind is to enhance our understanding of the way in which rogue pro-attitudes bypass the normal process of belief-formation so as to generate beliefs in an illegitimate manner. Davidson certainly defends the idea of splits in the mind on the grounds that it enables us to think of rogue pro-attitudes as influencing beliefs in a manner analogous to the way the pro-attitudes of one person can influence the beliefs of another. He argues that postulating splits in the mind enables us to make sense of hot irrationality as analogous to the following type of case. If John grows a beautiful flower because he wants Susan to visit his garden, and if Susan visits his garden to see his flower, then his pro-attitude influences her action even though his pro-attitude is not a reason for her action. According to Davidson, hot irrationality resembles a particular type of social interaction.

Davidson's analogy between hot irrationality and social interaction actually ignores a crucial difference between the two. Cases of hot irrationality involve people's pro-attitudes directly producing beliefs that must be contrary to their ideas of best belief. The type of social interaction highlighted by Davidson, in contrast, involves pro-attitudes indirectly producing beliefs that could be in accord with the believers' ideas of best belief. To see the importance of this distinction, consider the example of Paul. Paul once held a belief in God contrary to his belief about the nature of best belief, and he did so because of the illegitimate influence of his pro-attitude to the existence of God. Now, however, he believes God brought him to faith in this way; he regards his faith as a product of God acting through his pro-attitudes. Paul's belief in God has become a rational one quite consistent with his current concept of best belief. Perhaps he believes that the way he reached faith provides evidence of God's existence, or perhaps he points to the Bible for evidence that God exists and brings people to faith in the way he reached his faith; whatever the exact nature of his beliefs, they are consistent and so rational. Thus, Paul, like Peter, holds beliefs that arose because of the illegitimate influence of a pro-attitude, but Paul, unlike Peter, does not hold irrational beliefs. This crucial difference in their beliefs exists because of the different ways their pro-attitudes affect their beliefs. Peter's pro-attitude inspires his belief in God directly: it bypasses his reasoned assessment of beliefs to produce a subsystem of beliefs that does not fit in with his main system. Paul's pro-attitude, in contrast, inspires his belief in God only indirectly: it produced the set of circumstances he now takes to be a reasonable basis for faith in accord with his belief about the nature of best belief. Paul's pro-attitude might have created the circumstances in which he came to believe in God, but his belief in God now rests on his belief about how God entered his life or about the veracity of biblical testimony. Paul's faith in God now fits in with his main system of beliefs. The difference between the examples of Peter and of Paul points to the failure of Davidson's analogy. Whereas cases of hot irrationality occur only when pro-attitudes influence beliefs in a direct way, the type of social interaction he highlights can occur when the influence is an indirect one. Consider the example in which John grows a beautiful flower because he wants Susan to visit his garden. John's pro-attitude creates the circumstances in which Susan decides to visit his garden. She visits his garden, however, because she takes the flower to be a reason to do so, and this reason might be compatible with her beliefs about the nature of best belief. Her beliefs and actions are not the product of the influence of a rogue pro-attitude. Crucially, because social interaction thus cannot provide a model for hot irrationality, we gain nothing by postulating splits in the mind. The idea of splits in the mind adds nothing of substance to our analysis of hot irrationality.

Hot irrationality presupposes nothing other than a main system of beliefs and a rogue belief or set of beliefs centred on a rogue pro-attitude. Historians can explain a case of hot irrationality in much the same way as they do the distortions produced by the unconscious. For a start, they can explain the main system of beliefs as they do any normal web of beliefs, that is, as a product of the way the individual concerned developed an inherited tradition in response to specific dilemmas. Likewise, historians can explain the rogue belief or set of beliefs as they do the expressed beliefs produced by the activity of the unconscious, that is, by showing how they coalesce around the pro-attitude motivating them. Finally, historians can explain the place of the rogue belief or set of beliefs in the whole mind by reference to the operation of the rogue pro-attitude. This analysis of hot irrationality differs from the one given earlier of the unconscious principally with respect to the mechanism that enables pro-attitudes adversely to influence a web of beliefs. Pro-attitudes operating in the unconscious are able to influence one's beliefs precisely because a censor prevents one from realising they are doing so. In contrast, there is no clear mechanism by which to explain how pro-attitudes produce hot irrationalities – no censor prevents one realising what is going on.

Let us turn now to an analysis of cold irrationality. Sometimes people hold beliefs that are contrary to their belief about the nature of best belief simply because their reasoning is faulty. Reasoning is a skill, and, as with all skills, we can exercise it more or less competently; when we fall short of an ideal competence, we make mistakes. Cold irrationality exists because some of the mistakes people make when they reason are due to incompetence rather than rogue pro-attitudes. Some philosophers reject the dichotomy between a hot irrationality prompted by rogue pro-attitudes and a cold irrationality conceived as incompetence. They argue that the very process of reasoning encourages bad habits which give rise to irrationalities that we cannot describe either as motivated by a desire or as matters of incompetence.[15] They point out, for example, that people tend both to rely too much on evidence near to hand and to be too keen to retain an initial hypothesis after accepting evidence against it. To defend our analysis of irrationality, we must show that these types of stubborn reasoning are irrational only if they are motivated by a pro-attitude or matters of incompetence.

From our perspective, two types of stubborn reasoning do not even constitute cases of irrationality. The first is best described as a type of error. People can reason in a stubborn way without realising they are doing so, even believing they are treating evidence and hypotheses in non-stubborn ways. When they do so, they have a false view of their reasoning, and this may lead them to other false beliefs. None the less, their beliefs might still fit together as prescribed by their concept of best belief: their beliefs might be consistent and so rational. The crucial point here is that our concept of rationality allows for people having beliefs that are erroneous but rational. When philosophers describe stubborn

---

[15] D. Pears, *Motivated Irrationality* (Oxford: Clarendon Press, 1984).

reasoning as irrational, they usually point to the way in which it undermines objective rationality.[16] They suggest that stubborn reasoning represents a poor procedure for reaching true beliefs since it distorts our perceptions of things, our evaluations of the evidence, or both. They do not purport to show that stubborn reasoning leads inexorably to one's holding inconsistent beliefs. Our concern, however, lies exclusively with irrational beliefs defined in contrast to a conceptual presumption in favour of consistency. For our purposes, therefore, stubborn reasoning counts as irrational only if it entails inconsistency. No doubt stubborn reasoning often leads to false beliefs, but this does not establish that it leads to irrational ones. Instances of stubborn reasoning count as irrational only if people grasp the pitfalls of what they are doing.

The second type of stubborn reasoning that does not constitute a case of irrationality is best described as a type of rationality. People can understand the pitfalls of stubborn reasoning, but none the less choose to reason in that way because they believe that doing so generally leads to true beliefs. In these cases, their reasoning is in accord with their second-order beliefs and so is rational. People rarely sift through all the possible evidence before they arrive at a particular belief. Instead, they rely on various strategies for forming beliefs: they take short cuts by, say, accepting expert opinion, or adopting set approaches to problem-solving. To adopt such strategies need not be irrational since such strategies can cohere with the rest of one's beliefs. People may accept the opinion of experts, for instance, precisely because they think the experts are well informed whereas they themselves do not possess the technical background necessary to reach an informed opinion. Indeed, people may rationally adopt a strategy of belief-formation knowing full well that it can lead to errors or even entails systematic biases. They may do so, for instance, because they think they would make even more errors if they did not do so. Whenever people use stubborn reasoning because they think it represents a good strategy for forming beliefs, their reasoning fits in with their beliefs about best belief and so is rational. Instances of stubborn reasoning are irrational only if people indulge in them while also believing such reasoning to be a bad way of forming beliefs.

Stubborn reasoning is irrational only when people knowingly engage in it believing it to be a bad way of forming beliefs. If people believe that to favour initial hypotheses and the evidence immediately available is a poor way of reaching valid beliefs but none the less do these things, then

---

[16] However, it also has been argued that stubborn reasoning is in many ways a rational strategy of belief formation explicable in evolutionary terms. See Nozick, *Problem of Rationality*.

they are irrational. To defend my analysis of irrationality, therefore, I need to show only that these forms of stubborn reasoning are either motivated by a pro-attitude or matters of incompetence. Consider an example of the former. If people form beliefs as a result of a type of stubborn reasoning of which they disapprove simply because they cannot be bothered to go through the processes they think most likely to end in true beliefs, their stubborn reasoning is an instance of hot irrationality. A pro-attitude to the avoidance of effort can motivate irrationality: inordinate laziness can stop people giving what they consider suitable attention to things such as distant evidence and novel hypotheses. More generally, stubborn reasoning stands as a case of hot irrationality whenever it arises because a pro-attitude produces an unwillingness to reason as one thinks one should do. Thus, the only instances of stubborn reasoning left for us to account for are those in which people knowingly engage in stubborn reasoning without a motive for doing so and despite their disapproving of so doing. Surely, however, all these instances will represent examples of incompetence: surely people do something they disapprove of for no reason only if they are incompetent. Imagine, for instance, that Lucy disapproves of paying too much heed to evidence near at hand but none the less does so on a certain occasion for no discernible reason. Surely we would say she had made a mistake. Perhaps she failed to concentrate on what she was doing and so fell into a well-known trap; but falling into a well-known trap counts as a mistake. Perhaps we, and even Lucy herself, are so familiar with the trap she fell into that we can describe her mistake in terms of a common pattern; but what we thus describe still remains a pattern common to various mistakes. The fact is that when people disapprove of stubborn reasoning, they must want to avoid it, so when they engage in it for no discernible motive, they must be incompetent. All instances of irrationality, therefore, are either motivated by a rogue pro-attitude or a result of incompetence.

How can we explain a case of cold irrationality understood as unmotivated incompetence? We cannot really do so. Unmotivated incompetence must remain inexplicable. We cannot explain incompetence using the language of natural science because physicalism remains a mere aspiration. We cannot explain it by giving reasons for it because it is unmotivated: we cannot give reasons that are beliefs because the beliefs concerned are irrational, and we cannot give reasons that are pro-attitudes because the irrationality concerned is unmotivated. The very nature of cold irrationality, therefore, renders it inexplicable. Of course, we can describe the common traps people fall into, and we can show how these traps produce common patterns of incompetent reasoning, but the existence of such traps does not explain why people fall into them. The best we can do, therefore, is to assimilate a case of cold irrationality to a pattern that recurs in similar cases; but this is not to explain it. The best we can do is to describe the sort of mistake that arises when reasoning fails in a certain way, but this is not to explain why reasoning failed in that way on that particular occasion.

I have finished analysing the different types of distortion that disrupt a history of ideas told entirely in terms of sincere, conscious, rational beliefs. Our presumption in favour of sincere beliefs breaks down when pro-attitudes lead people to engage in deception. Our presumption in favour of conscious beliefs breaks down when pro-attitudes lead people to express beliefs other than their actual beliefs in acts of self-deception. Our presumption in favour of rational beliefs breaks down both when pro-attitudes illegitimately influence the reasoning process and when people make mistakes. As a rule, therefore, historians can explain distortions by reference to the pro-attitudes motivating them. The only exceptions to this rule are cases of cold irrationality, and these cases are inherently inexplicable. Explanations of distortions work by pointing to the influence of rogue pro-attitudes on the beliefs people express. Next, therefore, I will proceed to analyse the concept of a pro-attitude. So far I have introduced this concept twice, and, on both occasions, I did so in order to distinguish beliefs from motivated actions. The first time, I contrasted historians in general, who concern themselves in part with the pro-attitudes motivating actions, with historians of ideas, who initially concentrate exclusively on beliefs. The second time, I argued that when historians of ideas do refer to pro-attitudes, they do so in order to explain distorted beliefs which are motivated by rogue pro-attitudes. Clearly, therefore, the concept of a pro-attitude refers to motives for acting. By identifying motives with pro-attitudes, we at least raise a question about the reduction of motives to any one type of psychological state, such as desire.

Pro-attitudes are what motivate people to perform the actions they do. To develop further our analysis of distorted beliefs, we need to fill out this definition of pro-attitudes. We need to specify their object – the sorts of things people have pro-attitudes towards – and their origins –

the sorts of things that are capable of generating pro-attitudes. Let us begin by considering the objects of pro-attitudes: what sort of things do people have pro-attitudes towards? Earlier we defined the concept of a pro-attitude as a motive in contrast to a belief because the two have different directions of fit to the world: people want their beliefs to mirror the world, but the world to mirror their pro-attitudes. Because pro-attitudes thus motivate people to act in attempts to change specific states of affairs, it is these states of affairs that constitute the objects of pro-attitudes. This implies that a pro-attitude may fall under any one of three forms of description. We can describe some pro-attitudes by saying that people regard states of affairs as unacceptable, so that they have a positive preference for bringing them to an end: we might explain why Sarah went for a drink, for example, by saying she was lonely. We can describe other pro-attitudes by saying that people regard states of affairs as admirable, so that they have a positive preference for bringing them into being: we might explain why Sarah went for a drink, for example, by saying she wanted company. We can describe yet other pro-attitudes by saying that people regard one state of affairs as unacceptable and another as admirable, so that they have a positive preference both for bringing the one to an end and the other into being: we might explain why Sarah went for a drink, for example, by saying she was lonely and wanted company. We can identify any given pro-attitude, therefore, by reference to its object, where its object is a state of affairs someone is concerned to end, or to bring into being, or both. Actually, however, the object of a pro-attitude must be an understanding of a state of affairs since people necessarily adopt pro-attitudes towards objects as they understand them, not as they are. People necessarily want to change states of affairs from what they understand them to be to what they understand they might be, not from what they are to what they will be. To emphasise the constructed nature of the objects of pro-attitudes is not to imply that when people act on a pro-attitude they aim only to change their beliefs or their understanding of the world. The point of acting on a pro-attitude is to transform a state of affairs that actually exists in the world, but the point of acting on a given pro-attitude is not the same thing as the object of that pro-attitude. The object of a pro-attitude is its content, and this content must be an understanding of the world.

Let us turn now to the origins of pro-attitudes: what sort of things are capable of generating pro-attitudes? An inductive analysis of folk psychology will show that pro-attitudes can derive from any one of a reason, desire, or need. If we asked people what type of pro-attitude gave them a motive for acting as they did, they might legitimately reply by mentioning a reason, desire, or need. Of course, people can have mixed motives, but this implies only that several different pro-attitudes can motivate one action. It does not imply that any of the pro-attitudes concerned derive from something other than a reason, desire, or need. Similarly, people can have open or hidden motives, but this implies only that they can be willing or unwilling to acknowledge that a given pro-attitude prompted their action. It does not imply that the pro-attitudes they do or do not acknowledge derive from something other than a reason, desire, or need. All pro-attitudes derive from reasons, desires, or needs, and we will consider each in turn.

When a pro-attitude rests on a reason, we describe the motive for the relevant action as a conviction that a state of affairs is unacceptable, or admirable, or both. Reasons are convictions; they are beliefs about what is good and what is bad – products of the intellect, the result of the process of thinking. Moral convictions provide the clearest examples of reasons. For example, vegetarians who do not eat meat because they are convinced doing so is morally wrong have as a motive a pro-attitude based on a reason; they do not eat meat because their intellect tells them doing so is bad. Moral convictions, however, are not the only reasons capable of generating pro-attitudes. Reasons can be convictions about the way things are, or about what is appropriate, with no real moral content. For example, some Brahmins in India might not eat meat simply because members of their caste are vegetarians; not because they think eating meat is wrong, or because they think they should respect caste rules, but simply because that is the way things are for people like them. Similarly, boxers might shake hands before a fight because it is the appropriate thing to do; not because they think they ought to show respect for their opponents, or because they think they should conform to social norms, but simply because that is what is appropriate for people like them. Philosophers are inclined to overplay the role of conscious reflection and moral conviction in human affairs because these things play such a prominent role in their professional lives. In fact, however, people's motives often derive from their understanding of the done thing. For instance, people who do not believe in God might get married just because they are in love and people in love get married; or Sarah might go for a drink with a friend every Friday after work even when she does not feel like doing so just because that is what she does. The reasons that motivate such actions depend on convictions about social or personal norms, and we gain nothing by describing such convictions in the ethical terms of what the agent concerned thinks he ought to do.

When a pro-attitude rests on a desire, we describe the motive for the relevant action as a feeling that a state of affairs is unacceptable, or admirable, or both. Desires are emotions; they are sentiments about what is to be hoped and what is to be feared – they are products of the passions, a result of our feelings. The unity of consciousness means we can reflect on our desires, and when we do so, we might act on a desire we have thought about, even a desire we are convinced we have. Even when this happens, however, it remains the desire, understood as an emotion, rather than the reason, understood as a conviction, which provides the content of our motive. Sometimes we act because we desire something. For example, people who leave a light on at night because they are afraid of the dark have as a motive a pro-attitude based on a desire; they leave a light on because they fear the dark. Similarly, when Sarah goes out for a drink with a friend because she enjoys doing so, she acts on a desire for pleasure. Desires – whether or not they provide the motive for an action – are psychological states since the mind is the location of emotions and feelings no less than of beliefs and thoughts. I, however, will continue to avoid taking any one view of the metaphysical status of psychological states. As far as I am concerned, historians can conceive of desires as genuine mental states, or in purely functional terms, or as defined exclusively by reference to behaviour, or any other of a number of familiar ways.

When a pro-attitude rests on a need, we will describe the motive for the relevant action as a physiological impulse to end a state of affairs, or to bring a state of affairs into being, or both. Needs are requirements of the body; they arise out of physiological states the absence of which prevents the survival or normal functioning of the body. People automatically act to sustain themselves unless they definitely choose to do otherwise, and when they automatically act to sustain themselves, the pro-attitudes that prompt them to do so are physiological needs. For example, people who eat because they are starving, or sleep because they are tired, have as a motive a pro-attitude based on a need; they eat and sleep because their bodies need food and rest to survive, or, at the very least, to function normally. Similarly, we might say that some alcoholics go for a drink with their friends because of a need: their bodies require alcohol to function normally. It is important to recognise that we can explain actions by reference to needs only because we can unpack statements about needs as statements about physiological states we know to be essential to the survival or normal functioning of the body. We can accept needs as a possible source of motivation the content of which does not derive from folk psychology only because we can define them in the physiological terms of the natural sciences. Clearly, therefore, we cannot extend the concept of a physiological need to incorporate a psychological drive. All too often the concept of a drive represents a mistaken attempt to interpret the concept of a desire through the language of the natural sciences, rather than folk psychology.[17] To reject such a physicalist view of drives is, however, not to deny that people can legitimately use the word 'drive' to refer to something other than a need. It is just that when they do so, the things they describe as drives cannot be things people must satisfy somehow. Drives that are not needs must be things people can choose not to fulfil. They must resemble psychological emotions, not physiological needs. Moreover, because we have no reason to assume that people have psychological drives they must satisfy somehow, we would usually be well advised to translate any pseudo-scientific talk of drives back into folk psychology so as to avoid confusion about the status of the drives we are evoking. We should not say, for example, that people go skiing because they have a drive towards pleasure; after all, the absence of pleasure neither endangers survival nor prevents the normal functioning of the body. Instead, we should say they go skiing because they feel pleasure when they do so, and this feeling gives them a desire to do so. Needs can explain actions only because they have a physiological nature.

An analysis of folk psychology suggests that any one of a reason, desire, or need can give people a pro-attitude that prompts them to perform an action. A number of scholars, however, have tried to reduce all pro-attitudes to one or other of needs, desires, or reasons, arguing that only one or other of these things can move people to act. To defend a pluralist analysis of pro-attitudes, therefore, we must show that all of these reductionist programmes fail. Let us start with the idea that all pro-attitudes are needs. Because physicalists believe that all human actions have physiological causes, they often reduce desires to needs, drives, instincts or something else of the sort. Certainly Freud always remained wedded to a reductionism of this type. Initially he suggested that physiological tension constitutes a sort of pain that activates the

---

[17] Drive theory resembles Freud's theory of the instincts; it simply uses the word 'drive' to refer to what Freud called 'instinct', that is, a physiological impulse we must satisfy somehow through our behaviour.

mental processes which prompt people to act.[18] Later he suggested that
the basis of a causal explanation of all human action lay in the quasi-
physiological preservative and aggressive instincts.[19] All sorts of physicalists argue, with Freud, that our physiology lies behind not only our
needs, but also the desires and reasons that seem to motivate at least
some of our actions.

Really, however, we cannot reduce all pro-attitudes to physiological
states. It is true that we sometimes associate a specific physiological state
with a type of action: stomach contractions, for example, can indicate
hunger, which often prompts people to eat. None the less, the fact that
we sometimes associate a prior physiological state with a later action
does not sustain a physicalist reductionism. It establishes only that needs
can motivate actions, not that needs alone motivate actions. Any attempt
to associate all actions with prior physiological states confronts insurmountable obstacles. For a start, we cannot identify most types of action
with an antecedent physiological state: we know of no physiological state
that usually precedes shopping, or driving a car, or reading a book.
Moreover, even when we can identify an action with an antecedent
physiological state, this state rarely seems to be necessary to bring about
that action. Physiological states rarely constitute a necessary condition
for an action because people can act voluntarily in accord with a desire
or reason that lacks a physiological basis. People might choose to eat, for
example, even though they are not hungry because they feel like tasting a
particular dish or because they think they should try to put on weight,
and, in such cases, their eating will presumably not be preceded by
stomach contractions. Clearly, therefore, we cannot reduce all the pro-
attitudes that motivate actions to physiological states. Physicalists might
argue that even when people eat when they are not hungry, there are still
antecedent physiological states prompting them so to do. Yet because
physicalists cannot begin to describe these physiological states – indeed
because they have no evidence these states exist – here too physicalism
remains a mere aspiration, a research programme based on a faith in
natural science. If the aspiration ever became a reality, historians might
have to rethink their discipline, but until then historians must eschew all
forms of physicalist reductionism. At least for the moment, therefore, we
cannot unpack the concept of a pro-attitude solely in terms of physiological needs, drives, instincts, or anything else of the kind.

[18] Freud, 'Project'.
[19] See, in particular, S. Freud, 'Instincts and their vicissitudes', and 'Beyond the pleasure principle',
in *Works*, vol. XIV, pp. 109–40 and vol. XVIII, pp. 1–64.

The limitations of a purely physicalist analysis of pro-attitudes can be brought out in another way. Imagine we were uncertain what pro-attitude was motivating people to act in the way they were. How would we set about discovering what the relevant pro-attitudes were? Usually we would ask the people concerned why they acted as they did, although we also might investigate their actions more closely. We would not try to discover what pro-attitudes they had by means of physiological tests. Imagine, however, that we made a series of tests to discover all about the physiology of the people whose actions puzzled us. The results of the tests would still not tell us conclusively what pro-attitudes motivated their actions. Indeed, we might well trust the testimony of the people concerned even if it conflicted with the results of the tests. If they sincerely told us they were motivated by hunger, we might accept that they were motivated by hunger even if the results of the tests revealed no physiological evidence of hunger. We cannot discover what pro-attitudes someone has using physiological tests because the categorical structure of folk psychology rules out a physicalist reductionism. Folk psychology allows that people sometimes act because of their needs, but it also insists people have the capacity to act on their reasons and desires, neither of which can be defined in physiological terms.

Humeans often attempt to reduce all pro-attitudes to desires, conceived as emotions or dispositions, rather than to needs conceived as physiological states. The psychological reductionism of the Humeans avoids the objections that undermine its physicalist counterpart. The Humean position does not rely on an aspiration that would overturn folk psychology if it were realised, but rather on a particular analysis of folk psychology according to which all pro-attitudes derive ultimately from desires. Hume argued that reason alone does not have the power to move us to act; thus, because he paid little heed to the role of needs, he concluded that all motives must be desires defined as passions or emotions.[20] He reduced all pro-attitudes to desires on the grounds, first, that we act to realise a state of affairs only if we prefer it to another state of affairs, and, second, that reason alone cannot give us such preferences. His argument depends, therefore, on the belief that reason cannot give us preferences. To defend this belief, Hume argued that the objects of reason are always propositions, understood as descriptive statements which are either true or false. Thus, he continued, because

---

[20] Hume, *Treatise of Human Nature*, pp. 413–14.

propositions do not exist in time, reason cannot concern things in time, so it cannot influence our actions precisely because they do occur in time.

Hume's argument fails because of its inadequate characterisation of reason. When we reason, we do not merely contemplate propositions, we also take a stance towards them. When we reason, we do not just process statements as true or false, we also come to accept them as true or false. The stance we take towards a proposition, moreover, is a psychological state that exists in time. Thus, because reason leads us to take a stance in time, it can influence our actions in time. When our reason leads us to take a proposition as true or false, we give ourselves a motive for acting or not acting in a particular way. Hume's argument fails, therefore, because the objects of reason are not propositions, but rather our convictions about propositions, and although propositions cannot give us motives for action, convictions that a proposition is true or false can do so. Critics might object that the stance we take to a proposition is a matter of desire, not reason – a product of our emotions, not thought. Surely, however, their objection lacks plausibility. When we say that people are convinced of something, we should not conceive of their conviction as an emotion. Rather, remembering our presumption in favour of the rational, we should take their conviction to be a product of their reason, although, of course, we might think their reasoning was faulty. Imagine, for example, that James orders a vegetarian dish in a restaurant because he believes eating meat is unhealthy. Surely his conviction constitutes a thought that provides him with a reason to order a vegetarian dish, not an emotion that provides him with a desire so to do.

Humeans sometimes offer us a rather different argument in favour of the reduction of pro-attitudes to desires. Hume suggested that although reason can lead us to recognise something as a means to an end, it cannot commend an end to us.[21] We adopt the ends we do as emotional commitments rather than reasoned convictions. All human actions ultimately arise from desires because desires alone can give us our basic ends. If, for instance, we ask James why he ordered a vegetarian dish and he replies he did so because he thinks eating meat is unhealthy, we can ask him why he has this preference for being healthy; and if he says his preference rests on a belief that sickness is painful, we can ask him why he has a negative attitude to pain; and so we could go on until

---

[21] *Ibid.*, pp. 414–15.

finally he expresses a clear emotional commitment, perhaps saying he fears pain. Humeans argue that reasons can explain why people have pro-attitudes to things only in so far as those things help to satisfy some basic desire. Reasons cannot explain why we have a pro-attitude to things in themselves. To explain such basic preferences, we must refer to desires.

This second Humean argument for reducing pro-attitudes to desires is valid only if we deprive the concept of desire of almost all content to the point where we render the argument vacuous. Pro-attitudes differ from beliefs because they inspire actions to alter the world whereas beliefs attempt to grasp the world as it is. This difference, moreover, points to a parallel one between reason as commitment and reason as conviction. When our reason commits us to an attempt to realise something it gives us a pro-attitude. When it convinces us of the truth or falsity of something it gives us a belief. The second Humean argument relies on the claim that reason cannot take us from convictions to commitments. Humeans claim that we can commit ourselves to something only on the basis of a desire. Surely, however, their claim is true only if it is vacuous; otherwise it is false. Humeans can make their second argument work by definition: if they define reason in terms of conviction alone, and if they define desire to include reason as commitment, then of course reason cannot give us a pro-attitude. The argument loses its plausibility, however, once we break this charmed circle of definitions. Once we cease to define desire to include reason as commitment, we no longer have any reason to assume that the commitments we adopt as a result of our reason or thought are the same as those we adopt as a result of our emotions or feeling. Crucially, because the Humeans can make their reduction of pro-attitudes to desires work only by definition, it has no explanatory value. We cannot explain the committed nature of some of our reasons by reference to desire if we define desire to include the committed nature of some of our reasons. If all pro-attitudes by definition spring from the passions, any explanation of pro-attitudes in terms of the passions must be vacuous.

We can now provide a general critique of emotionalism understood as any attempt to reduce pro-attitudes to desires. All forms of emotionalism confront the difficulty that we can distinguish between thinking something desirable and actually desiring it: vegetarians can think abstaining from meat desirable while craving a bacon sandwich; and wealthy entrepreneurs can think higher taxes desirable without actually desiring them. This distinction gives rise to one between a reasoned commitment to what one thinks desirable and an actual desire. Thus, we cannot reduce pro-attitudes to desires because pro-attitudes can arise from reasoned commitments defined in contrast to desires. Emotionalists can overcome this difficulty only if they argue that we necessarily desire the things we think are desirable, but this argument is either vacuous or else false. If the things we think desirable are things we desire by definition, the argument is vacuous. If the things we think desirable are not things we desire by definition, the argument is false because we sometimes feel no desire for a thing we think desirable. Consider, for example, vegetarians who turn down a dish of meat because they believe eating meat is immoral. If we ask them why they believe this, they might say that all animals have a right to life. If we ask them why they act on this belief, they might say that they believe they should do what is right. Neither they nor we need refer to a desire in order to account for their action. Of course, we could say they desired to do right, but we need do so only if we already have decided we must describe all pro-attitudes as desires, and if we already have decided this, our reduction of pro-attitudes to desires is vacuous. If we define pro-attitudes in terms of desires, we will say that the vegetarians desire to do right, but we cannot explain their pro-attitude in terms of this desire. If we do not define pro-attitudes in terms of desires, we will say the vegetarians turned down the meat because their reason convinced them they ought to do so, and this conviction will explain their action.

Our general critique of emotionalism applies to analytical behaviourism just as cogently as it does to the Humean position. Analytical behaviourists reject the idea of desires as mental states in favour of dispositions to behave in certain ways, where these dispositions are defined exclusively by reference to behaviour. None the less, they still end up reducing pro-attitudes to dispositions understood as the psychological causes of all actions. Analytical behaviourists reduce pro-attitudes to dispositions conceived as a behaviourist equivalent to Humean desires. Gilbert Ryle, for example, proposes that we explain actions by reference to law-like propositions of the form 'the actor had a disposition to do that sort of thing in those sort of circumstances'.[22] Once again, however, the attempt to reduce pro-attitudes to dispositions is

---

[22] G. Ryle, *The Concept of Mind* (London: Hutchinson, 1949). Actually, Ryle seems to adopt a position even closer to that of Hume than the one discussed here. He argues not only that we can reduce pro-attitudes to the dispositional causes of actions, but also that desires (understood as feelings) cause the pro-attitudes (understood as motives) that we can reduce to the dispositional causes of actions.

either false or vacuous. Consider cases in which people act out of character. Imagine, for example, an extraordinarily selfish couple who on one notable occasion send a donation to Oxfam after having watched a television programme on famine in Africa. We cannot explain their action by reference to a disposition because the action is out of character; indeed, they cannot have a disposition to act in a humanitarian fashion in these sort of circumstances precisely because they would usually not do so. Thus, analytical behaviourists can tie actions that are out of character to dispositions only if they define pro-attitudes in terms of dispositions. If they do this, however, their reduction of pro-attitudes to dispositions becomes vacuous.

The rationalist equivalent of emotionalism and physicalism is the reduction of all pro-attitudes to reasons at the expense of desires and needs. Rationalism fails because things other than reason can give us pro-attitudes, sometimes even pro-attitudes contrary to those suggested by our reason. Our desires and needs sometimes override our reason so as to lead us to act in one way even though we think acting in another way would be preferable. A reason for performing an action encourages us to do so, but it does not impel us to do so. Even when our reason gives us a preference for a particular action, we might still perform a contrary action because of an emotional desire or physiological need. Someone might think something highly desirable, and even desire to desire it, and yet still not desire it, and so consciously choose to act on a contrary desire. Indeed, we often encounter just such behaviour. The overriding of reasons by desires or needs accounts for most of, quite possibly all of, the cases people describe in terms of weakness of the will. It is not really that the will is weak and so unable to compel the body to act in accord with one's reason. It is rather that a desire or need trumps one's reason so that the pro-attitude one acts on is not what one's reason would wish. Consider a case in which a desire overrides a reason. Jane thinks it highly desirable she stay in and work but none the less goes to a football match with her friends; her reason gives her one preference, her desires give her another, and she acts on the latter. Consider also a case in which a need overrides a reason: Bill thinks it highly desirable he stop smoking but none the less so craves a cigarette that he has one; his reason gives him one preference, his physiological needs give him another, and he acts on the latter. Rationalists who would reduce all pro-attitudes to reasons can account for these sorts of cases only if they argue that Jane and Bill have respectively a reason, not a desire, for going to watch the football, and a reason, not a need, for having a cigarette. But to argue this would be either to say something obviously false or to make rationalism true by definition and so entirely vacuous. Even a restricted rationalism that allows desires and needs can generate pro-attitudes only then to insist that reason can always trump desires and needs; even a restricted rationalism has difficulties accounting for the cases exemplified by Jane and Bill. A restricted rationalism can account for such cases only by evoking a complex analysis of weakness of the will to explain why and how reason sometimes fails to trump desires and needs. A complex analysis of weakness of the will becomes necessary, however, only if we adopt a rationalist position where we either assume that reason always triumphs over desire and need or equate what we will with the pro-attitudes generated by reason.[23] The periodic failure of reason to have its own way will seem strange to us only if we assume that reason alone can move us to act, or at least that reason can always trump any desire or need that might otherwise move us to act. Once we accept that any one of a reason, desire, or need can move us to act, we can explain the periodic failure of reason to have its own way simply by referring to the influence of desires and needs.

Physicalism, emotionalism, and rationalism all rest on the strange assumption that any acceptable account of human motivation must be a monistic one. Only a prior commitment to monism could lead philosophers to reject the pluralism implicit in folk psychology for an attempt to reduce all pro-attitudes to a particular psychological or physiological source. But why should we prefer a monistic to a pluralistic account of human motivation? What stands against our accepting the obvious plurality of our physical and mental requirements and capacities? People act on pro-attitudes, where a pro-attitude can derive from any one of a reason, desire, or need, and where all of reasons, desires, and needs are basic in that we cannot reduce any one of them to another of them or to anything else. Because needs, emotions, and thoughts can take all sorts of things as their subject matter, it is possible for a single object to be the subject of a need, desire, and reason. What is more, the unity of consciousness and the unity of mind and body imply that individuals can think about their emotions and needs, want to have certain needs and thoughts, and perhaps even need to have certain thoughts and emotions. None the less, the fact that our various physical and mental capacities can go to work on the same things and even on

---

[23] See respectively the account of the Socratic paradox in Plato, *Protagoras*, trans. C. Taylor (Oxford: Clarendon Press, 1991), ## 351–8; and D. Davidson, 'How is weakness of the will possible?', in *Essays on Actions and Events*, pp. 21–42.

one another does not imply that we can reduce any of these capacities to anything else. All of these capacities are basic. We can conclude, therefore, that a pro-attitude can derive from any one of a reason, desire, or need. People can act on motives generated by any one of a conviction that something is a good or bad thing, a feeling that something is a good or bad thing, or a need to have or to avoid something. Distorted beliefs can arise whenever any one of a reason, need, or desire takes the form of a pro-attitude that exercises an illegitimate influence on the beliefs someone expresses.

PURPOSIVE EXPLANATION

To complete a logic for the history of ideas, we need only to consider how historical explanations of distorted beliefs work. Given that explanations in the history of ideas do not embody the scientific concept of causation, we must specify the nature of the connections between distorted beliefs and the pro-attitudes that motivate them. How do pro-attitudes lead to actions? Earlier we found that all forms of explanation work by uncovering pertinent connections between entities or events. Now we will find that explanations of distorted beliefs rely on intentional, purposive connections. Historians tie actions back to the relevant pro-attitudes by showing that the pro-attitudes correspond to the intentions with which the actions were done. Similarly, historians explain someone's distorted belief by showing how his will led him to formulate that belief at the prompting of a rogue pro-attitude. Distorted beliefs are connected to the reasons, desires, and needs that generate them by a volitional connection established by the operation of a will. Volitional connections are what a will creates whenever it first decides to act on a pro-attitude and then does so. Volitional connections come into being whenever people first determine to act on a pro-attitude and then command themselves so to do. Thus, historians can take us from a need, emotion, or reason to a decision to act and on to the action itself by appealing to the appropriate volition.

When historians consider distorted beliefs, they still have to work with the language of folk psychology, not the physical language of the natural sciences. Indeed, the language they use to discuss deception, self-deception, and irrationality is parasitic on the one they use to discuss sincerity, the conscious, and the rational. They describe distortions by applying concepts such as pro-attitude, reason, and desire, concepts whose meanings derive from folk psychology. More importantly, when they apply these concepts to cases of deception, self-deception, and irrationality, they do so using criteria of application centred on a normative notion of rationality. They try to show how a particular distortion relates rationally, or at least quasi-rationally, to the rogue pro-attitude that prompted it. Certainly, for example, the failure of the politician to mention the incompetence of the government represents a rational way of trying to enhance its popularity, the cancer patient's denial of the likelihood of his dying is a quasi-rational response to his fear of death, and Peter's belief in God is a quasi-rational fulfilment of his wish. Historians explain distortions by ascribing psychological states to people using criteria centred on a concept of rationality, a concept with no place in the natural sciences. Because the physical language of the natural sciences does not cover distorted beliefs, we cannot describe distorted beliefs as products of causes in contrast to normal beliefs viewed as products of reason.[24] When scholars distinguish distorted beliefs from normal ones in this way, they imply that historians should explain distorted and normal beliefs using different languages. They would have historians explain distorted beliefs using a quasi-scientific language incorporating the idea of a physically necessary link between it and its cause. In contrast, we have found that historians should explain all beliefs, whether distorted or not, by deploying folk psychology. What we need to identify, therefore, is the nature of the connection folk psychology postulates between a rogue pro-attitude and the distortion it prompts.

We say a person performed an action X because he believed Y and had pro-attitude Z. We say that Paul added sage to the stew because he thought that doing so would improve its taste and he had a preference for improving its taste. What is the nature of the connection between, on the one hand, the action, and, on the other hand, the belief and the pro-attitude? Clearly the connection cannot be a physically necessary one if only because the concepts involved derive from a folk psychology in which the idea of physical necessity has no place. Some philosophers, however, present the connection between an action and the relevant beliefs and pro-attitudes as one of logical necessity. Davidson, for example, argues that the action follows deductively from the belief and the pro-attitude taken as premises.[25] If we specify the belief and pro-

---

[24] Contrast A. MacIntyre, 'Rationality and the explanation of action', in *Against the Self-Images of the Age: Essays on Ideology and Philosophy* (London: Duckworth, 1971), pp. 244–59.

[25] Davidson, 'Actions, reasons, and causes', in *Essays on Actions and Events*, pp. 3–19. Also see G. Anscombe, *Intention* (Oxford: Basil Blackwell, 1957).

attitude in the right way, they do indeed seem to lead logically to something akin to the action. We can see how a pro-attitude towards a state of affairs could combine with a belief that doing something will bring that state of affairs into being to give one grounds for doing that thing. If, for instance, Paul has a pro-attitude towards improving the taste of the stew, and if he believes adding sage to the stew will improve its taste, then he has grounds for adding sage to the stew. Surely, however, there remains a gap between his having grounds for doing so and his actually doing so; surely his having grounds for doing so does not make it logically necessary that he does so. One consequence of ignoring the gap between grounds for an action and the action itself, in the way Davidson does, is to render the concept of the will effectively redundant. The relevant pro-attitude, conceived as a motive, leads directly to the action. No space remains between motive and action in which to insert a will that forms an intention to act in accord with the pro-attitude. Indeed, the analysis of intentionality as a practical syllogism appeals to philosophers, especially those who are attracted to behaviourism, precisely because it leaves no room for the will. If one defines an intention not as an intention to do X (a decision made prior to an action) but rather as intention in doing X (pro-attitudes and beliefs instanced in the action), then by definition the intention produces the action in a way which excludes the need for a decision to act. Thus, philosophers such as Davidson conclude that the intentionality of actions lies solely in their relationship to the relevant beliefs and pro-attitudes, not in a special psychological state or capacity which takes one from the beliefs and pro-attitudes to the actions. The intentionality of actions lies in the fact that they are done because of beliefs and pro-attitudes, not in the existence of a distinctive will to do them.

Actually, however, the relationship between actions and the pro-attitudes that motivate them cannot be one of logical necessity. It cannot be so simply because we do not act on all pertinent pairs of pro-attitudes and beliefs. People might have a pro-attitude towards a state of affairs, and a belief that performing a particular action will bring the state of affairs into being, and yet they might still not act in that way. The pro-attitude and the belief do not necessarily result in the associated action. People might not have time to do the action, they might have other grounds for not doing it, they might find an alternative action preferable, or they might just be lazy; for any number of reasons, they might not act on the pro-attitude and the belief. Paul, for example, might want to improve the taste of the stew, and he might believe adding sage to it will improve its taste, but he still might not add sage to it; he might be in too much of a hurry, he might be allergic to sage, or he might attempt to improve its taste by adding chilli and not believe in mixing sage with chilli. Because every intention takes over from a pro-attitude, we always can relate intentions back to pro-attitudes, which can make the concept of an intention appear redundant. None the less, not all pro-attitudes lead to intentions, so we need a concept such as intention to denote the special stance we adopt towards a pro-attitude when we decide to act on it. The fact is that practical syllogisms give us only grounds for doing things, where there might be grounds for not doing them, or grounds for doing different things, and this means that the conclusions of practical syllogisms cannot be actions. A practical syllogism that takes beliefs and a pro-attitude as its premises has as its conclusion only grounds for an action, not the action itself, and there is a gap between the two, a gap we can fill only by evoking the operation of the will. Of course, Davidson might accept practical syllogisms give people only prima facie, as opposed to all-out, propositions in favour of actions, and still try to argue for a logically necessary relationship between actions and the relevant beliefs and pro-attitudes.[26] They might do so by identifying their all-out propositions with actions themselves rather than psychological states consequent upon deciding to act in a particular way. There are, however, as we will see, two insurmountable problems with such a move. The first is that it ignores the way we can decide now to do something in the future: it cannot accommodate future intentions.[27] The second is that it ignores our phenomenological awareness of a psychological act of commanding which often accompanies our actions: it cannot accommodate our conception of ourselves as willing our own actions.

To define the nature of a volitional connection, therefore, we must analyse the operation of a will as it moves from pro-attitudes to actions. Volitional connections arise as a consequence of a will playing a dual role. They emerge as the movement of someone's will takes him from having grounds for performing an action first to deciding to do so and second to commanding himself to do so. The decisions and commands of the will line the path from simply having pro-attitudes and beliefs to acting upon them. It is only by appealing to the will understood in terms

---

[26] D. Davidson, 'Intending', in *Essays on Actions and Events*, pp. 83–102.
[27] Compare M. Bratman, 'Davidson's theory of intention', in E. LePore and B. McLaughlin (eds.), *Actions and Events: Perspectives on the Philosophy of Donald Davidson* (Oxford: Basil Blackwell, 1985), pp. 14–28.

of this dual capacity that we can explain actions. We can fill out the concept of a volitional connection, therefore, by examining what happens when people decide to do something and then command themselves to do it.

Let us start with the capacity of the will to form intentions to act by making appropriate decisions. Whereas our beliefs and pro-attitudes give us all sorts of grounds for doing all sorts of things, our will selects the particular actions we are to perform from among the alternatives thus presented to us. Our will forms an intention to act by deciding which action we should perform out of the many we have grounds for performing. We have to postulate the will here because there is a space separating pro-attitudes from intentions as evidenced by those of our pro-attitudes we decide not to act on. John, for example, might have a desire, and so a motive, to kill Peter in that Peter killed his brother, and yet he might still decide not to do so. Some philosophers try to close this gap between pro-attitudes and intentions by analysing intentions as the products of a sort of algorithm applied to all the diverse pro-attitudes relevant to a particular action. They conceive of the will as reaching a decision simply by weighing up the comparative strengths of all the reasons, desires, and needs that would be satisfied or frustrated by various possible actions. This idea of the will as a calculating machine, however, has little to recommend it. For a start, our phenomenological awareness is of a much greater gap than this between pro-attitudes and intentions. We feel we are free to decide which pro-attitudes to act upon irrespective of the outcome of any algorithm one might apply to them. In addition, this phenomenological awareness of our freedom of decision gains support from the way we form and utilise intentions to do things in the future. To co-ordinate our actions over time in accord with complex plans, we have to be able to do more than compute our preferences as they are at the moment. We have to be able to follow past commitments for future purposes even when our current preferences would have us do otherwise. Surely, therefore, we should conceive of the will reaching a decision in an unrestricted process in which previously formed intentions, current preferences, and future possibilities all interact with one another. When our will makes a decision, it withdraws from the immediacy of our pro-attitudes to choose from among them in the light not only of their respective strengths, but also of things such as our long-term plans. The decisions it thereby makes give us our intentions.

Let us turn now to the capacity of the will to initiate actions by issuing commands. Although our decisions give us intentions, we can act on such intentions only because of the ability of our will to command us so to do. We act at our own insistence, and this insistence is neither a pro-attitude nor an intention, but rather a command, a command that initiates something such as a bodily movement or an impression in the mind. Our phenomenological experience recognises a type of psychological event corresponding uniquely to the performance of actions. When we act, we feel ourselves to be not just intending to do so, as we might intend to do something in the future, but also commanding ourselves to do so right then and there. Once our will decides to do something, that thing does not just happen more or less spontaneously. We know it does not do so because we have intentions we do not act on. John, for example, might intend to kill Peter, and he might act to bring about a situation in which he could shoot him, but at the critical moment he might still not pull the trigger of the gun. Once we have decided to do something, therefore, we still have to command ourselves to do it. To bridge this gap between intentions and commands, we again have to postulate the will; we have to ascribe to the will an ability to initiate new states of affairs by commanding the body or mind to do things. A will can instigate a movement of the body, a calling to mind of a particular memory, and other such things. When we deliberately bring about a new state of affairs, we have a phenomenological experience of our will commanding us so to do. It is true that the action we actually perform need not correspond to the one we have commanded ourselves to perform. John might command himself to pull the trigger but lack the force required to do so, or he might mistakenly move a finger other than the one on the trigger. None the less, this gap between command and result does not imply that the action we actually perform is not a product of a command. It is just that the command does not have the required result. A will initiates an action by issuing a command so as to bring about a movement of the body or an impression of the mind.

Volitional connections consist, therefore, of a decision and a command made by a will. These volitional connections cannot be physically necessary because they are postulated within a folk psychology in which the concept of physical necessity has no place. They cannot be logically necessary because we do not decide to act on all our pro-attitudes, and we do not command ourselves to act on all our intentions. They cannot be arbitrary because we bring them into being for reasons. Although volitional connections thus resemble conditional ones in that their location in a folk psychology concerned with human affairs divorces them from both the necessary and the arbitrary, they still differ from conditional ones. Conditional connections link beliefs that pick up on themes contained in one another. The stance the agent takes towards the two objects is the same – the agent believes X and Y – but the two objects have different content – X and Y have themes in common but they are not the same. Volitional connections, in contrast, link commands back to decisions and decisions back to pro-attitudes. The content of the objects is the same – the agent commands himself to do X having decided to do X having had a preference for something he believed would be brought about by doing X – but the stance the agent takes towards them differs – to command differs from to decide which, in turn, differs from to prefer. Whereas conditional connections link different contents to which people take the same stance, volitional connections link similar contents to which people take a different stance. We can conclude, therefore, that volitional connections come into being when a will operates so as to transform one's stance towards an act from being favourable to it to a decision to do it and then on to a command to do it. Historians can explain a distorted belief by reference to the way someone willed himself to believe that belief at the prompting of a rogue pro-attitude. No doubt historians are unable to say much about the way the will operates: they can say little other than that the will did operate with a particular result. That they are unable to do so, however, is not a failing so much as a necessary consequence of the nature of a will. A will can bring something new into being.

Explanations in the history of ideas work by evoking conditional or volitional connections. The distinction between these connections and those found in science, mathematics, and the like, suggests that explanation in the history of ideas constitutes a type of narrative. The forms of explanation appropriate to the history of ideas provide the basis of narrative structures in that they relate entities and events to one another in an intelligible and often temporal manner without evoking the idea of necessity.[28] Historians of ideas offer us meaningful stories about the past. They relate beliefs to one another in synchronic webs and diachronic sequences by highlighting appropriate conditional and volitional connections. The history of ideas deploys, therefore, the same types of narrative structure we find in other accounts of human affairs, including works of fiction. To say this is not to assimilate history to fiction. The

---

[28] In contrast, scientism suggests all explanations must invoke physically-necessary covering laws, so narrative cannot be a form of explanation unless it constitutes a 'sketchy' version of the covering law model. See, most famously, C. Hempel, 'The function of general laws in history', *Journal of Philosophy* 39 (1942), 35–48.

difference between the two, however, is not that the former does not deploy narrative structures of the type associated with the latter. It is rather that the narrative structures they deploy have different relationships to our knowledge of the world. Historians offer us narratives that they believe retell the way in which things really did happen in the past, whereas writers of fiction do not. Historians cannot ignore the facts, although as we have seen no fact is simply given to them. They cannot ignore what happened, or invent what happened, as can writers of fiction.

The fear remains, however, that all narratives are constructed in part by the imagination of the writer, so if the history of ideas relies on narrative, it lacks proper epistemic legitimacy. Even scholars who defend history as narrative have expressed this sort of fear. Louis Mink, for example, doubted whether one could resolve the dilemma that although historical narrative 'claims to represent . . . the real complexity of the past', as narrative it must be an 'imaginative construction, which cannot defend its claim to truth'.[29] Indeed, some scholars who defend history as narrative embrace the idea that a dependence on narrative implies that history disrupts the past instead of representing it. White, for example, defends his sceptical conclusion that an aesthetic judgement alone decides which form of reasoning a historian should adopt by arguing that historians endow the past with meaning by imposing narratives upon it. The type of narrative historians should adopt cannot depend on facts about the past: it depends instead on their aesthetic judgement as to which genre of literary figuration to project on to the facts.[30] Crucially, however, an anthropological epistemology allows us to dispel the scepticism surrounding an analysis of history as narrative. We can accept that historical narratives are in part imaginative constructs, and still defend their epistemic legitimacy; after all, a rejection of given facts implies that all knowledge is constructed in part by prior theories. Although historians of ideas postulate certain links between historical entities and events, they do so not at random or for aesthetic reasons, but because these links are given to them by the folk psychology we accept as true.

All knowledge rests in part on prior theories we accept as true.

[29] L. Mink, 'Narrative form as a cognitive instrument', in *The Writing of History*, ed. R. Canary and H. Kozicki (Madison, Wis.: University of Wisconsin Press, 1978), p. 145.
[30] See, in particular, H. White, 'The question of narrative in contemporary historical theory', in *The Content of the Form: Narrative Discourse and Historical Representation* (Baltimore: Johns Hopkins University Press, 1987), pp. 26–57.

Among the prior theories on which historians rely are those given by folk psychology. Indeed, the past does not present itself to historians as a series of isolated facts upon which they impose a narrative in order to bring the facts to order. Rather, the past, like all experience, presents itself as an already structured set of facts. Historians cannot grasp facts about the past save in their relation to one another and also to the other theories they hold true. They cannot experience the past apart from the categories given them by folk psychology. The past they experience already has a narrative structure.[31] Once we thus accept the legitimacy of historians postulating conditional and volitional connections, we can allow for the way in which they select objects for inclusion in their narratives. Critics might argue that if, as I have said, we experience the past as having a narrative structure, historians would need only to record the narratives they experienced, whereas actually they struggle to organise and convey their view of the past, which implies that they cannot experience it as having a narrative structure. Really, however, when historians struggle to organise their material, they do so not at random or for aesthetic reasons, but because they are trying to expand their knowledge by tracing the conditional and volitional connections that enable them to explain more and more of their chosen field. Similarly, when they struggle to convey their material, they do so in order to make their view of the past convincing. They try to show how their narrative does better than its rivals judged by the sort of criteria of comparison we identified earlier. To say that the history of ideas relies on narrative is not in any way, therefore, to undermine its epistemic legitimacy.

CONCLUSION

I have completed the analysis of the form of explanation historians should adopt for distorted beliefs. Historians should explain distorted beliefs by showing how someone's will led him to express or adopt the relevant beliefs at the prompting of a rogue pro-attitude. Here I analysed deception, self-deception, and irrationality, so as to show that they all occurred because of the illegitimate influence of a rogue pro-attitude on beliefs. To begin, I argued that deception occurs when a pro-attitude

[31] Several phenomenologists emphasise that we experience history as narrative. Typically, however, they do so as a result of an analysis of temporality, not of folk psychology. See, in particular, P. Ricœur, *Time and Narrative*, 3 vols., trans. K. McLaughlin and D. Pellauer (Chicago: University of Chicago Press, 1984–88).

leads someone to express beliefs he does not hold in an attempt to obtain a preferred effect. From the perspective of the deceiver, the pro-attitude plays the quite legitimate role of grounds for action: it only influences what the deceiver does, not what he believes. From the perspective of the audience, however, the pro-attitude plays the illegitimate role of grounds for a belief: it influences the beliefs the deceiver expresses to them. Next I deduced the nature of self-deception from the idea of a disjunction between conscious and unconscious beliefs. Self-deception occurs when a rogue pro-attitude leads people to repress their actual beliefs in their unconscious while consciously avowing alternative beliefs clustered around that pro-attitude. Because I constructed this concept of the unconscious from the nature of self-deception alone, it was a considerably broader one than Freud's: it avoided his problematic commitments to physicalism, the primacy of childhood, and other such theories. Finally, I deduced the nature of irrationality from the idea of an unwanted inconsistency of belief. Irrationality occurs either as a result of an inexplicable mistake or as a result of a pro-attitude leading people to hold beliefs contrary to their own concept of best belief.

The concepts of deception, the unconscious, and hot irrationality, are universal in that I deduced them as logical consequences of the grammar of our concepts. Within my concept of a distortion, therefore, one might identify various more precisely defined phenomena. On the one hand, one might identify a special type of distortion by reference to the sort of pro-attitude motivating it. Perhaps, for example, one might begin to devise a sociological theory of ideology by reference to distortions based on a pro-attitude to political or social power.[32] On the other hand, one might identify a special type of distortion by reference to its social context and then go on to devise sociological theories about the effects it has. Perhaps, for example, one might begin to devise a theory of the stability of political regimes by reference to the levels of trust and deception existing between government and people.[33] Alternatively one might begin to explore how certain types of social co-operation encourage people to adopt certain unconscious or irrational beliefs.[34] Although such theories would be most welcome, I will not try to devise them. Once again I will observe only that any distinctive type of distortion would have to fit within the framework set by my logical analysis of

---

[32] See M. Bevir, 'Ideology as distorted belief', *Journal of Political Ideologies* 1 (1996), 107–22.
[33] Compare J. Dunn, *Political Obligation in Its Historical Context* (Cambridge: Cambridge University Press, 1980).
[34] Compare S. Freud, *Civilisation and its Discontents*, *Works*, vol. XXI, pp. 57–146.

distortions as such. A special type of deception, unconscious belief, or irrationality would have to possess the generic features I have described in addition to any others more specific to it.

One of the properties common to all distorted beliefs, except instances of cold irrationality, is that they are motivated by a rogue pro-attitude. This is why historians can explain cases of deception, self-deception, and hot irrationality by referring to the pro-attitudes motivating them. A series of inductive arguments based on the nature of folk psychology showed that pro-attitudes can be any one of a reason, desire, or need. A reason is a conviction and so a product of thought. A desire is an emotion and so a product of feeling. A need is a physiological requirement understood in terms of the normal functioning of the body. Historians can explain distorted beliefs, therefore, by showing how any one of a reason, desire, or need played the illegitimate role of grounds for belief rather than the legitimate role of grounds for action. Whenever historians explain distorted beliefs in this way, they postulate a volitional connection between the rogue pro-attitude and the distortion it engendered. A series of inductive arguments based on the grammar of folk psychology enabled me to fill out the concept of a volitional connection in terms of the operation of a will. It is the will that takes one from pro-attitudes to actions; it does so by making a decision and then issuing a command to act in accord with that decision.

This analysis of volitional connections completed our study of the forms of explanation appropriate to the history of ideas. The history of ideas has dominant and subsidiary forms of explanatory reasoning. The dominant form applies to sincere, conscious and rational beliefs, following the presumptions folk psychology gives us in favour of such beliefs. It works by uncovering the conditional connections relating individual beliefs to webs of belief, and webs of belief to traditions and dilemmas. There are three subsidiary forms of explanation depending on whether the distortion is a case of deception, the unconscious, or irrationality. All three work in part, however, by uncovering the volitional connections relating distorted beliefs back to the pro-attitudes motivating them. Historians of ideas should adopt whichever form of explanation is appropriate to the particular object they want to explain.

CHAPTER 8

Conclusion

All historical inquiries start from relics from the past that are available to us in the present. Historians have before them a collection of source material consisting of books, newspapers, works of art, government reports, census data, and other such things. Because this source material comes from the past, it can provide evidence of the nature of the past. None the less, because it is not itself the past, historians use it to postulate historical objects; they tease out its secrets in an interpretative process. To postulate any one historical object, however, historians also have to postulate other such objects and to relate them to one another in a narrative structure. Historians of ideas, of course, concern themselves exclusively with ideas. They look only at what relics from the past tell us about historical meanings, not what they tell us about other historical objects. Like all historians, however, they use relics from the past to devise narratives that relate various historical objects to one another. The logic of the history of ideas concerns the forms of reasoning historians ought to use to do this. It examines the forms of justification and explanation appropriate to the discipline: it examines, first, the way historians should defend the narratives they tell, and, second, the way they should relate the objects they postulate to one another in a narra-tive.

Clearly a logic of the history of ideas must apply to itself. If we believe that a given form of explanation applies to beliefs, we must accept that our belief can be explained using just that form of explanation. Similar-ly, if we believe that a given form of justification operates on all knowledge, we must accept that our argument needs to be justified using that form of justification. The purpose of this conclusion is, therefore, not just to reiterate my earlier arguments, but also to show how my logic of the history of ideas applies to itself. To begin, I will consider my earlier arguments from the point of view of the form of explanation I have defended. I will try to show how my conclusions arise out of traditions, the dilemmas they face, and the debates they encourage. In doing so, of course, I will go a long way towards locating my conclusions within certain research programmes. Later, however, I will explicitly consider my earlier arguments from the point of view of the form of justification I have defended. More particularly, I will try to show how my conclusions open up new avenues of research in a progressive manner.

One tradition in which I can locate my arguments is that of philosophers who have renounced the idea of given, self-evident truths. Although one can overstate the case, various philosophical movements of the twentieth century – pragmatism, much phenomenology following Martin Heidegger, Wittgenstein's later work, and now, of course, a more self-conscious post-modernism – have crept, or even leapt, towards a rejection of not only pure experience but also pure reason.[1] The adherents of these movements have rejected traditional concepts of certainty for more anthropocentric epistemologies or a more or less irrationalist relativism. My arguments represent an extension of this anti-foundationalist tradition of philosophy to the logic of the history of ideas. I adopted a version of Wittgenstein's view of analytic philosophy as the grammar of our concepts, and then explored the forms of reasoning appropriate to the history of ideas in terms of such a philosophy. To highlight a particular debt to Wittgenstein in this way is, however, to point to debates between anti-foundationalists. It is to locate myself in what sometimes gets described as the post-analytic section of anti-foundationalism. On the one hand, my rejection of logics of discovery, and also my affirmation of narrative, resemble positions adopted by others, including LaCapra, who have written on the philosophy of history from within a broad anti-foundationalist tradition.[2] On the other hand, however, my opposition to relativism, and also my intentionalist theory of meaning, stand in contrast to positions adopted by just the same people in so far as they are inspired by the post-structuralist or post-modern sections of the anti-foundationalist tradition.[3] In the context of anti-foundationalism, I have defended both an anthropocentric concept of objectivity against a

---

[1] Compare Rorty, *Philosophy and the Mirror of Nature*, particularly pp. 5–13.
[2] For a review of a number of works that approach the history of ideas from an anti-foundationalist perspective, see J. Toews, 'Intellectual history after the linguistic turn: the autonomy of meaning and the irreducibility of experience', *American Historical Review* 92 (1987), 879–907.
[3] LaCapra draws on post-Freudian psycho-analysis to challenge intentionalism in a way I have argued we cannot do because of our adherence to folk psychology. See, in particular, D. LaCapra, 'History and psychoanalysis', *Critical Inquiry* 13 (1987), 222–51.

post-modern relativism, and also a space for conscious and rational human agency against a post-structuralist focus on the unconscious and social determinants of beliefs.

My form of justification for the history of ideas avoided both the objectivist belief in given truths renounced by all anti-foundationalists and the sceptical relativism adopted by many post-modernists. I rejected the idea of facts given to us outside of, or independent of, all theoretical frameworks. Although historians cannot be certain of the truth or falsity of their view of a historical meaning, however, they can reach an objective understanding that they have good reason to take as more or less true. Here I argued that historians can attain objective knowledge through a process of criticising and comparing rival sets of theories against criteria of accuracy, comprehensiveness, consistency, progressiveness, fruitfulness, and openness. Historians have good reason to take as more or less true the objective understandings at which they thereby arrive because our ability to act in the world guarantees that our perceptions are more or less accurate, which implies that the theories that best account for our perceptions are more or less true. Because there are no given facts, historical understanding must be holistic: because what we accept as a fact depends on the theories we hold true, any meaning historians postulate necessarily relates to the other meanings they postulate, where all these inter-connected meanings then fit together to form an integral part of their webs of belief. Objectivity in history must depend, therefore, on a comparison between whole sets of theories. It must be webs of historical theories that provide the material for the process of criticism and comparison which leads us to objective knowledge of the past. A historical understanding can never be objective in and of itself, but only by virtue of its place in a broader web. This means that the objectivity of any particular historical understanding is always tentative in two respects: first, the web to which it belongs might change so as to lead us to modify it; and, second, another web could develop so as to lead us to reject the web to which it belongs. None the less, we should not mistake a tentative stance towards the truth of the knowledge we accept as objective for a sceptical rejection of the rationality of our taking anything to be true. Historians can defend their view of the past by showing how it compares favourably with its rivals when judged against the criteria I have specified.

Because the objective status of a historical understanding depends on its relationship to a broader web, historians will do well to relate their understanding of any one work to their understanding of various others.

This does not imply that a study of the context of a work is either necessary or sufficient to ensure an objective grasp of its meaning. It implies only that historians who wish to defend a particular understanding of a work must do so in terms of their understanding of various other works. They must relate the various historical objects they postulate to one another in an illuminating manner. Thus, a concern with justification in the history of ideas leads us on to a study of explanation therein.[4] To defend an understanding of any one work, historians must relate it to other works; they must weave numerous historical objects into a single tapestry, showing how some objects explain others, which explain others, and so on; they must develop a narrative that moves from object to object through time. In the history of ideas, the objects to be explained are beliefs, and an analysis of beliefs shows that historians should adopt presumptions in favour of sincere, conscious, and rational beliefs. These presumptions imply only that historians should ascribe beliefs to people in accord with norms in favour of these types of belief, not that they never can ascribe other types of belief to people. Indeed, historians should ascribe insincere, unconscious, or irrational beliefs to people whenever doing so is part of an objective account of the past. Thus, a concern with explanation in the history of ideas points back to a study of justification therein. Here, however, an analysis of objectivity as a product of a comparison between rival webs of beliefs precludes our specifying necessary or sufficient conditions under which historians may postulate distorted beliefs.

My form of explanation for the history of ideas avoided both the notion of autonomy renounced by all anti-foundationalists and the hostility to the subject or author adopted by many post-structuralists. Consider the form of explanation I proposed for sincere, conscious, and rational beliefs. I rejected the idea of explaining such beliefs by reference to the allegedly pure experiences or pure reasoning of the individual in question. Individuals can exercise their reason and have their experiences only in the context of their existing webs of belief, webs of belief which influence the content of their reason and their experience. Historians, therefore, can begin to explain why someone held a particular belief by relating it to his other beliefs. They can explain a belief by showing how it fitted into an inter-connected web of beliefs that makes sense of it. Similarly, historians can begin to explain why someone held a particular web of beliefs by locating it in the tradition to which it

---

[4] On the interpenetration of explanation and understanding, see Ricœur, *Interpretation Theory*, p. 72.

belongs. Just as webs of belief provide the background against which individuals exercise their reason and have experiences, so traditions provide the background against which individuals come to adopt the webs of belief they do. Although historians cannot explain beliefs by referring to pure experiences or pure reasoning, they must allow for the active role played by individuals in developing their webs of belief. We should not mistake a rejection of autonomy for a hostility to agency. We should not mistake a rejection of the atomistic view of the subject for a hostility to the very notion of the subject. Individuals possess a faculty of thought which enables them to exercise their reason in local contexts. They can extend and modify the webs of belief they inherit in a way which precludes our reducing their beliefs to a tradition or any other type of social structure. Historians can explain fully why someone held a web of beliefs, therefore, only by showing how he developed the tradition from which he set out. They can do this, moreover, by relating the way in which he developed the tradition to the dilemmas he faced. A dilemma is an authoritative understanding that poses a question of the web of beliefs in which it arises. Historians explain changes of belief by showing how the new web of beliefs resolves a dilemma, that is, by showing how it hooks the understanding within a dilemma on to suitable parts of the old web of beliefs. Distortions occur when the process of belief-formation rests not on an attempt to resolve a dilemma, but rather on a rogue pro-attitude. Distorted beliefs appear when pro-attitudes act as grounds for belief, not grounds for action, and so lead people to depart from their proper concern to arrive at objective beliefs. Historians can explain cases of deception, self-deception, and irrationality, therefore, by reference to the pro-attitudes that motivate them, where pro-attitudes themselves can derive from any one of needs, desires, or reasons.

The place of my conclusions within an anti-foundationalist tradition appears also in my analysis of the connections that sustain explanations in the history of ideas. Like other anti-foundationalists, I identified explanation in the history of ideas as a type of narrative, but unlike many of them, I did not equate such narratives with subjective impositions that disrupt the past. The threads that bind the tapestries historians weave out of historical objects are conditional and volitional, not necessary or arbitrary. Historical narratives do not progress inevitably from one object to another with each being necessitated by its predecessor and making necessary its successor. Nor do historical narratives stumble haphazardly from one object to another with no object having a significant relationship to those adjacent to it. On the contrary, beliefs, webs of belief, traditions, and dilemmas, are connected conditionally to one another. The content of each includes themes picked up by the content of those adjacent to it. Historical narratives progress, therefore, by following themes from object to object. Historians can give rational explanations of objects by highlighting the themes that connect them to others. Similarly, pro-attitudes, decisions, commands to oneself, and actions are connected volitionally to one another. A will takes the content of one and transforms the stance the person concerned takes to it so as to produce another. Historical narratives progress, therefore, by following the operation of a will as it takes us from object to object. Historians can give purposive explanations of objects by highlighting a change in the stance someone takes towards a given content. Although historians of ideas thus construct narratives by postulating conditional and volitional connections between objects, their doing so does not constitute an imposition of subjective structures on to the past. Rather, our shared commitment to folk psychology enables historians to assume that all beliefs, traditions, pro-attitudes, actions, and the like are connected to others in the very ways they thus postulate.

To explain the positions I have adopted in debates within anti-foundationalism, we have to locate my arguments in a different tradition, namely, modern idealism. Modern idealism derives from Hegel, and, more immediately, philosophers influenced by him such as Benedetto Croce in Italy, and F. H. Bradley, T. H. Green and R. G. Collingwood in Britain, and, to take a different and more problematic route, Arthur Schopenhauer and Wittgenstein.[5] Although these philosophers owed a clear debt to Hegel, they were, at least to some extent, critical of his intellectualism. Most of them did not share Hegel's faith in an objective reason working through history. In general, however, they rejected his intellectualism because they gave a more significant role than did he to things other than reason in human affairs, not because they rejected the very idea of a pure, objective reason. My arguments represent, therefore, an attempt to modify the tradition of modern idealism in response to the dilemma posed by anti-foundationalism understood as the rejection of the very idea of pure reason or final truth.

Perhaps the most important theme I have taken from modern idealism is a commitment to the history of ideas as central to all the human sciences. In addition, however, my debt to modern idealism appears

---

[5] On Wittgenstein's relationship to Schopenhauer, see Hacker, *Insight and Illusion*, pp. 81–107.

in a strong commitment to at least local reasoning. This commitment led me away from anti-foundationalists more heavily indebted to post-modernism and post-structuralism. It led me to adopt an anthro-pocentric analysis of objectivity in contrast to their sceptical relativism, and a view of individuals as rational agents rather than mere products of a determining social structure, unconscious will, or something else of the sort. Equally, however, I modified modern idealism – or rather I adopted certain positions in debates within it – to accommodate the insights of anti-foundationalism. Here my arguments come into close proximity with those of Skinner, who draws on Collingwood and Wittgenstein to reject the intimations of pure reason in the work of philosophers such as Lovejoy and Strauss.[6] Like Skinner, I opposed accounts of the history of ideas as the study of either eternal presences or an epic tradition embodying logical connections, accounts which respectively have too Platonic and too Hegelian an aura. So my form of justification for the history of ideas embraced a belief in local reason while avoiding postulat-ing a pure reason or final truth. I rejected the idea of pure reason by denying that historians could be certain of any truth about the past. Yet I defended the idea of local reasoning by arguing that historians could arrive at objective knowledge of the past by criticising and comparing sets of theories against the criteria specified. The objective knowledge at which they thus arrive must remain tentative and local because it constitutes a decision about the comparative merits of the rival sets of theories currently available. My form of explanation for the history of ideas also embraced local reason while rejecting pure reason. I rejected the idea of a pure reason or final truth by denying that historians can explain beliefs in a way which presupposes the autonomy of the individ-ual, and also by insisting that traditions are contingent products of individual agency, not hypostatised entities with an inner logic of their own. Yet I defended the idea of local reasoning by arguing that historical meanings derive from the beliefs of actual individuals rather than a social structure, and that the process of ascribing beliefs to people embodies a norm in favour of rationality understood as consistency.

Historians of ideas recreate historical objects from the relics of the past available to them in the present. They give rational and purposive explanations of these objects by highlighting the conditional and voli-tional connections that relate them to each other in narratives. And they criticise and compare rival narratives to obtain objective knowledge of

---

[6] Skinner, 'Meaning and understanding'.

the past. To what extent does this analysis of the logic of the history of ideas constitute an adequate, let alone complete, theory of culture? To ask this question is to point to the need to assess my conclusions in terms of the criteria I have argued govern the ascription of objectivity to theories. Most of my arguments have been designed to establish the accuracy and consistency of my logic of the history of ideas. They establish its accuracy principally by showing how it derives from various languages, notably folk psychology, which we must accept since we use them to describe the world. They establish its consistency principally by showing how the positions it incorporates hang together around central commitments to theories like semantic holism. In addition, some of my arguments have been designed to show the comprehensiveness of my logic. They have done so both by relating it to languages such as folk psychology and by locating it in broader research programmes, notably that associated with an anti-foundationalist rejection of given truths.

In locating my logic of the history of ideas in broader research programmes, I have extended, taken positions within, and perhaps even modified, these programmes. To recognise this is to raise the question of the value of my intervention in the anti-foundationalist, or more specifically the post-analytic, tradition. The fruitfulness of this intervention is, of course, something for time and the work of others to reveal. None the less, I want to go some way towards demonstrating the progressive nature of my intervention by showing how it suggests novel hypotheses so as to open up new avenues for research.

Consider first the ways in which one might extend my logic of the history of ideas to history in general. My analysis of distorted beliefs already provides the basis of a form of explanation for human actions. Historians should explain actions by reference to the beliefs and pro-attitudes that motivate them, where they should explain the relevant beliefs in the way I have described, and the relevant pro-attitudes by referring to the reasons, desires, and needs from which they derive. In addition, historians can go a long way towards explaining the consequences of an action by describing how others understood it and how their understanding of it led them to act in certain ways. Here historians can explain why people understood an action as they did, and so acted as they did, using those forms of explanation that apply to beliefs and actions in general. My logic provides us, therefore, with the basis of a general logic of history covering not only ideas or beliefs, but also actions, institutions, and the like. In addition, of course, my logic also brings to the fore several philosophical questions. One might ask: what precisely is the status of the knowledge given us by the grammar of our concepts? How does post-analytic philosophy relate to other traditions such as phenomenology? How should we link semantic, linguistic, and hermeneutic meanings to each other so as to arrive at a unified theory of meaning?

Consider next the way my logic points to hypotheses and areas for research in sociology as well as philosophy. For a start, one might try to devise sociological theories to explain how different types of tradition emerge, develop, and decline. My arguments suggest that open traditions, those which recognise our capacity for agency and actively encourage innovation, are likely to develop more rapidly than those that do not do so. We cannot say that open traditions necessarily develop more rapidly than closed ones, however, for two reasons: first, the speed at which a tradition develops also depends on factors such as the extent to which changes in the world push new beliefs on its adherents; and, second, when and how people change their beliefs is something we can neither predict nor bring under some covering law. Still, any sociological theory at which we thus arrived would help us to answer various questions about the relationship between different types of tradition and wider social formations. We might ask, for example: do certain social formations push new beliefs on people in a way likely to increase the speed of intellectual change? Are some social formations particularly conducive to the development of open traditions that value human agency? Do certain traditions promote the forms of behaviour associated with particular social formations?

In addition, one might try to use my logic to devise sociological theories to explain how different types of dilemma affect different types of tradition. My arguments suggest that an encounter with another way of life is likely to produce more dramatic change than is the discovery of a new fact or theory within a tradition. Even when people encounter another way of life, however, they will not replicate it, but rather graft parts of it on to themes found in their own tradition. My logic leads me to suspect, therefore, that we cannot have a general theory of societal evolution. Any adequate theory of modernisation should allow for the nature of modernity varying across traditions and ways of life. My arguments also suggest that open traditions will encounter more dilemmas and challenges to authority than closed ones, but that they will be less likely to need to make dramatic changes to incorporate the dilemmas they do encounter. Perhaps we might be able, therefore, to devise new theories of things such as political stability by being more sensitive to the importance and indeterminacy of beliefs. Any sociological theory at which we thus arrived would help us answer questions about the relationships between different types of traditions, dilemmas, and social formations. We might ask, for example: do different social formations promote different patterns of modernisation? Do some social formations encourage challenges to authority in a way which makes them especially unstable? Do different social formations promote different ways of responding to challenges to authority?

Finally, one might try to use my logic to devise sociological theories to account for the incidence and effects of different types of distorted beliefs. My arguments suggest that we might base a critical theory of ideology on an analysis of the way in which a preference for power can lead people to express beliefs other than their actual ones. To complete such a theory of ideology, however, we would have to explore how distorted beliefs are adopted by others as sincere, conscious, and rational beliefs. Any sociological theory at which we thus arrived would help us to answer questions about the relationship between types of distortion and different social formations. We might ask, for example: do certain social formations promote political cultures of deception or of trust? Are certain social formations especially likely to generate ideologies? Do irrational beliefs give rise to particular types of social formation?

The main purpose of my logic, however, is to promote a particular way of doing the history of ideas. My principal aim has been to describe how historians of ideas should explain the historical objects they postulate and justify the narratives they tell. The main question to ask of my logic, therefore, is: does it help historians of ideas to make better sense of the relics from the past available to them? Only time can tell whether or not it does.

Bibliography

Acton, H., 'Tradition and some other forms of order', *Proceedings of the Aristotelian Society* 53 (1952–53), 1–28.

Amacher, P., *Freud's Neurological Education and Its Influence on Psychoanalytic Theory*, New York: International Universities Press, 1965.

Anscombe, G., *Intention*, Oxford: Basil Blackwell, 1957.

Arendt, H., *The Life of the Mind*, 2 vols., ed. M. McCarthy, New York: Harcourt Brace Jovanovich, 1978.

Austin, J., *How to Do Things with Words*, ed. J. Urmson and M. Sbisa, Oxford: Clarendon Press, 1975.

Ayer, A., *Language, Truth and Logic*, London: Victor Gollancz, 1936.

Ayer, A. (ed.), *Logical Positivism*, Glencoe, Ill.: Free Press, 1959.

Bates, D., 'Rediscovering Collingwood's spiritual history (in and out of context)', *History and Theory* 35 (1996), 29–55.

Baudrillard, J., *Simulations*, trans. P. Foss, P. Patton, and P. Beitchman, New York: Semiotext[e], 1983.

Bernstein, R., *Beyond Objectivism and Relativism: Science, Hermeneutics, and Praxis*, Philadelphia: University of Pennsylvania Press, 1983.

Besant, A., *Four Great Religions*, London: Theosophical Publishing, n.d.

Bevir, M., 'The errors of linguistic contextualism', *History and Theory* 31 (1992), 276–98.

'Are there perennial problems in political theory?', *Political Studies* 42 (1994), 662–75.

'Objectivity in history', *History and Theory* 33 (1994), 328–44.

'Ideology as distorted belief', *Journal of Political Ideologies* 1 (1996), 107–22.

'The individual and society', *Political Studies* 44 (1996), 102–14.

'Meaning, truth and phenomenology', *Teorema* 16 (1997), 61–76.

'Mind and method in the history of ideas', *History and Theory* 36 (1997), 167–89.

Bleicher, J. (ed.), *Contemporary Hermeneutics: Hermeneutics and Method, Philosophy and Critique*, London: Routledge & Kegan Paul, 1980.

Bloom, A., *The Closing of the American Mind*, New York: Simon & Schuster, 1987.

Bogen, J., *Wittgenstein's Philosophy of Language: Some Aspects of Its Development*,

London: Routledge & Kegan Paul, 1972.

Bouwsma, W., 'Intellectual history in the 1980s: from history of ideas to history of meaning', *Journal of Interdisciplinary History* 12 (1981), 279–91.

Bratman, M., 'Davidson's theory of intention', in E. LePore and B. McLaughlin (eds.), *Actions and Events: Perspectives on the Philosophy of Donald Davidson*, Oxford: Basil Blackwell, 1985, 14–28.

Burge, T., 'Individualism and the mental', in P. French, T. Uehling, Jr, and H. Wettstein (eds.), *Studies in Metaphysics*, Midwest Studies in Philosophy 4, Minneapolis: University of Minnesota Press, 1979, 73–121.

Burke, E., *Reflections on the Revolution in France*, ed. C. O'Brien, Harmondsworth, Middlesex: Penguin, 1968.

Carnap, R., *The Logical Syntax of Language*, London: Routledge & Kegan Paul, 1937.

'The old and the new logic', in A. Ayer (ed.), *Logical Positivism*, Glencoe, Ill.: Free Press, 1959, 133–46.

Chomsky, N., *Reflections on Language*, London: Temple Smith, 1976.

Cohen, L., 'Do illocutionary forces exist?', *Philosophical Quarterly* 14 (1964), 118–37.

Collingwood, R., *An Essay on Metaphysics*, Oxford: Clarendon Press, 1940.

The Idea of History, ed. T. Knox, Oxford: Clarendon Press, 1946.

An Autobiography, intro. S. Toulmin, Oxford: Oxford University Press, 1978.

Condren, C., *The Status and Appraisal of Classic Texts*, Princeton: Princeton University Press, 1985.

Cummins, R., *The Nature of Psychological Explanation*, Cambridge, Mass.: Massachusetts Institute of Technology Press, 1983.

Davidson, D., *Essays on Actions and Events*, Oxford: Clarendon Press, 1980.

'Paradoxes of irrationality', in R. Wollheim and J. Hopkins (eds.), *Philosophical Essays on Freud*, Cambridge: Cambridge University Press, 1982, 289–305.

Inquiries into Truth and Interpretation, Oxford: Clarendon Press, 1984.

'A nice derangement of epitaphs', in E. LePore (ed.), *Truth and Interpretation: Perspectives on the Philosophy of Donald Davidson*, Oxford: Basil Blackwell, 1987, 433–46.

'A coherence theory of truth and knowledge', in E. LePore (ed.), *Truth and Interpretation: Perspectives on the Philosophy of Donald Davidson*, Oxford: Basil Blackwell, 1987, 307–19.

Dennett, D., 'Intentional systems', in *Brainstorms: Philosophical Essays on Mind and Psychology*, Brighton, Sussex: Harvester Press, 1981, 3–22.

Derrida, J., *Speech and Phenomena, and Other Essays on Husserl's Theory of Signs*, trans. D. Allison, Evanston, Ill.: Northwestern University Press, 1973.

Of Grammatology, trans. G. Spivak, Baltimore: Johns Hopkins University Press, 1976.

Spurs: Nietzsche's Styles, trans. B. Harlow, Chicago: University of Chicago Press, 1979.

'Difference', in *Margins of Philosophy*, trans. A. Bass, Brighton, Sussex:

Harvester Press, 1982, 1–27.

'Signature, event, context', in *Limited Inc.*, ed. G. Graff, trans. S. Weber and J. Mehlman, Evanston, Ill.: Northwestern University Press, 1988, 1–23.

Dilthey, W., *Selected Writings*, ed. and trans. H. Rickman, Cambridge: Cambridge University Press, 1976.

Dray, W., *Laws and Explanation in History*, Oxford: Oxford University Press, 1957.

Drury, S., *The Political Ideas of Leo Strauss*, New York: St Martin's Press, 1988.

Dunn, J., *The Political Thought of John Locke*, Cambridge: Cambridge University Press, 1969.

Political Obligation in Its Historical Context, Cambridge: Cambridge University Press, 1980.

Eagleton, T., *Literary Theory: An Introduction*, Oxford: Basil Blackwell, 1983.

Fann, K. (ed.), *Wittgenstein: The Man and His Philosophy*, New York: Dell, 1967.

Festinger, L., *A Theory of Cognitive Dissonance*, Stanford: Stanford University Press, 1957.

Fish, S., *Is There a Text in This Class?*, Cambridge, Mass.: Harvard University Press, 1980.

Fisher, S. and Greenberg, R., *The Scientific Credibility of Freud's Theories and Therapy*, Hassocks, Sussex: Harvester Press, 1977.

Foucault, M., *The Order of Things: An Archaeology of the Human Sciences*, London: Tavistock, 1970.

The Archaeology of Knowledge, trans. A. Sheridan-Smith, London: Tavistock, 1972.

'Nietzsche, genealogy, history', in *Language, Counter-Memory, Practice: Selected Interviews and Essays*, trans. D. Bouchard and S. Simon, Oxford: Basil Blackwell, 1977, 139–64.

'What is an author?', *Language, Counter-Memory, Practice*, trans. D. Bouchard and S. Simon, Oxford: Basil Blackwell, 1977, 113–38.

Power/Knowledge: Selected Interviews and Other Writings 1972–77, ed. C. Gordon, Brighton, Sussex: Harvester Press, 1980.

Frege, G., *The Foundations of Arithmetic: A Logico-Mathematical Enquiry into the Concept of Number*, trans. J. Austin, Oxford: Basil Blackwell, 1950.

French, P., Uehling, T., Jr, and Wettstein, H. (eds.), *Studies in Metaphysics*, Midwest Studies in Philosophy 4, Minneapolis: University of Minnesota Press, 1979.

Freud, S., *The Standard Edition of the Complete Psychological Works of Sigmund Freud*, ed. and trans. J. Strachey, 24 vols., London: Hogarth, 1953–74.

Gadamer, H.-G., *Truth and Method*, trans. W. Glen-Doepel, London: Sheed & Ward, 1979.

Goldman, A., *Epistemology and Cognition*, Cambridge, Mass.: Harvard University Press, 1986.

Gramsci, A., *Selections from the Prison Notebooks*, ed. and trans. Q. Hoare and G. Smith, London: Lawrence & Wishart, 1971.

Gunnell, J., 'The myth of the tradition', *American Political Science Review* 72 (1978),

122–34.

Political Theory: Tradition and Interpretation, Cambridge, Mass.: Winthrop Publishers, 1979.

'Interpretation and the history of political theory: apology and epistemology', *American Political Science Review* 76 (1982), 317–27.

Gutting, G., *Michel Foucault's Archaeology of Scientific Reason*, Cambridge: Cambridge University Press, 1989.

Habermas, J., 'The hermeneutic claim to universality', in J. Bleicher (ed.), *Contemporary Hermeneutics: Hermeneutics and Method, Philosophy and Critique*, London: Routledge & Kegan Paul, 1980, 181–211.

The Theory of Communicative Action, 2 vols., trans. T. McCarthy, Boston: Beacon Press, 1984–87.

The Philosophical Discourse of Modernity, trans. F. Lawrence, Cambridge: Polity Press, 1987.

Hacker, P., 'Semantic holism: Frege and Wittgenstein', in C. Luckhardt (ed.), *Wittgenstein: Sources and Perspectives*, Hassocks, Sussex: Harvester Press, 1979, 213–42.

Insight and Illusion: Themes in the Philosophy of Wittgenstein, Oxford: Clarendon Press, 1986.

Hacking, I. (ed.), *Scientific Revolutions*, Oxford: Oxford University Press, 1981.

Hegel, G., *The Philosophy of History*, trans. J. Sibree, intro. C. Friedrich, New York: Dover Publications, 1956.

Hempel, C., 'The function of general laws in history', *Journal of Philosophy* 39 (1942), 35–48.

Hesse, M., 'Habermas and the force of dialectical argument', *History of European Ideas* 21 (1995), 367–78.

Hirsch, E., *Validity in Interpretation*, New Haven, Conn.: Yale University Press, 1967.

'Three dimensions in hermeneutics', *New Literary History* 3 (1971–72), 246–60.

Hume, D., *A Treatise of Human Nature*, ed. L. Selby-Bigge, rev. P. Nidditch, Oxford: Clarendon Press, 1978.

Husserl, E., *Ideas: General Introduction to Pure Phenomenology*, trans. W. Gibson, London: George Allen & Unwin, 1931.

James, W., *Pragmatism: A New Name for Some Old Ways of Thinking*, New York: Longman, Green, 1907.

Jevons, W., *The Theory of Political Economy*, ed. R. Collison Black, Harmondsworth, Middlesex: Penguin, 1970.

Juhl, P., *Interpretation*, Princeton: Princeton University Press, 1980.

Kant, I., *Critique of Pure Reason*, trans. N. Kemp Smith, London: Macmillan, 1964.

Keane, J., 'More theses on the philosophy of history', in J. Tully (ed.), *Meaning and Context: Quentin Skinner and His Critics*, Cambridge: Polity Press, 1988, 204–17.

Kirk, R., *Translation Determined*, Oxford: Oxford University Press, 1986.

Knapp, S. and Michaels, W., 'Against theory (literary criticism)', *Critical Inquiry*

8 (1982), 723–42.

Kripke, S., *Wittgenstein on Rules and Private Language*, Oxford: Basil Blackwell, 1982.

Kuhn, T., *The Structure of Scientific Revolutions*, Chicago: University of Chicago Press, 1970.

'Reflections on my critics', in I. Lakatos and A. Musgrave (eds.), *Criticism and the Growth of Knowledge*, Cambridge: Cambridge University Press, 1970, 231–78.

'Second thoughts on paradigms', in F. Suppe (ed.), *The Structure of Scientific Theories*, Urbana, Ill.: University of Illinois Press, 1974, 459–82.

'A function for thought experiments', in I. Hacking (ed.), *Scientific Revolutions*, Oxford: Oxford University Press, 1981, 6–27.

Lacan, J., 'The function and field of speech and language in psychoanalysis', in *Ecrits: A Selection*, trans. A. Sheridan, London: Tavistock, 1977, 30–113.

'The agency of the letter in the unconscious or reason since Freud', *Ecrits: A Selection*, trans. A. Sheridan, London Tavistock, 1977, 146–78.

LaCapra, D., *Rethinking Intellectual History: Texts, Contexts, Language*, Ithaca, N.Y.: Cornell University Press, 1983.

History and Criticism, Ithaca, N.Y.: Cornell University Press, 1985.

'History and psychoanalysis', *Critical Inquiry* 13 (1987), 222–51.

Lakatos, I., 'Falsification and the methodology of scientific research programmes', in *Philosophical Writings*, vol. I: *The Methodology of Scientific Research Programmes*, Cambridge: Cambridge University Press, 1978, 8–101.

Lakatos, I. and Musgrave, A. (eds.), *Criticism and the Growth of Knowledge*, Cambridge: Cambridge University Press, 1970.

Laslett, P. and Runciman, W. (eds.), *Philosophy, Politics and Society*, second series, Oxford: Basil Blackwell, 1962.

Laudan, L., *Progress and Its Problems*, Berkeley: University of California Press, 1977.

Lear, J., 'Leaving the world alone', *Journal of Philosophy* 79 (1982), 382–403.

Leavis, F., 'The responsible critic: or the function of criticism at any time', in *A Selection from Scrutiny*, 2 vols., Cambridge: Cambridge University Press, 1968, vol. II, 280–303.

LePore, E. (ed.), *Truth and Interpretation: Perspectives on the Philosophy of Donald Davidson*, Oxford: Basil Blackwell, 1987.

LePore, E. and McLaughlin, B. (eds.), *Actions and Events: Perspectives on the Philosophy of Donald Davidson*, Oxford: Basil Blackwell, 1985.

Lewis, D., *Convention*, Cambridge, Mass.: Harvard University Press, 1969.

'Radical interpretation', in *Philosophical Papers*, vol. 1, New York: Oxford University Press, 1983, 108–18.

Lilla, M., 'On Goodman, Putnam, and Rorty: the return to the given', *Partisan Review* 51 (1984), 220–35.

Lipton, P., *Inference to the Best Explanation*, London: Routledge, 1991.

Lockyer, A., '"Traditions" as context in the history of political theory', *Political Studies* 27 (1979), 201–17.

Loewenberg, P., 'Psychoanalytic models of history: Freud and after', in W. Runyan (ed.), *Psychology and Historical Interpretation*, New York: Oxford University Press, 1980, 126–56.

Lormand, E., 'How to be a meaning holist', *Journal of Philosophy* 93 (1996), 51–73.

Lovejoy, A., *The Great Chain of Being: A Study of the History of an Idea*, Cambridge, Mass.: Harvard University Press, 1936.

'The historiography of ideas', in *Essays in the History of Ideas*, Baltimore: Johns Hopkins University Press, 1948, 1–13.

Luckhardt, C. (ed.), *Wittgenstein: Sources and Perspectives*, Hassocks, Sussex: Harvester Press, 1979.

Lukes, S., 'Some problems about rationality', in B. Wilson (ed.), *Rationality*, Oxford: Basil Blackwell, 1970, 194–213.

Individualism, Oxford: Basil Blackwell, 1973.

Lynch, M., 'Three models of conceptual schemes', *Inquiry* 40 (1997), 407–26.

MacIntyre, A., 'Rationality and the explanation of action', in *Against the Self-Images of the Age: Essays on Ideology and Philosophy*, London: Duckworth, 1971, 244–59.

'Epistemological crises, dramatic narrative, and the philosophy of science', *The Monist* 60 (1977), 453–72.

Whose Justice? Which Rationality?, London: Duckworth, 1988.

Macpherson, C., *The Political Theory of Possessive Individualism*, Oxford: Oxford University Press, 1962.

McGinn, C., 'Charity, interpretation, and belief', *Journal of Philosophy* 74 (1977), 521–35.

McKendrick, N. (ed.), *Historical Perspectives: Essays in Honour of J. H. Plumb*, London: Europa Publications, 1974.

Mandelbaum, M., 'The history of ideas, intellectual history, and the history of philosophy', *History and Theory* 4 (1965), Beiheft 5: *The Historiography of the History of Philosophy*, 31–66.

Marx, K., 'Preface to *A Critique of Political Economy*', in *Karl Marx: Selected Writings*, ed. D. McLellan, Oxford: Oxford University Press, 1977, 388–91.

Megill, A., 'Recounting the past: "description", explanation, and narrative in historiography', *American Historical Review* 94 (1989), 627–53.

Mink, L., 'Narrative form as a cognitive instrument', in *The Writing of History*, ed. R. Canary and H. Kozicki, Madison, Wis.: University of Wisconsin Press, 1978, 129–40.

Morton, A., 'Folk psychology is not a predictive device', *Mind* 105 (1996), 119–37.

Moser, P., *Knowledge and Evidence*, Cambridge: Cambridge University Press, 1989.

Namier, L., 'Human nature in politics', in *Personalities and Powers*, London: Hamish Hamilton, 1955, 1–7.

Newell, R., *The Concept of Philosophy*, London: Methuen, 1967.

Nietzsche, F., *Beyond Good and Evil*, trans. W. Kaufman, New York: Vintage, 1960.

Nozick, R., *The Nature of Rationality*, Princeton: Princeton University Press, 1993.

Oakeshott, M., 'Rationalism in politics', in *Rationalism in Politics and Other Essays*, Oxford: Oxford University Press, 1962, 1–36.

On Human Conduct, Oxford: Clarendon Press, 1975.

'Historical events', in *On History and Other Essays*, Oxford: Basil Blackwell, 1983, 45–96.

Olsen, C., 'Knowledge of one's own intentional actions', *Philosophical Quarterly* 19 (1969), 324–36.

Palmer, R., *Hermeneutics: Interpretation Theory in Schleiermacher, Dilthey, Heidegger, and Gadamer*, Evanston, Ill.: Northwestern University Press, 1969.

Pears, D., *Motivated Irrationality*, Oxford: Clarendon Press, 1984.

Philips, D., 'Philosophy, theology, and the reality of god', *Philosophical Quarterly* 13 (1963), 344–50.

The Concept of Prayer, London: Routledge & Kegan Paul, 1967.

Plato, *Protagoras*, trans. C. Taylor, Oxford: Clarendon Press, 1991.

Pocock, J., 'The history of political thought: a methodological enquiry', in P. Laslett and W. Runciman (eds.), *Philosophy, Politics and Society*, second series, Oxford: Basil Blackwell, 1962, 180–202.

Politics, Language and Time, London: Methuen, 1972.

The Machiavellian Moment: Florentine Political Thought and the Atlantic Republican Tradition, Princeton: Princeton University Press, 1975.

'Prophet and inquisitor', *Political Theory* 3 (1975), 385–401.

Virtue, Commerce and History, Cambridge: Cambridge University Press, 1985.

Pomper, P., *The Structure of Mind in History: Five Major Figures in Psycho-history*, New York: Columbia University Press, 1985.

Popper, K., *Poverty of Historicism*, London: Routledge & Kegan Paul, 1957.

The Logic of Scientific Discovery, New York: Basic Books, 1959.

The Open Society and Its Enemies, 2 vols., London: Routledge & Kegan Paul, 1966.

Objective Knowledge: An Evolutionary Approach, Oxford: Clarendon Press, 1972.

'Science: conjectures and refutations', *Conjectures and Refutations: The Growth of Scientific Knowledge*, London: Routledge & Kegan Paul, 1972, 33–65.

Putnam, H., 'The logic of quantum mechanics', in *Philosophical Papers*, 3 vols., Cambridge: Cambridge University Press, 1975–83, vol I: *Mathematics, Matter and Method*, 174–97.

'It ain't neccessarily so', in *Philosophical Papers*, 3 vols., Cambridge: Cambridge University Press, 1975–83, vol I: *Mathematics, Matter and Method*, 237–49.

'The meaning of meaning', in *Philosophical Papers*, 3 vols., Cambridge: Cambridge University Press, 1975–83, vol. II: *Mind, Language and Reality*, 215–71.

'The nature of mental states', in *Philosophical Papers*, 3 vols., Cambridge: Cambridge University Press, 1975–83, vol. II: *Mind, Language and Reality*, 429–40.

'Analyticity and apriority: beyond Wittgenstein and Quine', in *Philosophical Papers*, 3 vols., Cambridge: Cambridge University Press, 1975–83, vol III:

Realism and Reason, 115–38.
Reason, Truth, and History, Cambridge: Cambridge University Press, 1981.
Representation and Reality, Cambridge, Mass.: Massachusetts Institute of Technology Press, 1988.
Quine, W., *Word and Object*, Cambridge, Mass.: Massachusetts Institute of Technology Press, 1960.
'Two dogmas of empiricism', in *From a Logical Point of View*, Cambridge, Mass.: Harvard University Press, 1961, 20–46.
'Epistemology naturalized', in *Ontological Relativity and Other Essays*, New York: Columbia University Press, 1969, 69–90.
Philosophy of Logic, Englewood Cliffs, N.J.: Prentice-Hall, 1970.
The Pursuit of Truth, Cambridge, Mass.: Harvard University Press, 1990.
Quine, W. and Ullian, J., *The Web of Belief*, New York: Random House, 1970.
Rawls, J., *A Theory of Justice*, Oxford: Clarendon Press, 1972.
Richard, M., *Propositional Attitudes: An Essay on Thoughts and How We Ascribe Them*, Cambridge: Cambridge University Press, 1990.
Richards, I., *Practical Criticism*, London: Routledge & Kegan Paul, 1929.
Ricœur, P., *Interpretation Theory: Discourse and the Surplus of Meaning*, Fort Worth, Tex.: Texas Christian University Press, 1976.
Time and Narrative, 3 vols., trans. K. McLaughlin and D. Pellauer, Chicago: University of Chicago Press, 1984–88.
Rorty, R., 'The world well lost', *Journal of Philosophy* 69 (1972), 649–65.
Philosophy and the Mirror of Nature, Princeton: Princeton University Press, 1979.
'On ethnocentrism: a reply to Clifford Geertz', *Michigan Quarterly Review* 25 (1986), 525–34.
Roth, P., *Meaning and Method in the Social Sciences*, Ithaca, N.Y.: Cornell University Press, 1987.
'Narrative explanation: the case of history', *History and Theory* 27 (1988), 1–13.
Rudder, L., *Saving Belief: A Critique of Physicalism*, Princeton: Princeton University Press, 1987.
Runyan, W., 'Alternatives to psychoanalytic psychobiography', in W. Runyan (ed.), *Psychology and Historical Interpretation*, New York: Oxford University Press, 1980, 219–44.
Runyan, W. (ed.), *Psychology and Historical Interpretation*, New York: Oxford University Press, 1980.
Russell, B., 'Knowledge by acquaintance and knowledge by description', *Proceedings of the Aristotelian Society* 11 (1911), 108–28.
'The philosophy of logical atomism', in *Logic and Knowledge*, ed. R. Marsh, London: George Allen & Unwin, 1956, 175–281.
'The philosophy of logical analysis', in *History of Western Philosophy*, London: George Allen & Unwin, 1971, 783–9.
Ryan, A., 'Locke and the dictatorship of the bourgeoisie', *Political Studies* 13 (1965), 219–30.
Ryle, G., *The Concept of Mind*, London: Hutchinson, 1949.
'Categories', in *Collected Papers*, vol. II: *Collected Essays 1929–1968*, London:

Hutchinson, 1971, 170–84.

'Philosophical argument', in *Collected Papers*, vol. II: *Collected Essays 1929–1968*, London: Hutchinson, 1971, 194–211.

Salmon, N. and Soames, S. (eds.), *Propositions and Attitudes*, New York: Oxford University Press, 1988.

Sartre, J.-P., *Being and Nothingness: An Essay on Phenomenological Ontology*, trans. H. Barnes, London: Methuen, 1981.

Saussure, F. de, *Course in General Linguistics*, ed. C. Bally and A. Sechehaye, trans. W. Baskin, New York: McGraw-Hill, 1966.

Schleiermacher, F., *Hermeneutics: The Hand Written Manuscripts*, ed. H. Kimmerle, trans. J. Duke and J. Forstman, Missoula, Mont.: Scholars Press, 1977.

Searle, J., *Minds, Brains and Science*, Cambridge, Mass.: Harvard University Press, 1984.

Sheridan, R., *The Rivals*, ed. E. Duthie, London: E. Benn, 1979.

Skinner, Q., 'The limits of historical explanation', *Philosophy* 41 (1966), 199–215.

'Conventions and the understanding of speech-acts', *Philosophical Quarterly* 20 (1970), 118–38.

'On performing and explaining linguistic actions', *Philosophical Quarterly* 21 (1971), 1–21.

'The principles and practice of opposition: the case of Bolingbroke versus Walpole', in N. McKendrick (ed.), *Historical Perspectives: Essays in Honour of J. H. Plumb*, London: Europa Publications, 1974, 93–128.

The Foundations of Modern Political Thought, 2 vols., Cambridge: Cambridge University Press, 1978.

'Meaning and understanding in the history of ideas', in J. Tully (ed.), *Meaning and Context: Quentin Skinner and His Critics*, Cambridge: Polity Press, 1988, 29–67.

'Motives, intentions, and the interpretation of texts', in J. Tully (ed.), *Meaning and Context: Quentin Skinner and His Critics*, Cambridge: Polity Press, 1988, 68–78.

'"Social meaning" and the explanation of social action', in J. Tully (ed.), *Meaning and Context: Quentin Skinner and His Critics*, Cambridge: Polity Press, 1988, 79–96.

'Some problems in the analysis of political thought and action', in J. Tully (ed.), *Meaning and Context: Quentin Skinner and His Critics*, Cambridge: Polity Press, 1988, 97–118.

'A reply to my critics', in J. Tully (ed.), *Meaning and Context: Quentin Skinner and His Critics*, Cambridge: Polity Press, 1988, 231–88.

Smith, M., 'The Humean theory of motivation', *Mind* 96 (1987), 36–61.

Stannard, D., *Shrinking History: On Freud and the Failure of Psychohistory*, Oxford: Oxford University Press, 1980.

Stich, S., *From Folk Psychology to Cognitive Science*, Cambridge, Mass.: Massachusetts Institute of Technology Press, 1983.

Strauss, L., 'Persecution and the art of writing', in *Persecution and the Art of*

Writing, Glencoe, Ill.: Free Press, 1952, 22–37.
Natural Right and History, Chicago: University of Chicago Press, 1953.
'On a forgotten kind of writing', in *What is Political Philosophy?*, Glencoe, Ill.: Free Press, 1959, 221–32.
'Political philosophy and history', in *What is Political Philosophy?*, Glencoe, Ill.: Free Press, 1959, 56–77.
Strawson, P., 'Intention and convention in speech-acts', *Philosophical Review* 73 (1964), 439–60.
Suppe, F. (ed.), *The Structure of Scientific Theories*, Urbana, Ill.: University of Illinois Press, 1974.
Thompson, M., 'Reception theory and the interpretation of historical meaning', *History and Theory* 32 (1993), 248–72.
Toews, J., 'Intellectual history after the linguistic turn: the autonomy of meaning and the irreducibility of experience', *American Historical Review* 92 (1987), 879–907.
Toulmin, S., *Human Understanding: The Collective Use and Evolution of Concepts*, Princeton: Princeton University Press, 1972.
Tully, J., *A Discourse on Property: John Locke and His Adversaries*, Cambridge: Cambridge University Press, 1980.
'The pen is a mighty sword: Quentin Skinner's analysis of politics', in J. Tully (ed.), *Meaning and Context: Quentin Skinner and His Critics*, Cambridge: Polity Press, 1988, 7–25.
Tully, J. (ed.), *Meaning and Context: Quentin Skinner and His Critics*, Cambridge: Polity Press, 1988.
van Parijs, P., *Evolutionary Explanation in the Social Sciences: An Emerging Paradigm*, London: Tavistock, 1981.
von Wright, G., *Explanation and Understanding*, London: Routledge & Kegan Paul, 1971.
White, H., *Metahistory: The Historical Imagination in Nineteenth-Century Europe*, Baltimore: Johns Hopkins University Press, 1973.
'The question of narrative in contemporary historical theory', *The Content of the Form: Narrative Discourse and Historical Representation*, Baltimore: Johns Hopkins University Press, 1987, 26–57.
Wilson, B. (ed.), *Rationality*, Oxford: Basil Blackwell, 1970.
Wimsatt, W., 'History and criticism: a problematic relationship', in W. Wimsatt (ed.), *The Verbal Icon: Studies in the Meaning of Poetry*, Lexington, Ky.: University of Kentucky Press, 1954, 253–65.
Wimsatt, W. and M. Beardsley, 'The intentional fallacy', in W. Wimsatt (ed.) *The Verbal Icon: Studies in the Meaning of Poetry*, Lexington, Ky.: University of Kentucky Press, 1954, 3–18.
Winch, P., *The Idea of a Social Science*, London: Routledge & Kegan Paul, 1958.
'Understanding a primitive society', in *Ethics and Action*, London: Routledge & Kegan Paul, 1972, 8–49.
Wisdom, J., 'A feature of Wittgenstein's technique', in K. Fann (ed.), *Wittgenstein: The Man and His Philosophy*, New York: Dell, 1967, 353–65.

Wittgenstein, L., *Tractatus Logico-Philosophicus*, trans. D. Pears and B. McGuiness, London: Routledge & Kegan Paul, 1960.
The Blue and Brown Books, Oxford: Basil Blackwell, 1969.
Philosophical Investigations, trans. G. Anscombe, Oxford: Basil Blackwell, 1972.
On Certainty, trans. D. Paul and G. Anscombe, Oxford: Basil Blackwell, 1974.
Philosophical Grammar, ed. R. Rhees, trans. A. Kenny, Oxford: Basil Blackwell, 1974.
Remarks on the Foundations of Mathematics, ed. G. Anscombe, R. Rhees, and G. von Wright, Oxford: Basil Blackwell, 1978.
'Conversations on Freud', in R. Wollheim and J. Hopkins (eds.), *Philosophical Essays on Freud*, Cambridge: Cambridge University Press, 1982, 1–11.
Wood, N., *John Locke and Agrarian Capitalism*, Berkeley: University of California Press, 1984.
Wollheim, R. and Hopkins, J. (eds.), *Philosophical Essays on Freud*, Cambridge: Cambridge University Press, 1982.
Wright, C., *Wittgenstein on the Foundations of Mathematics*, London: Duckworth, 1980.

Index

action
  beliefs and pro-attitudes as constituents of, 28, 130, 134, 140–2, 172
  historical explanation of, 140–2, 316
  relationship of pro-attitudes to, 299–304
  speech–acts as, 134–5, 139
  see also Skinner, Quentin; speech–act theory
agency, 188–9, 221, 313
  and conceptual change, 223–4
  and traditions, 196–9, 200, 229
anarchism, 205
anomaly *see* Kuhn, Thomas
anti-foundationalism, 3n., 5n., 310–14
  irrationalist, 6
  and irreducibility of dilemmas, 245
  and knowledge, 6n., 125
  and objectivity as comparison, 112
  see also philosophy; post-modernism
argument
  deductive, 19–22
    conventionalist view of, 21
    role of examples in, 24–5
  inductive, 19n., 22–4
    conventionalist view of, 23
    role of examples in, 24–5
    role of intuitions in, 22–5
  philosophical
    foundations of, 16–19
    method, 19–26
authors
  prior purposes of, 68–70, 76
  see also intentions, authorial; readers

Bachelard, Gaston, 37
behaviourism, 57, 119, 120, 295–6
beliefs, 247
  actual and expressed, 130, 267–70, 272, 276–8
  attribution of, 129–30
  changes of, 221–7, 230–1, 234–40

and anthropological epistemology, 221
conscious, 153–8, 159, 270, 271, 272, 277, 278
  conceptual priority of, 128–9, 151–3, 156–7, 172, 173
distinguished from motives, 131–4, 139
distorted, 265–6, 308, 312, 313, 318
  and pro-attitudes, 266–7
and experience, 243–7
explanation of, 28–9, 176–7, 187–93, 194–9, 262–3, 265
  and dilemmas, 177
  role of traditions in, 213–18
expressed, 128–9, 130–1, 137, 139, 172, 176
expressive, 167
functionalist view of, 182–3
literal, 166
objective, 162–5, 168
  and semantic holism, 190–1
and pro-attitudes as constituents of action, 28, 130, 134, 140–2, 172
rational,
  absolute priority of, 160–1
  conceptual priority of, 128–9, 158–63, 172–3
  instrumental concept of, 165–7
  and semantic holism, 162, 262–3
  see also irrationality; rationality
rogue, 282–3, 281
  see also pro–attitudes, rogue
sincere, conceptual priority of, 29, 128–9, 172, 173
traditions as sum of, 203–7
as webs, 5–6, 165, 213–18
  and conditional connections, 258–9, 262, 314
  and dilemmas, 226–7, 229–31, 235–7, 238–43, 313
  and historical explanation, 29, 178, 192–3, 225–7, 219
  rationality of, 189–91

330

.